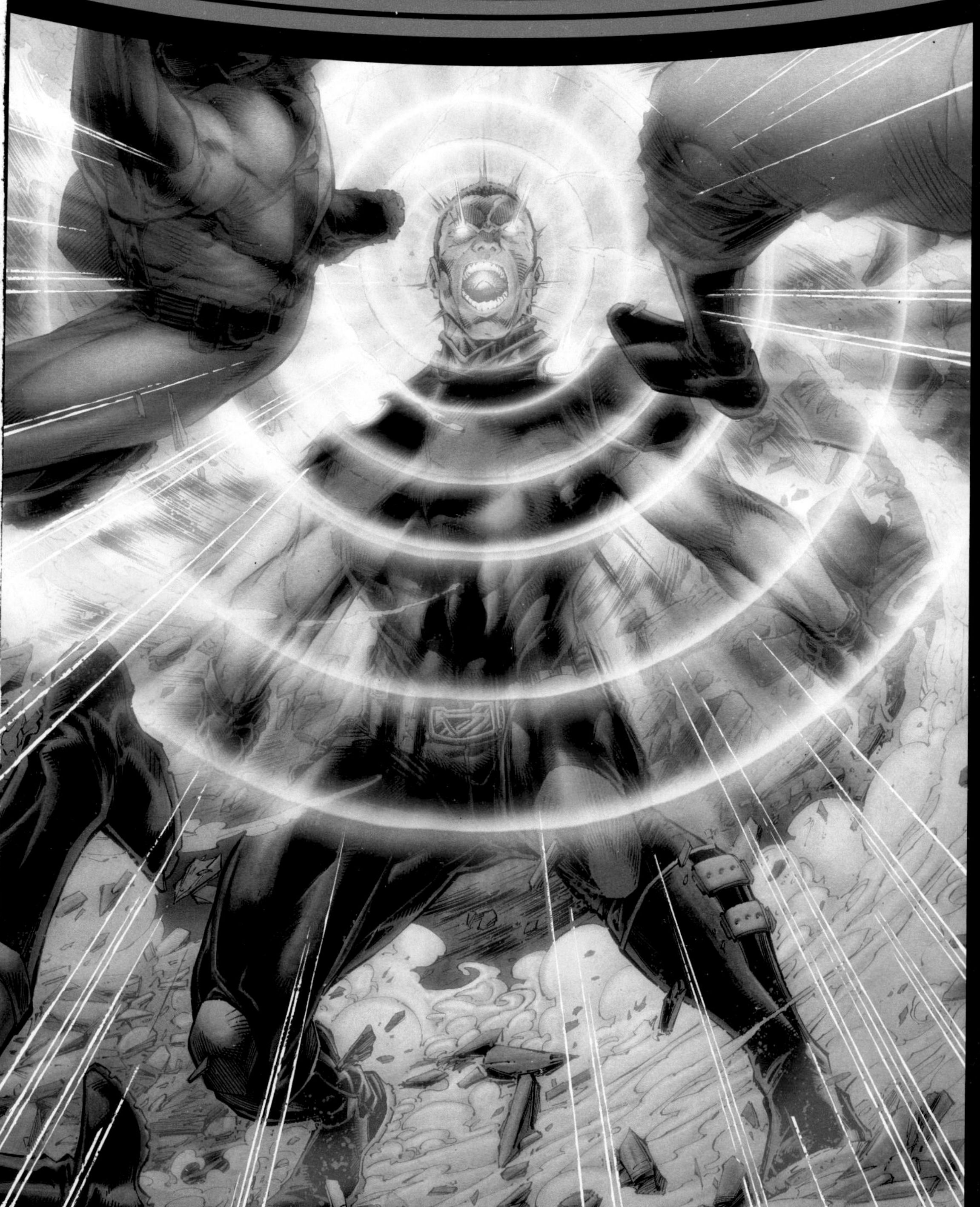

TITANS

VOL. 2 MADE IN MANHATTAN

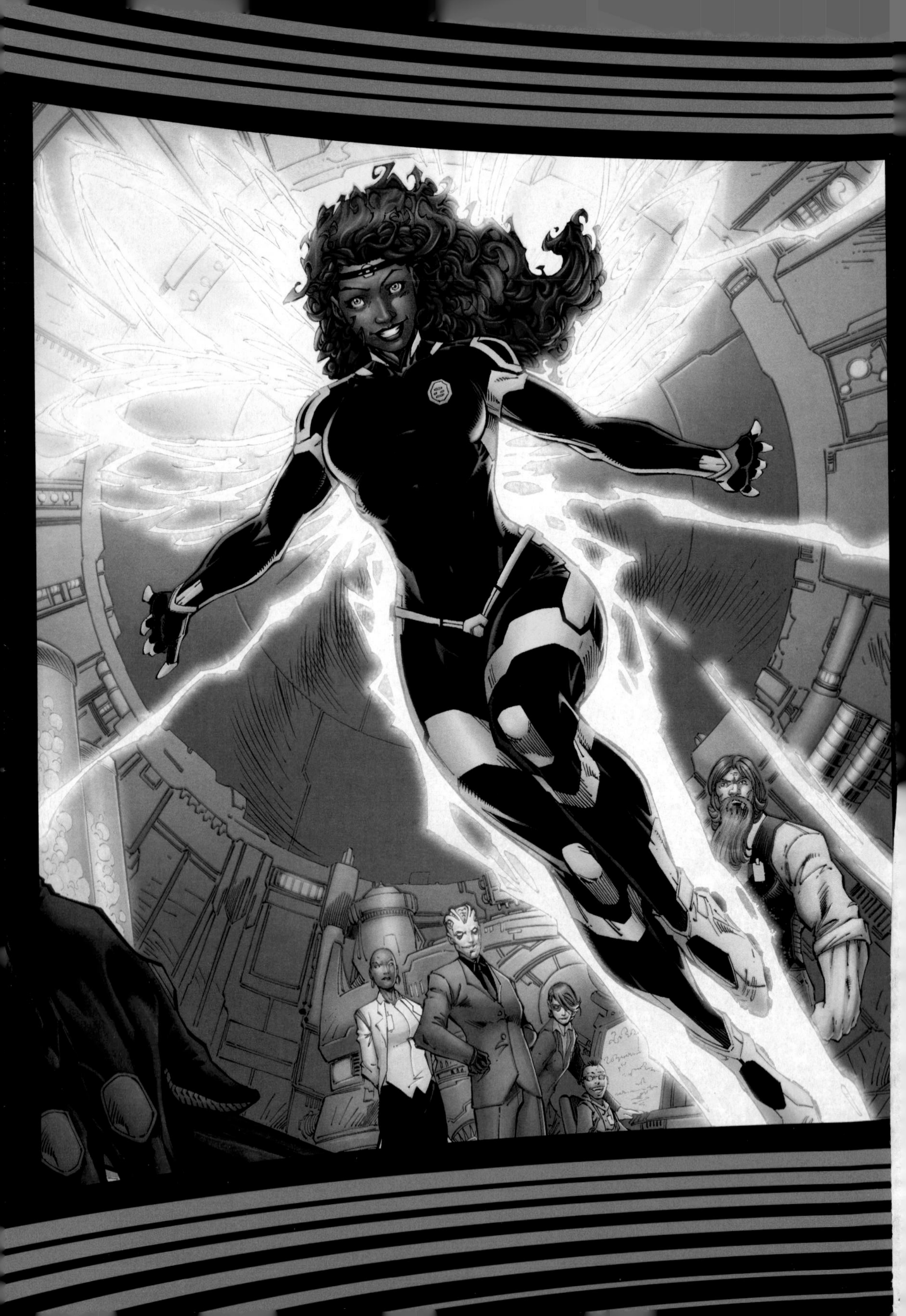

TITANS

VOL. 2 MADE IN MANHATTAN

DAN ABNETT

JAMES ASMUS

writers

BRETT BOOTH
NORM RAPMUND
MINKYU JUNG
LEE WEEKS

REILLY BROWN

SCOTT HANNA

artists

ANDREW DALHOUSE
ADRIANO LUCAS
JOHN KALISZ

TONY AVIÑA

colorists

CARLOS M. MANGUAL
COREY BREEN

JOSH REED

letterers

BRETT BOOTH, NORM RAPMUND
& ANDREW DALHOUSE

collection cover artists

BUMBLEBEE created by BOB ROZAKIS and JOSÉ DELBO
THE FEARSOME FIVE created by Marv Wolfman and George Pérez
SUPERMAN created by JERRY SIEGEL and JOE SHUSTER
By special arrangement with the JERRY SIEGEL family

ALEX ANTONE Editor - Original Series ✳ **BRITTANY HOLZHERR** Associate Editor - Original Series
JEB WOODARD Group Editor - Collected Editions ✳ **ROBIN WILDMAN** Editor - Collected Edition
STEVE COOK Design Director - Books ✳ **SHANNON STEWART** Publication Design

BOB HARRAS Senior VP - Editor-in-Chief, DC Comics

DIANE NELSON President ✳ **DAN DiDIO** Publisher ✳ **JIM LEE** Publisher ✳ **GEOFF JOHNS** President & Chief Creative Officer
AMIT DESAI Executive VP - Business & Marketing Strategy, Direct to Consumer & Global Franchise Management
SAM ADES Senior VP - Direct to Consumer ✳ **BOBBIE CHASE** VP - Talent Development ✳ **MARK CHIARELLO** Senior VP - Art, Design & Collected Editions
JOHN CUNNINGHAM Senior VP - Sales & Trade Marketing ✳ **ANNE DePIES** Senior VP - Business Strategy, Finance & Administration
DON FALLETTI VP - Manufacturing Operations ✳ **LAWRENCE GANEM** VP - Editorial Administration & Talent Relations
ALISON GILL Senior VP - Manufacturing & Operations ✳ **HANK KANALZ** Senior VP - Editorial Strategy & Administration
JAY KOGAN VP - Legal Affairs ✳ **THOMAS LOFTUS** VP - Business Affairs ✳ **JACK MAHAN** VP - Business Affairs
NICK J. NAPOLITANO VP - Manufacturing Administration ✳ **EDDIE SCANNELL** VP - Consumer Marketing
COURTNEY SIMMONS Senior VP - Publicity & Communications ✳ **JIM (SKI) SOKOLOWSKI** VP - Comic Book Specialty Sales & Trade Marketing
NANCY SPEARS VP - Mass, Book, Digital Sales & Trade Marketing

TITANS VOLUME 2: MADE IN MANHATTAN

Published by DC Comics. Compilation and all new material Copyright © 2017 DC Comics.
All Rights Reserved. Originally published in single magazine form in TITANS 7-10, TITANS ANNUAL 1, DC REBIRTH HOLIDAY SPECIAL 1.
Copyright © 2016, 2017 DC Comics. All Rights Reserved. All characters, their distinctive likenesses and related elements featured in this publication
are trademarks of DC Comics. The stories, characters and incidents featured in this publication are entirely fictional.
DC Comics does not read or accept unsolicited submissions of ideas, stories or artwork.

DC Comics, 2900 West Alameda Ave., Burbank, CA 91505
Printed by LSC Communications, Kendallville, IN, USA. 8/18/17. First Printing.
ISBN: 978-1-4012-7377-4

Library of Congress Cataloging-in-Publication Data is available.

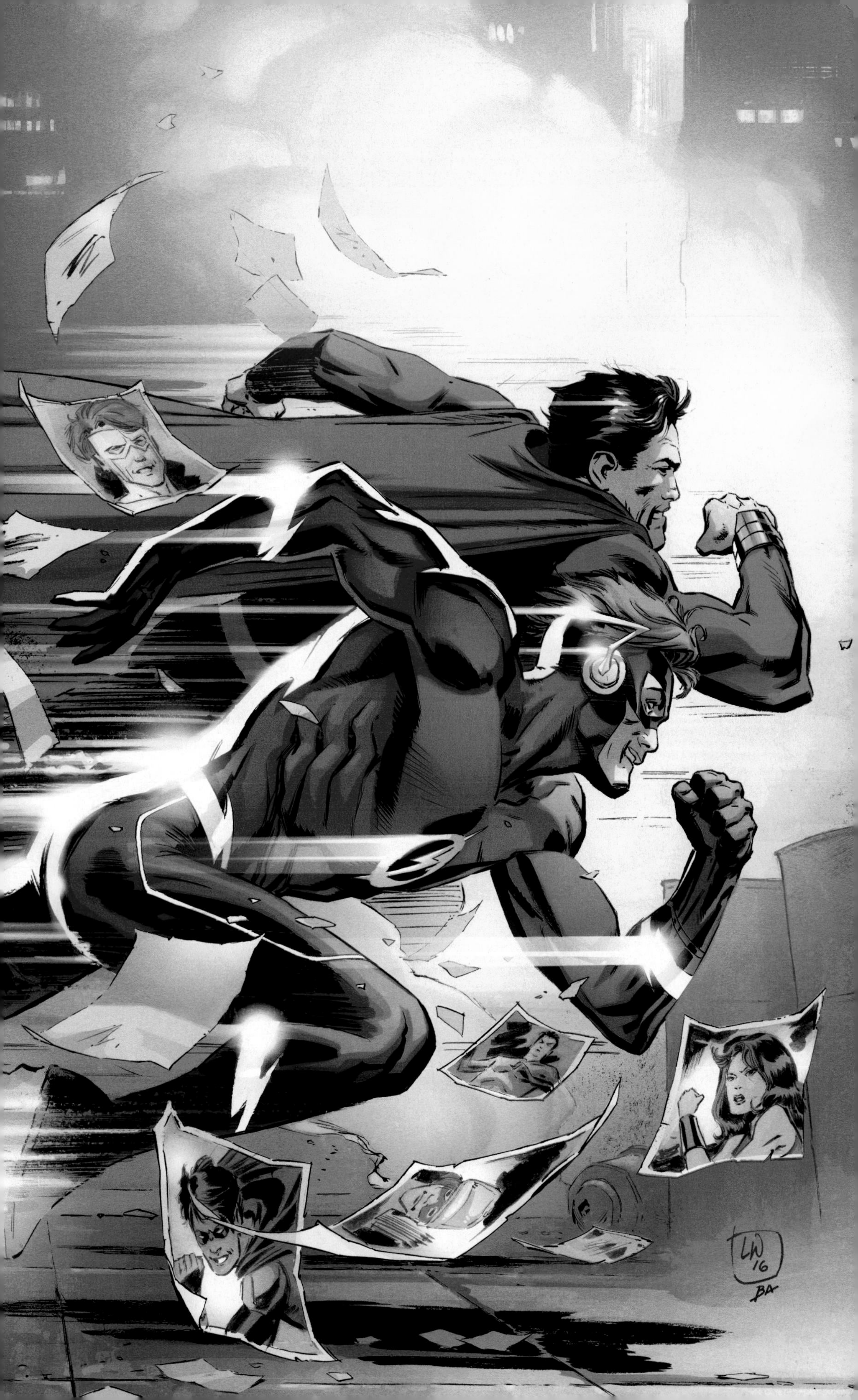

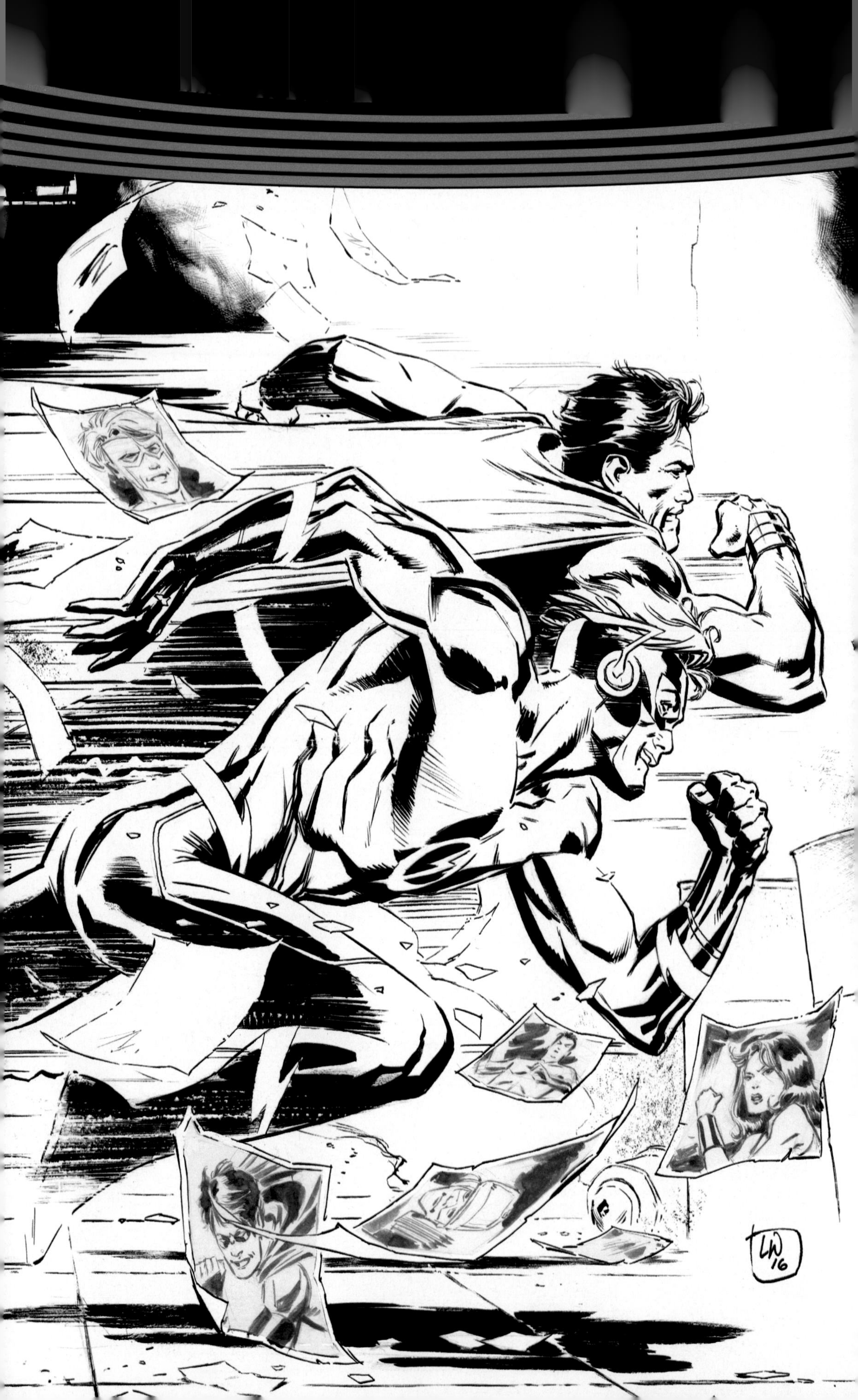
LW 16

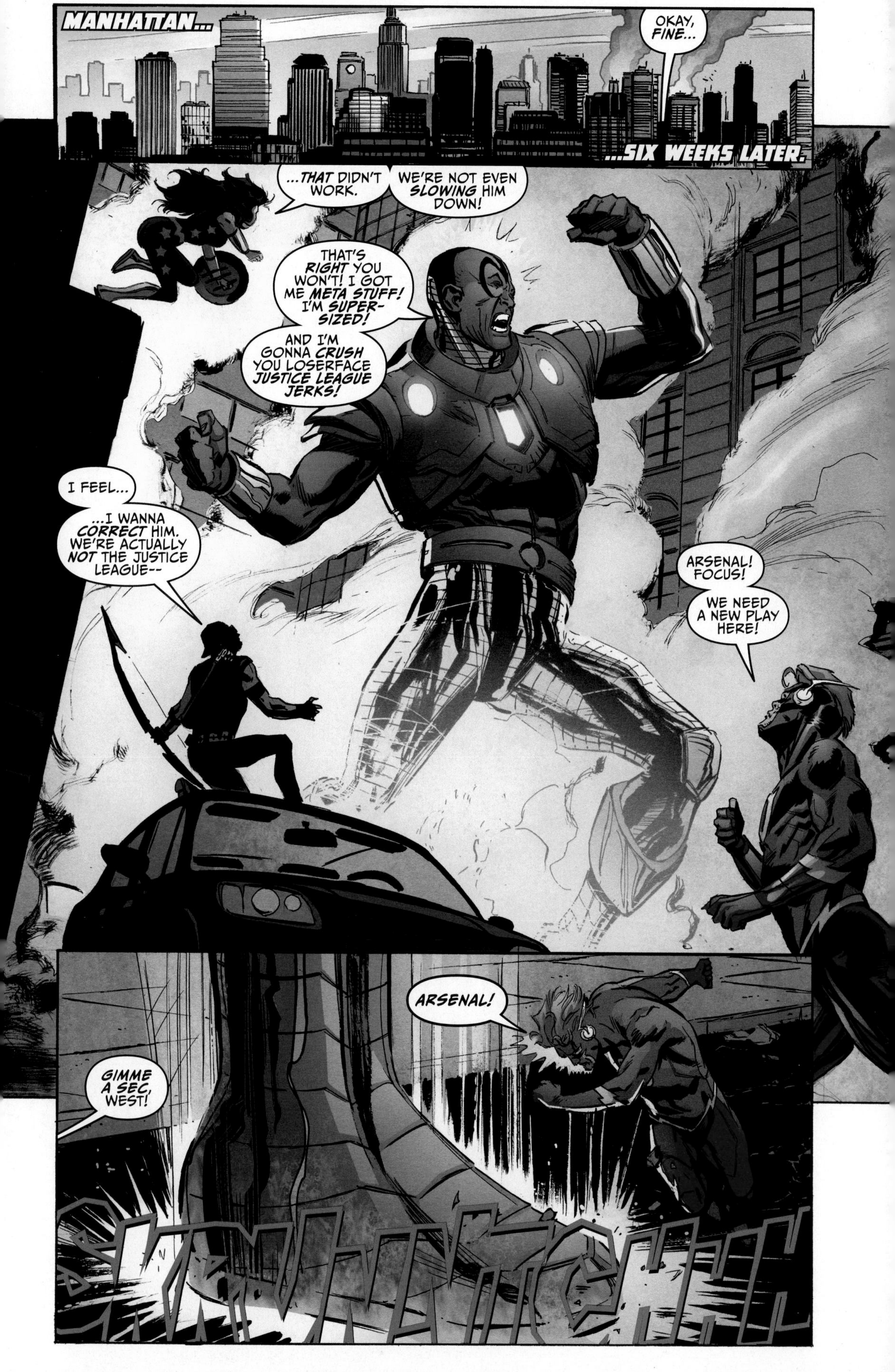
MANHATTAN...
OKAY, FINE...
...SIX WEEKS LATER.
...THAT DIDN'T WORK.
WE'RE NOT EVEN SLOWING HIM DOWN!
THAT'S RIGHT YOU WON'T! I GOT ME META STUFF! I'M SUPER-SIZED!
AND I'M GONNA CRUSH YOU LOSERFACE JUSTICE LEAGUE JERKS!
I FEEL...
...I WANNA CORRECT HIM. WE'RE ACTUALLY NOT THE JUSTICE LEAGUE--
ARSENAL! FOCUS!
WE NEED A NEW PLAY HERE!
ARSENAL!
GIMME A SEC, WEST!

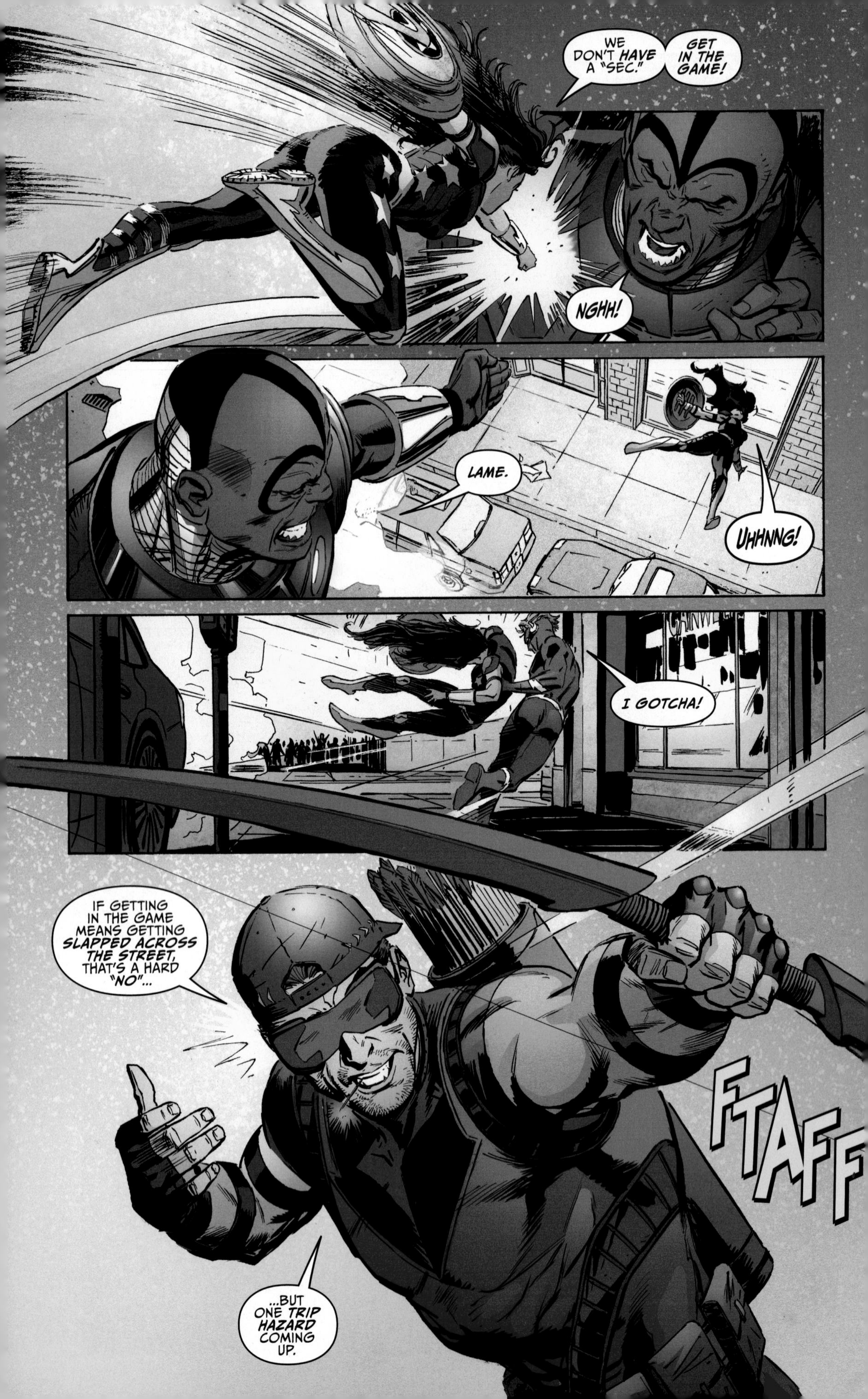
WE DON'T HAVE A "SEC."
GET IN THE GAME!
NGHH!
LAME.
UHHNNG!
I GOTCHA!
IF GETTING IN THE GAME MEANS GETTING SLAPPED ACROSS THE STREET, THAT'S A HARD "NO"...
FTAFF
...BUT ONE TRIP HAZARD COMING UP.

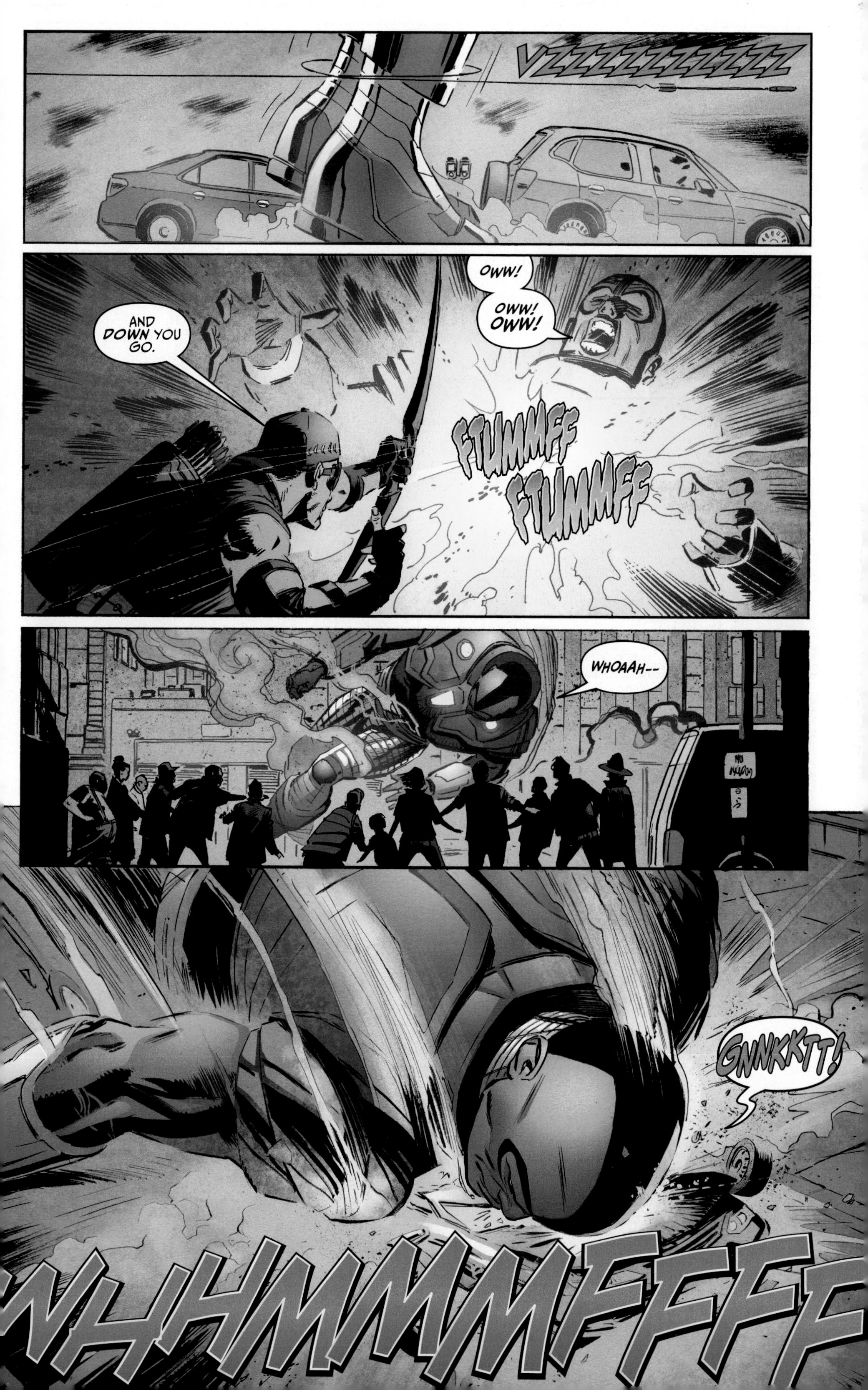
VZZZZZZZZZZZZ
AND DOWN YOU GO.
OWW!
OWW! OWW!
FTUMMFF FTUMMFF
WHOAAH--
GNNKKTT!
WHHMMMMFFFF

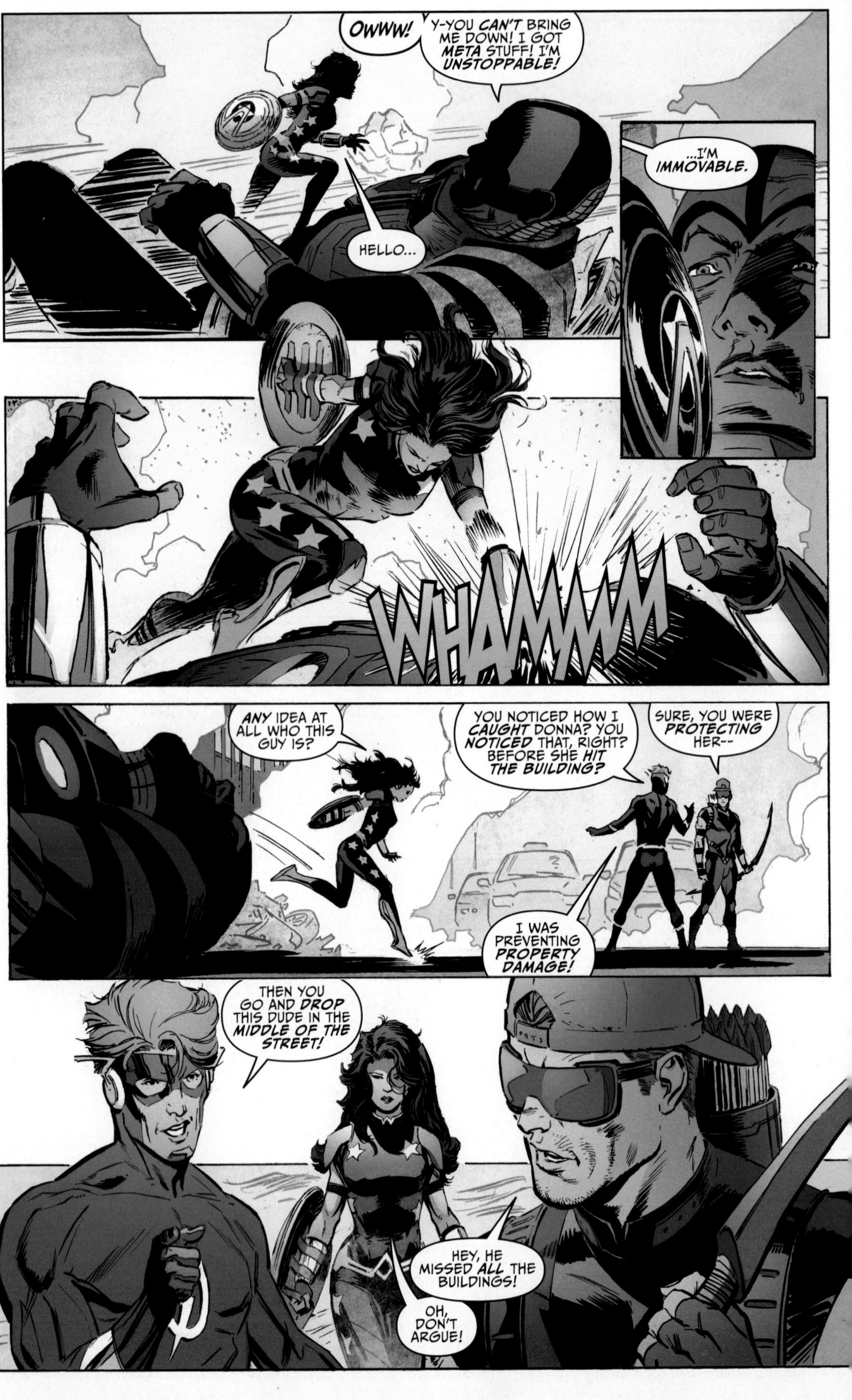
OWWW!
Y-YOU CAN'T BRING ME DOWN! I GOT META STUFF! I'M UNSTOPPABLE!
HELLO...
...I'M IMMOVABLE.
WHAMMM
ANY IDEA AT ALL WHO THIS GUY IS?
YOU NOTICED HOW I CAUGHT DONNA? YOU NOTICED THAT, RIGHT? BEFORE SHE HIT THE BUILDING?
SURE, YOU WERE PROTECTING HER--
I WAS PREVENTING PROPERTY DAMAGE!
THEN YOU GO AND DROP THIS DUDE IN THE MIDDLE OF THE STREET!
HEY, HE MISSED ALL THE BUILDINGS!
OH, DON'T ARGUE!

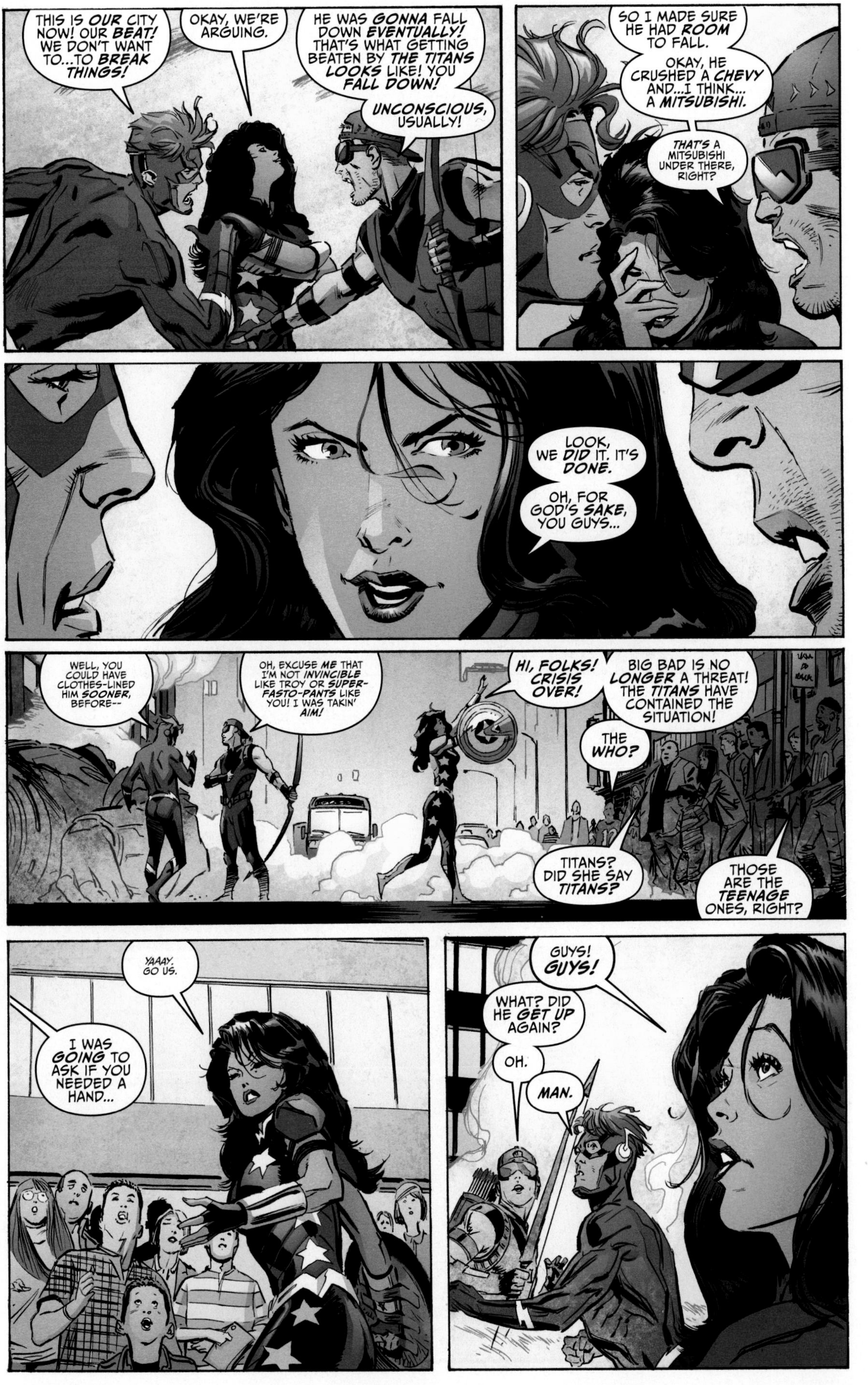
THIS IS *OUR* CITY NOW! OUR *BEAT!* WE DON'T WANT TO...TO *BREAK THINGS!*
OKAY, WE'RE ARGUING.
HE WAS *GONNA* FALL DOWN *EVENTUALLY!* THAT'S WHAT GETTING BEATEN BY *THE TITANS LOOKS* LIKE! YOU *FALL DOWN!*
UNCONSCIOUS, USUALLY!
SO I MADE SURE HE HAD *ROOM* TO FALL.
OKAY, HE CRUSHED A *CHEVY* AND...I THINK... A *MITSUBISHI.*
THAT'S A MITSUBISHI UNDER THERE, RIGHT?
LOOK, WE *DID* IT. IT'S *DONE.*
OH, FOR GOD'S *SAKE,* YOU GUYS...
WELL, YOU COULD HAVE CLOTHES-LINED HIM *SOONER,* BEFORE--
OH, EXCUSE *ME* THAT I'M NOT *INVINCIBLE* LIKE TROY OR *SUPER-FASTO-PANTS* LIKE YOU! I WAS TAKIN' *AIM!*
HI, FOLKS! CRISIS OVER!
BIG BAD IS NO *LONGER* A THREAT! THE *TITANS* HAVE CONTAINED THE SITUATION!
THE *WHO?*
TITANS? DID SHE SAY *TITANS?*
THOSE ARE THE *TEENAGE* ONES, RIGHT?
YAAAY. GO US.
I WAS *GOING* TO ASK IF YOU NEEDED A HAND...
GUYS! *GUYS!*
WHAT? DID HE *GET UP* AGAIN?
OH.
MAN.

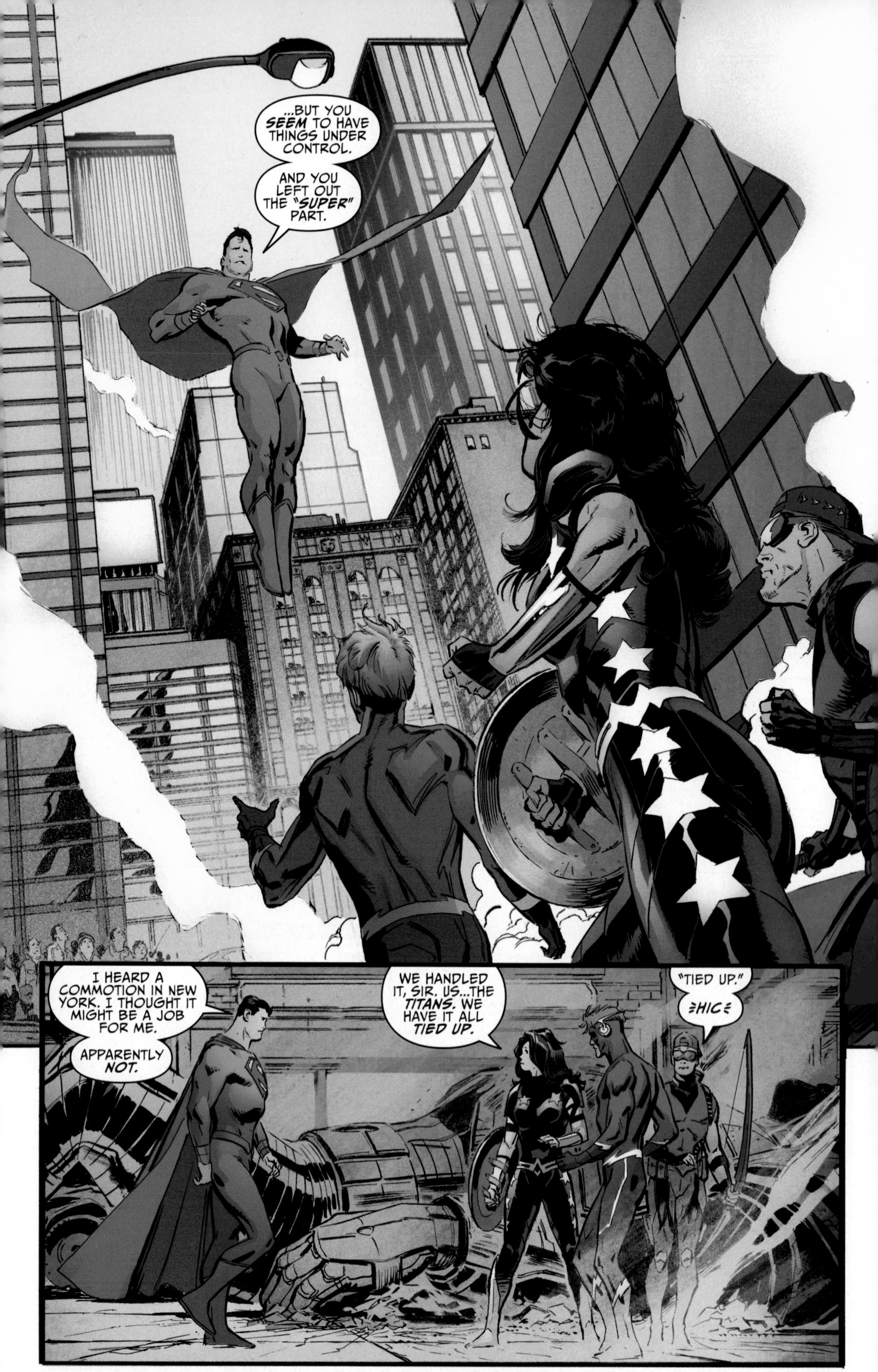
...BUT YOU SEEM TO HAVE THINGS UNDER CONTROL.
AND YOU LEFT OUT THE "SUPER" PART.
I HEARD A COMMOTION IN NEW YORK. I THOUGHT IT MIGHT BE A JOB FOR ME.
APPARENTLY NOT.
WE HANDLED IT, SIR. US...THE TITANS. WE HAVE IT ALL TIED UP.
"TIED UP."
HIC

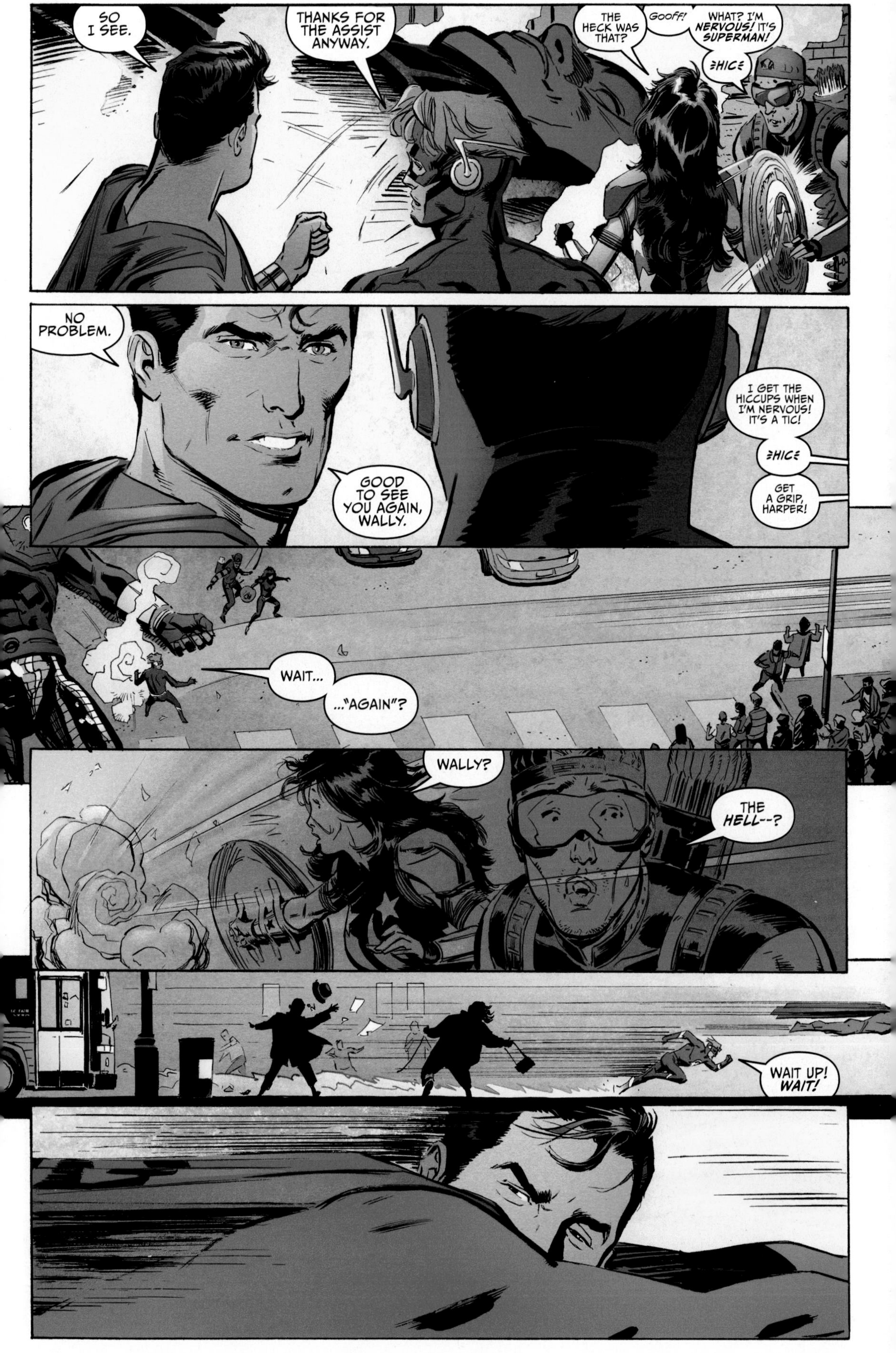
SO I SEE.
THANKS FOR THE ASSIST ANYWAY.
THE HECK WAS THAT?
Gooff!
WHAT? I'M NERVOUS! IT'S SUPERMAN!
HIC
NO PROBLEM.
GOOD TO SEE YOU AGAIN, WALLY.
I GET THE HICCUPS WHEN I'M NERVOUS! IT'S A TIC!
HIC
GET A GRIP, HARPER!
WAIT...
..."AGAIN"?
WALLY?
THE HELL--?
WAIT UP! WAIT!

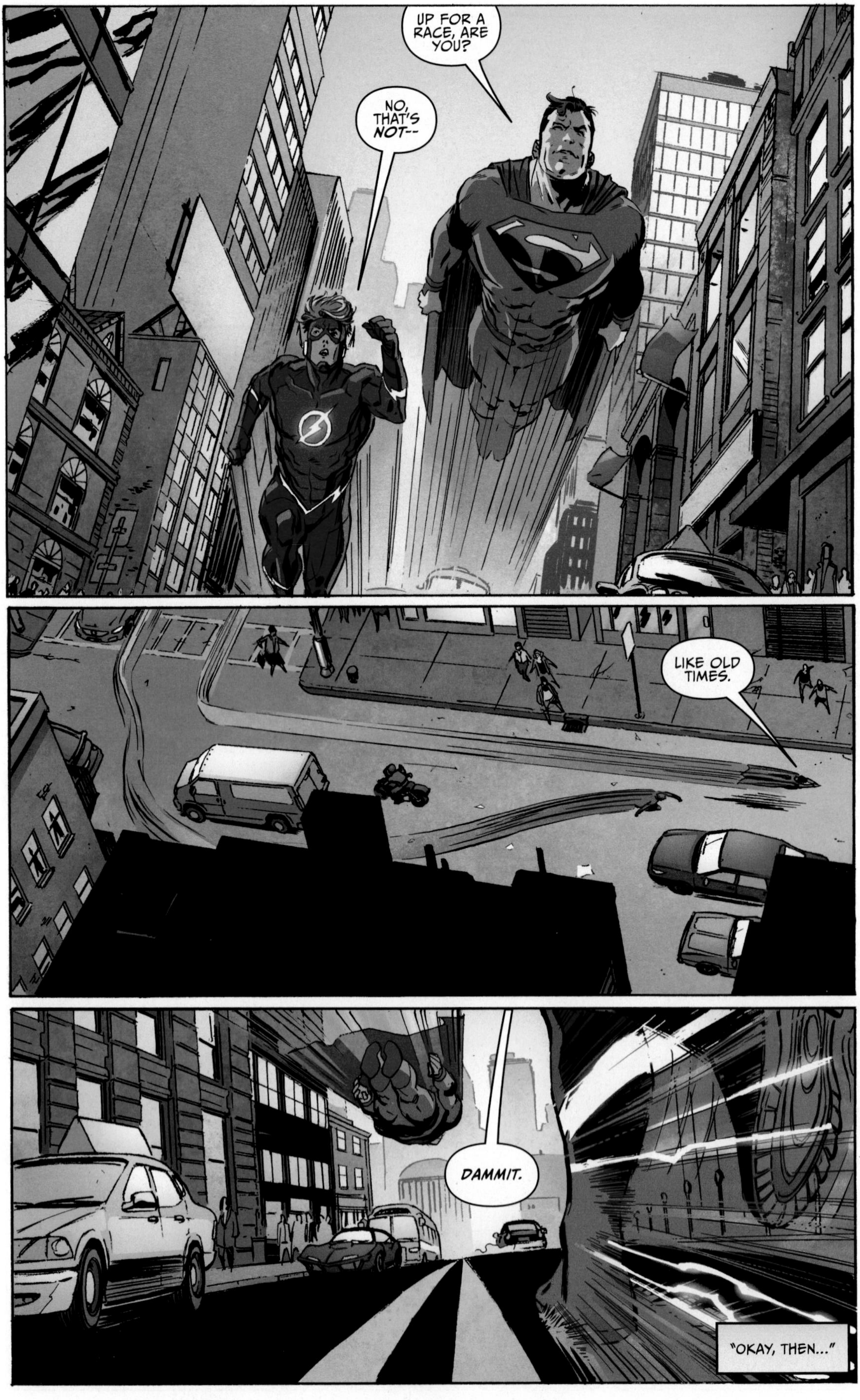
UP FOR A RACE, ARE YOU?
NO, THAT'S NOT--
LIKE OLD TIMES.
DAMMIT.
"OKAY, THEN..."

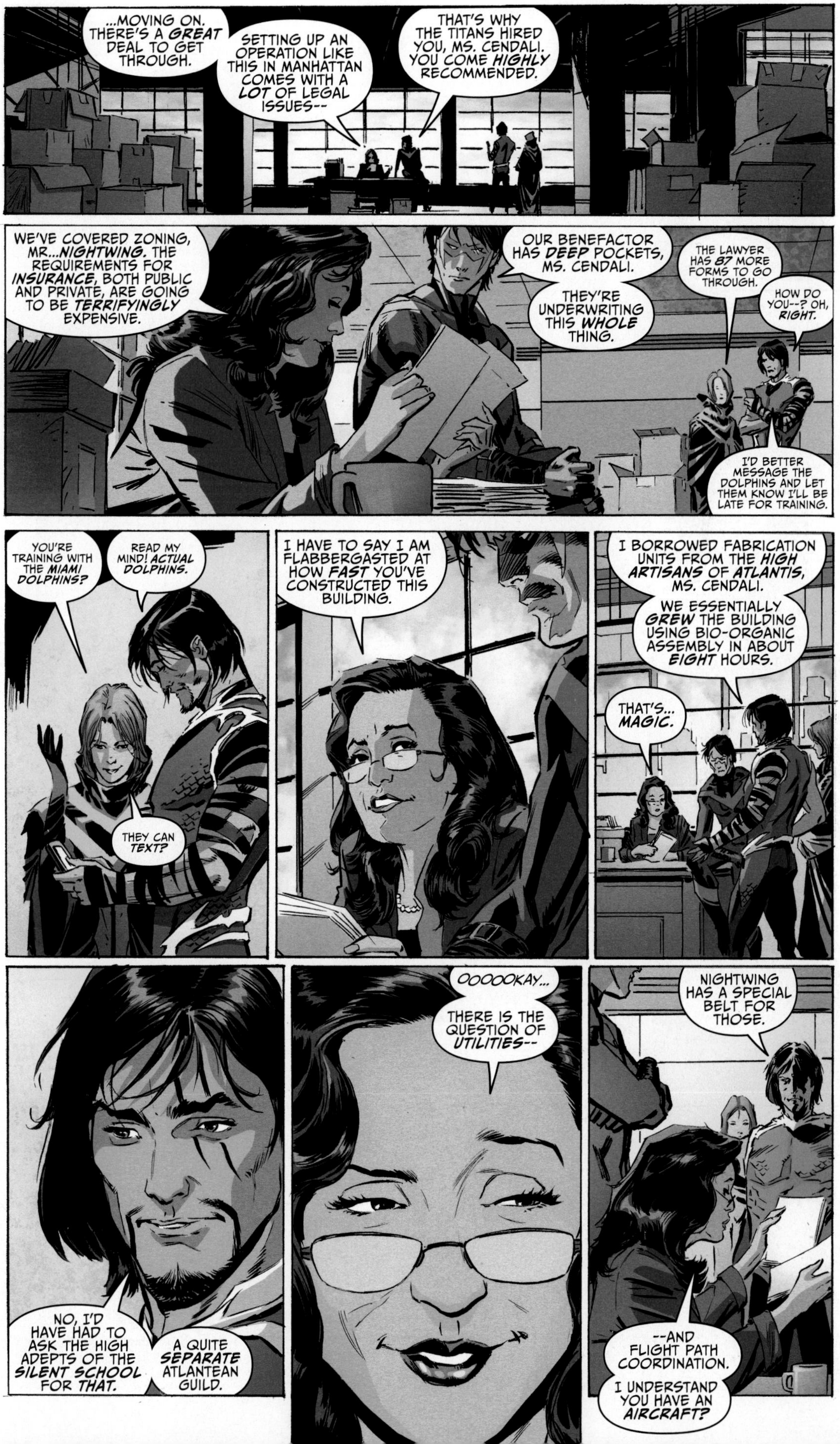

...MOVING ON. THERE'S A GREAT DEAL TO GET THROUGH.
SETTING UP AN OPERATION LIKE THIS IN MANHATTAN COMES WITH A LOT OF LEGAL ISSUES--
THAT'S WHY THE TITANS HIRED YOU, MS. CENDALI. YOU COME HIGHLY RECOMMENDED.
WE'VE COVERED ZONING, MR...NIGHTWING. THE REQUIREMENTS FOR INSURANCE, BOTH PUBLIC AND PRIVATE, ARE GOING TO BE TERRIFYINGLY EXPENSIVE.
OUR BENEFACTOR HAS DEEP POCKETS, MS. CENDALI.
THEY'RE UNDERWRITING THIS WHOLE THING.
THE LAWYER HAS 87 MORE FORMS TO GO THROUGH.
HOW DO YOU--? OH, RIGHT.
I'D BETTER MESSAGE THE DOLPHINS AND LET THEM KNOW I'LL BE LATE FOR TRAINING.
YOU'RE TRAINING WITH THE MIAMI DOLPHINS?
READ MY MIND! ACTUAL DOLPHINS.
THEY CAN TEXT?
I HAVE TO SAY I AM FLABBERGASTED AT HOW FAST YOU'VE CONSTRUCTED THIS BUILDING.
I BORROWED FABRICATION UNITS FROM THE HIGH ARTISANS OF ATLANTIS, MS. CENDALI.
WE ESSENTIALLY GREW THE BUILDING USING BIO-ORGANIC ASSEMBLY IN ABOUT EIGHT HOURS.
THAT'S... MAGIC.
NO, I'D HAVE HAD TO ASK THE HIGH ADEPTS OF THE SILENT SCHOOL FOR THAT.
A QUITE SEPARATE ATLANTEAN GUILD.
OOOOOKAY...
THERE IS THE QUESTION OF UTILITIES--
NIGHTWING HAS A SPECIAL BELT FOR THOSE.
--AND FLIGHT PATH COORDINATION.
I UNDERSTAND YOU HAVE AN AIRCRAFT?

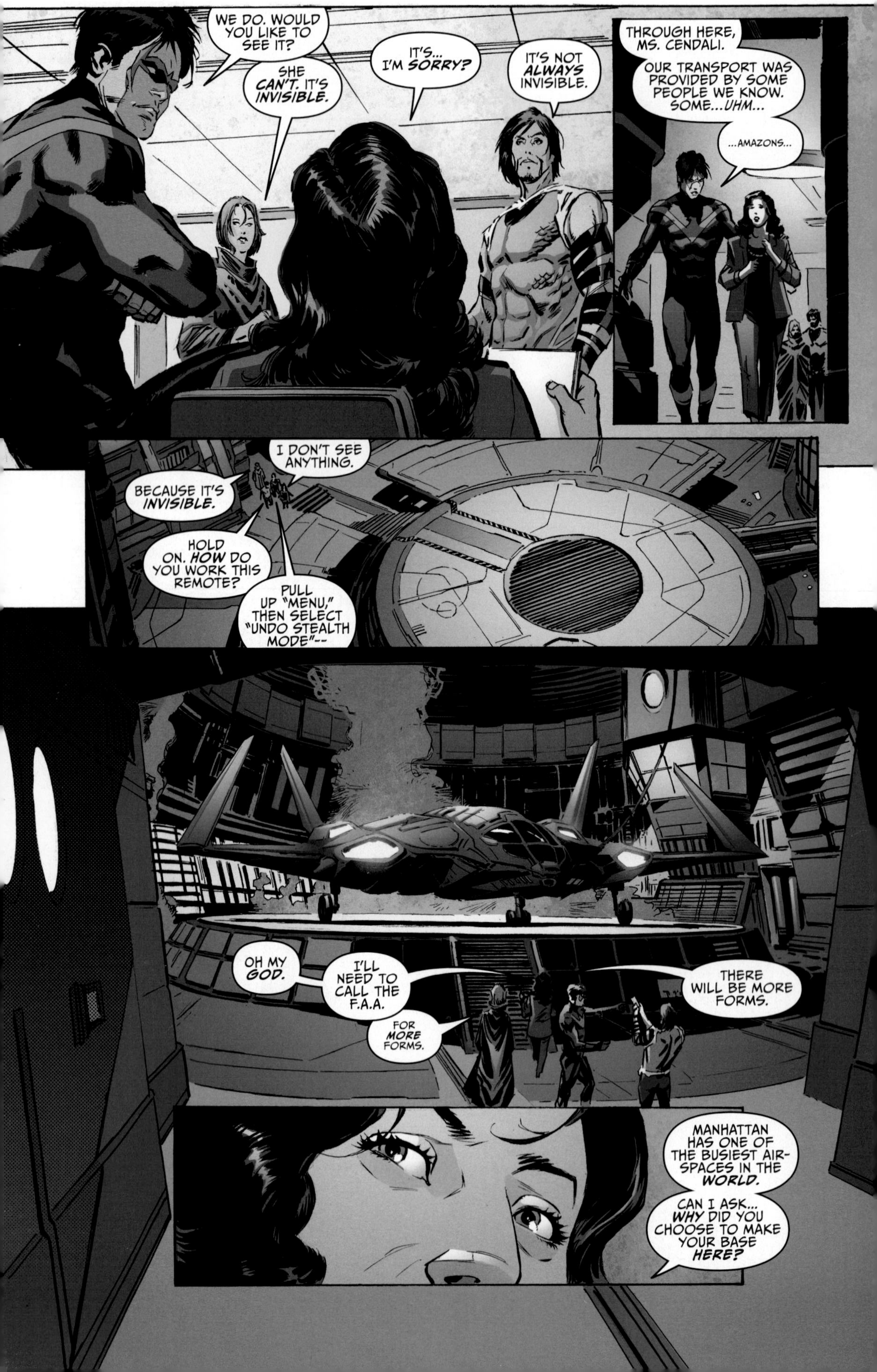
WE DO. WOULD YOU LIKE TO SEE IT?
SHE CAN'T. IT'S INVISIBLE.
IT'S... I'M SORRY?
IT'S NOT ALWAYS INVISIBLE.
THROUGH HERE, MS. CENDALI.
OUR TRANSPORT WAS PROVIDED BY SOME PEOPLE WE KNOW. SOME...UHM...
...AMAZONS...
I DON'T SEE ANYTHING.
BECAUSE IT'S INVISIBLE.
HOLD ON. HOW DO YOU WORK THIS REMOTE?
PULL UP "MENU," THEN SELECT "UNDO STEALTH MODE"--
OH MY GOD.
I'LL NEED TO CALL THE F.A.A.
FOR MORE FORMS.
THERE WILL BE MORE FORMS.
MANHATTAN HAS ONE OF THE BUSIEST AIR-SPACES IN THE WORLD.
CAN I ASK... WHY DID YOU CHOOSE TO MAKE YOUR BASE HERE?

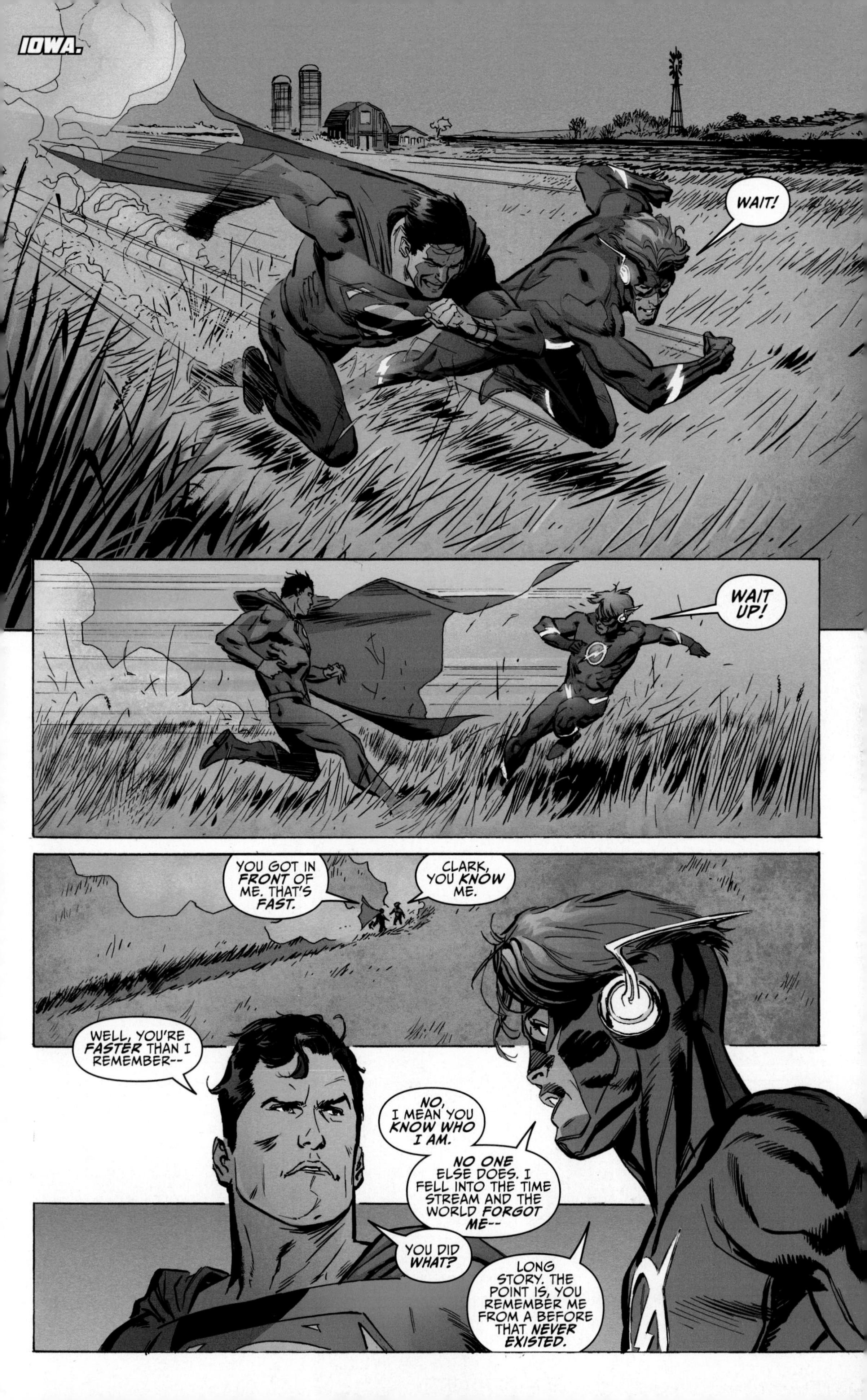
IOWA.
WAIT!
WAIT UP!
YOU GOT IN FRONT OF ME. THAT'S FAST.
CLARK, YOU KNOW ME.
WELL, YOU'RE FASTER THAN I REMEMBER--
NO, I MEAN YOU KNOW WHO I AM.
NO ONE ELSE DOES. I FELL INTO THE TIME STREAM AND THE WORLD FORGOT ME--
YOU DID WHAT?
LONG STORY. THE POINT IS, YOU REMEMBER ME FROM A BEFORE THAT NEVER EXISTED.

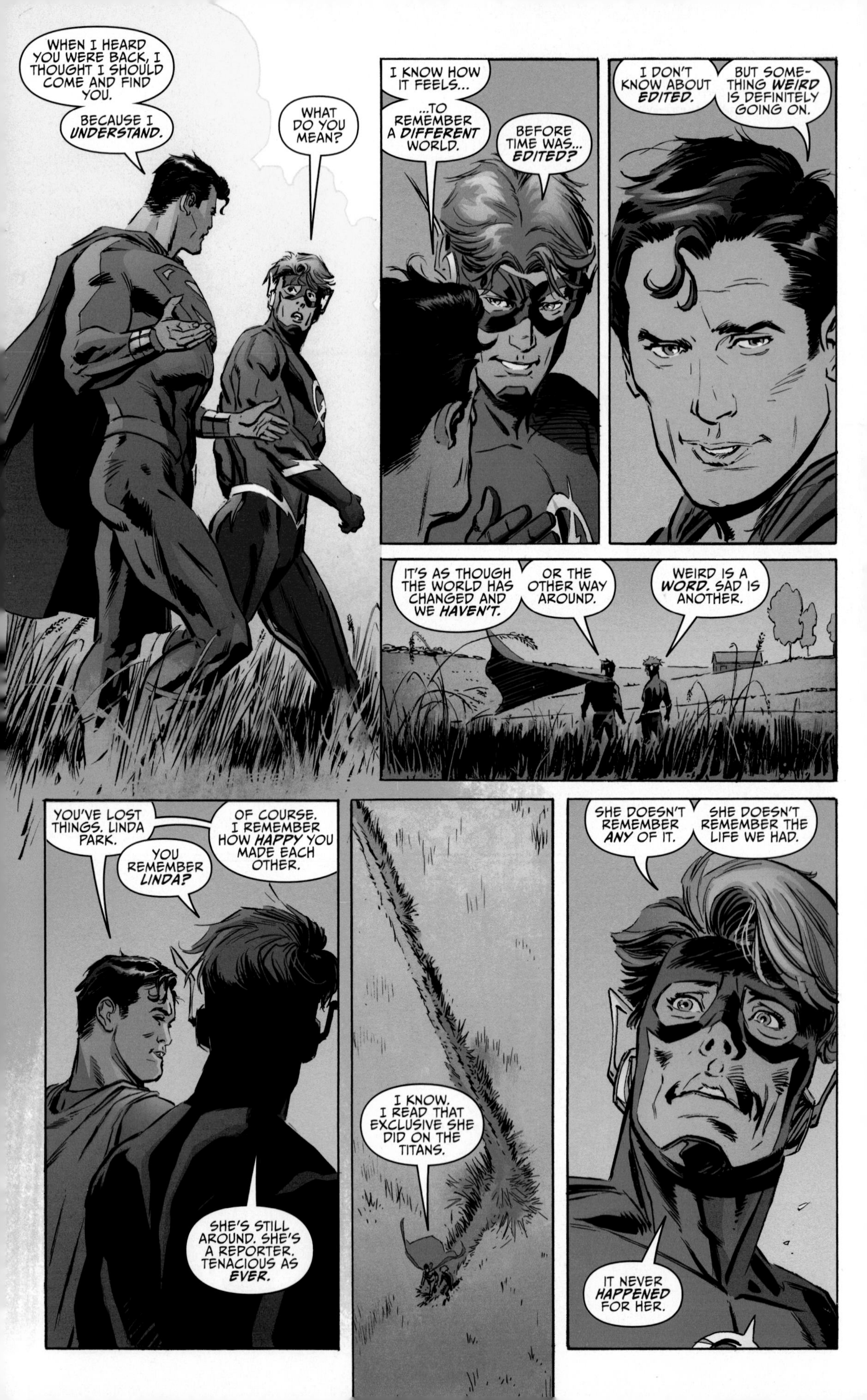
WHEN I HEARD YOU WERE BACK, I THOUGHT I SHOULD COME AND FIND YOU.
BECAUSE I UNDERSTAND.
WHAT DO YOU MEAN?
I KNOW HOW IT FEELS...
...TO REMEMBER A DIFFERENT WORLD.
BEFORE TIME WAS... EDITED?
I DON'T KNOW ABOUT EDITED.
BUT SOMETHING WEIRD IS DEFINITELY GOING ON.
IT'S AS THOUGH THE WORLD HAS CHANGED AND WE HAVEN'T.
OR THE OTHER WAY AROUND.
WEIRD IS A WORD. SAD IS ANOTHER.
YOU'VE LOST THINGS. LINDA PARK.
YOU REMEMBER LINDA?
OF COURSE. I REMEMBER HOW HAPPY YOU MADE EACH OTHER.
SHE'S STILL AROUND. SHE'S A REPORTER. TENACIOUS AS EVER.
I KNOW. I READ THAT EXCLUSIVE SHE DID ON THE TITANS.
SHE DOESN'T REMEMBER ANY OF IT.
SHE DOESN'T REMEMBER THE LIFE WE HAD.
IT NEVER HAPPENED FOR HER.

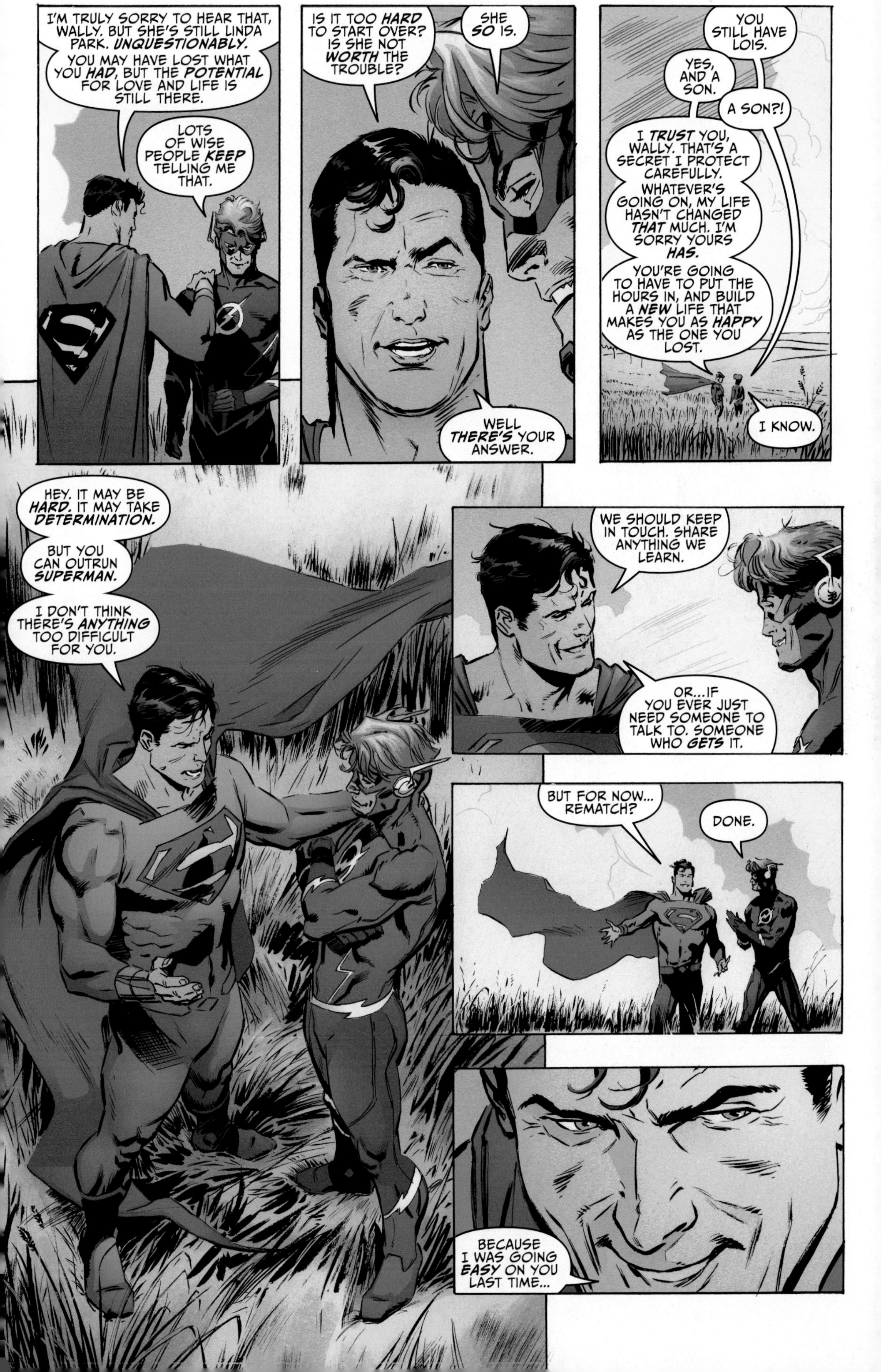
I'M TRULY SORRY TO HEAR THAT, WALLY. BUT SHE'S STILL LINDA PARK. UNQUESTIONABLY.
YOU MAY HAVE LOST WHAT YOU HAD, BUT THE POTENTIAL FOR LOVE AND LIFE IS STILL THERE.
LOTS OF WISE PEOPLE KEEP TELLING ME THAT.
IS IT TOO HARD TO START OVER? IS SHE NOT WORTH THE TROUBLE?
SHE SO IS.
WELL THERE'S YOUR ANSWER.
YOU STILL HAVE LOIS.
YES, AND A SON.
A SON?!
I TRUST YOU, WALLY. THAT'S A SECRET I PROTECT CAREFULLY.
WHATEVER'S GOING ON, MY LIFE HASN'T CHANGED THAT MUCH. I'M SORRY YOURS HAS.
YOU'RE GOING TO HAVE TO PUT THE HOURS IN, AND BUILD A NEW LIFE THAT MAKES YOU AS HAPPY AS THE ONE YOU LOST.
I KNOW.
HEY. IT MAY BE HARD. IT MAY TAKE DETERMINATION.
BUT YOU CAN OUTRUN SUPERMAN.
I DON'T THINK THERE'S ANYTHING TOO DIFFICULT FOR YOU.
WE SHOULD KEEP IN TOUCH. SHARE ANYTHING WE LEARN.
OR...IF YOU EVER JUST NEED SOMEONE TO TALK TO. SOMEONE WHO GETS IT.
BUT FOR NOW... REMATCH?
DONE.
BECAUSE I WAS GOING EASY ON YOU LAST TIME...

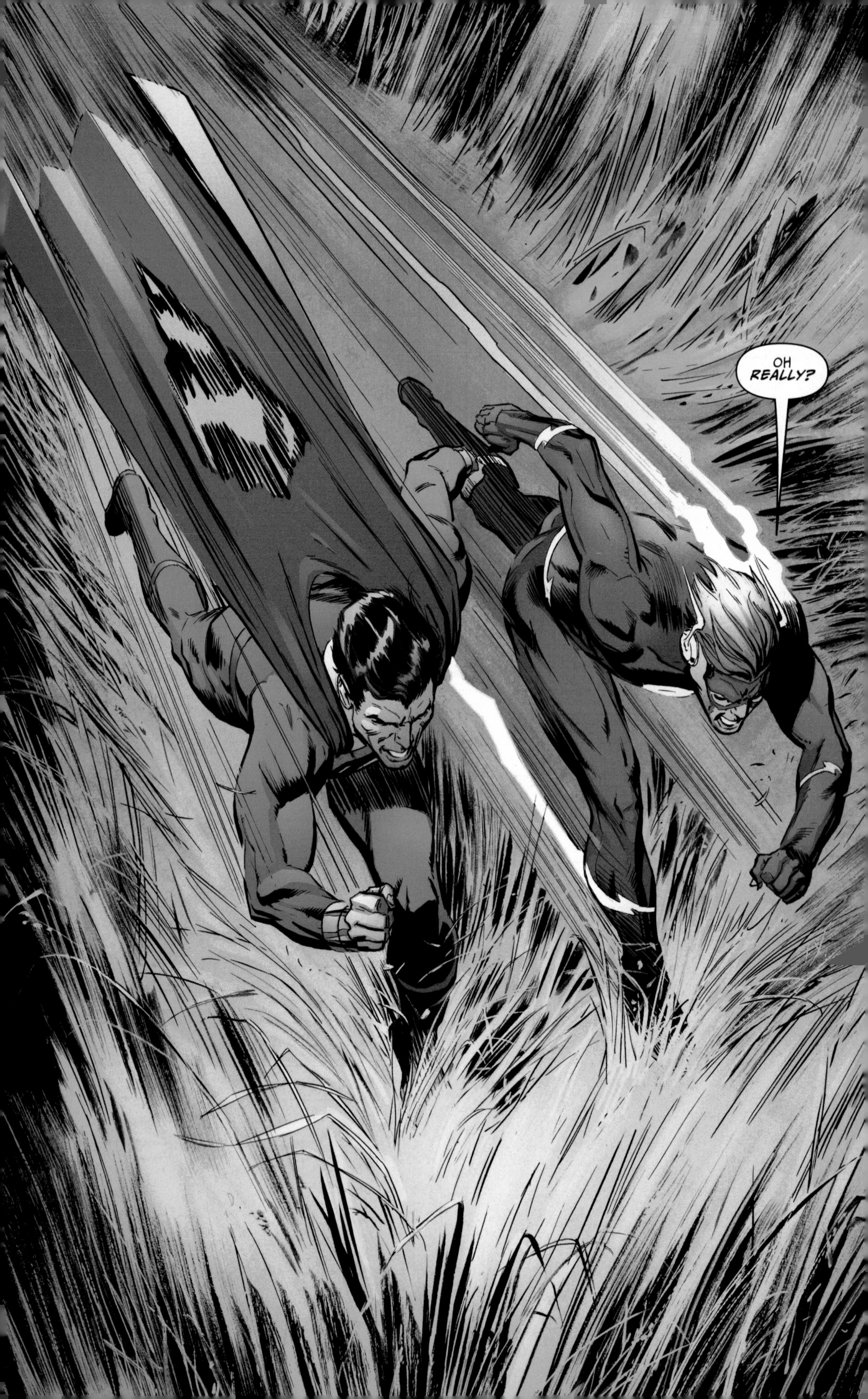
OH *REALLY?*

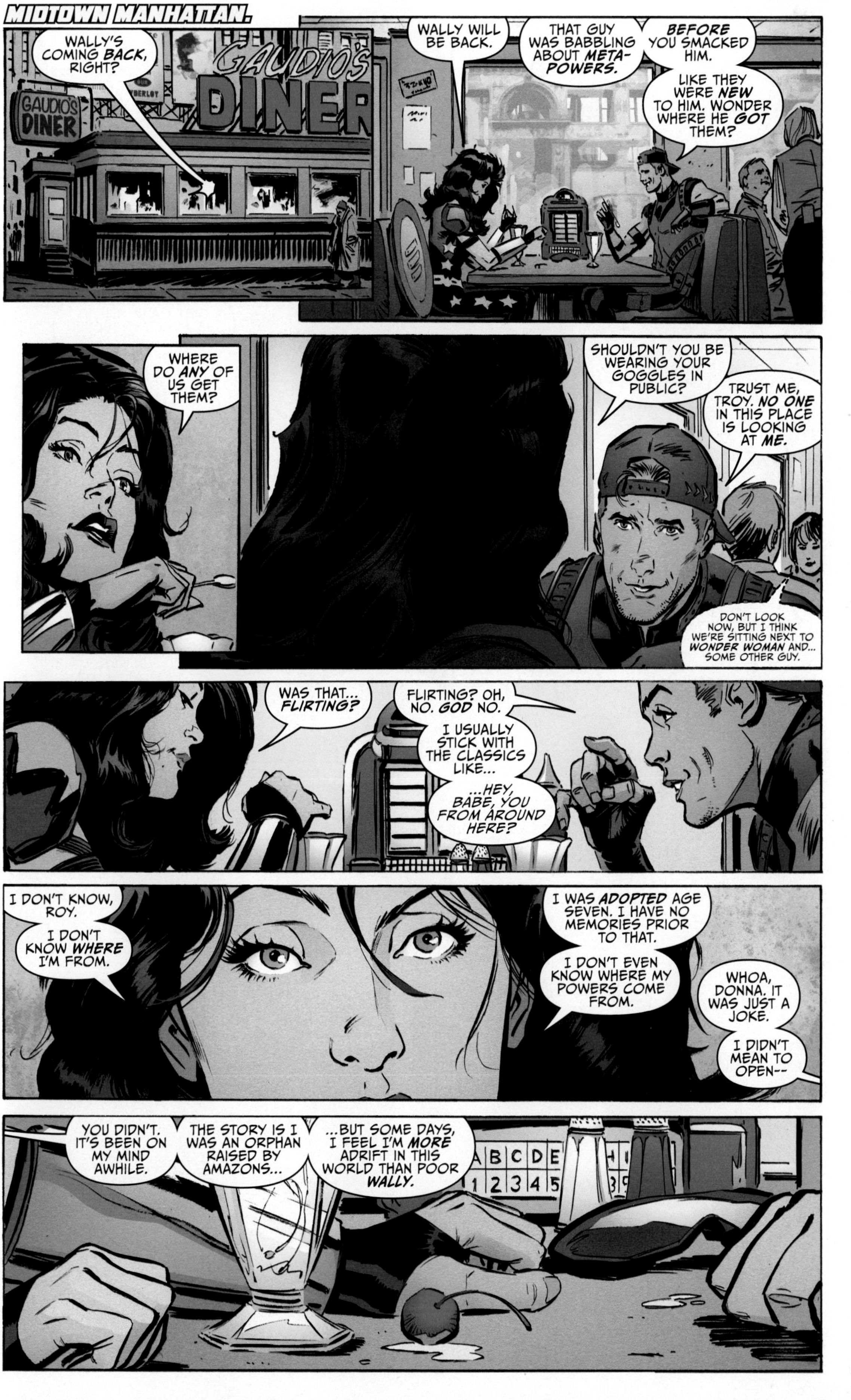
MIDTOWN MANHATTAN.
GAUDIO'S DINER
GAUDIO'S DINER
WALLY'S COMING BACK, RIGHT?
WALLY WILL BE BACK.
THAT GUY WAS BABBLING ABOUT META-POWERS.
BEFORE YOU SMACKED HIM.
LIKE THEY WERE NEW TO HIM. WONDER WHERE HE GOT THEM?
WHERE DO ANY OF US GET THEM?
SHOULDN'T YOU BE WEARING YOUR GOGGLES IN PUBLIC?
TRUST ME, TROY. NO ONE IN THIS PLACE IS LOOKING AT ME.
DON'T LOOK NOW, BUT I THINK WE'RE SITTING NEXT TO WONDER WOMAN AND... SOME OTHER GUY.
WAS THAT... FLIRTING?
FLIRTING? OH, NO. GOD NO.
I USUALLY STICK WITH THE CLASSICS LIKE...
...HEY, BABE, YOU FROM AROUND HERE?
I DON'T KNOW, ROY.
I DON'T KNOW WHERE I'M FROM.
I WAS ADOPTED AGE SEVEN. I HAVE NO MEMORIES PRIOR TO THAT.
I DON'T EVEN KNOW WHERE MY POWERS COME FROM.
WHOA, DONNA. IT WAS JUST A JOKE.
I DIDN'T MEAN TO OPEN--
YOU DIDN'T. IT'S BEEN ON MY MIND AWHILE.
THE STORY IS I WAS AN ORPHAN RAISED BY AMAZONS...
...BUT SOME DAYS, I FEEL I'M MORE ADRIFT IN THIS WORLD THAN POOR WALLY.
A B C D E
1 2 3 4 5

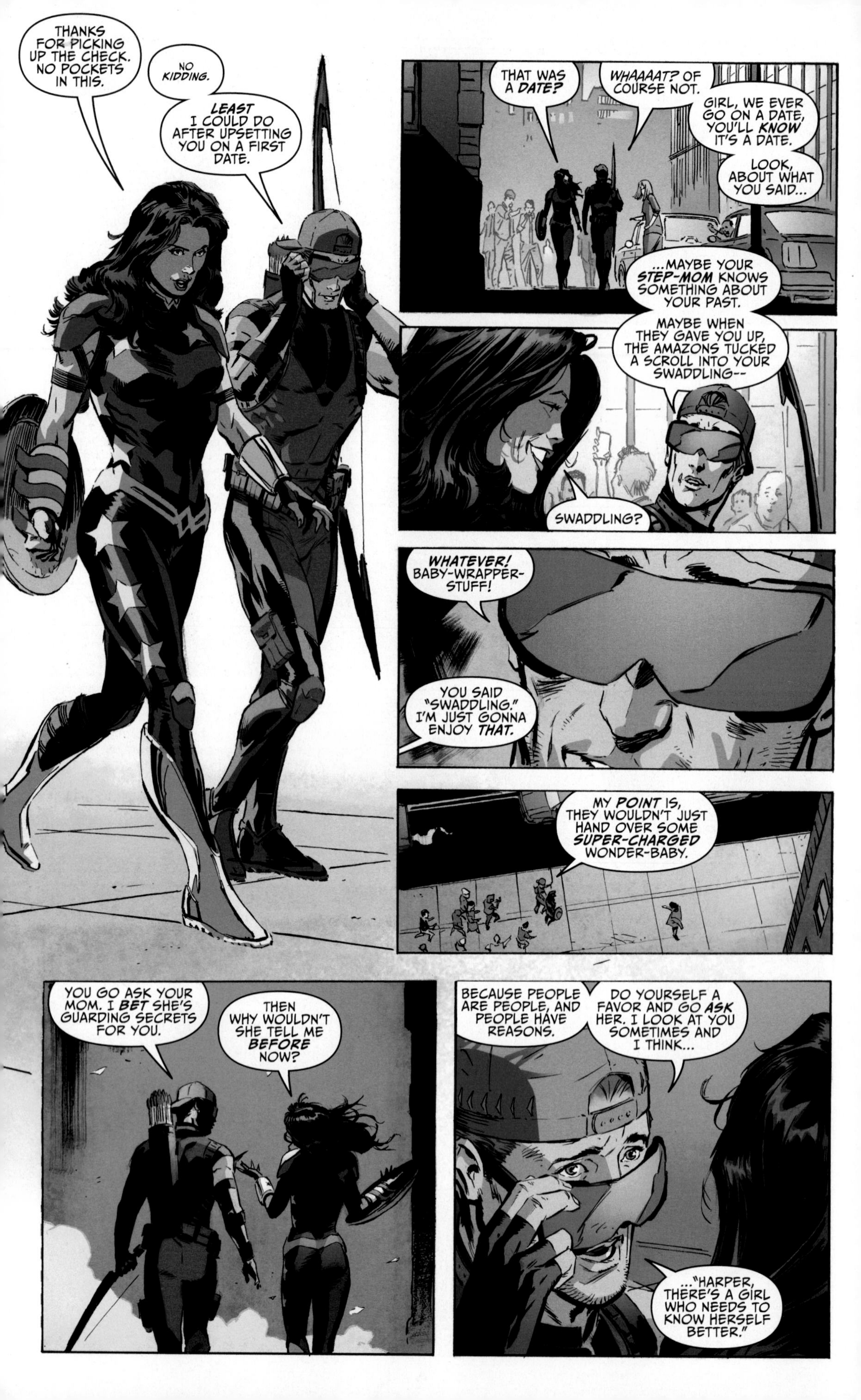
THANKS FOR PICKING UP THE CHECK. NO POCKETS IN THIS.
NO KIDDING.
LEAST I COULD DO AFTER UPSETTING YOU ON A FIRST DATE.
THAT WAS A DATE?
WHAAAAT? OF COURSE NOT.
GIRL, WE EVER GO ON A DATE, YOU'LL KNOW IT'S A DATE.
LOOK, ABOUT WHAT YOU SAID...
...MAYBE YOUR STEP-MOM KNOWS SOMETHING ABOUT YOUR PAST.
MAYBE WHEN THEY GAVE YOU UP, THE AMAZONS TUCKED A SCROLL INTO YOUR SWADDLING--
SWADDLING?
WHATEVER! BABY-WRAPPER-STUFF!
YOU SAID "SWADDLING." I'M JUST GONNA ENJOY THAT.
MY POINT IS, THEY WOULDN'T JUST HAND OVER SOME SUPER-CHARGED WONDER-BABY.
YOU GO ASK YOUR MOM. I BET SHE'S GUARDING SECRETS FOR YOU.
THEN WHY WOULDN'T SHE TELL ME BEFORE NOW?
BECAUSE PEOPLE ARE PEOPLE, AND PEOPLE HAVE REASONS.
DO YOURSELF A FAVOR AND GO ASK HER. I LOOK AT YOU SOMETIMES AND I THINK...
..."HARPER, THERE'S A GIRL WHO NEEDS TO KNOW HERSELF BETTER."

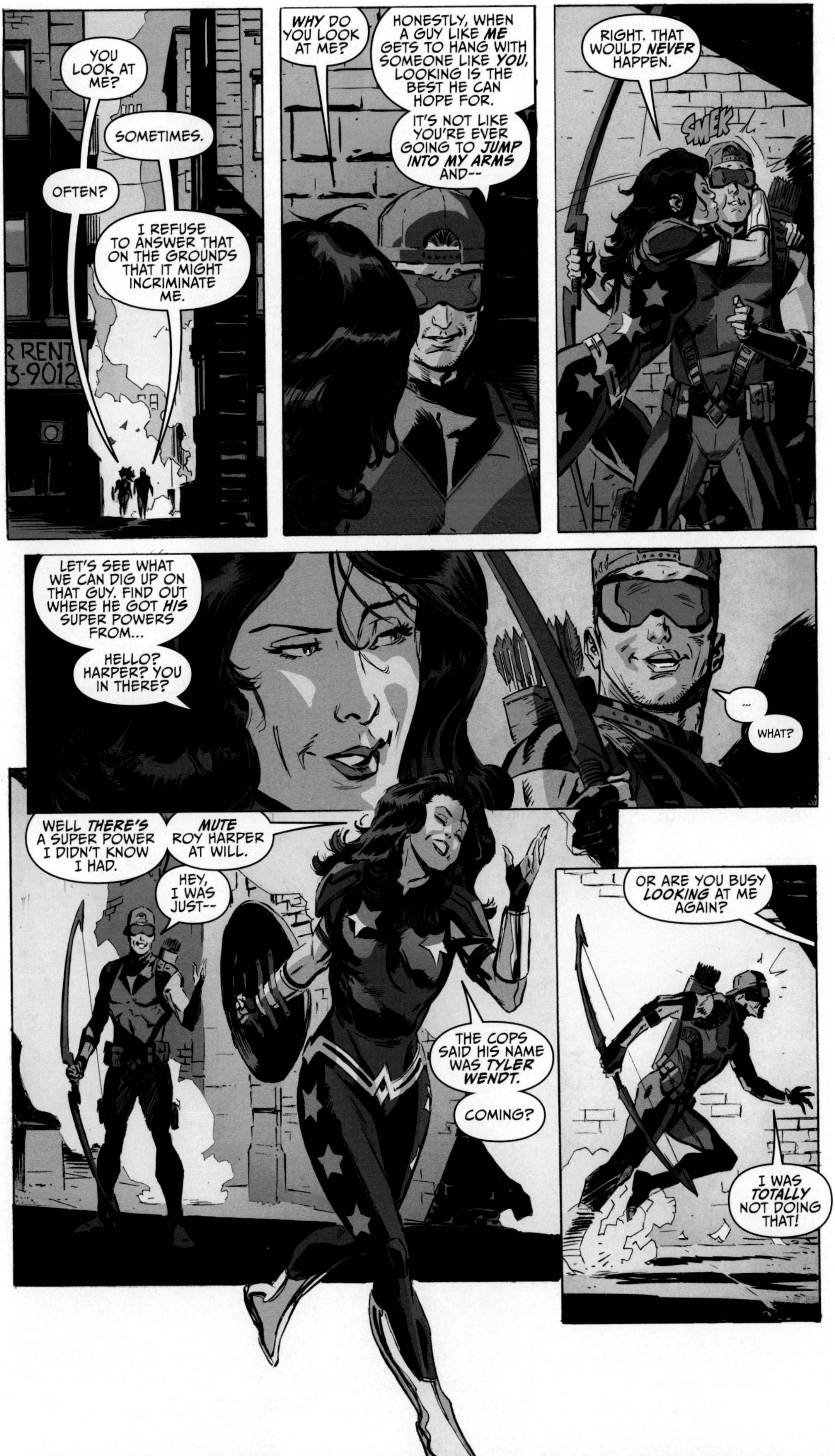
YOU LOOK AT ME?
SOMETIMES.
OFTEN?
I REFUSE TO ANSWER THAT ON THE GROUNDS THAT IT MIGHT INCRIMINATE ME.
R RENT
3-9012
WHY DO YOU LOOK AT ME?
HONESTLY, WHEN A GUY LIKE ME GETS TO HANG WITH SOMEONE LIKE YOU, LOOKING IS THE BEST HE CAN HOPE FOR.
IT'S NOT LIKE YOU'RE EVER GOING TO JUMP INTO MY ARMS AND--
RIGHT. THAT WOULD NEVER HAPPEN.
SMEK
LET'S SEE WHAT WE CAN DIG UP ON THAT GUY. FIND OUT WHERE HE GOT HIS SUPER POWERS FROM...
HELLO? HARPER? YOU IN THERE?
...
WHAT?
WELL THERE'S A SUPER POWER I DIDN'T KNOW I HAD.
MUTE ROY HARPER AT WILL.
HEY, I WAS JUST--
THE COPS SAID HIS NAME WAS TYLER WENDT.
COMING?
OR ARE YOU BUSY LOOKING AT ME AGAIN?
I WAS TOTALLY NOT DOING THAT!

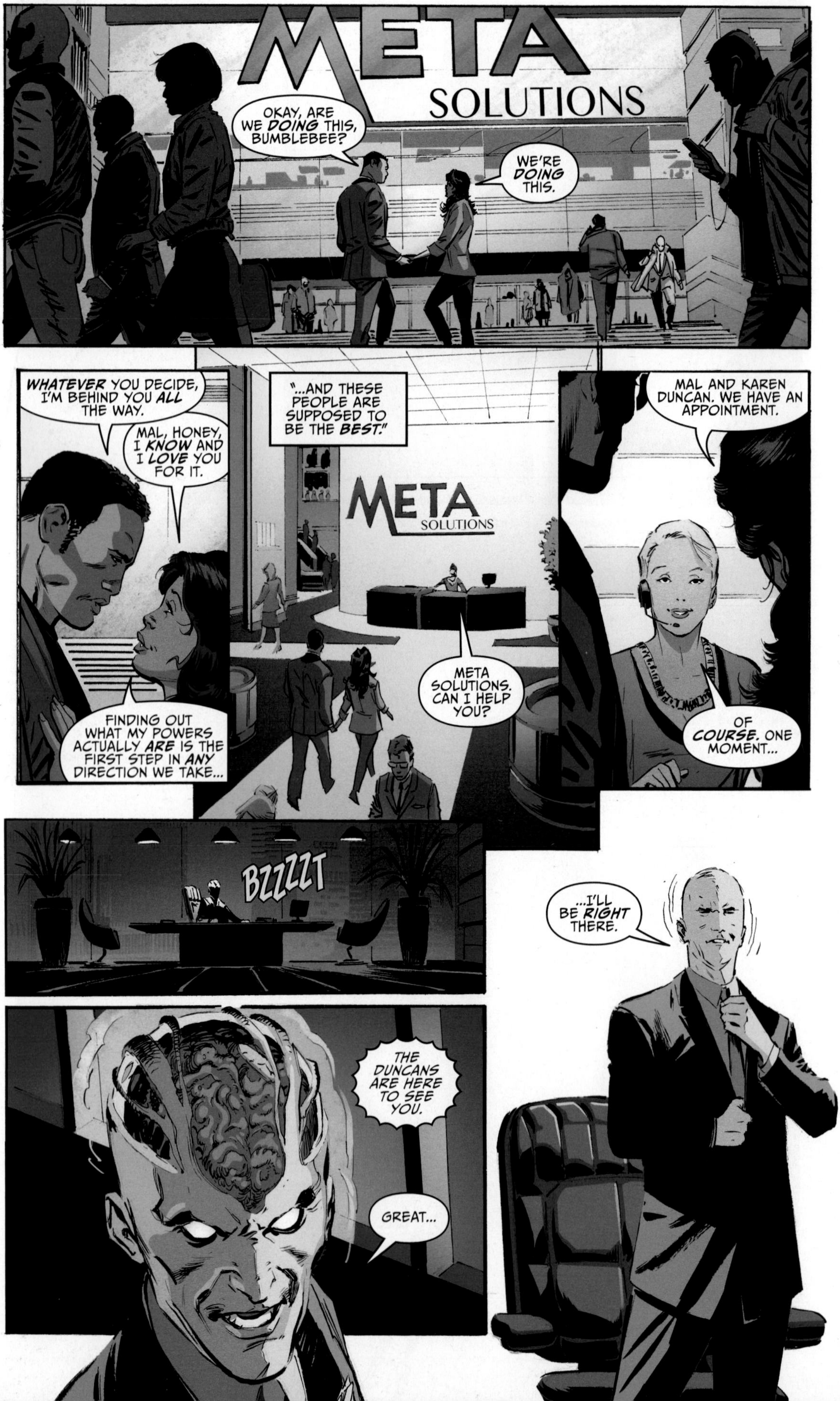
META
SOLUTIONS
OKAY, ARE WE *DOING* THIS, BUMBLEBEE?
WE'RE *DOING* THIS.
WHATEVER YOU DECIDE, I'M BEHIND YOU *ALL* THE WAY.
MAL, HONEY, I *KNOW* AND I *LOVE* YOU FOR IT.
FINDING OUT WHAT MY POWERS ACTUALLY *ARE* IS THE FIRST STEP IN *ANY* DIRECTION WE TAKE...
"...AND THESE PEOPLE ARE SUPPOSED TO BE THE *BEST.*"
META SOLUTIONS
META SOLUTIONS. CAN I HELP YOU?
MAL AND KAREN DUNCAN. WE HAVE AN APPOINTMENT.
OF *COURSE.* ONE MOMENT...
BZZZZT
THE DUNCANS ARE HERE TO SEE YOU.
GREAT...
...I'LL BE *RIGHT* THERE.

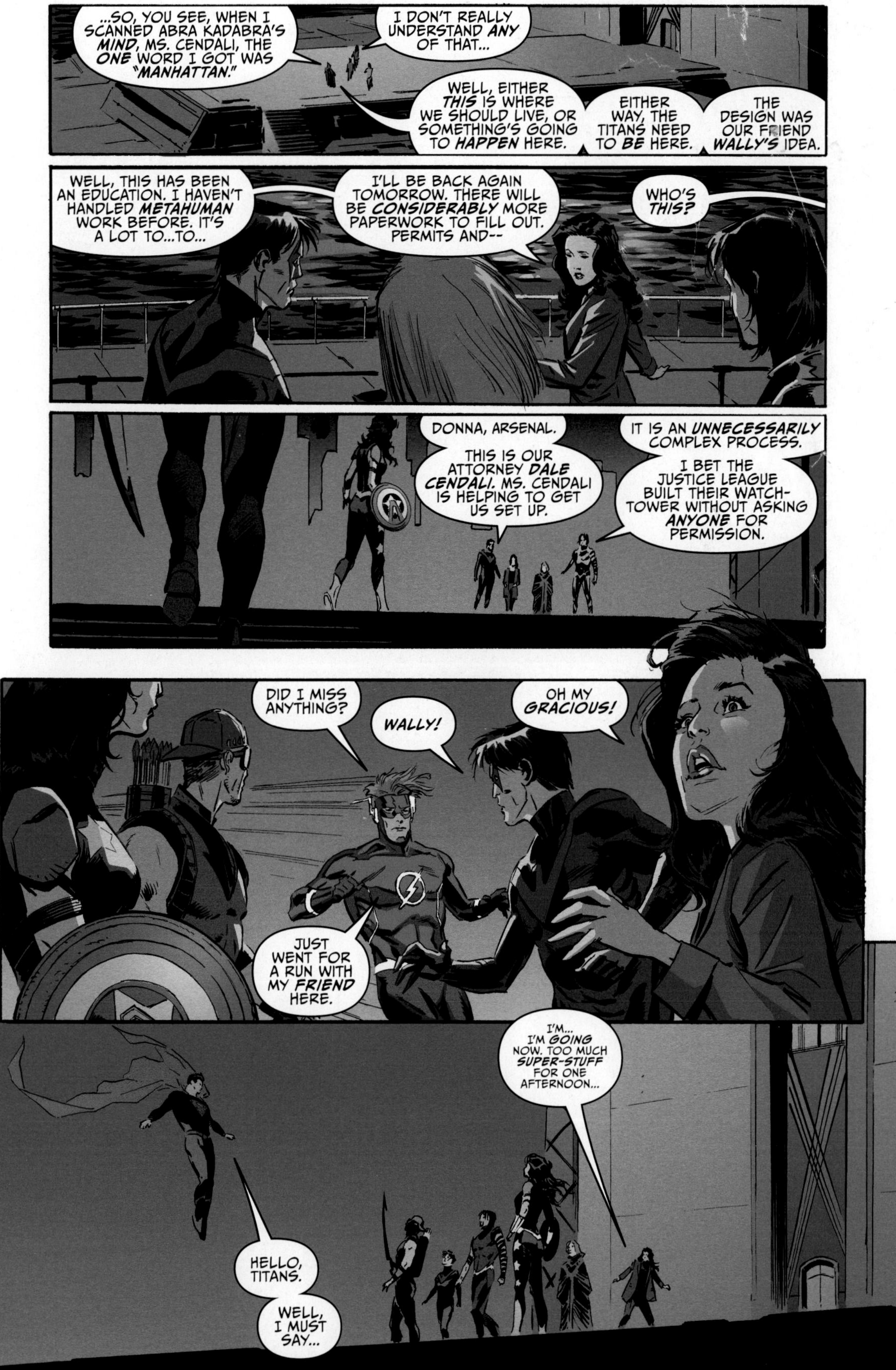
...SO, YOU SEE, WHEN I SCANNED ABRA KADABRA'S MIND, MS. CENDALI, THE ONE WORD I GOT WAS "MANHATTAN."
I DON'T REALLY UNDERSTAND ANY OF THAT...
WELL, EITHER THIS IS WHERE WE SHOULD LIVE, OR SOMETHING'S GOING TO HAPPEN HERE.
EITHER WAY, THE TITANS NEED TO BE HERE.
THE DESIGN WAS OUR FRIEND WALLY'S IDEA.
WELL, THIS HAS BEEN AN EDUCATION. I HAVEN'T HANDLED METAHUMAN WORK BEFORE. IT'S A LOT TO...TO...
I'LL BE BACK AGAIN TOMORROW. THERE WILL BE CONSIDERABLY MORE PAPERWORK TO FILL OUT. PERMITS AND--
WHO'S THIS?
DONNA, ARSENAL.
THIS IS OUR ATTORNEY DALE CENDALI. MS. CENDALI IS HELPING TO GET US SET UP.
IT IS AN UNNECESSARILY COMPLEX PROCESS.
I BET THE JUSTICE LEAGUE BUILT THEIR WATCH-TOWER WITHOUT ASKING ANYONE FOR PERMISSION.
DID I MISS ANYTHING?
WALLY!
OH MY GRACIOUS!
JUST WENT FOR A RUN WITH MY FRIEND HERE.
I'M... I'M GOING NOW. TOO MUCH SUPER-STUFF FOR ONE AFTERNOON...
HELLO, TITANS.
WELL, I MUST SAY...

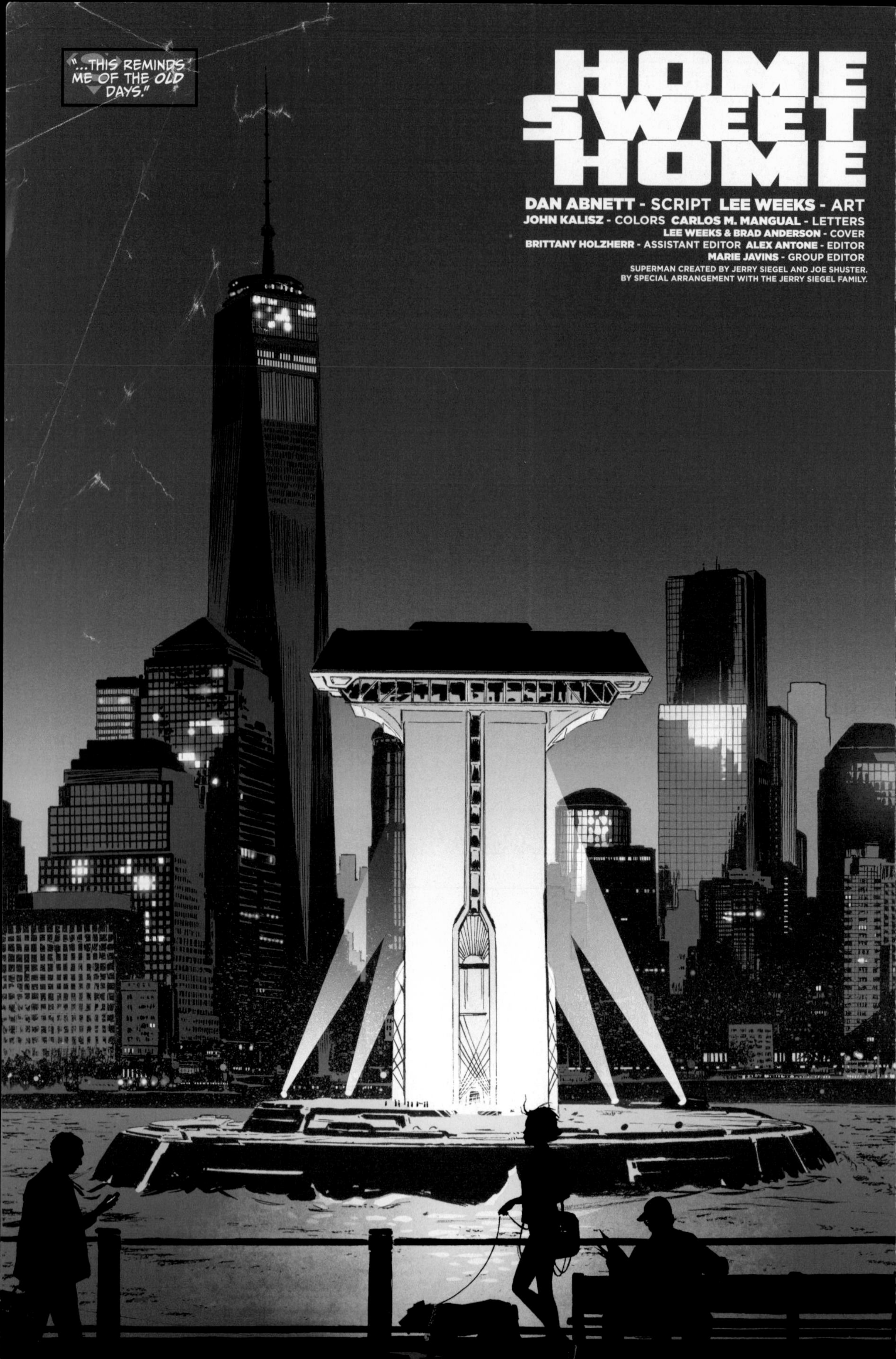
"...THIS REMINDS ME OF THE OLD DAYS."
HOME SWEET HOME
DAN ABNETT - SCRIPT LEE WEEKS - ART
JOHN KALISZ - COLORS CARLOS M. MANGUAL - LETTERS
LEE WEEKS & BRAD ANDERSON - COVER
BRITTANY HOLZHERR - ASSISTANT EDITOR ALEX ANTONE - EDITOR
MARIE JAVINS - GROUP EDITOR
SUPERMAN CREATED BY JERRY SIEGEL AND JOE SHUSTER.
BY SPECIAL ARRANGEMENT WITH THE JERRY SIEGEL FAMILY.

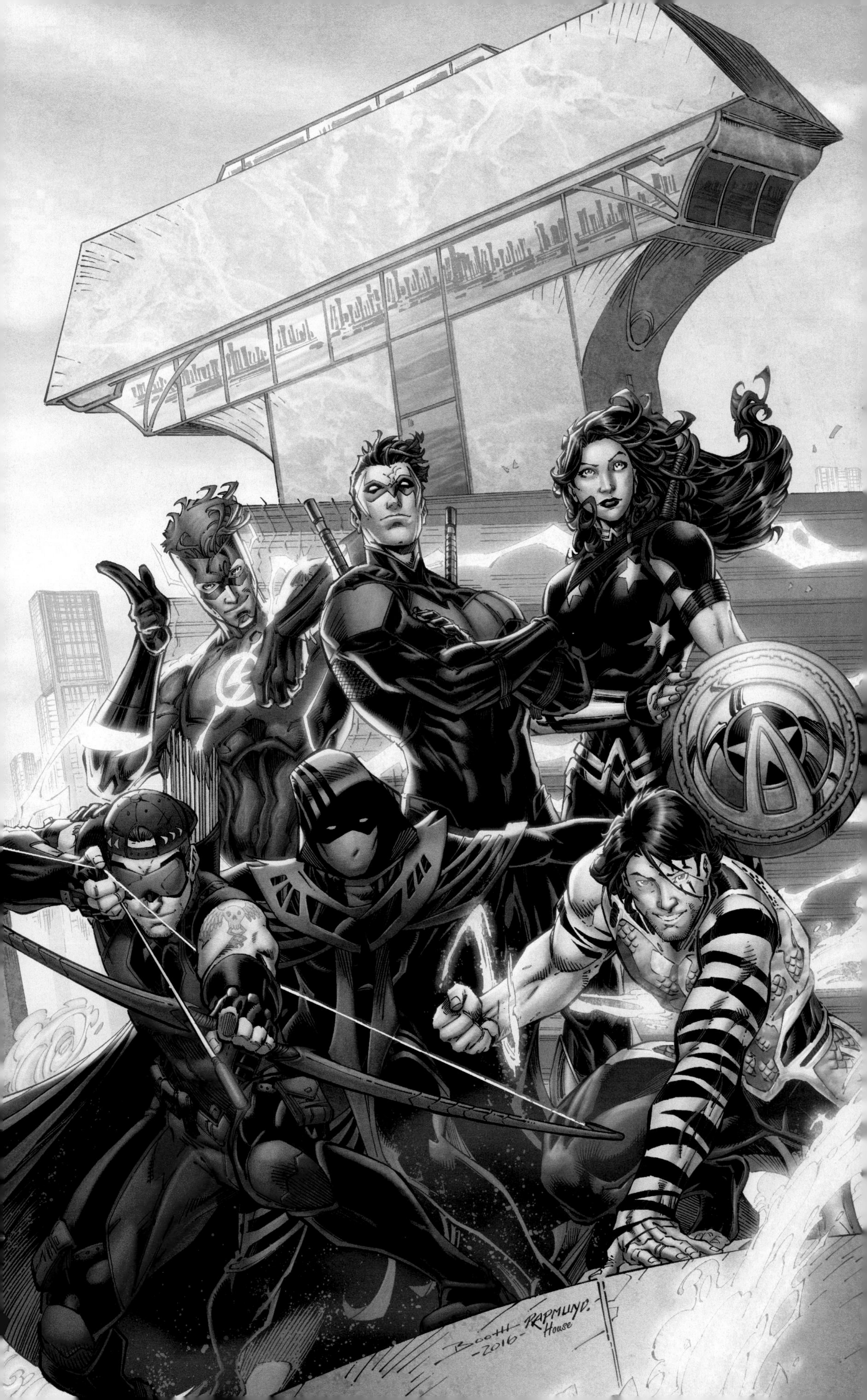
BOOTH
-2016-
RAPMUND
House

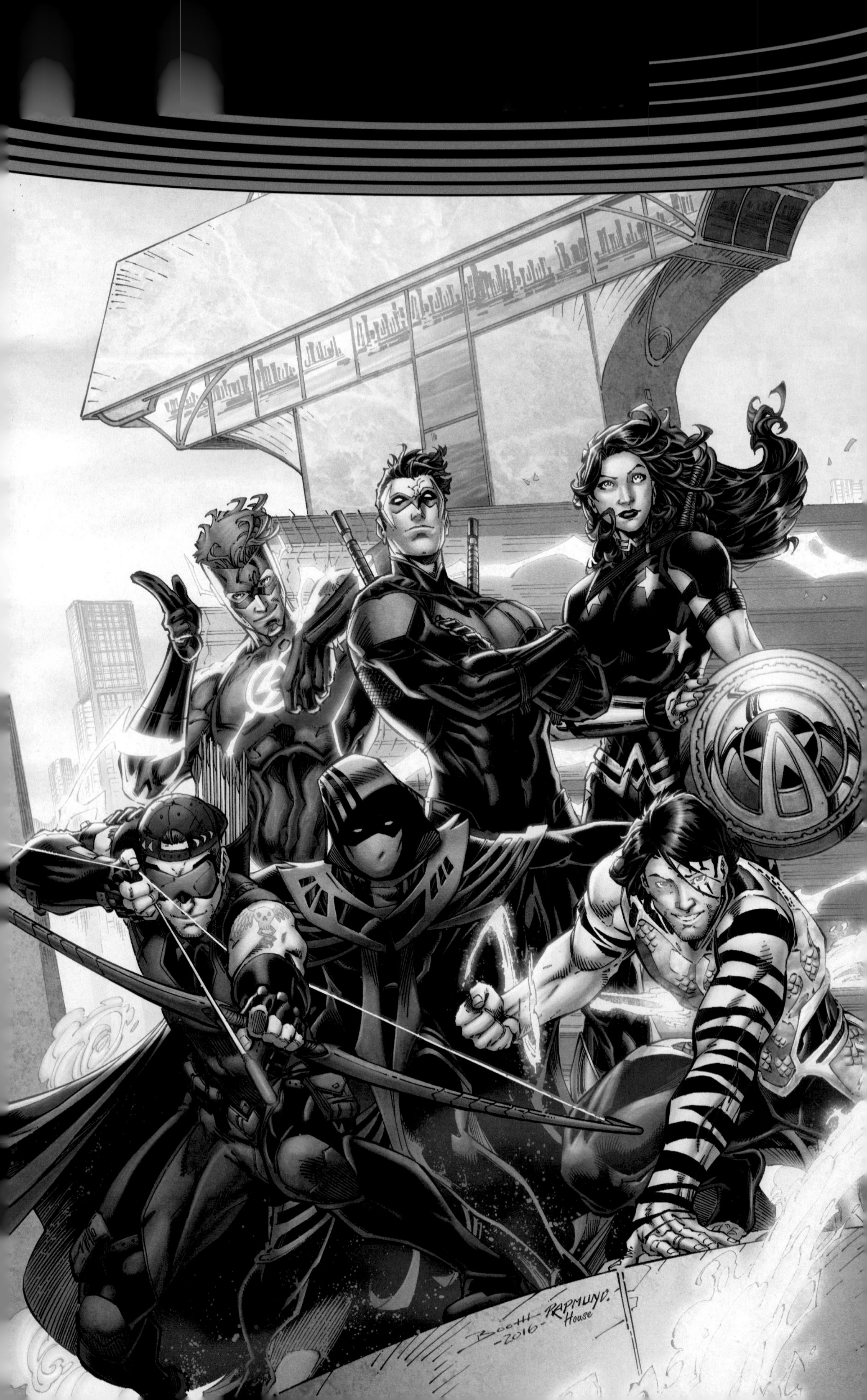
BOOTH
-2016-
RAPMUND
House

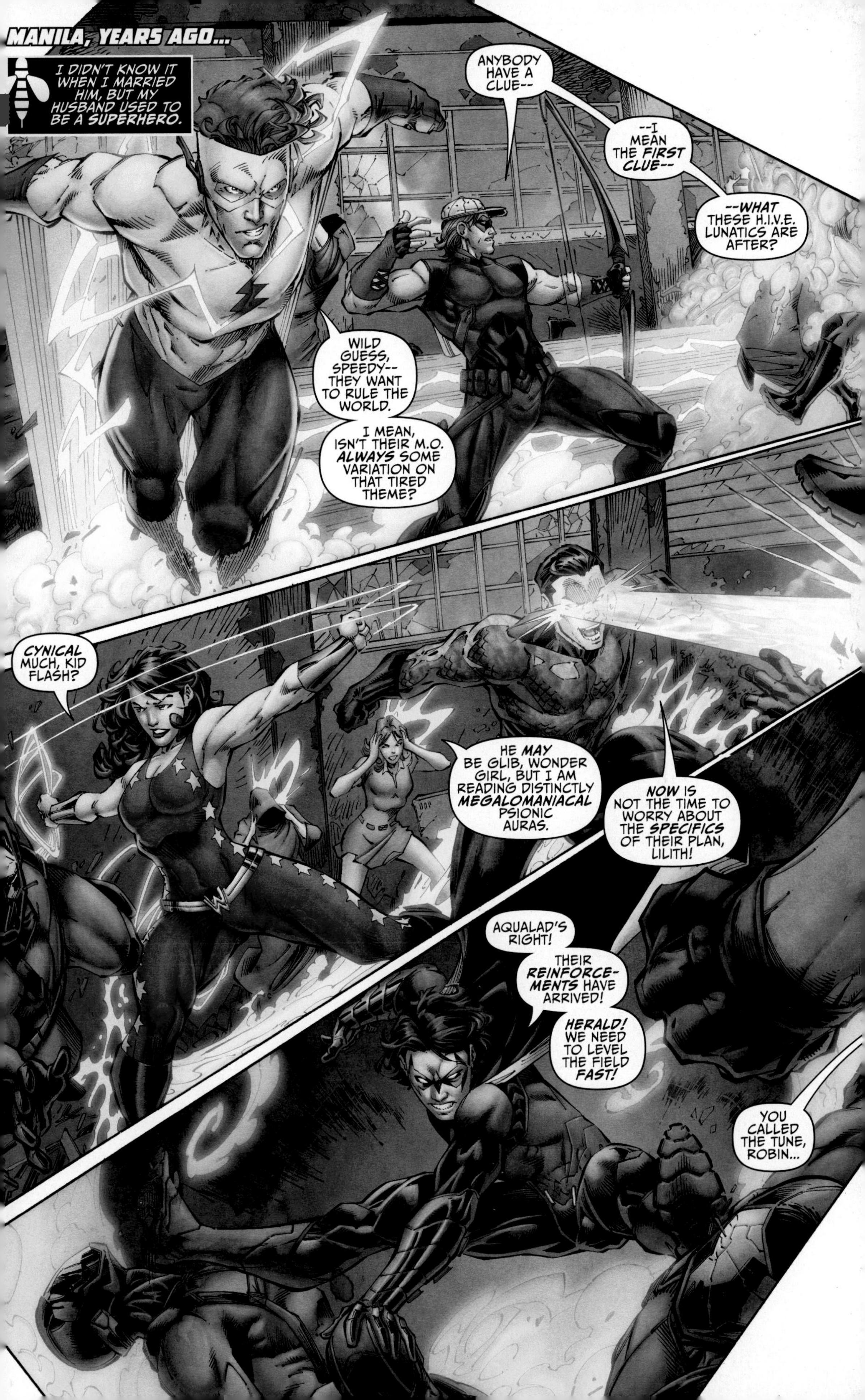
MANILA, YEARS AGO...
I DIDN'T KNOW IT WHEN I MARRIED HIM, BUT MY HUSBAND USED TO BE A SUPERHERO.
ANYBODY HAVE A CLUE--
--I MEAN THE FIRST CLUE--
--WHAT THESE H.I.V.E. LUNATICS ARE AFTER?
WILD GUESS, SPEEDY-- THEY WANT TO RULE THE WORLD.
I MEAN, ISN'T THEIR M.O. ALWAYS SOME VARIATION ON THAT TIRED THEME?
CYNICAL MUCH, KID FLASH?
HE MAY BE GLIB, WONDER GIRL, BUT I AM READING DISTINCTLY MEGALOMANIACAL PSIONIC AURAS.
NOW IS NOT THE TIME TO WORRY ABOUT THE SPECIFICS OF THEIR PLAN, LILITH!
AQUALAD'S RIGHT!
THEIR REINFORCEMENTS HAVE ARRIVED!
HERALD! WE NEED TO LEVEL THE FIELD FAST!
YOU CALLED THE TUNE, ROBIN...

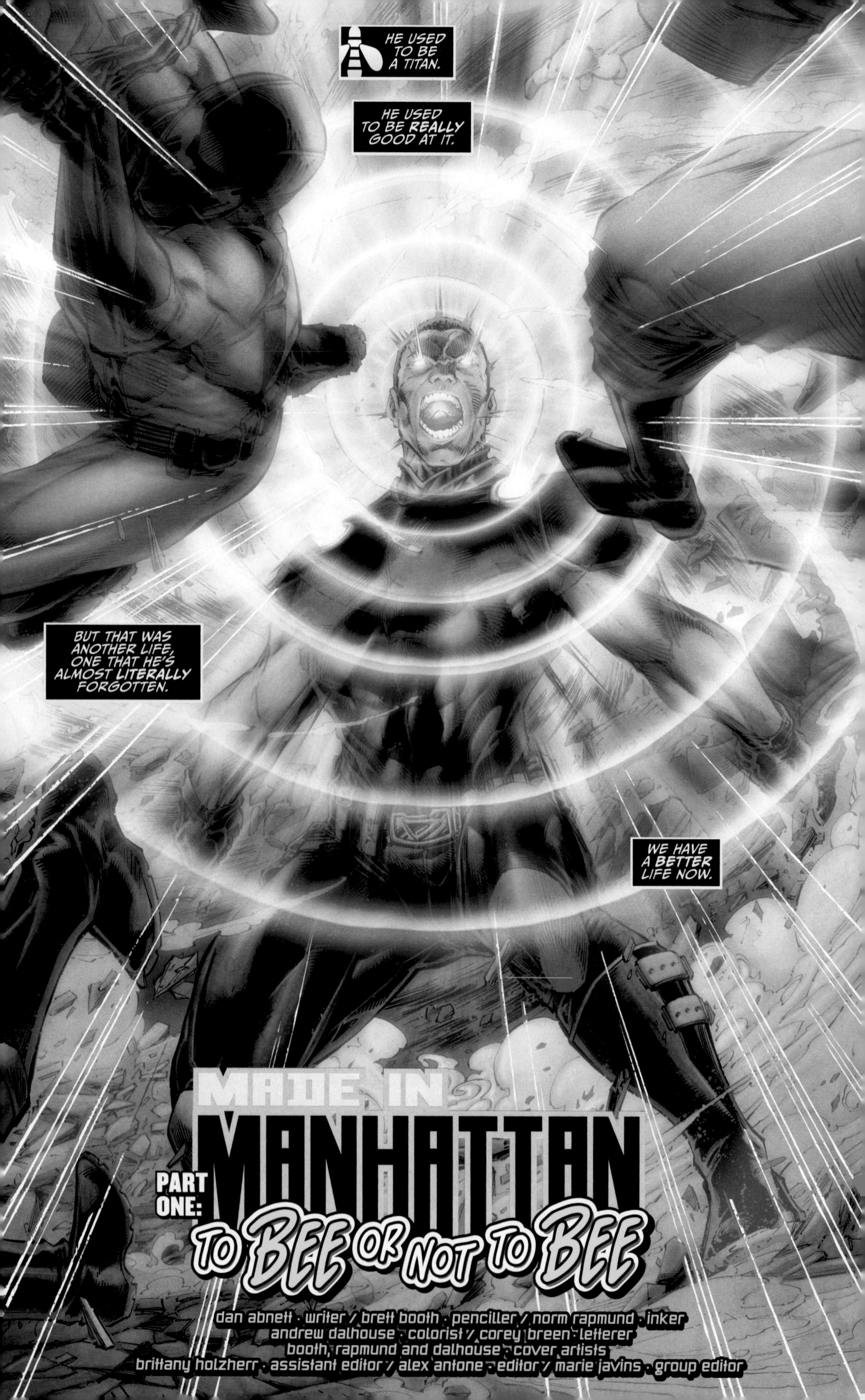
HE USED TO BE A TITAN.
HE USED TO BE REALLY GOOD AT IT.
BUT THAT WAS ANOTHER LIFE, ONE THAT HE'S ALMOST LITERALLY FORGOTTEN.
WE HAVE A BETTER LIFE NOW.
MADE IN MANHATTAN
PART ONE: TO BEE OR NOT TO BEE
dan abnett · writer / brett booth · penciller / norm rapmund · inker
andrew dalhouse · colorist / corey breen · letterer
booth, rapmund and dalhouse · cover artists
brittany holzherr · assistant editor / alex antone · editor / marie javins · group editor

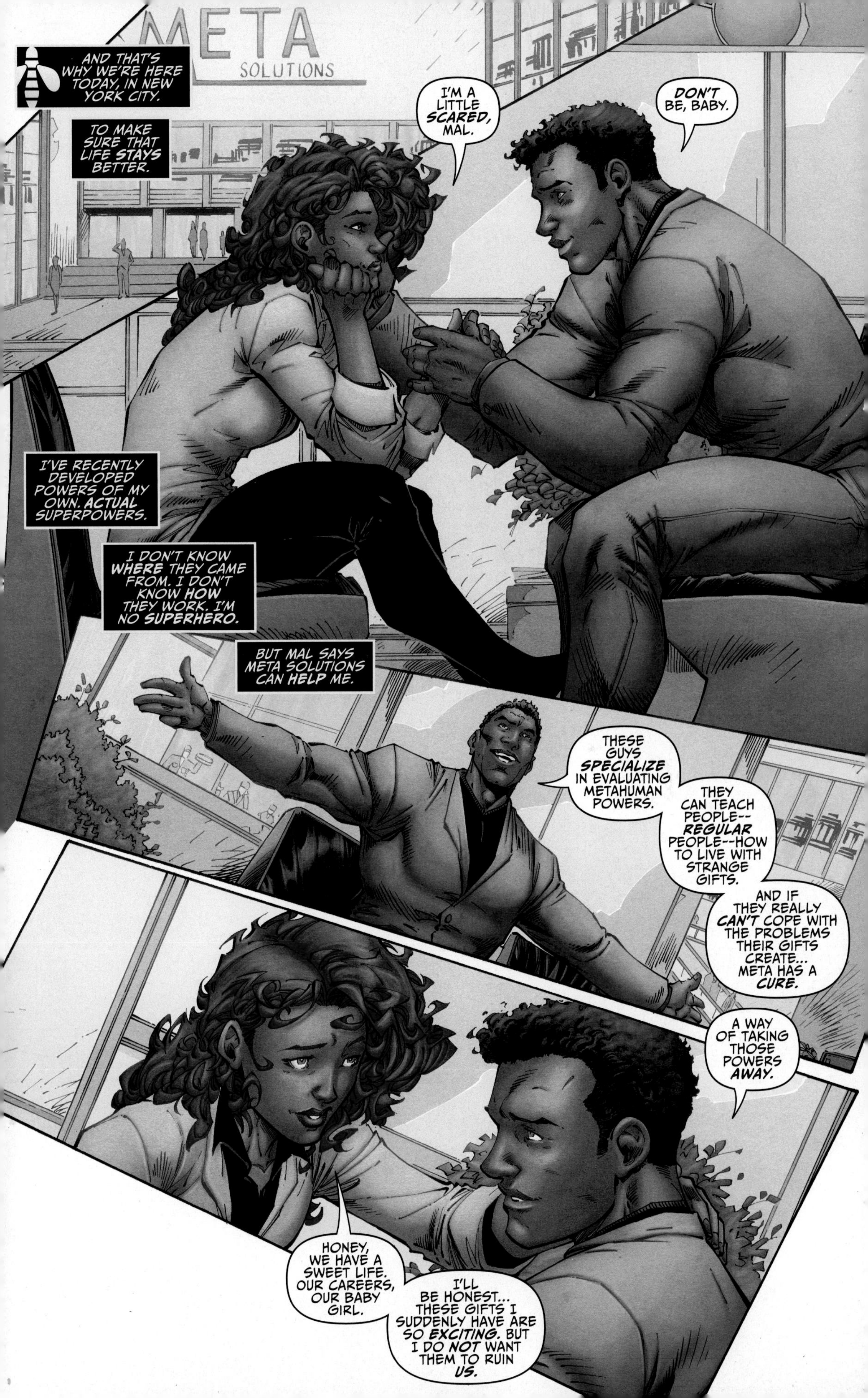
META
SOLUTIONS
AND THAT'S WHY WE'RE HERE TODAY, IN NEW YORK CITY.
TO MAKE SURE THAT LIFE STAYS BETTER.
I'M A LITTLE SCARED, MAL.
DON'T BE, BABY.
I'VE RECENTLY DEVELOPED POWERS OF MY OWN. ACTUAL SUPERPOWERS.
I DON'T KNOW WHERE THEY CAME FROM. I DON'T KNOW HOW THEY WORK. I'M NO SUPERHERO.
BUT MAL SAYS META SOLUTIONS CAN HELP ME.
THESE GUYS SPECIALIZE IN EVALUATING METAHUMAN POWERS.
THEY CAN TEACH PEOPLE-- REGULAR PEOPLE--HOW TO LIVE WITH STRANGE GIFTS.
AND IF THEY REALLY CAN'T COPE WITH THE PROBLEMS THEIR GIFTS CREATE... META HAS A CURE.
A WAY OF TAKING THOSE POWERS AWAY.
HONEY, WE HAVE A SWEET LIFE. OUR CAREERS, OUR BABY GIRL.
I'LL BE HONEST... THESE GIFTS I SUDDENLY HAVE ARE SO EXCITING. BUT I DO NOT WANT THEM TO RUIN US.

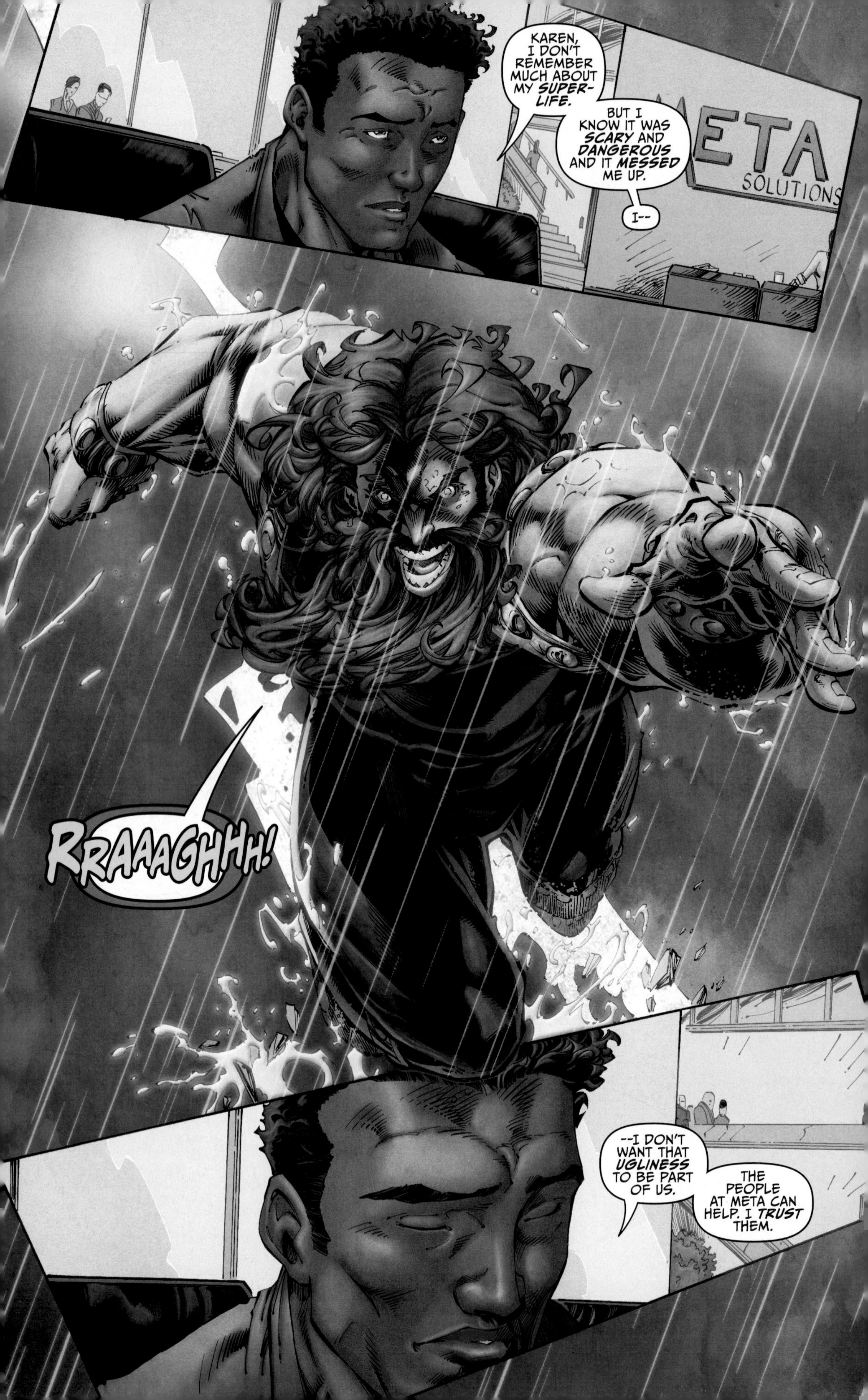
KAREN, I DON'T REMEMBER MUCH ABOUT MY SUPER-LIFE.
BUT I KNOW IT WAS SCARY AND DANGEROUS AND IT MESSED ME UP.
I--
META SOLUTIONS
RRAAAGHHH!
--I DON'T WANT THAT UGLINESS TO BE PART OF US.
THE PEOPLE AT META CAN HELP. I TRUST THEM.

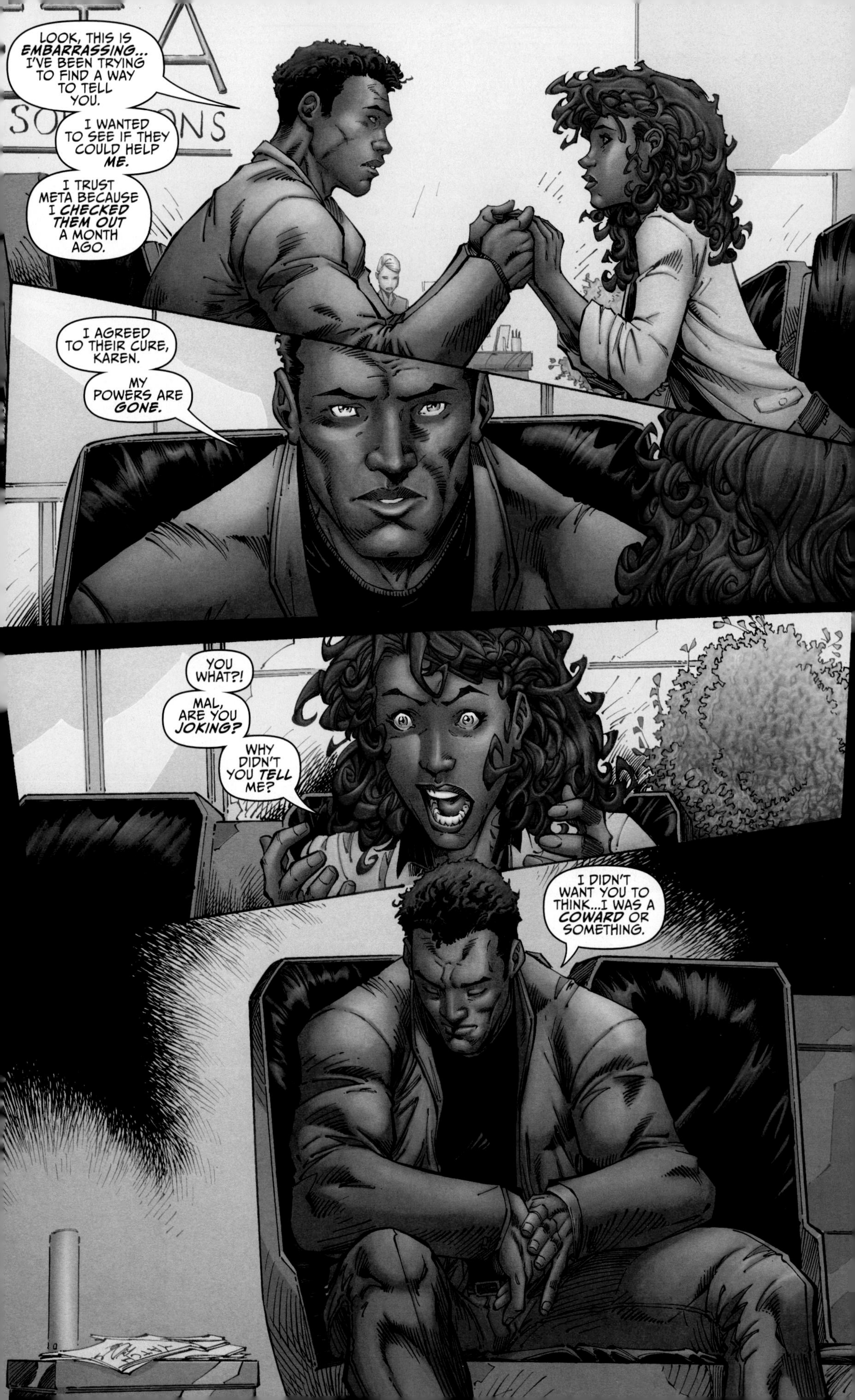
LOOK, THIS IS EMBARRASSING... I'VE BEEN TRYING TO FIND A WAY TO TELL YOU.
I WANTED TO SEE IF THEY COULD HELP ME.
I TRUST META BECAUSE I CHECKED THEM OUT A MONTH AGO.
I AGREED TO THEIR CURE, KAREN.
MY POWERS ARE GONE.
YOU WHAT?!
MAL, ARE YOU JOKING?
WHY DIDN'T YOU TELL ME?
I DIDN'T WANT YOU TO THINK...I WAS A COWARD OR SOMETHING.

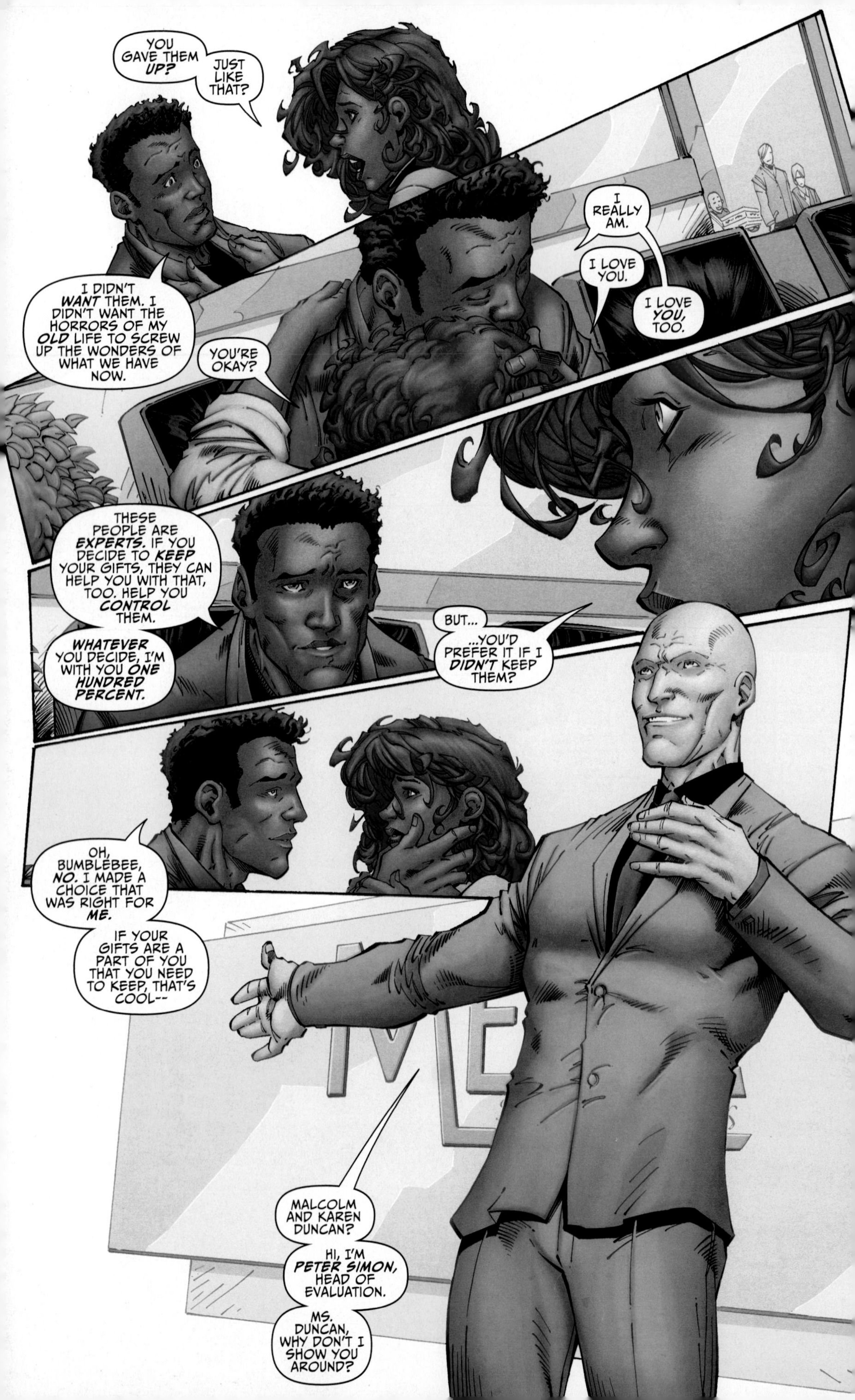
YOU GAVE THEM UP?
JUST LIKE THAT?
I DIDN'T WANT THEM. I DIDN'T WANT THE HORRORS OF MY OLD LIFE TO SCREW UP THE WONDERS OF WHAT WE HAVE NOW.
YOU'RE OKAY?
I REALLY AM.
I LOVE YOU.
I LOVE YOU, TOO.
THESE PEOPLE ARE EXPERTS. IF YOU DECIDE TO KEEP YOUR GIFTS, THEY CAN HELP YOU WITH THAT, TOO. HELP YOU CONTROL THEM.
WHATEVER YOU DECIDE, I'M WITH YOU ONE HUNDRED PERCENT.
BUT...
...YOU'D PREFER IT IF I DIDN'T KEEP THEM?
OH, BUMBLEBEE, NO. I MADE A CHOICE THAT WAS RIGHT FOR ME.
IF YOUR GIFTS ARE A PART OF YOU THAT YOU NEED TO KEEP, THAT'S COOL--
MALCOLM AND KAREN DUNCAN?
HI, I'M PETER SIMON, HEAD OF EVALUATION.
MS. DUNCAN, WHY DON'T I SHOW YOU AROUND?

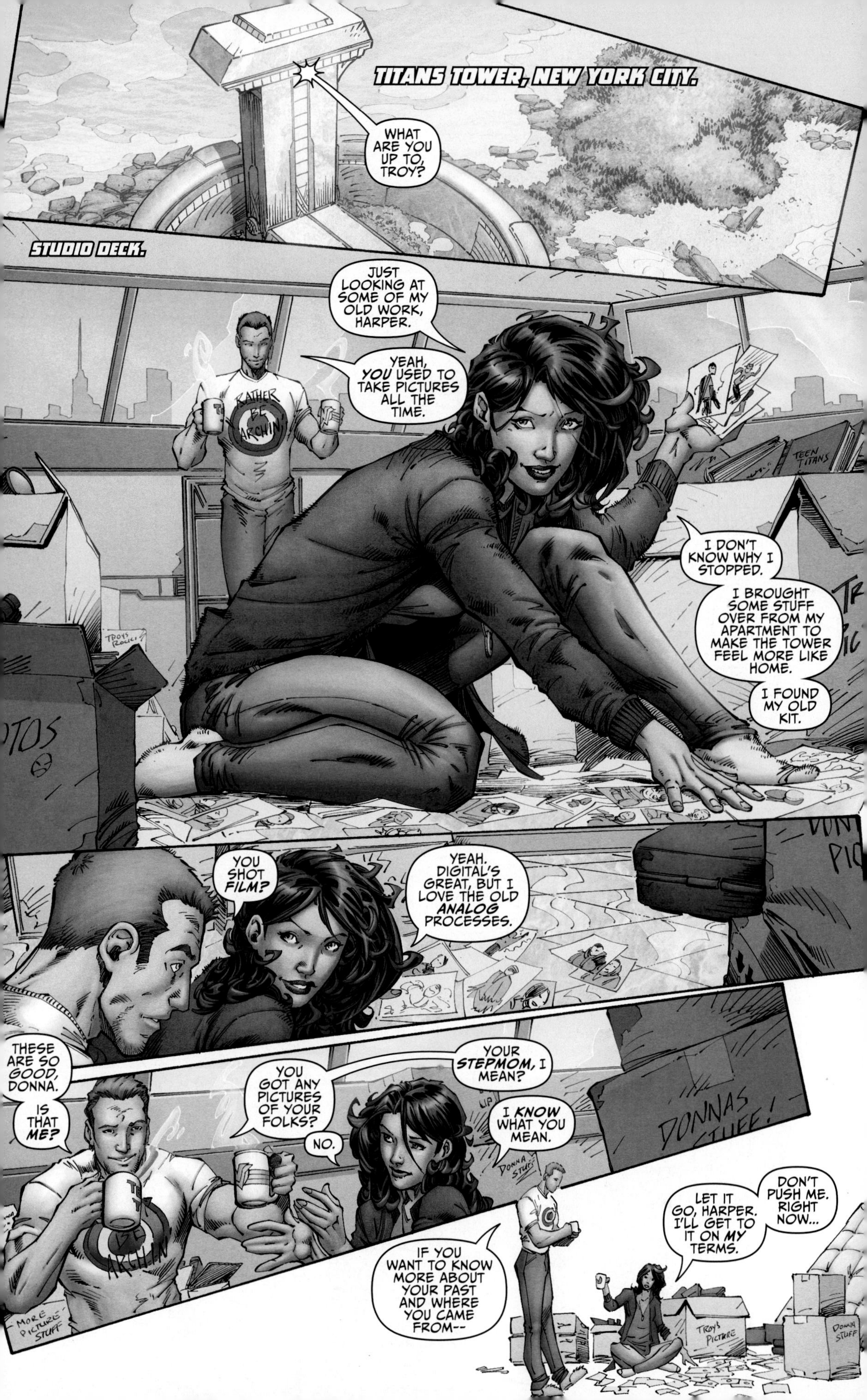
TITANS TOWER, NEW YORK CITY.
WHAT ARE YOU UP TO, TROY?
STUDIO DECK.
JUST LOOKING AT SOME OF MY OLD WORK, HARPER.
YEAH, YOU USED TO TAKE PICTURES ALL THE TIME.
TEEN TITANS
I DON'T KNOW WHY I STOPPED.
I BROUGHT SOME STUFF OVER FROM MY APARTMENT TO MAKE THE TOWER FEEL MORE LIKE HOME.
I FOUND MY OLD KIT.
YOU SHOT FILM?
YEAH. DIGITAL'S GREAT, BUT I LOVE THE OLD ANALOG PROCESSES.
THESE ARE SO GOOD, DONNA.
IS THAT ME?
YOU GOT ANY PICTURES OF YOUR FOLKS?
NO.
YOUR STEPMOM, I MEAN?
I KNOW WHAT YOU MEAN.
DONNAS STUFF!
IF YOU WANT TO KNOW MORE ABOUT YOUR PAST AND WHERE YOU CAME FROM--
LET IT GO, HARPER. I'LL GET TO IT ON MY TERMS.
DON'T PUSH ME. RIGHT NOW...

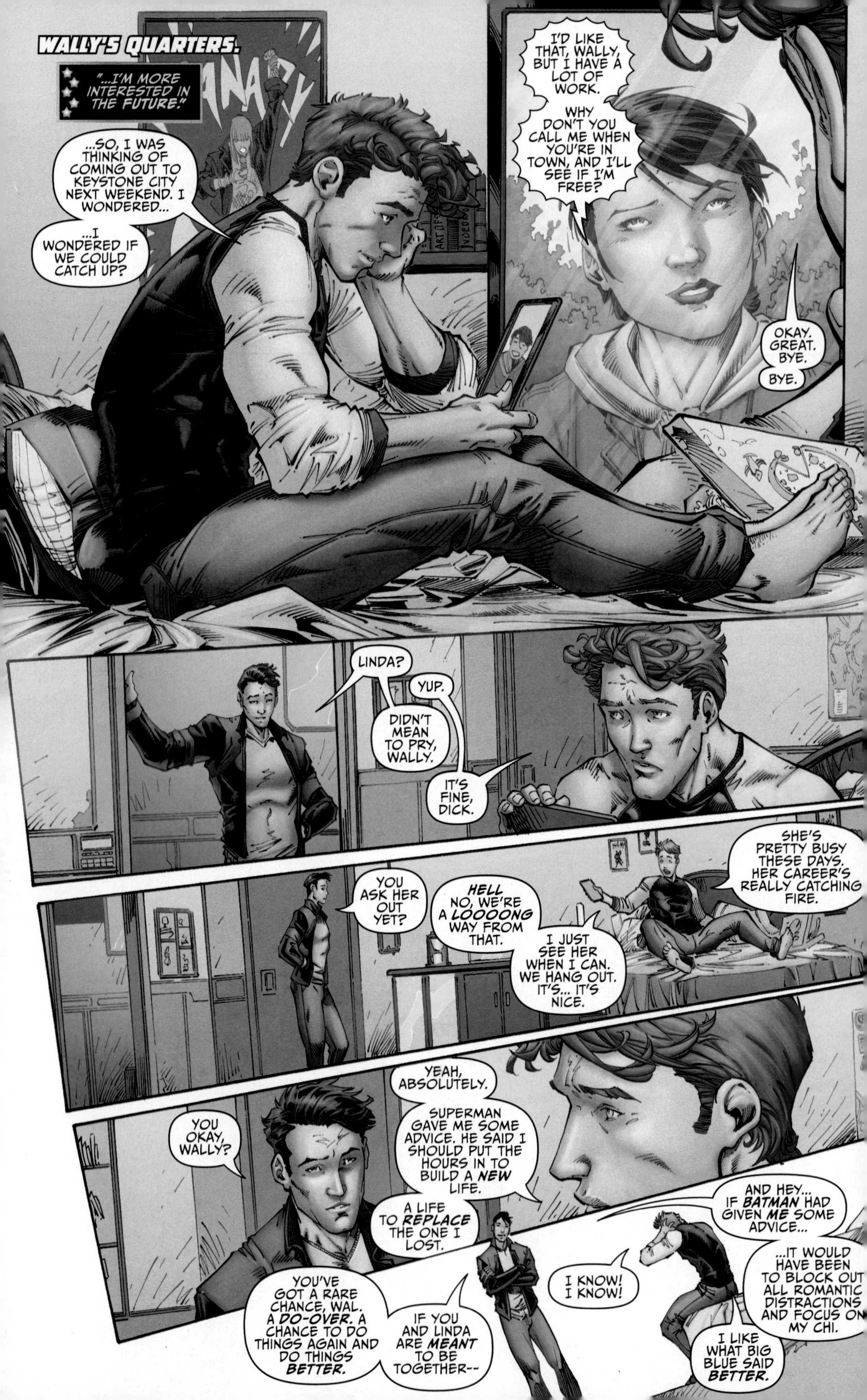
WALLY'S QUARTERS.
"...I'M MORE INTERESTED IN THE FUTURE."
...SO, I WAS THINKING OF COMING OUT TO KEYSTONE CITY NEXT WEEKEND. I WONDERED...
...I WONDERED IF WE COULD CATCH UP?
I'D LIKE THAT, WALLY, BUT I HAVE A LOT OF WORK.
WHY DON'T YOU CALL ME WHEN YOU'RE IN TOWN, AND I'LL SEE IF I'M FREE?
OKAY. GREAT. BYE.
BYE.
LINDA?
YUP.
DIDN'T MEAN TO PRY, WALLY.
IT'S FINE, DICK.
YOU ASK HER OUT YET?
HELL NO, WE'RE A LOOOONG WAY FROM THAT.
I JUST SEE HER WHEN I CAN. WE HANG OUT. IT'S... IT'S NICE.
SHE'S PRETTY BUSY THESE DAYS. HER CAREER'S REALLY CATCHING FIRE.
YOU OKAY, WALLY?
YEAH, ABSOLUTELY.
SUPERMAN GAVE ME SOME ADVICE. HE SAID I SHOULD PUT THE HOURS IN TO BUILD A NEW LIFE.
A LIFE TO REPLACE THE ONE I LOST.
YOU'VE GOT A RARE CHANCE, WAL. A DO-OVER. A CHANCE TO DO THINGS AGAIN AND DO THINGS BETTER.
IF YOU AND LINDA ARE MEANT TO BE TOGETHER--
I KNOW! I KNOW!
AND HEY... IF BATMAN HAD GIVEN ME SOME ADVICE...
...IT WOULD HAVE BEEN TO BLOCK OUT ALL ROMANTIC DISTRACTIONS AND FOCUS ON MY CHI.
I LIKE WHAT BIG BLUE SAID BETTER.

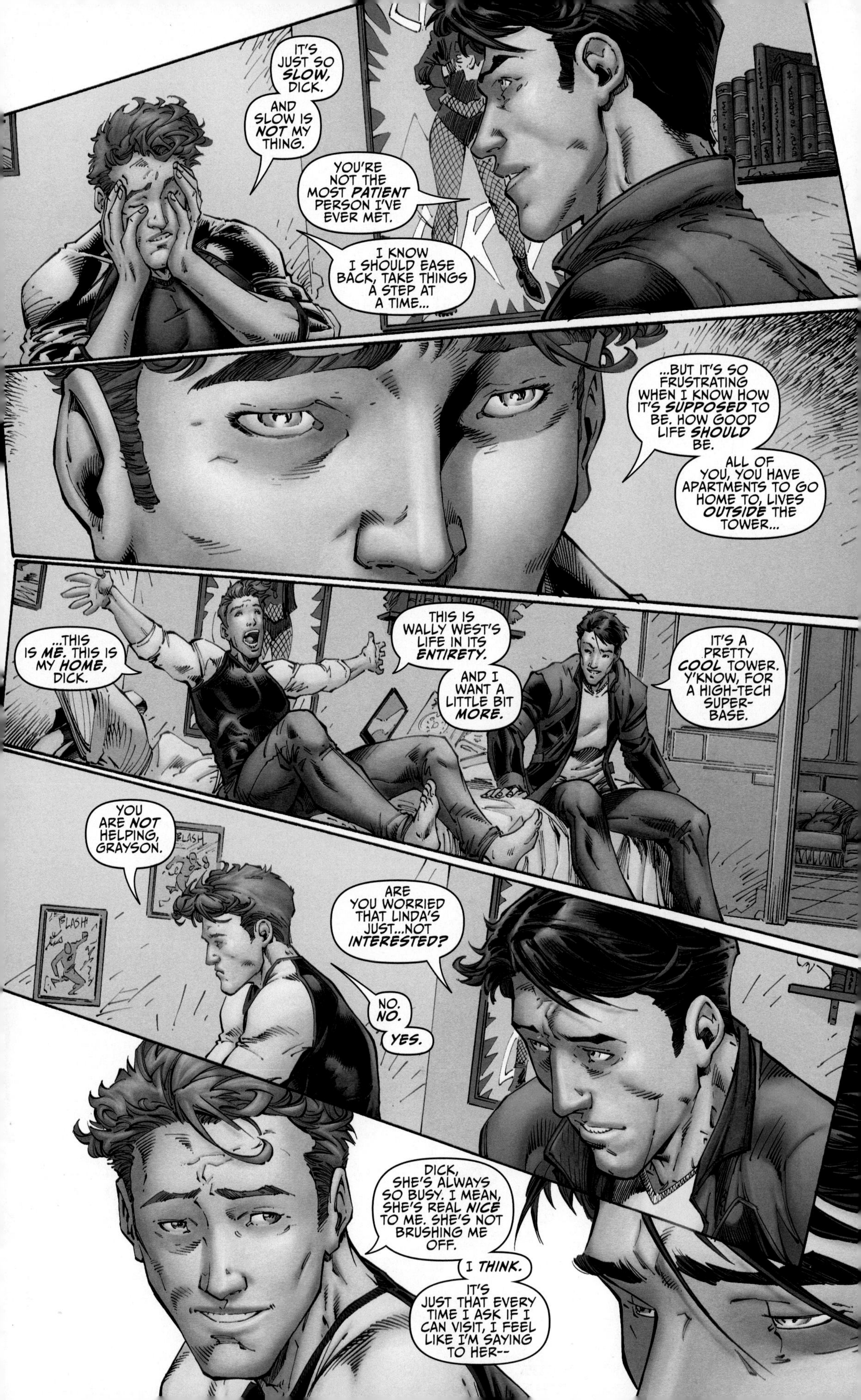
IT'S JUST SO SLOW, DICK.
AND SLOW IS NOT MY THING.
YOU'RE NOT THE MOST PATIENT PERSON I'VE EVER MET.
I KNOW I SHOULD EASE BACK, TAKE THINGS A STEP AT A TIME...
...BUT IT'S SO FRUSTRATING WHEN I KNOW HOW IT'S SUPPOSED TO BE. HOW GOOD LIFE SHOULD BE.
ALL OF YOU, YOU HAVE APARTMENTS TO GO HOME TO, LIVES OUTSIDE THE TOWER...
...THIS IS ME. THIS IS MY HOME, DICK.
THIS IS WALLY WEST'S LIFE IN ITS ENTIRETY.
AND I WANT A LITTLE BIT MORE.
IT'S A PRETTY COOL TOWER. Y'KNOW, FOR A HIGH-TECH SUPER-BASE.
YOU ARE NOT HELPING, GRAYSON.
ARE YOU WORRIED THAT LINDA'S JUST...NOT INTERESTED?
NO. NO. YES.
DICK, SHE'S ALWAYS SO BUSY. I MEAN, SHE'S REAL NICE TO ME. SHE'S NOT BRUSHING ME OFF.
I THINK.
IT'S JUST THAT EVERY TIME I ASK IF I CAN VISIT, I FEEL LIKE I'M SAYING TO HER--

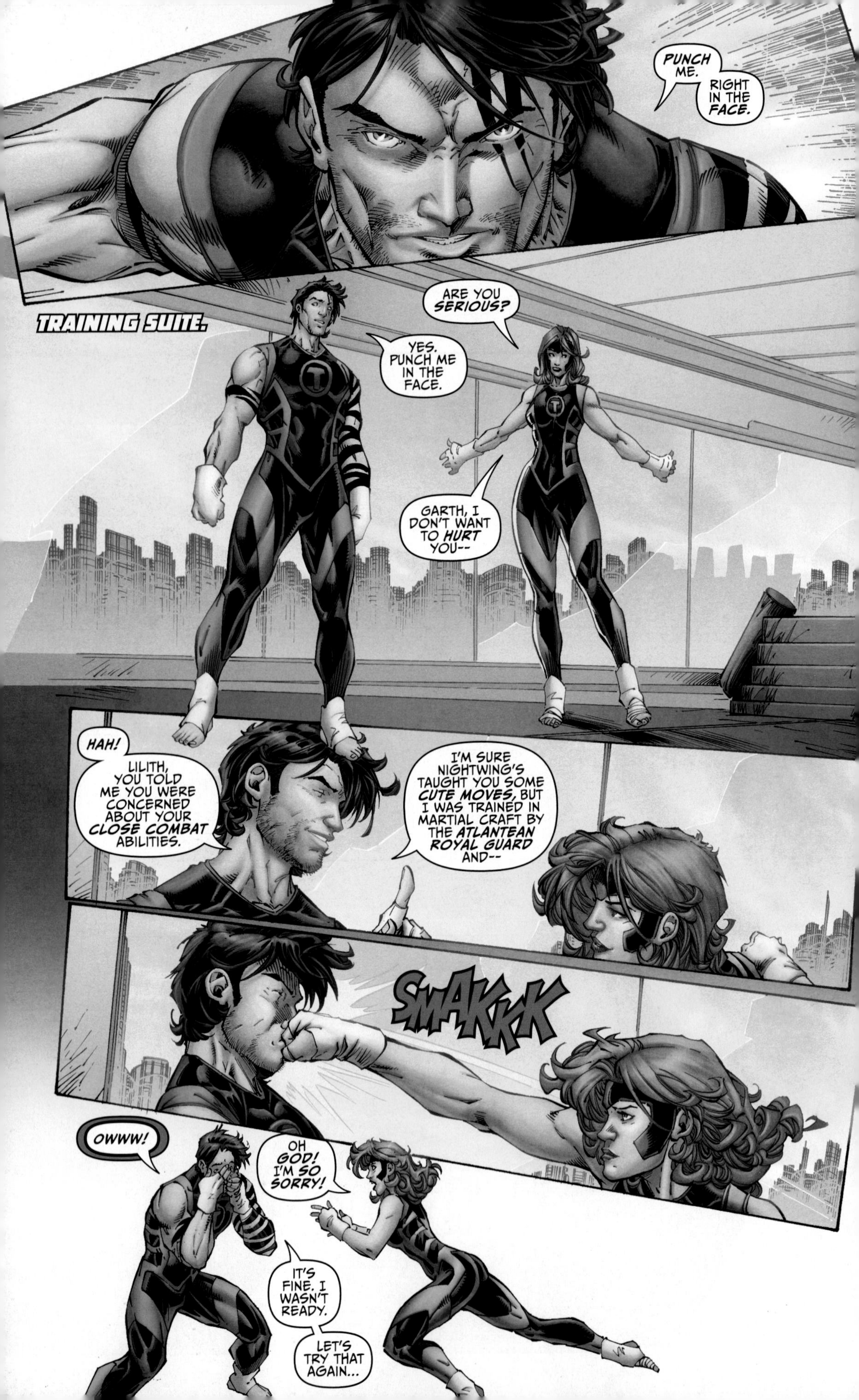
PUNCH ME.
RIGHT IN THE FACE.
TRAINING SUITE.
ARE YOU SERIOUS?
YES. PUNCH ME IN THE FACE.
GARTH, I DON'T WANT TO HURT YOU--
HAH!
LILITH, YOU TOLD ME YOU WERE CONCERNED ABOUT YOUR CLOSE COMBAT ABILITIES.
I'M SURE NIGHTWING'S TAUGHT YOU SOME CUTE MOVES, BUT I WAS TRAINED IN MARTIAL CRAFT BY THE ATLANTEAN ROYAL GUARD AND--
SMAKKK
OWWW!
OH GOD! I'M SO SORRY!
IT'S FINE. I WASN'T READY.
LET'S TRY THAT AGAIN...

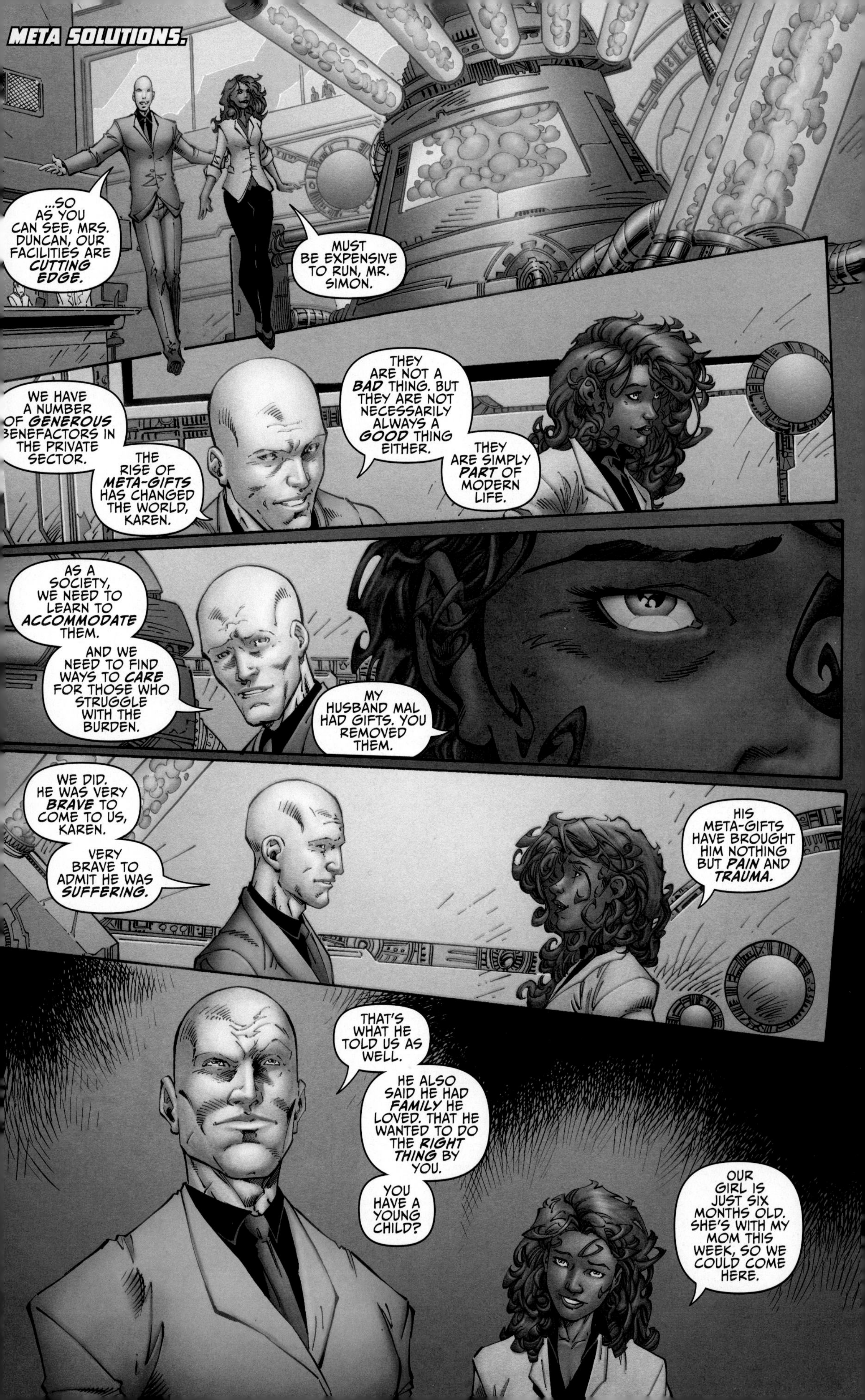
META SOLUTIONS.
...SO AS YOU CAN SEE, MRS. DUNCAN, OUR FACILITIES ARE CUTTING EDGE.
MUST BE EXPENSIVE TO RUN, MR. SIMON.
WE HAVE A NUMBER OF GENEROUS BENEFACTORS IN THE PRIVATE SECTOR.
THE RISE OF META-GIFTS HAS CHANGED THE WORLD, KAREN.
THEY ARE NOT A BAD THING. BUT THEY ARE NOT NECESSARILY ALWAYS A GOOD THING EITHER.
THEY ARE SIMPLY PART OF MODERN LIFE.
AS A SOCIETY, WE NEED TO LEARN TO ACCOMMODATE THEM.
AND WE NEED TO FIND WAYS TO CARE FOR THOSE WHO STRUGGLE WITH THE BURDEN.
MY HUSBAND MAL HAD GIFTS. YOU REMOVED THEM.
WE DID. HE WAS VERY BRAVE TO COME TO US, KAREN.
VERY BRAVE TO ADMIT HE WAS SUFFERING.
HIS META-GIFTS HAVE BROUGHT HIM NOTHING BUT PAIN AND TRAUMA.
THAT'S WHAT HE TOLD US AS WELL.
HE ALSO SAID HE HAD FAMILY HE LOVED. THAT HE WANTED TO DO THE RIGHT THING BY YOU.
YOU HAVE A YOUNG CHILD?
OUR GIRL IS JUST SIX MONTHS OLD. SHE'S WITH MY MOM THIS WEEK, SO WE COULD COME HERE.

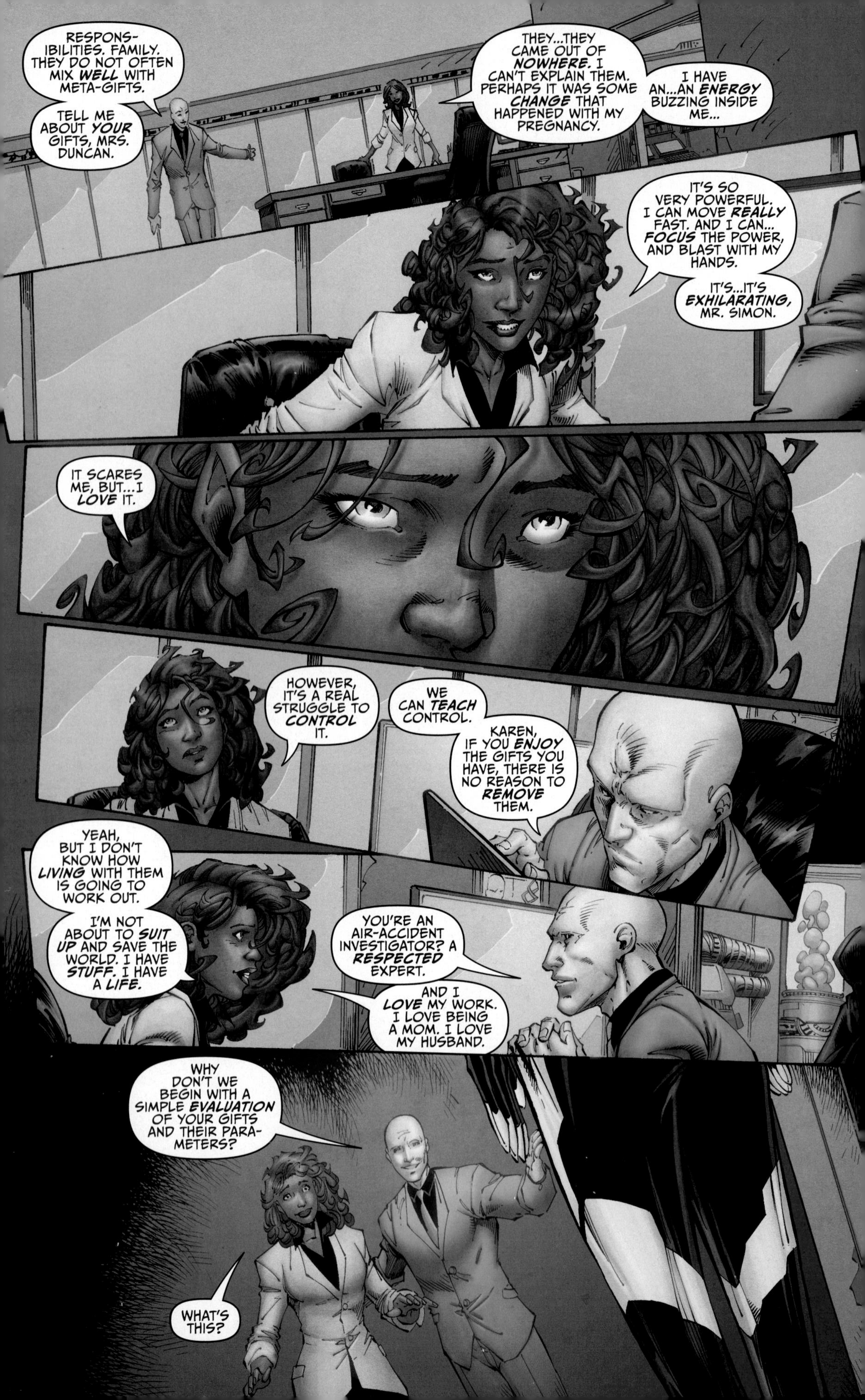
RESPONS-IBILITIES. FAMILY. THEY DO NOT OFTEN MIX WELL WITH META-GIFTS.
TELL ME ABOUT YOUR GIFTS, MRS. DUNCAN.
THEY...THEY CAME OUT OF NOWHERE. I CAN'T EXPLAIN THEM. PERHAPS IT WAS SOME CHANGE THAT HAPPENED WITH MY PREGNANCY.
I HAVE AN...AN ENERGY BUZZING INSIDE ME...
IT'S SO VERY POWERFUL. I CAN MOVE REALLY FAST. AND I CAN... FOCUS THE POWER, AND BLAST WITH MY HANDS.
IT'S...IT'S EXHILARATING, MR. SIMON.
IT SCARES ME, BUT...I LOVE IT.
HOWEVER, IT'S A REAL STRUGGLE TO CONTROL IT.
WE CAN TEACH CONTROL.
KAREN, IF YOU ENJOY THE GIFTS YOU HAVE, THERE IS NO REASON TO REMOVE THEM.
YEAH, BUT I DON'T KNOW HOW LIVING WITH THEM IS GOING TO WORK OUT.
I'M NOT ABOUT TO SUIT UP AND SAVE THE WORLD. I HAVE STUFF. I HAVE A LIFE.
YOU'RE AN AIR-ACCIDENT INVESTIGATOR? A RESPECTED EXPERT.
AND I LOVE MY WORK. I LOVE BEING A MOM. I LOVE MY HUSBAND.
WHY DON'T WE BEGIN WITH A SIMPLE EVALUATION OF YOUR GIFTS AND THEIR PARA-METERS?
WHAT'S THIS?

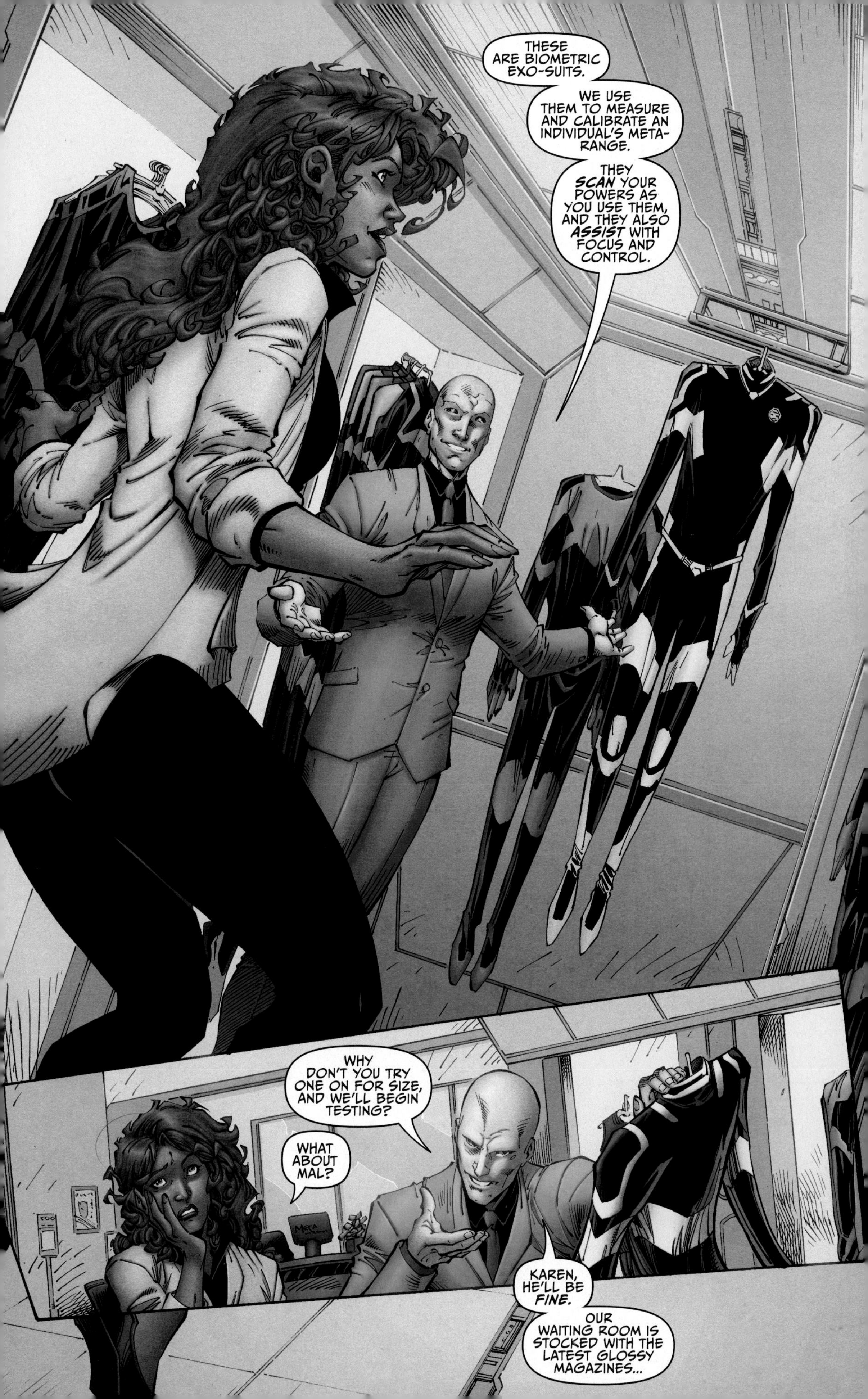
THESE ARE BIOMETRIC EXO-SUITS.
WE USE THEM TO MEASURE AND CALIBRATE AN INDIVIDUAL'S META-RANGE.
THEY *SCAN* YOUR POWERS AS YOU USE THEM, AND THEY ALSO *ASSIST* WITH FOCUS AND CONTROL.
WHY DON'T YOU TRY ONE ON FOR SIZE, AND WE'LL BEGIN TESTING?
WHAT ABOUT MAL?
KAREN, HE'LL BE *FINE.*
OUR WAITING ROOM IS STOCKED WITH THE LATEST GLOSSY MAGAZINES...

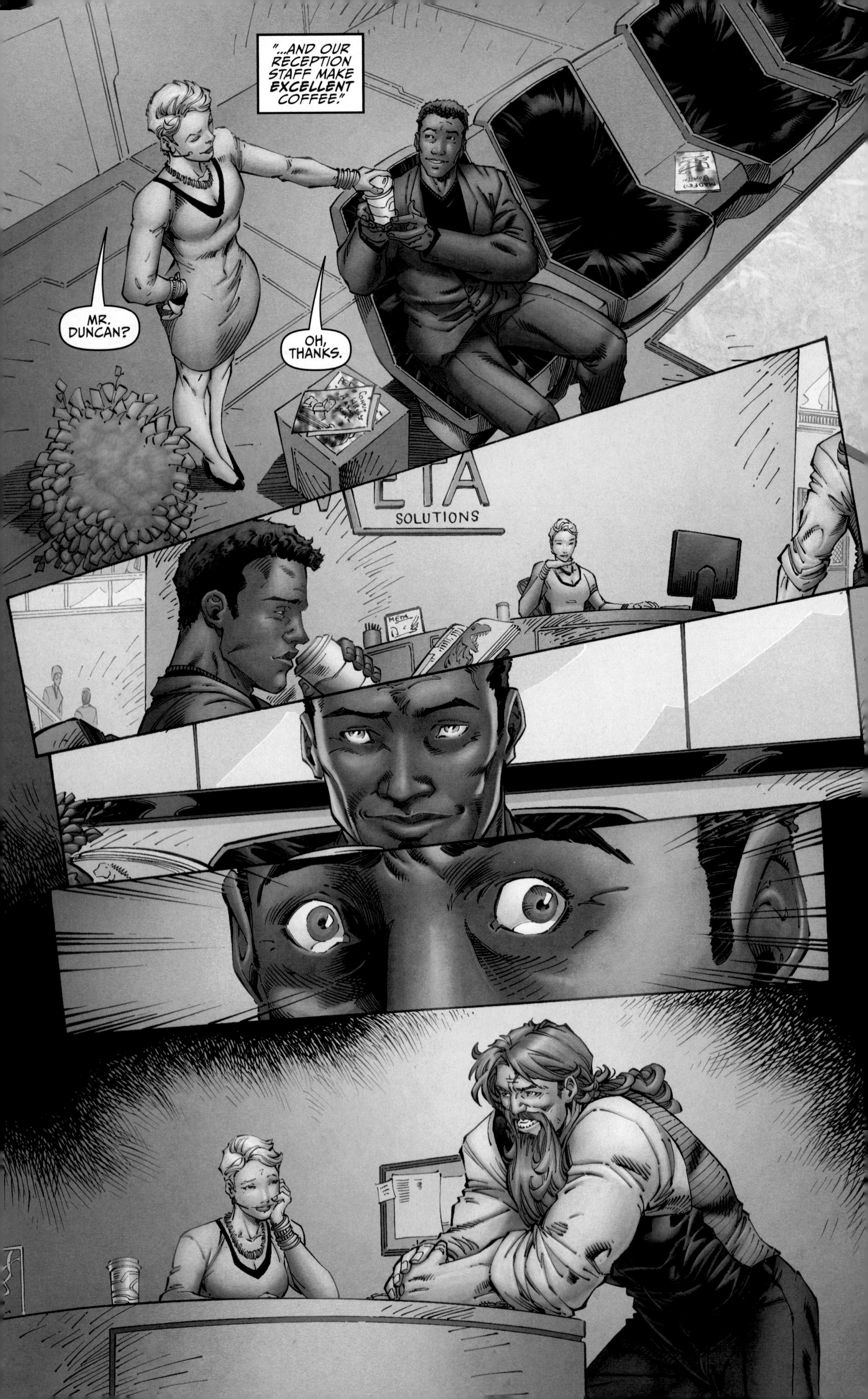
"...AND OUR RECEPTION STAFF MAKE EXCELLENT COFFEE."
MR. DUNCAN?
OH, THANKS.
META SOLUTIONS

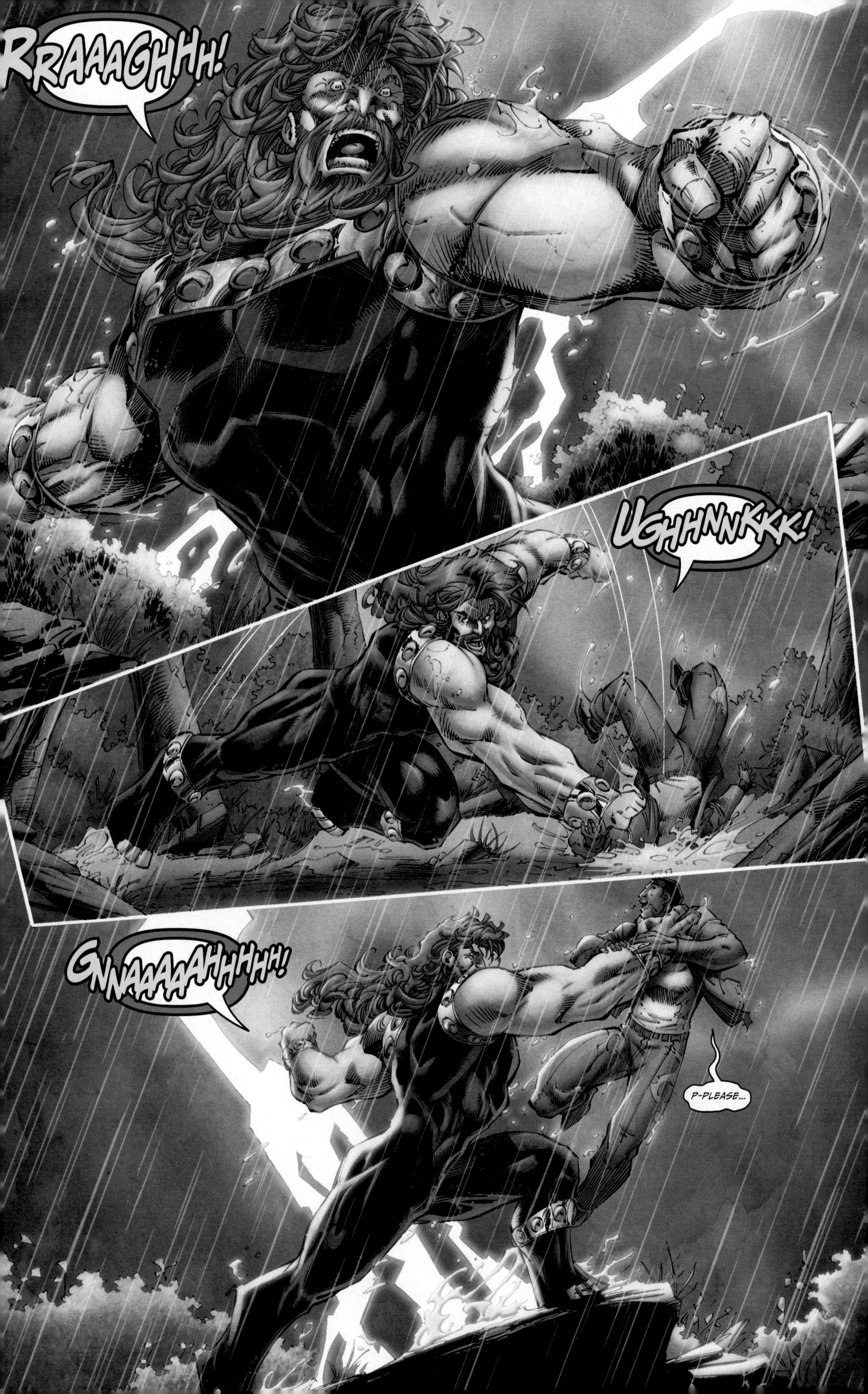
RRAAAGHHH!
UGHHNNKKK!
GNNAAAAAHHHHH!
P-PLEASE...

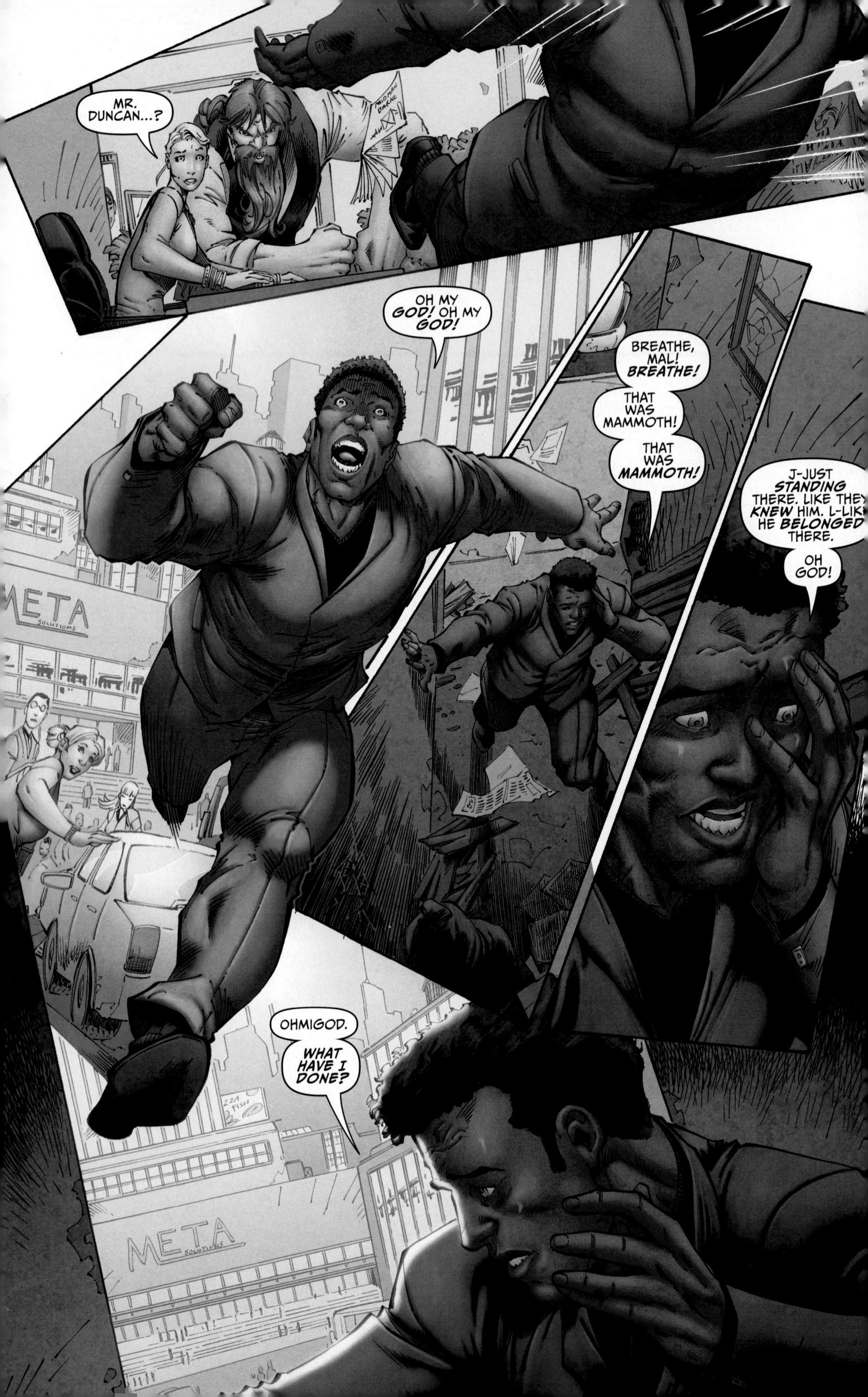
MR. DUNCAN...?
OH MY GOD! OH MY GOD!
BREATHE, MAL! BREATHE!
THAT WAS MAMMOTH!
THAT WAS MAMMOTH!
J-JUST STANDING THERE. LIKE THEY KNEW HIM. L-LIKE HE BELONGED THERE.
OH GOD!
OHMIGOD.
WHAT HAVE I DONE?
META SOLUTIONS
META SOLUTIONS

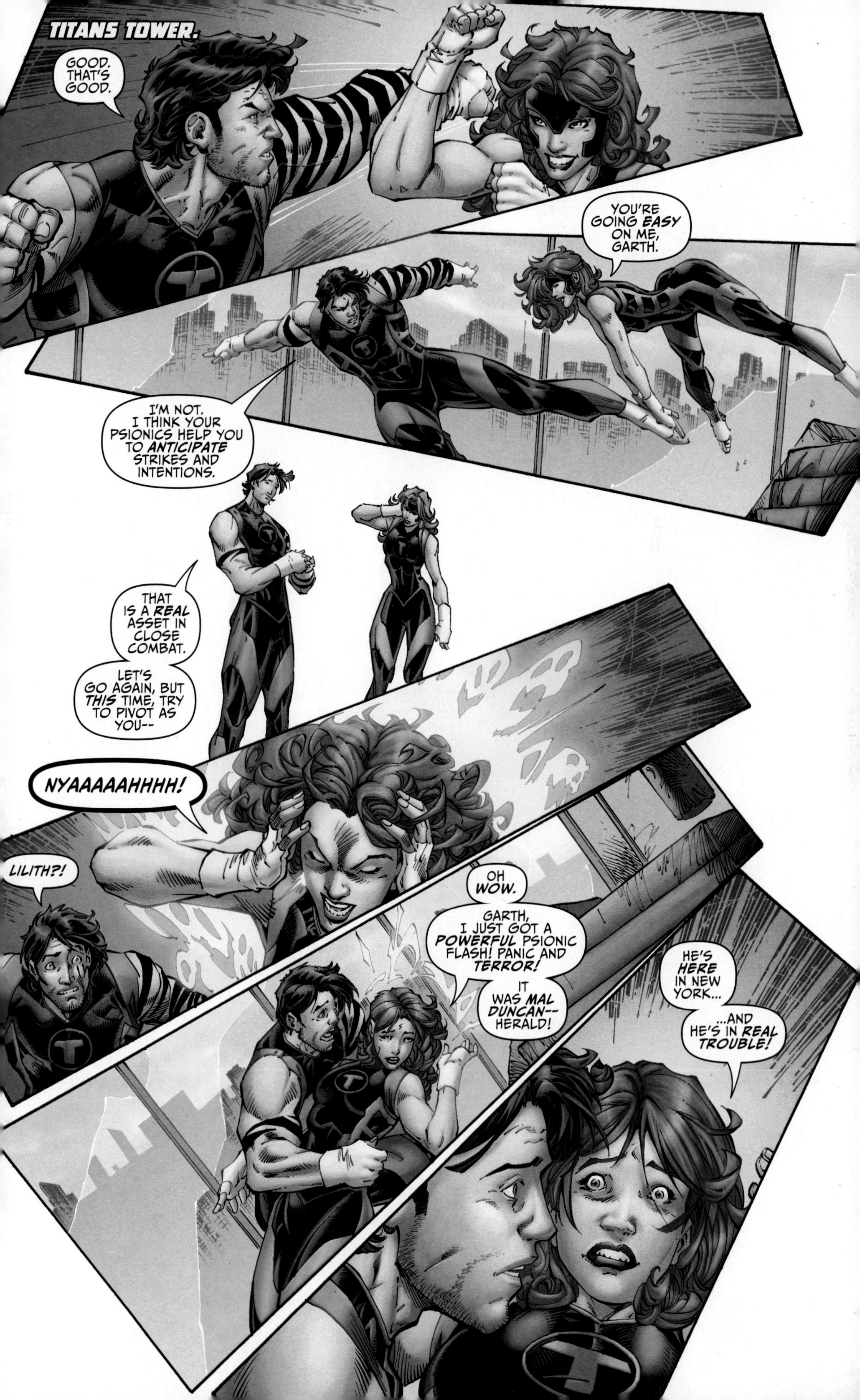
TITANS TOWER.
GOOD. THAT'S GOOD.
YOU'RE GOING EASY ON ME, GARTH.
I'M NOT. I THINK YOUR PSIONICS HELP YOU TO ANTICIPATE STRIKES AND INTENTIONS.
THAT IS A REAL ASSET IN CLOSE COMBAT.
LET'S GO AGAIN, BUT THIS TIME, TRY TO PIVOT AS YOU--
NYAAAAAHHHH!
LILITH?!
OH WOW.
GARTH, I JUST GOT A POWERFUL PSIONIC FLASH! PANIC AND TERROR!
IT WAS MAL DUNCAN-- HERALD!
HE'S HERE IN NEW YORK...
...AND HE'S IN REAL TROUBLE!

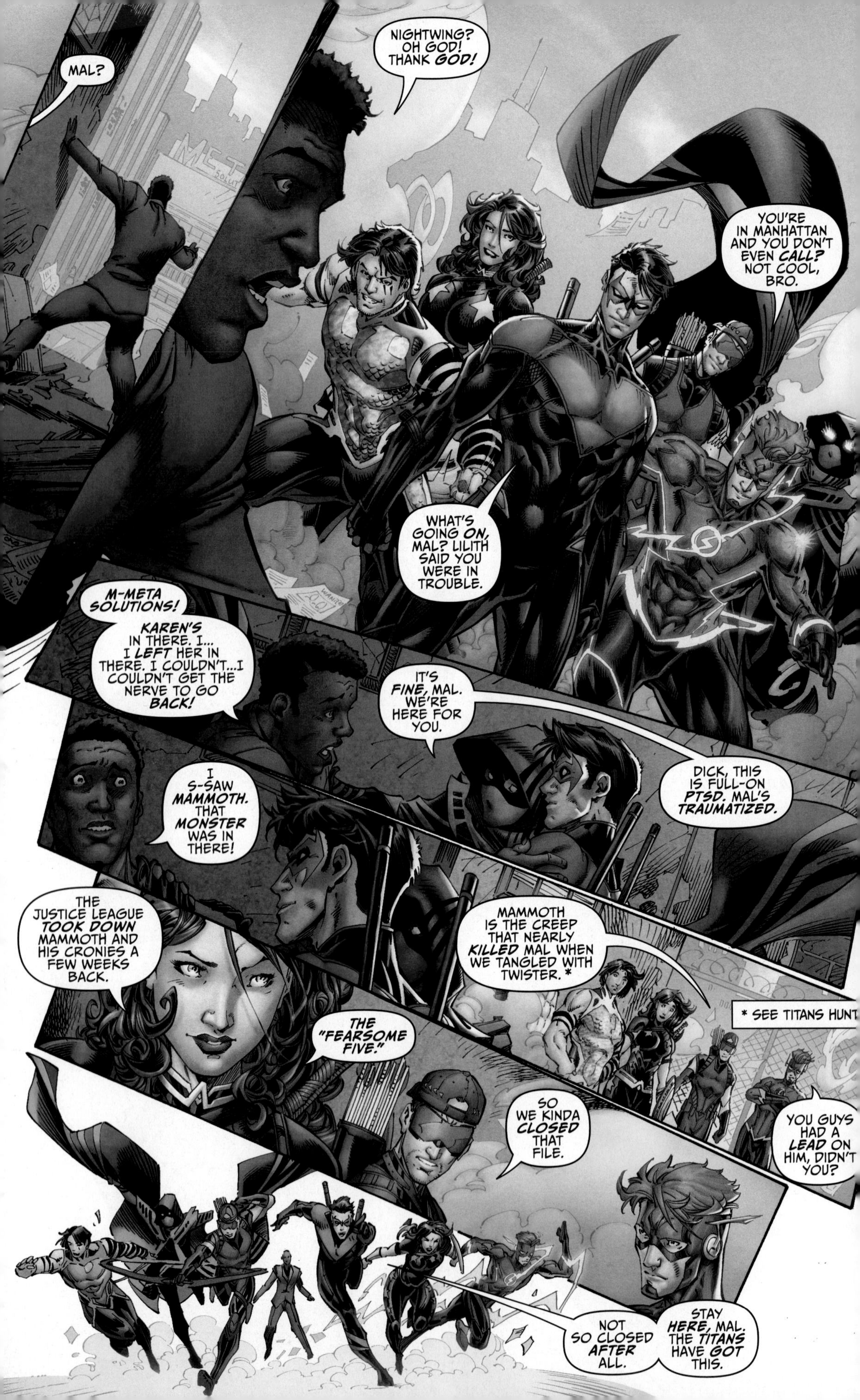
MAL?
NIGHTWING? OH GOD! THANK GOD!
YOU'RE IN MANHATTAN AND YOU DON'T EVEN CALL? NOT COOL, BRO.
WHAT'S GOING ON, MAL? LILITH SAID YOU WERE IN TROUBLE.
M-META SOLUTIONS!
KAREN'S IN THERE. I... I LEFT HER IN THERE. I COULDN'T...I COULDN'T GET THE NERVE TO GO BACK!
IT'S FINE, MAL. WE'RE HERE FOR YOU.
I S-SAW MAMMOTH. THAT MONSTER WAS IN THERE!
DICK, THIS IS FULL-ON PTSD. MAL'S TRAUMATIZED.
THE JUSTICE LEAGUE TOOK DOWN MAMMOTH AND HIS CRONIES A FEW WEEKS BACK.
MAMMOTH IS THE CREEP THAT NEARLY KILLED MAL WHEN WE TANGLED WITH TWISTER. *
* SEE TITANS HUNT
THE "FEARSOME FIVE."
SO WE KINDA CLOSED THAT FILE.
YOU GUYS HAD A LEAD ON HIM, DIDN'T YOU?
NOT SO CLOSED AFTER ALL.
STAY HERE, MAL. THE TITANS HAVE GOT THIS.

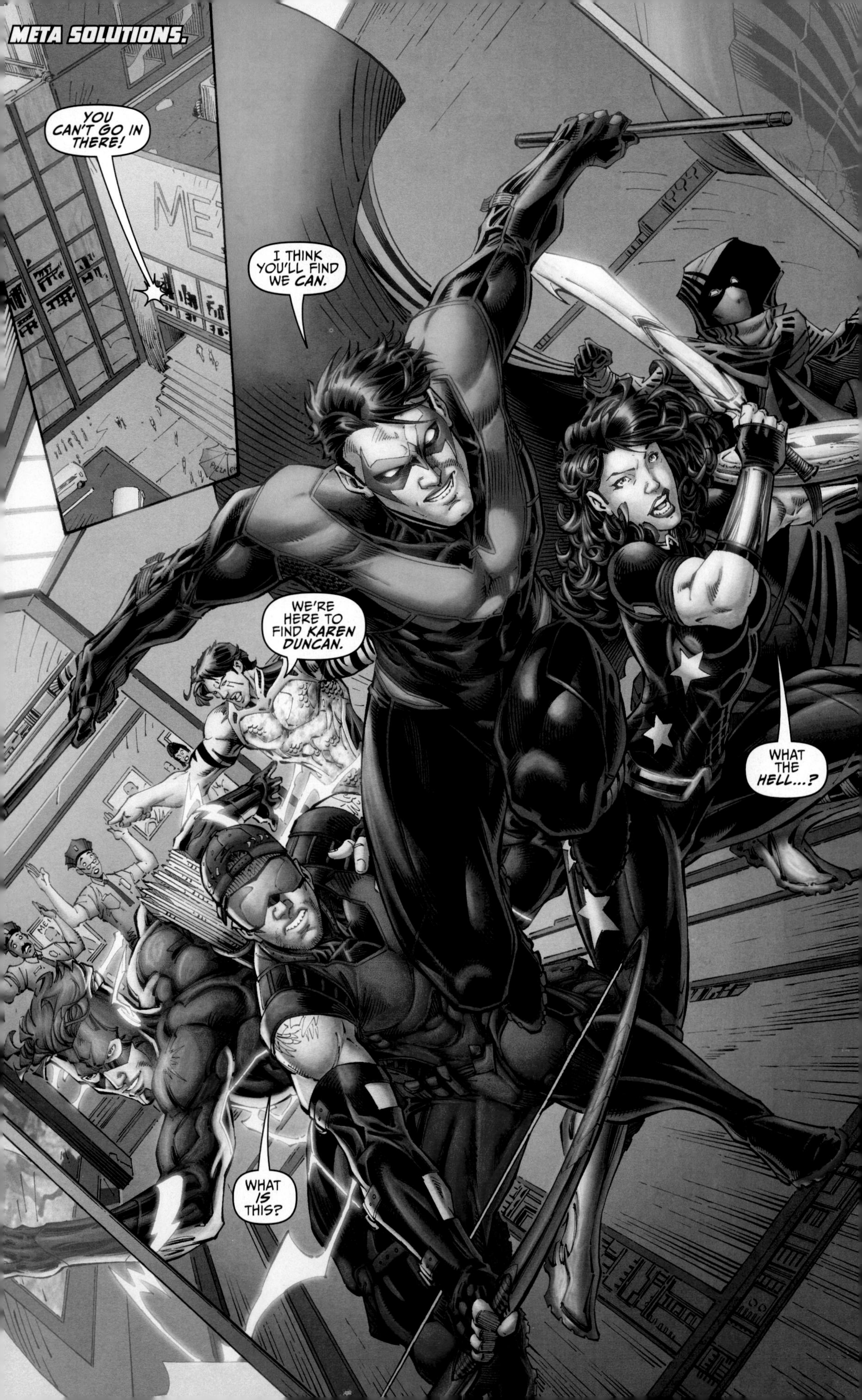
META SOLUTIONS.
YOU CAN'T GO IN THERE!
I THINK YOU'LL FIND WE CAN.
WE'RE HERE TO FIND KAREN DUNCAN.
WHAT THE HELL...?
WHAT IS THIS?

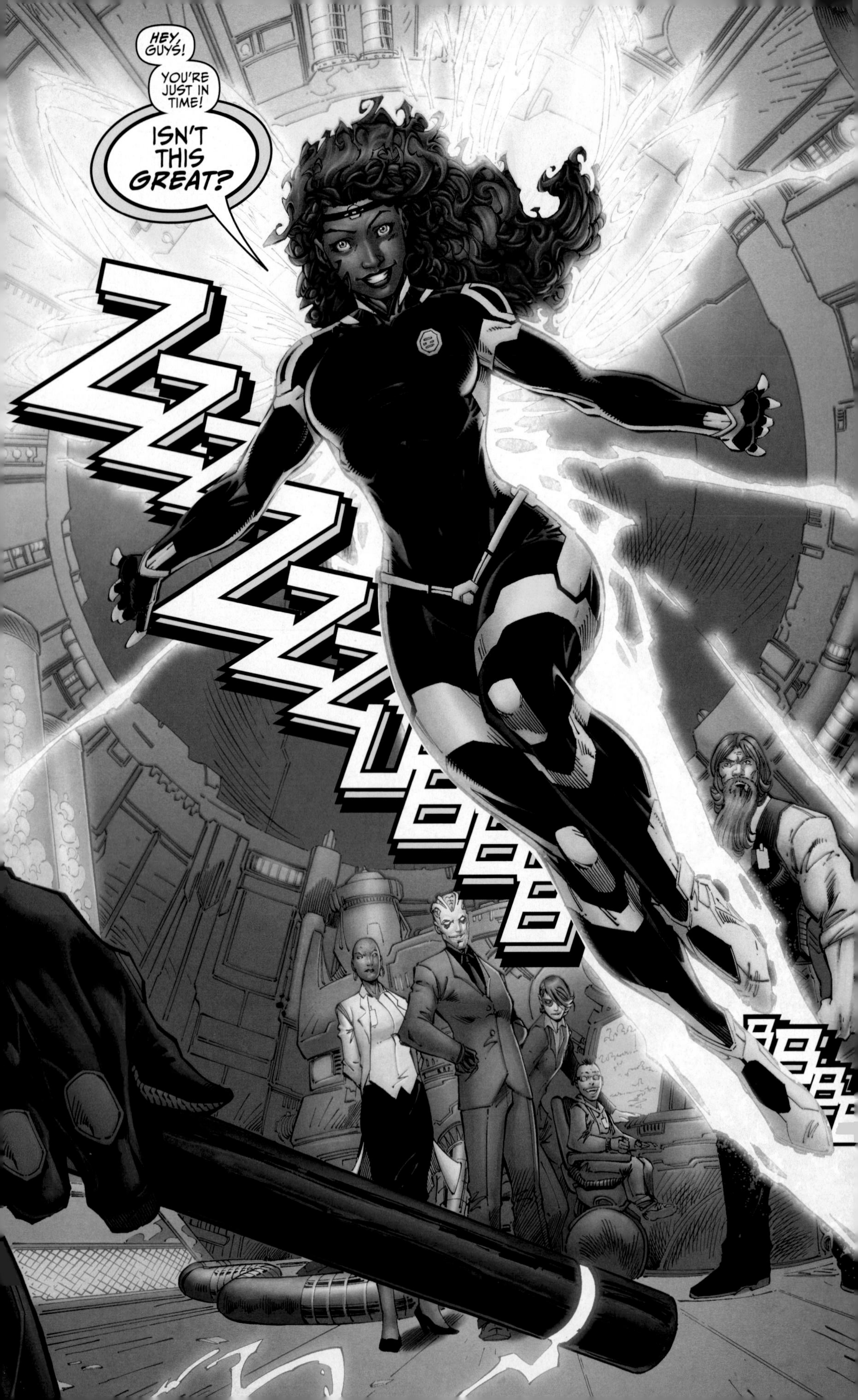
HEY, GUYS!
YOU'RE JUST IN TIME!
ISN'T THIS GREAT?
ZZZZZUBBBBB

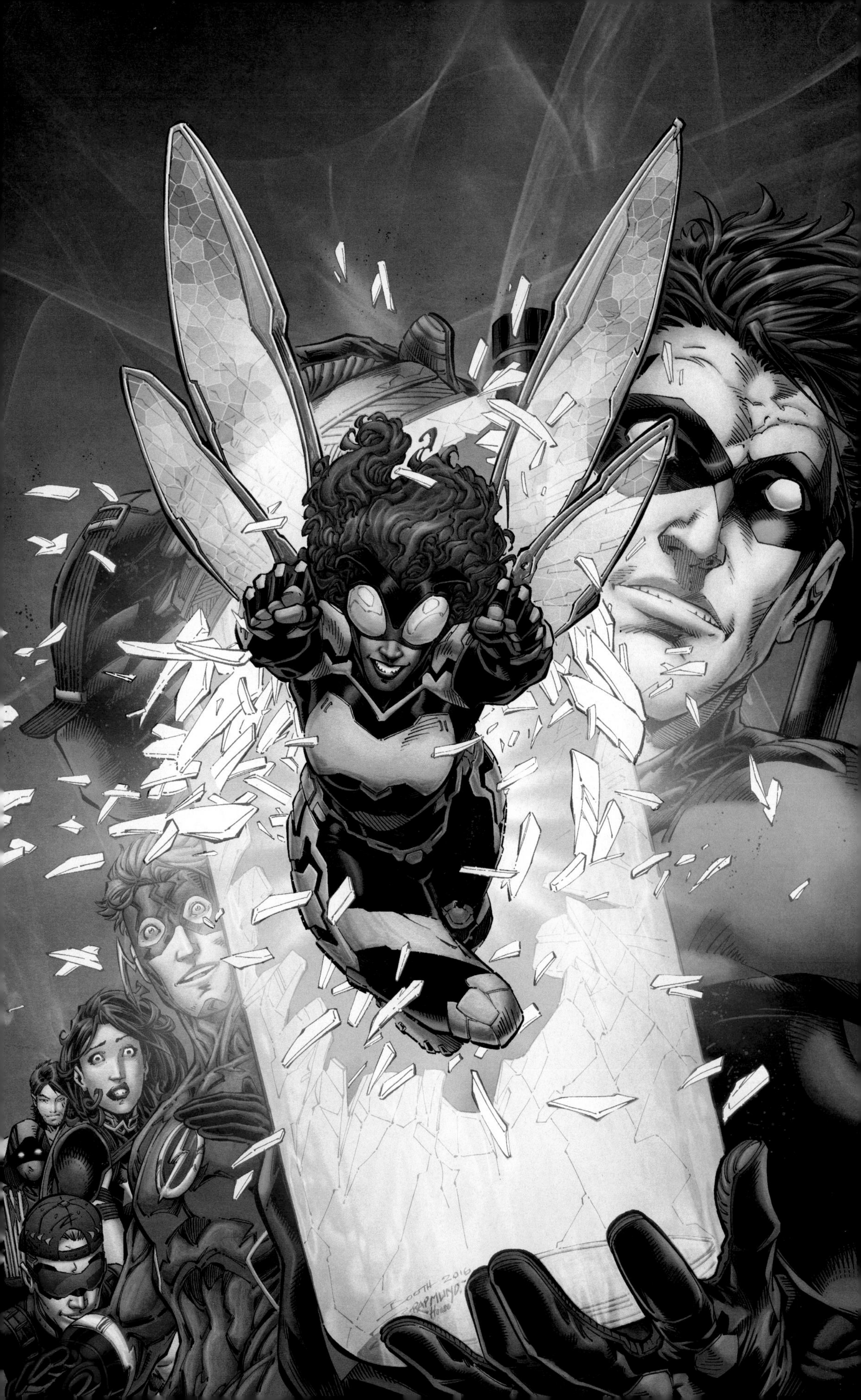

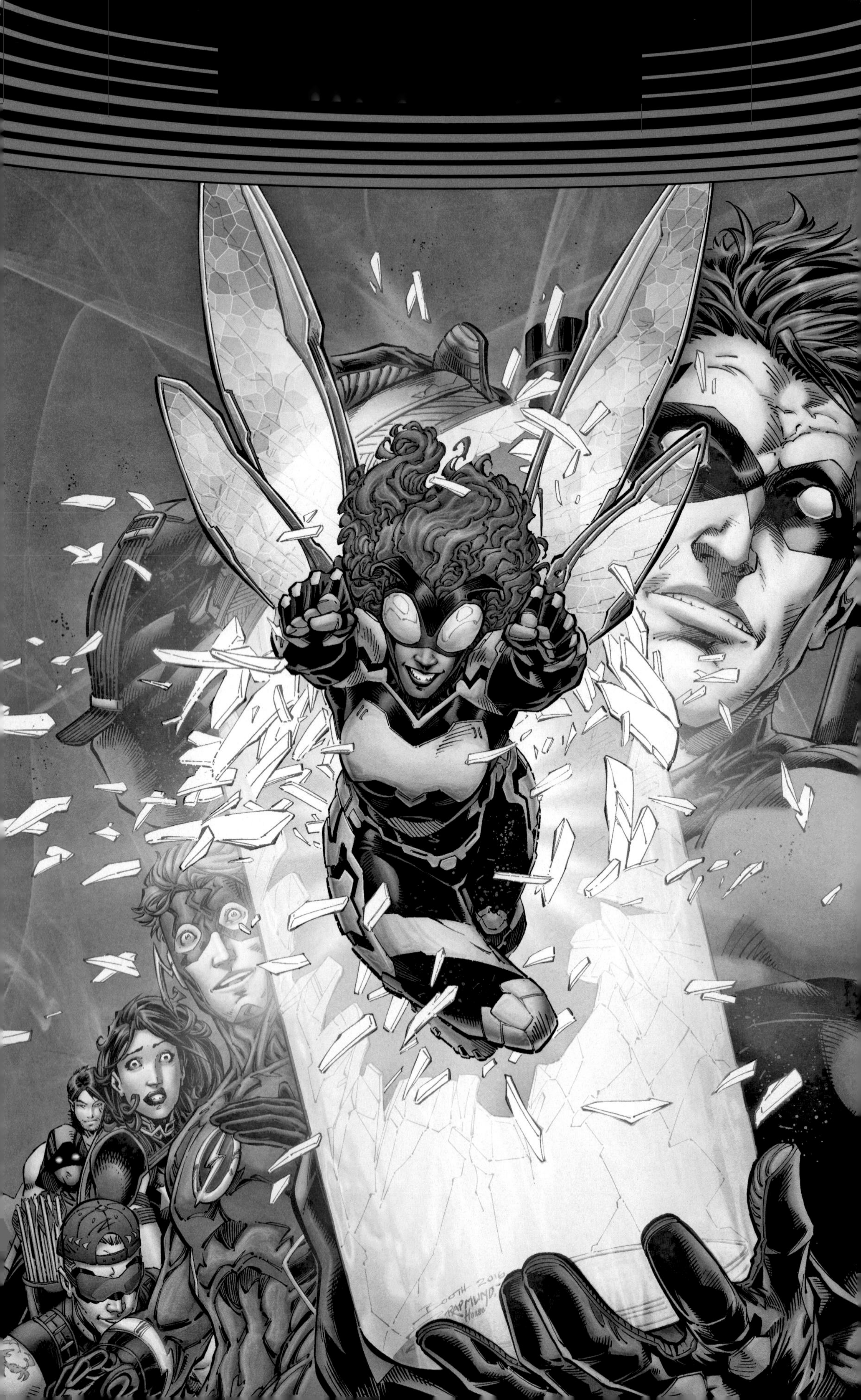

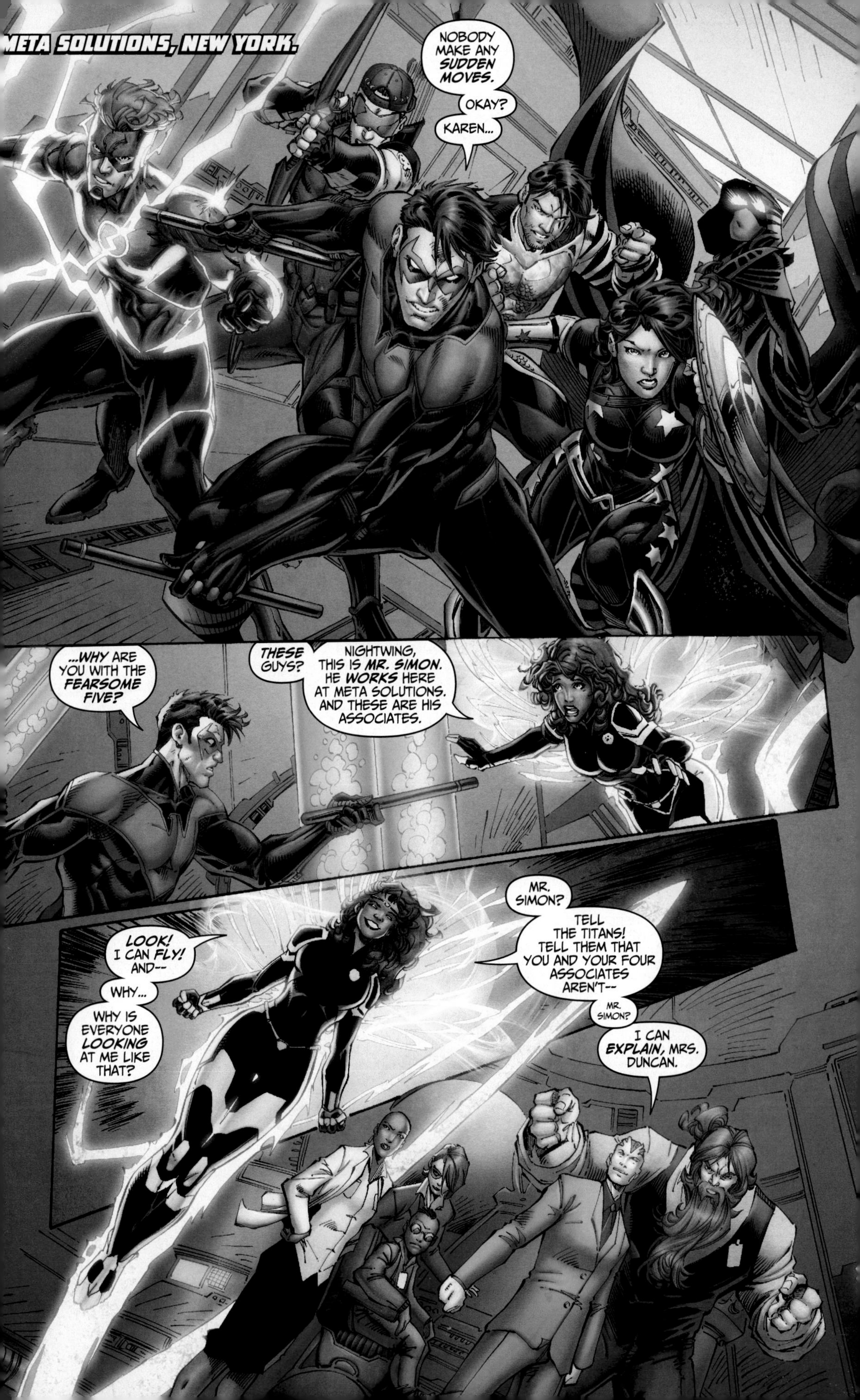
META SOLUTIONS, NEW YORK.
NOBODY MAKE ANY SUDDEN MOVES.
OKAY?
KAREN...
...WHY ARE YOU WITH THE FEARSOME FIVE?
THESE GUYS?
NIGHTWING, THIS IS MR. SIMON. HE WORKS HERE AT META SOLUTIONS. AND THESE ARE HIS ASSOCIATES.
LOOK! I CAN FLY! AND--
WHY...
WHY IS EVERYONE LOOKING AT ME LIKE THAT?
MR. SIMON?
TELL THE TITANS! TELL THEM THAT YOU AND YOUR FOUR ASSOCIATES AREN'T--
MR. SIMON?
I CAN EXPLAIN, MRS. DUNCAN.

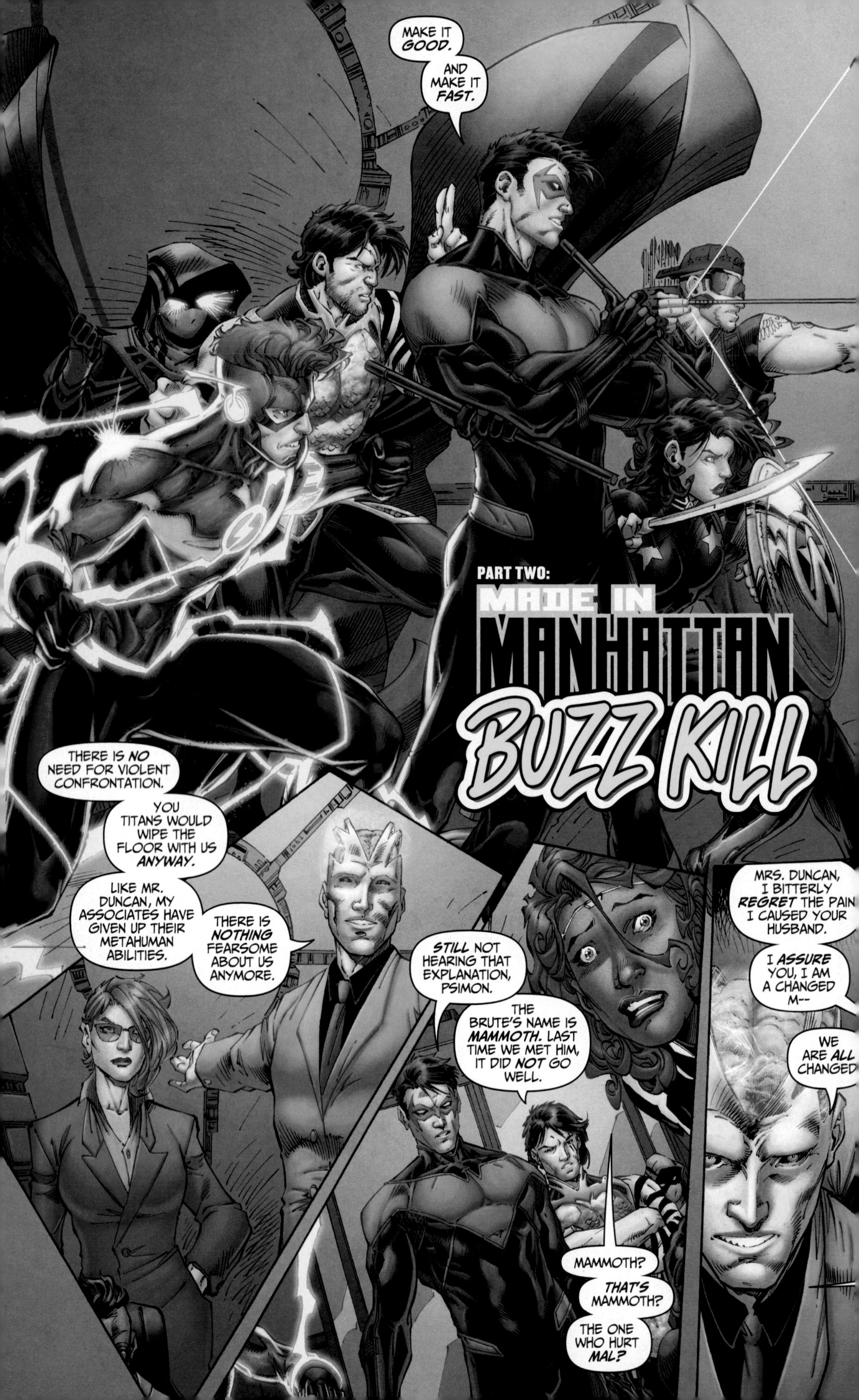

MAKE IT GOOD.
AND MAKE IT FAST.
PART TWO:
MADE IN MANHATTAN
BUZZ KILL
THERE IS NO NEED FOR VIOLENT CONFRONTATION.
YOU TITANS WOULD WIPE THE FLOOR WITH US ANYWAY.
LIKE MR. DUNCAN, MY ASSOCIATES HAVE GIVEN UP THEIR METAHUMAN ABILITIES.
THERE IS NOTHING FEARSOME ABOUT US ANYMORE.
STILL NOT HEARING THAT EXPLANATION, PSIMON.
THE BRUTE'S NAME IS MAMMOTH. LAST TIME WE MET HIM, IT DID NOT GO WELL.
MAMMOTH?
THAT'S MAMMOTH?
THE ONE WHO HURT MAL?
MRS. DUNCAN, I BITTERLY REGRET THE PAIN I CAUSED YOUR HUSBAND.
I ASSURE YOU, I AM A CHANGED M--
WE ARE ALL CHANGED.

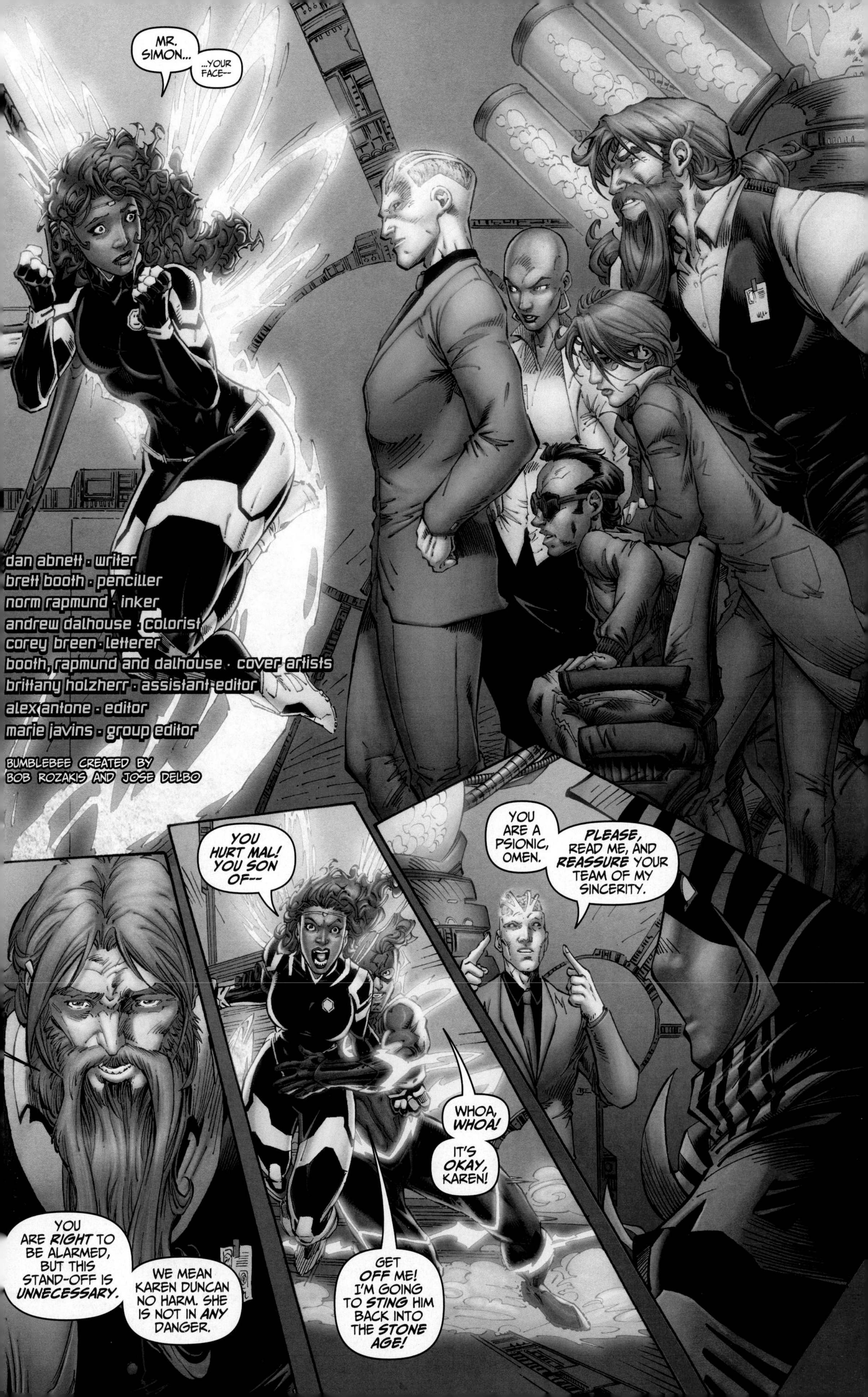

MR. SIMON...
...YOUR FACE--
dan abnett · writer
brett booth · penciller
norm rapmund · inker
andrew dalhouse · colorist
corey breen · letterer
booth, rapmund and dalhouse · cover artists
brittany holzherr · assistant editor
alex antone · editor
marie javins · group editor
BUMBLEBEE CREATED BY BOB ROZAKIS AND JOSE DELBO
YOU HURT MAL! YOU SON OF--
YOU ARE A PSIONIC, OMEN.
PLEASE, READ ME, AND REASSURE YOUR TEAM OF MY SINCERITY.
WHOA, WHOA!
IT'S OKAY, KAREN!
GET OFF ME! I'M GOING TO STING HIM BACK INTO THE STONE AGE!
YOU ARE RIGHT TO BE ALARMED, BUT THIS STAND-OFF IS UNNECESSARY.
WE MEAN KAREN DUNCAN NO HARM. SHE IS NOT IN ANY DANGER.

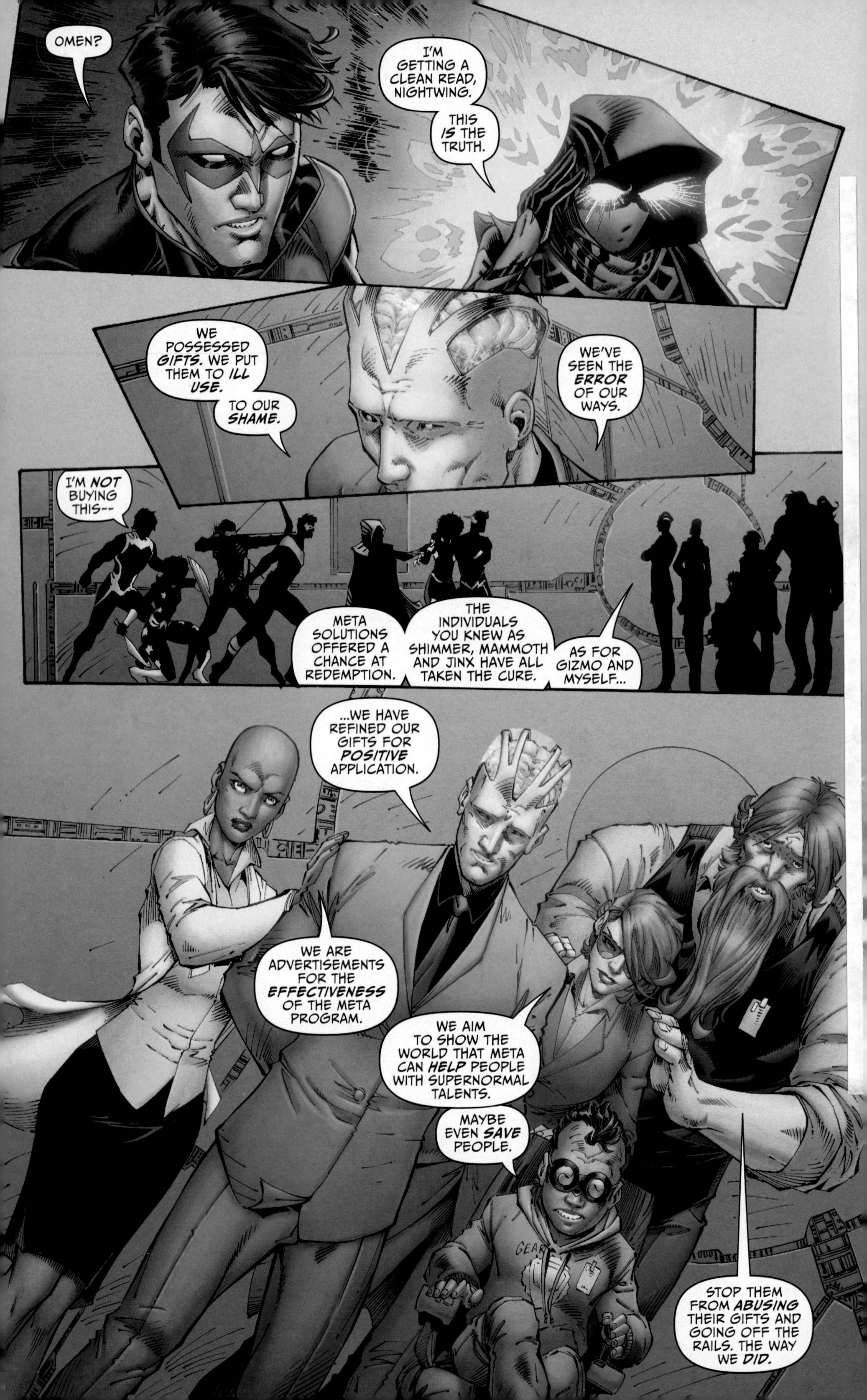
OMEN?
I'M GETTING A CLEAN READ, NIGHTWING.
THIS *IS* THE TRUTH.
WE POSSESSED *GIFTS.* WE PUT THEM TO *ILL USE.*
TO OUR *SHAME.*
WE'VE SEEN THE *ERROR* OF OUR WAYS.
I'M *NOT* BUYING THIS--
META SOLUTIONS OFFERED A CHANCE AT REDEMPTION.
THE INDIVIDUALS YOU KNEW AS SHIMMER, MAMMOTH AND JINX HAVE ALL TAKEN THE CURE.
AS FOR GIZMO AND MYSELF...
...WE HAVE REFINED OUR GIFTS FOR *POSITIVE* APPLICATION.
WE ARE ADVERTISEMENTS FOR THE *EFFECTIVENESS* OF THE META PROGRAM.
WE AIM TO SHOW THE WORLD THAT META CAN *HELP* PEOPLE WITH SUPERNORMAL TALENTS.
MAYBE EVEN *SAVE* PEOPLE.
STOP THEM FROM *ABUSING* THEIR GIFTS AND GOING OFF THE RAILS. THE WAY WE *DID.*

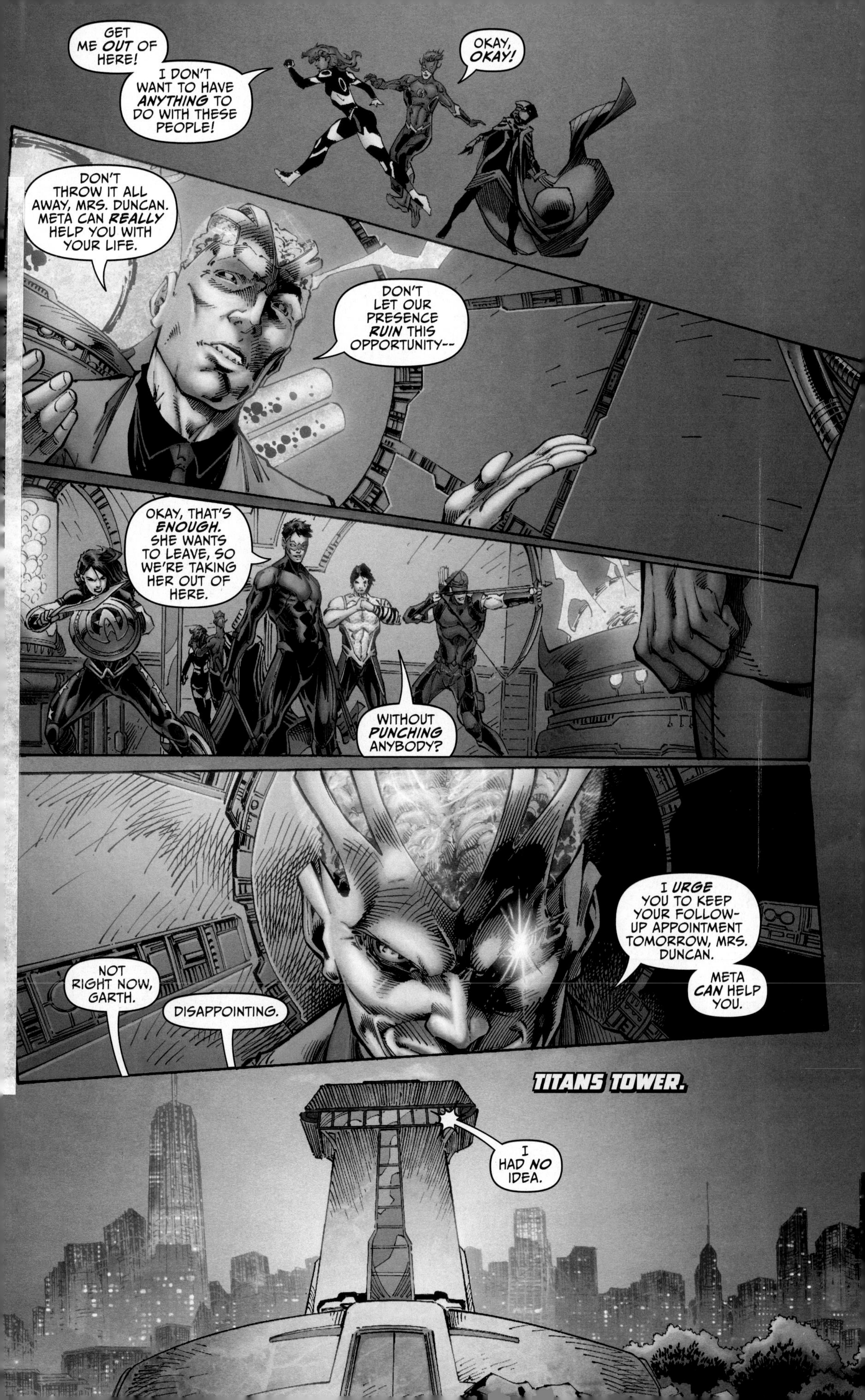
GET ME *OUT* OF HERE!
I DON'T WANT TO HAVE *ANYTHING* TO DO WITH THESE PEOPLE!
OKAY, *OKAY!*
DON'T THROW IT ALL AWAY, MRS. DUNCAN. META CAN *REALLY* HELP YOU WITH YOUR LIFE.
DON'T LET OUR PRESENCE *RUIN* THIS OPPORTUNITY--
OKAY, THAT'S *ENOUGH.* SHE WANTS TO LEAVE, SO WE'RE TAKING HER OUT OF HERE.
WITHOUT *PUNCHING* ANYBODY?
I *URGE* YOU TO KEEP YOUR FOLLOW-UP APPOINTMENT TOMORROW, MRS. DUNCAN.
META *CAN* HELP YOU.
NOT RIGHT NOW, GARTH.
DISAPPOINTING.
TITANS TOWER.
I HAD *NO* IDEA.

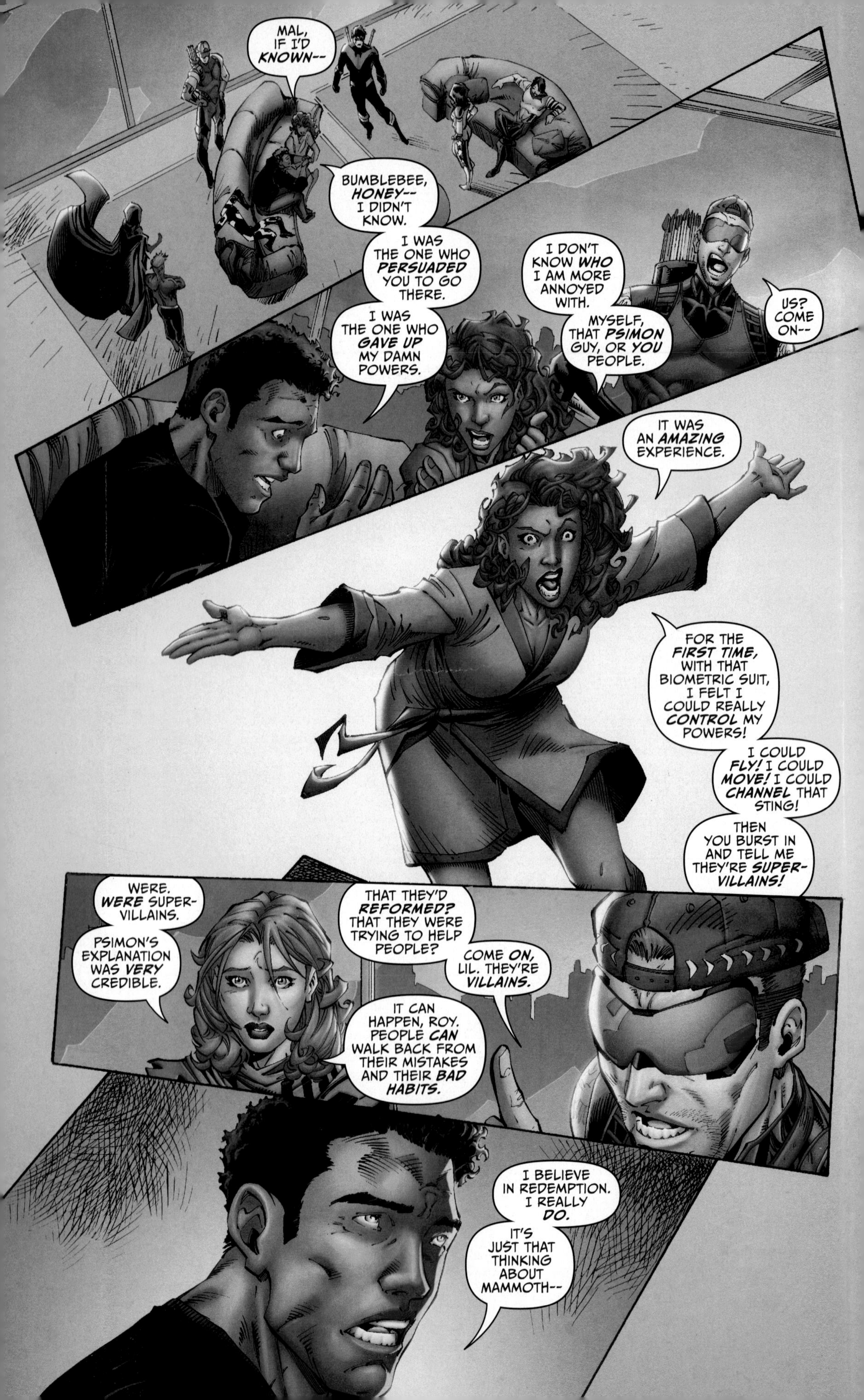
MAL, IF I'D KNOWN--
BUMBLEBEE, HONEY-- I DIDN'T KNOW.
I WAS THE ONE WHO PERSUADED YOU TO GO THERE.
I WAS THE ONE WHO GAVE UP MY DAMN POWERS.
I DON'T KNOW WHO I AM MORE ANNOYED WITH.
MYSELF, THAT PSIMON GUY, OR YOU PEOPLE.
US? COME ON--
IT WAS AN AMAZING EXPERIENCE.
FOR THE FIRST TIME, WITH THAT BIOMETRIC SUIT, I FELT I COULD REALLY CONTROL MY POWERS!
I COULD FLY! I COULD MOVE! I COULD CHANNEL THAT STING!
THEN YOU BURST IN AND TELL ME THEY'RE SUPER-VILLAINS!
WERE. WERE SUPER-VILLAINS.
PSIMON'S EXPLANATION WAS VERY CREDIBLE.
THAT THEY'D REFORMED? THAT THEY WERE TRYING TO HELP PEOPLE?
COME ON, LIL. THEY'RE VILLAINS.
IT CAN HAPPEN, ROY. PEOPLE CAN WALK BACK FROM THEIR MISTAKES AND THEIR BAD HABITS.
I BELIEVE IN REDEMPTION. I REALLY DO.
IT'S JUST THAT THINKING ABOUT MAMMOTH--

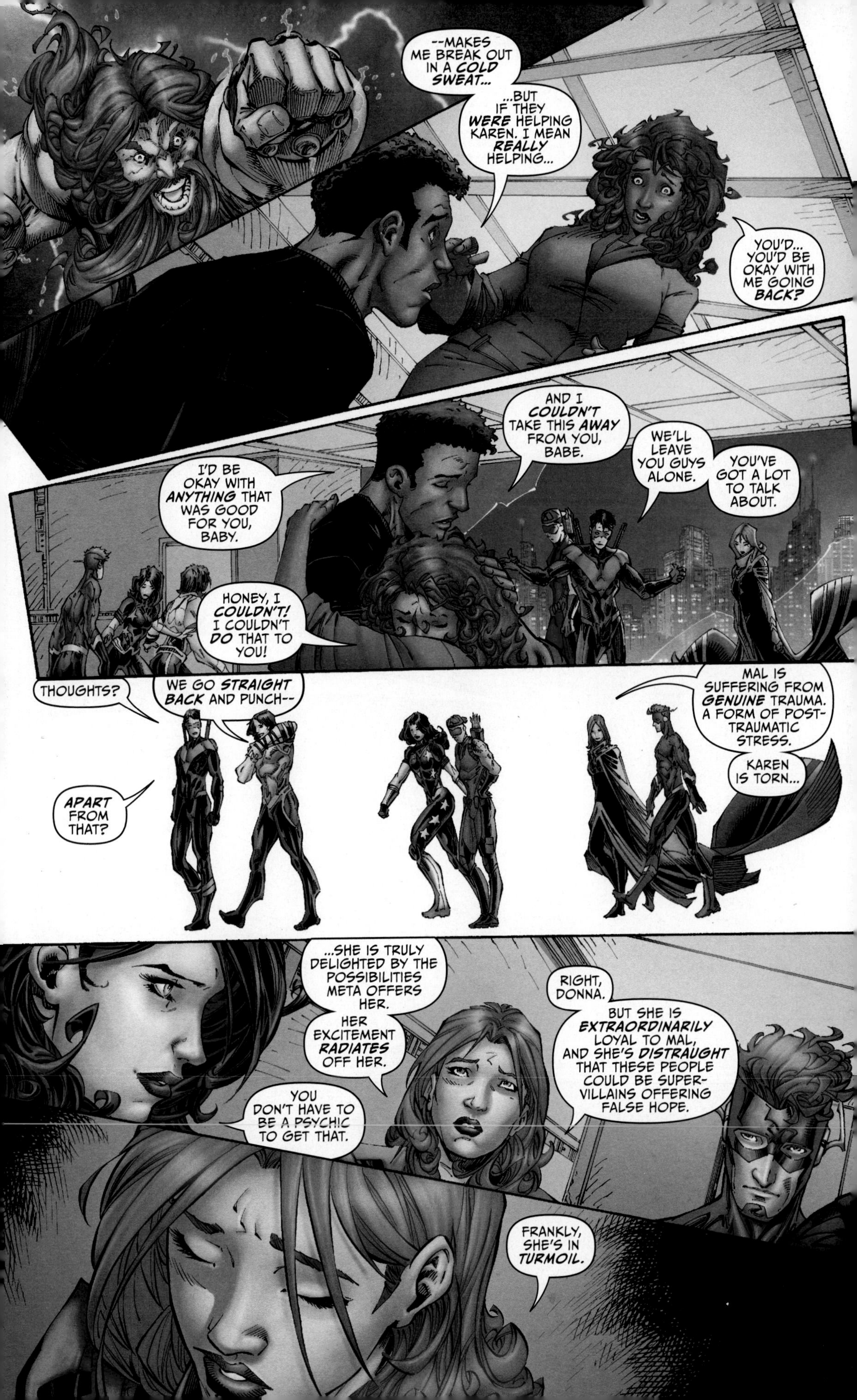
--MAKES ME BREAK OUT IN A COLD SWEAT...
...BUT IF THEY WERE HELPING KAREN. I MEAN REALLY HELPING...
YOU'D... YOU'D BE OKAY WITH ME GOING BACK?
I'D BE OKAY WITH ANYTHING THAT WAS GOOD FOR YOU, BABY.
AND I COULDN'T TAKE THIS AWAY FROM YOU, BABE.
HONEY, I COULDN'T! I COULDN'T DO THAT TO YOU!
WE'LL LEAVE YOU GUYS ALONE.
YOU'VE GOT A LOT TO TALK ABOUT.
THOUGHTS?
WE GO STRAIGHT BACK AND PUNCH--
APART FROM THAT?
MAL IS SUFFERING FROM GENUINE TRAUMA. A FORM OF POST-TRAUMATIC STRESS.
KAREN IS TORN...
...SHE IS TRULY DELIGHTED BY THE POSSIBILITIES META OFFERS HER.
HER EXCITEMENT RADIATES OFF HER.
YOU DON'T HAVE TO BE A PSYCHIC TO GET THAT.
RIGHT, DONNA.
BUT SHE IS EXTRAORDINARILY LOYAL TO MAL, AND SHE'S DISTRAUGHT THAT THESE PEOPLE COULD BE SUPER-VILLAINS OFFERING FALSE HOPE.
FRANKLY, SHE'S IN TURMOIL.

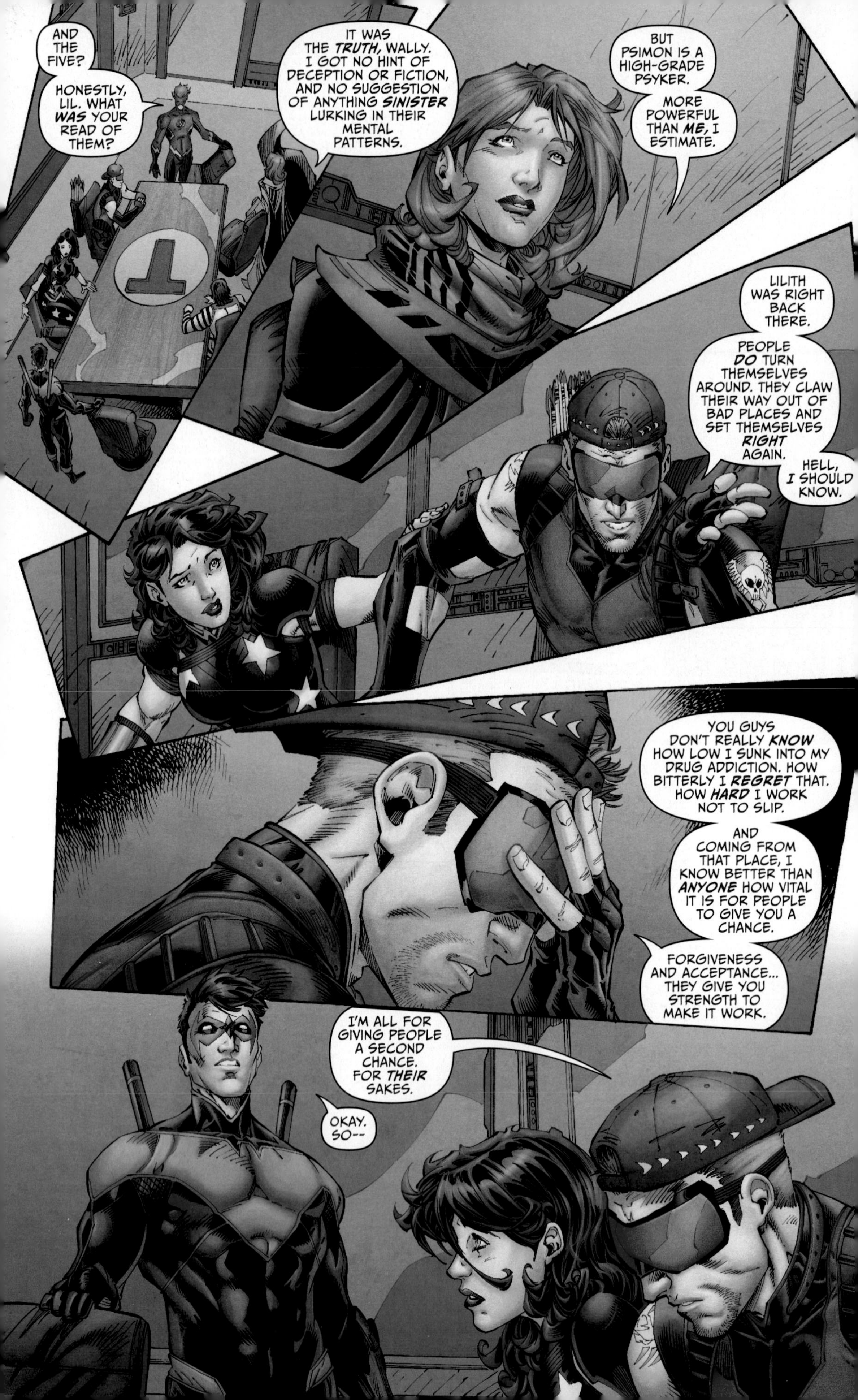
AND THE FIVE?
HONESTLY, LIL. WHAT WAS YOUR READ OF THEM?
IT WAS THE TRUTH, WALLY. I GOT NO HINT OF DECEPTION OR FICTION, AND NO SUGGESTION OF ANYTHING SINISTER LURKING IN THEIR MENTAL PATTERNS.
BUT PSIMON IS A HIGH-GRADE PSYKER.
MORE POWERFUL THAN ME, I ESTIMATE.
LILITH WAS RIGHT BACK THERE.
PEOPLE DO TURN THEMSELVES AROUND. THEY CLAW THEIR WAY OUT OF BAD PLACES AND SET THEMSELVES RIGHT AGAIN.
HELL, I SHOULD KNOW.
YOU GUYS DON'T REALLY KNOW HOW LOW I SUNK INTO MY DRUG ADDICTION. HOW BITTERLY I REGRET THAT. HOW HARD I WORK NOT TO SLIP.
AND COMING FROM THAT PLACE, I KNOW BETTER THAN ANYONE HOW VITAL IT IS FOR PEOPLE TO GIVE YOU A CHANCE.
FORGIVENESS AND ACCEPTANCE... THEY GIVE YOU STRENGTH TO MAKE IT WORK.
I'M ALL FOR GIVING PEOPLE A SECOND CHANCE. FOR THEIR SAKES.
OKAY. SO--

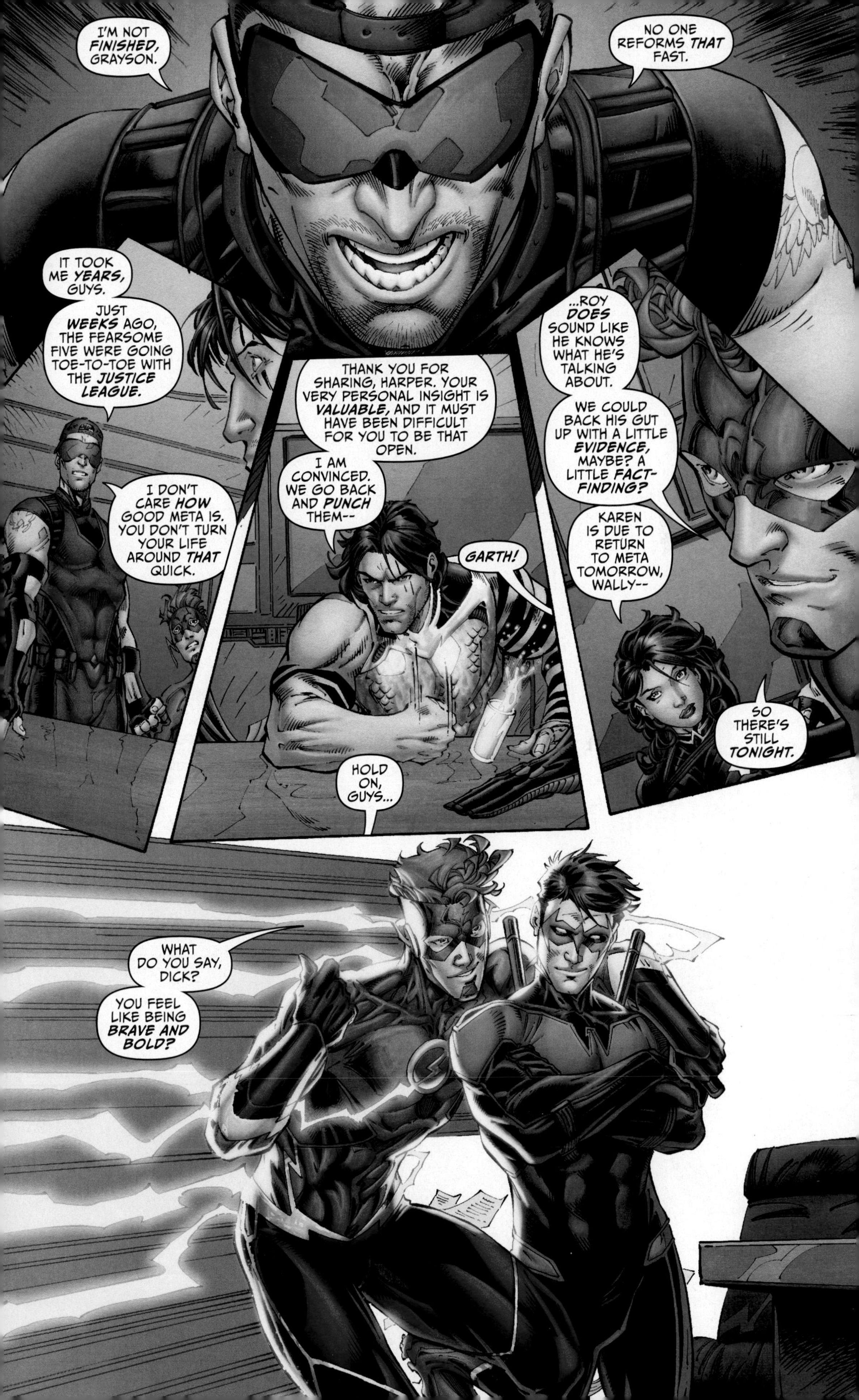

I'M NOT FINISHED, GRAYSON.
NO ONE REFORMS THAT FAST.
IT TOOK ME YEARS, GUYS.
JUST WEEKS AGO, THE FEARSOME FIVE WERE GOING TOE-TO-TOE WITH THE JUSTICE LEAGUE.
I DON'T CARE HOW GOOD META IS. YOU DON'T TURN YOUR LIFE AROUND THAT QUICK.
THANK YOU FOR SHARING, HARPER. YOUR VERY PERSONAL INSIGHT IS VALUABLE, AND IT MUST HAVE BEEN DIFFICULT FOR YOU TO BE THAT OPEN.
I AM CONVINCED. WE GO BACK AND PUNCH THEM--
GARTH!
HOLD ON, GUYS...
...ROY DOES SOUND LIKE HE KNOWS WHAT HE'S TALKING ABOUT.
WE COULD BACK HIS GUT UP WITH A LITTLE EVIDENCE, MAYBE? A LITTLE FACT-FINDING?
KAREN IS DUE TO RETURN TO META TOMORROW, WALLY--
SO THERE'S STILL TONIGHT.
WHAT DO YOU SAY, DICK?
YOU FEEL LIKE BEING BRAVE AND BOLD?

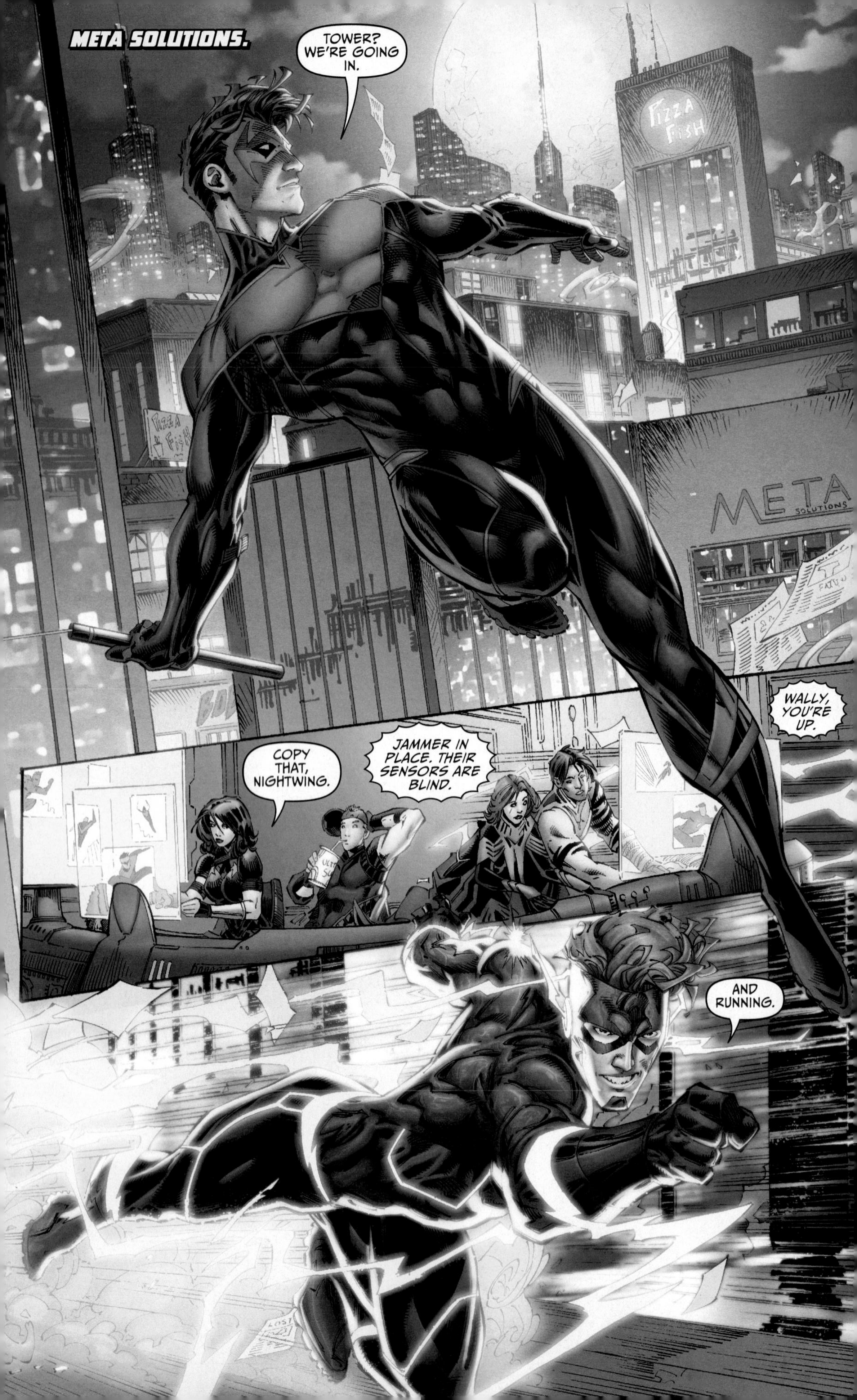

META SOLUTIONS.
TOWER? WE'RE GOING IN.
PIZZA FISH
META SOLUTIONS
WALLY, YOU'RE UP.
COPY THAT, NIGHTWING.
JAMMER IN PLACE. THEIR SENSORS ARE BLIND.
AND RUNNING.

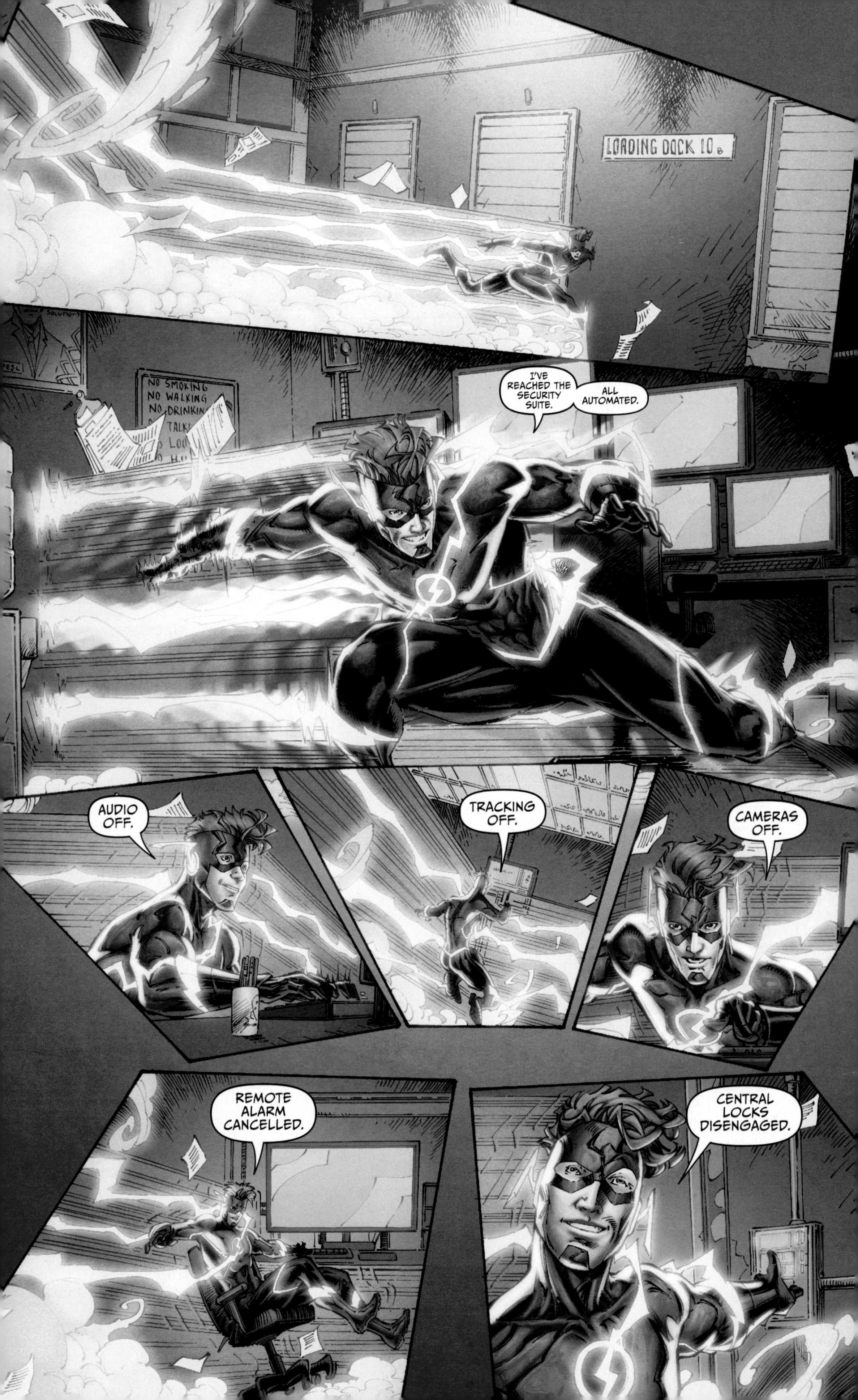
LOADING DOCK 10B
NO SMOKING
NO WALKING
NO DRINKIN
I'VE REACHED THE SECURITY SUITE.
ALL AUTOMATED.
AUDIO OFF.
TRACKING OFF.
CAMERAS OFF.
REMOTE ALARM CANCELLED.
CENTRAL LOCKS DISENGAGED.

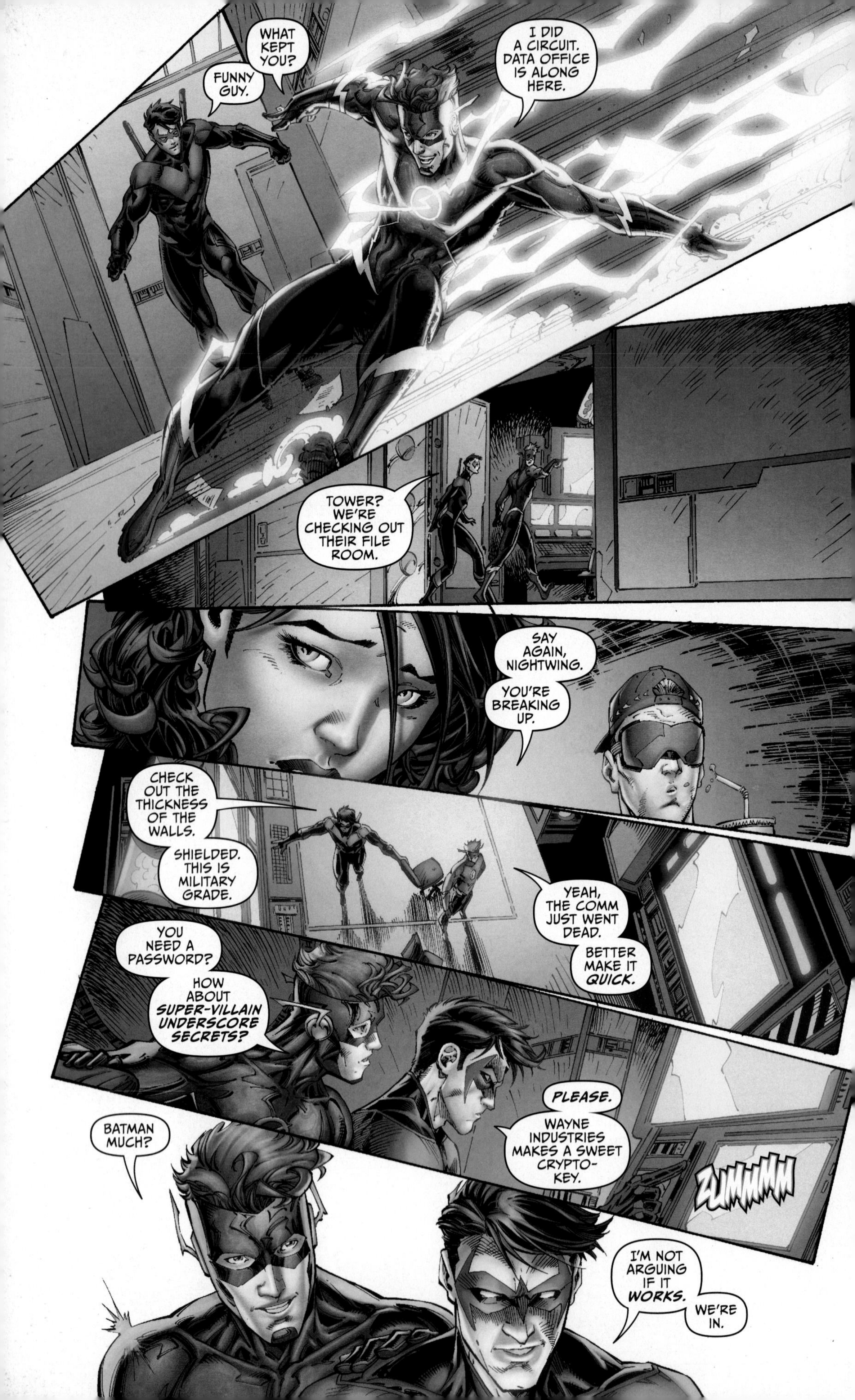
WHAT KEPT YOU?
FUNNY GUY.
I DID A CIRCUIT. DATA OFFICE IS ALONG HERE.
TOWER? WE'RE CHECKING OUT THEIR FILE ROOM.
SAY AGAIN, NIGHTWING.
YOU'RE BREAKING UP.
CHECK OUT THE THICKNESS OF THE WALLS.
SHIELDED. THIS IS MILITARY GRADE.
YEAH, THE COMM JUST WENT DEAD.
BETTER MAKE IT *QUICK.*
YOU NEED A PASSWORD?
HOW ABOUT *SUPER-VILLAIN UNDERSCORE SECRETS?*
PLEASE.
WAYNE INDUSTRIES MAKES A SWEET CRYPTO-KEY.
ZUMMMM
BATMAN MUCH?
I'M NOT ARGUING IF IT *WORKS.*
WE'RE IN.

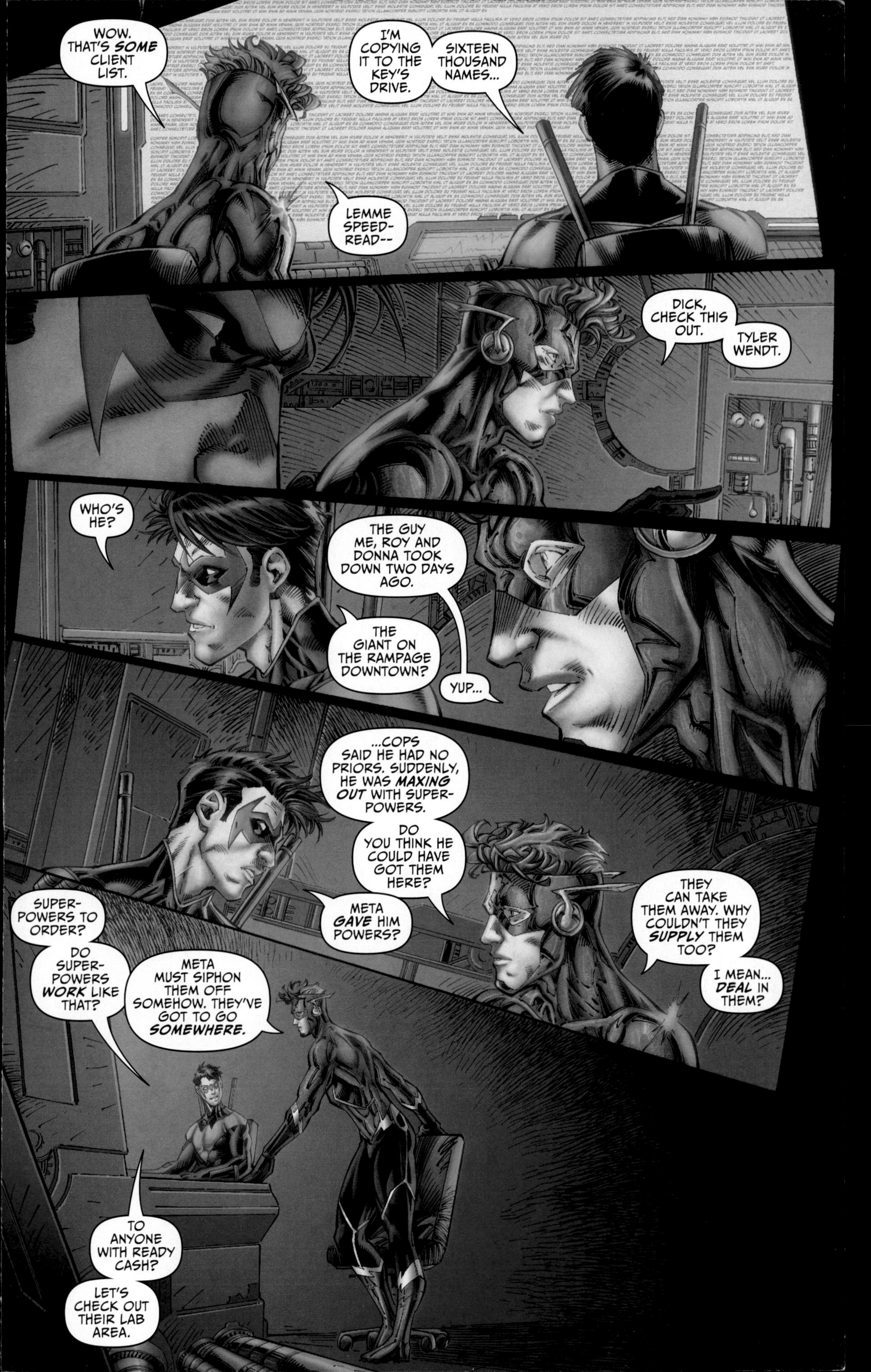

WOW. THAT'S SOME CLIENT LIST.
I'M COPYING IT TO THE KEY'S DRIVE.
SIXTEEN THOUSAND NAMES...
LEMME SPEED-READ--
DICK, CHECK THIS OUT.
TYLER WENDT.
WHO'S HE?
THE GUY ME, ROY AND DONNA TOOK DOWN TWO DAYS AGO.
THE GIANT ON THE RAMPAGE DOWNTOWN?
YUP...
...COPS SAID HE HAD NO PRIORS. SUDDENLY, HE WAS MAXING OUT WITH SUPER-POWERS.
DO YOU THINK HE COULD HAVE GOT THEM HERE?
META GAVE HIM POWERS?
THEY CAN TAKE THEM AWAY. WHY COULDN'T THEY SUPPLY THEM TOO?
I MEAN... DEAL IN THEM?
SUPER-POWERS TO ORDER?
DO SUPER-POWERS WORK LIKE THAT?
META MUST SIPHON THEM OFF SOMEHOW. THEY'VE GOT TO GO SOMEWHERE.
TO ANYONE WITH READY CASH?
LET'S CHECK OUT THEIR LAB AREA.

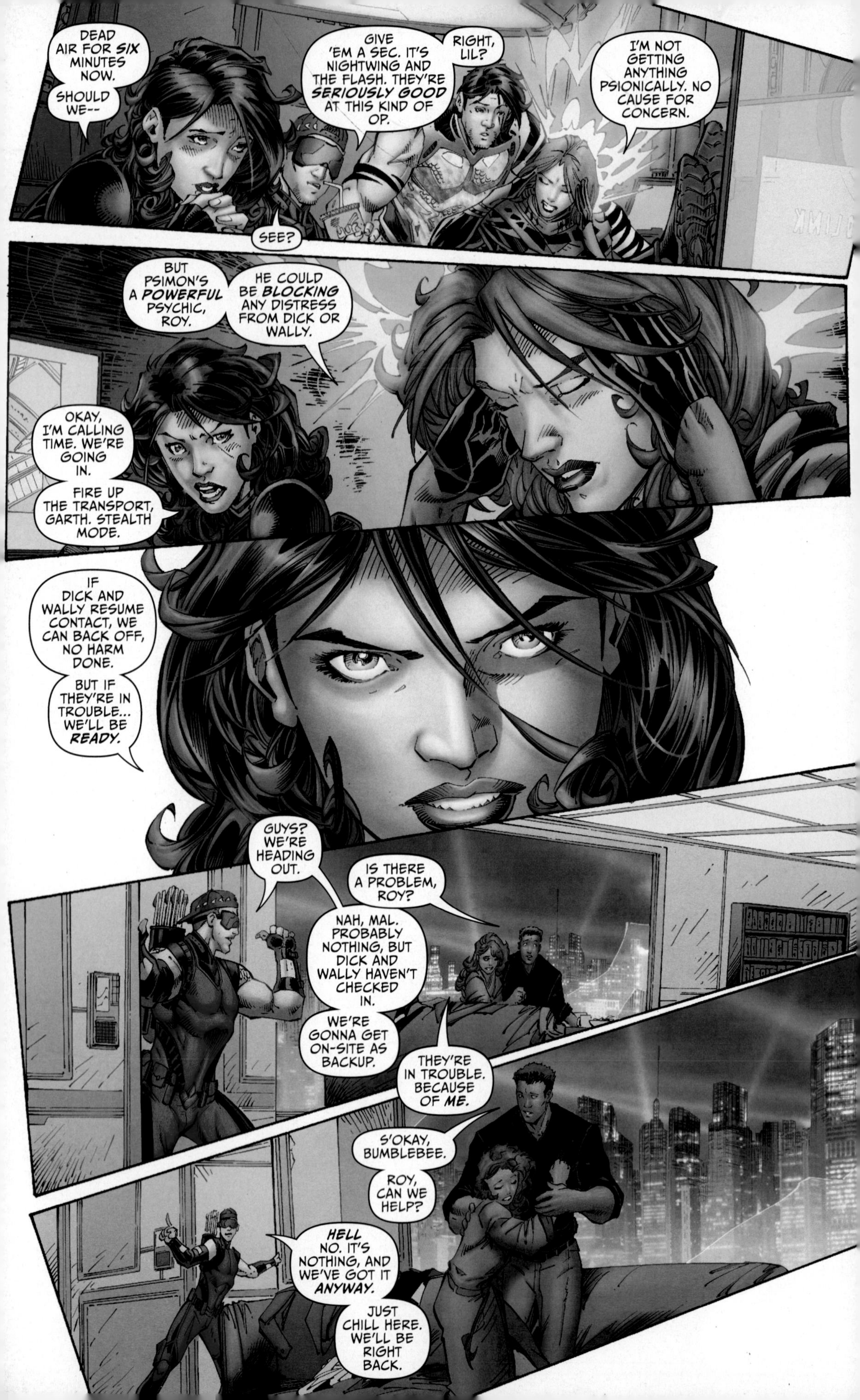

DEAD AIR FOR *SIX* MINUTES NOW.
SHOULD WE--
GIVE 'EM A SEC. IT'S NIGHTWING AND THE FLASH. THEY'RE *SERIOUSLY GOOD* AT THIS KIND OF OP.
RIGHT, LIL?
SEE?
I'M NOT GETTING ANYTHING PSIONICALLY. NO CAUSE FOR CONCERN.
BUT PSIMON'S A *POWERFUL* PSYCHIC, ROY.
HE COULD BE *BLOCKING* ANY DISTRESS FROM DICK OR WALLY.
OKAY, I'M CALLING TIME. WE'RE GOING IN.
FIRE UP THE TRANSPORT, GARTH. STEALTH MODE.
IF DICK AND WALLY RESUME CONTACT, WE CAN BACK OFF, NO HARM DONE.
BUT IF THEY'RE IN TROUBLE... WE'LL BE *READY.*
GUYS? WE'RE HEADING OUT.
IS THERE A PROBLEM, ROY?
NAH, MAL. PROBABLY NOTHING, BUT DICK AND WALLY HAVEN'T CHECKED IN.
WE'RE GONNA GET ON-SITE AS BACKUP.
THEY'RE IN TROUBLE. BECAUSE OF *ME.*
S'OKAY, BUMBLEBEE.
ROY, CAN WE HELP?
HELL NO. IT'S NOTHING, AND WE'VE GOT IT *ANYWAY.*
JUST CHILL HERE. WE'LL BE RIGHT BACK.

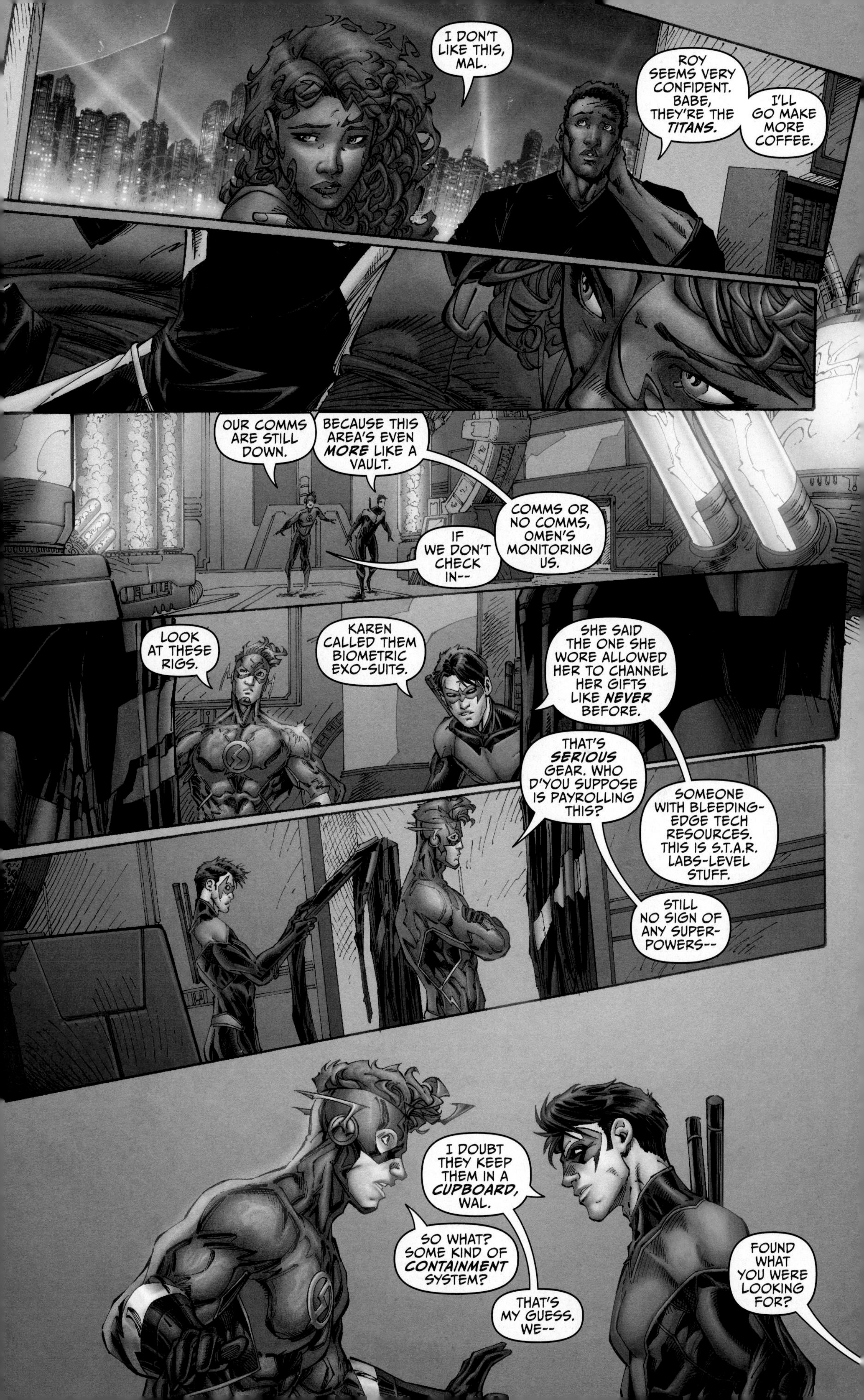
I DON'T LIKE THIS, MAL.
ROY SEEMS VERY CONFIDENT. BABE, THEY'RE THE *TITANS.*
I'LL GO MAKE MORE COFFEE.
OUR COMMS ARE STILL DOWN.
BECAUSE THIS AREA'S EVEN *MORE* LIKE A VAULT.
COMMS OR NO COMMS, OMEN'S MONITORING US.
IF WE DON'T CHECK IN--
LOOK AT THESE RIGS.
KAREN CALLED THEM BIOMETRIC EXO-SUITS.
SHE SAID THE ONE SHE WORE ALLOWED HER TO CHANNEL HER GIFTS LIKE *NEVER* BEFORE.
THAT'S *SERIOUS* GEAR. WHO D'YOU SUPPOSE IS PAYROLLING THIS?
SOMEONE WITH BLEEDING-EDGE TECH RESOURCES. THIS IS S.T.A.R. LABS-LEVEL STUFF.
STILL NO SIGN OF ANY SUPER-POWERS--
I DOUBT THEY KEEP THEM IN A *CUPBOARD,* WAL.
SO WHAT? SOME KIND OF *CONTAINMENT* SYSTEM?
THAT'S MY GUESS. WE--
FOUND WHAT YOU WERE LOOKING FOR?

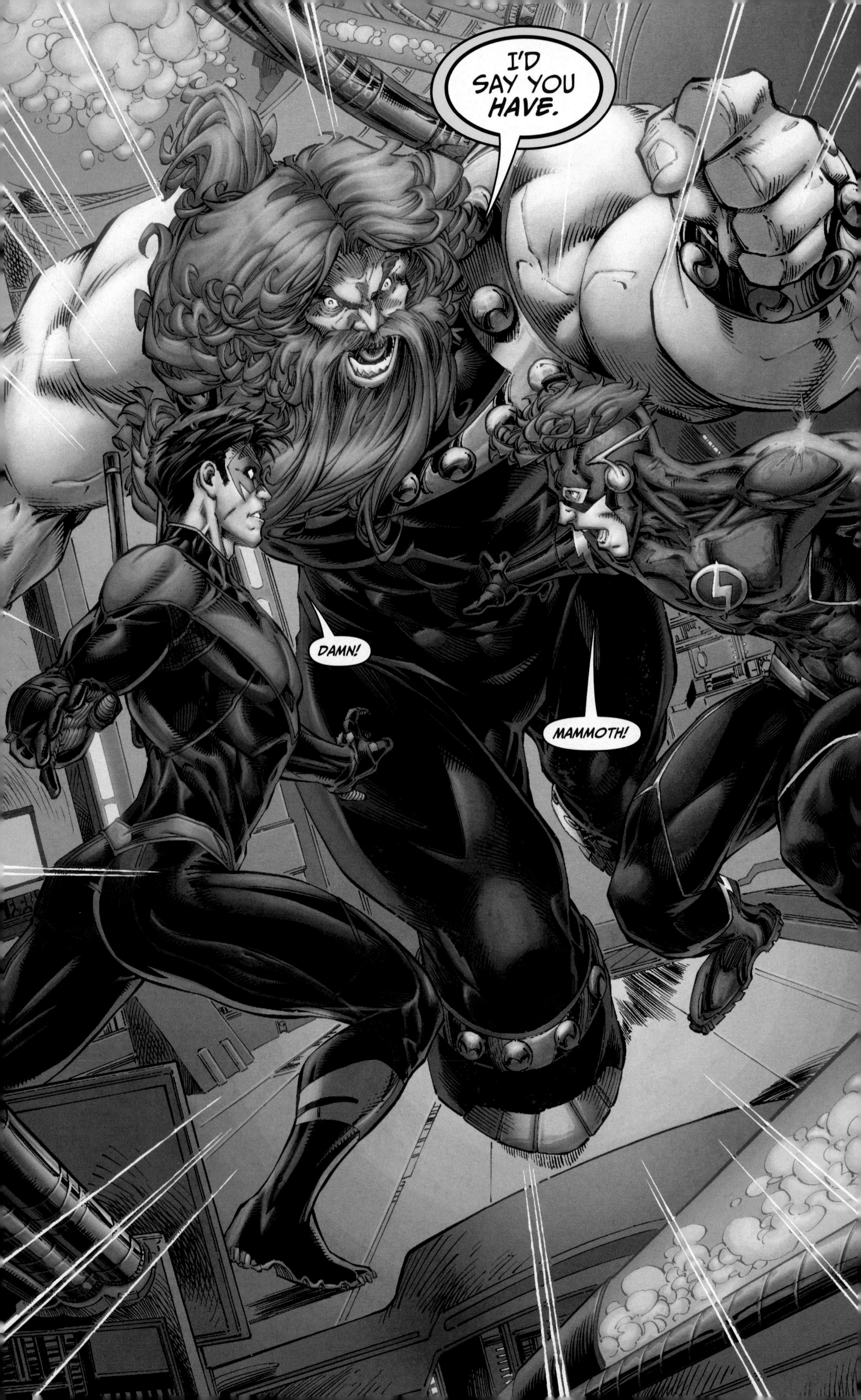
I'D SAY YOU HAVE.
DAMN!
MAMMOTH!

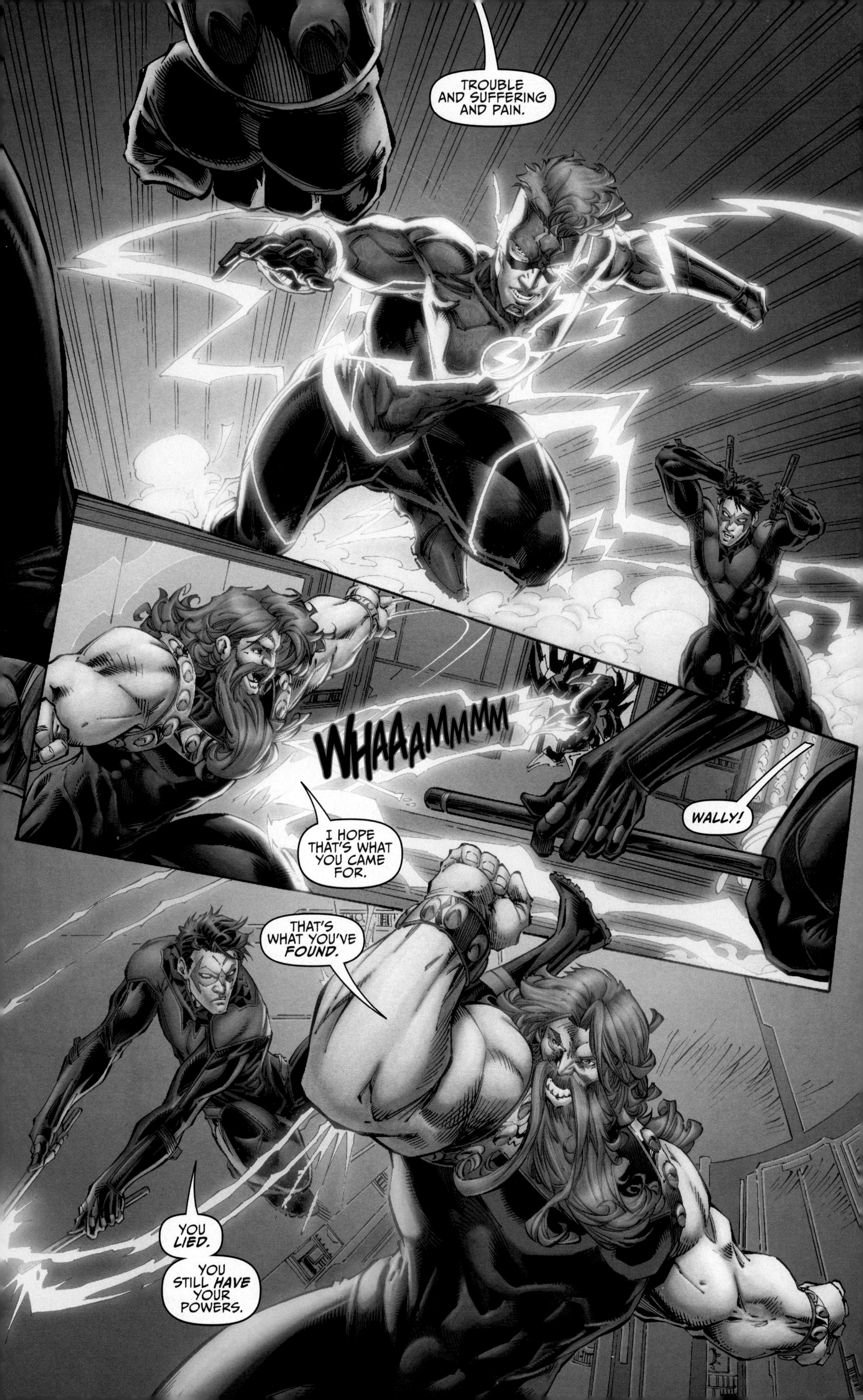
TROUBLE AND SUFFERING AND PAIN.
WHAAAMMMM
I HOPE THAT'S WHAT YOU CAME FOR.
WALLY!
THAT'S WHAT YOU'VE FOUND.
YOU LIED.
YOU STILL HAVE YOUR POWERS.

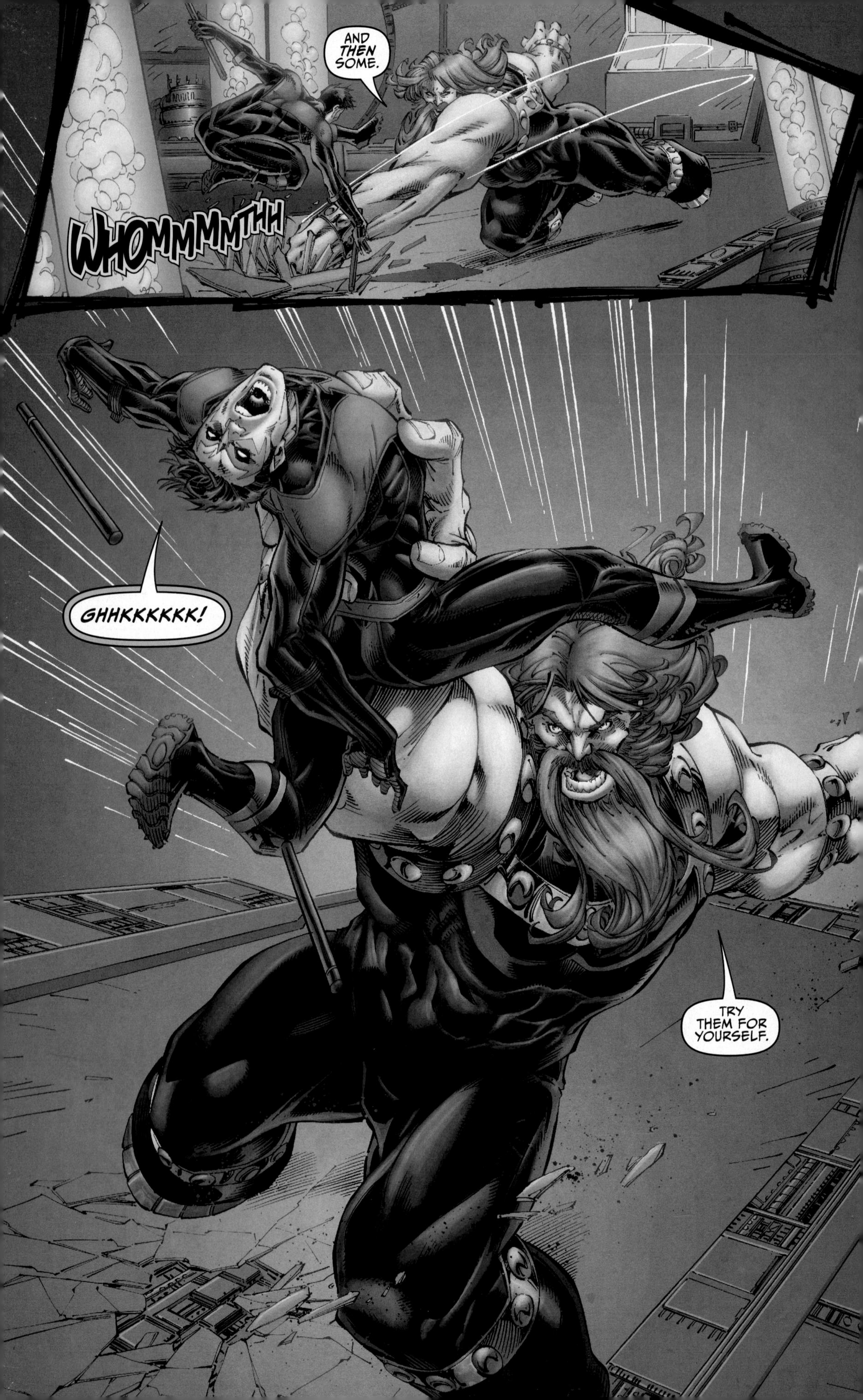
AND THEN SOME.
WHOMMMMTHH
GHHKKKKKK!
TRY THEM FOR YOURSELF.

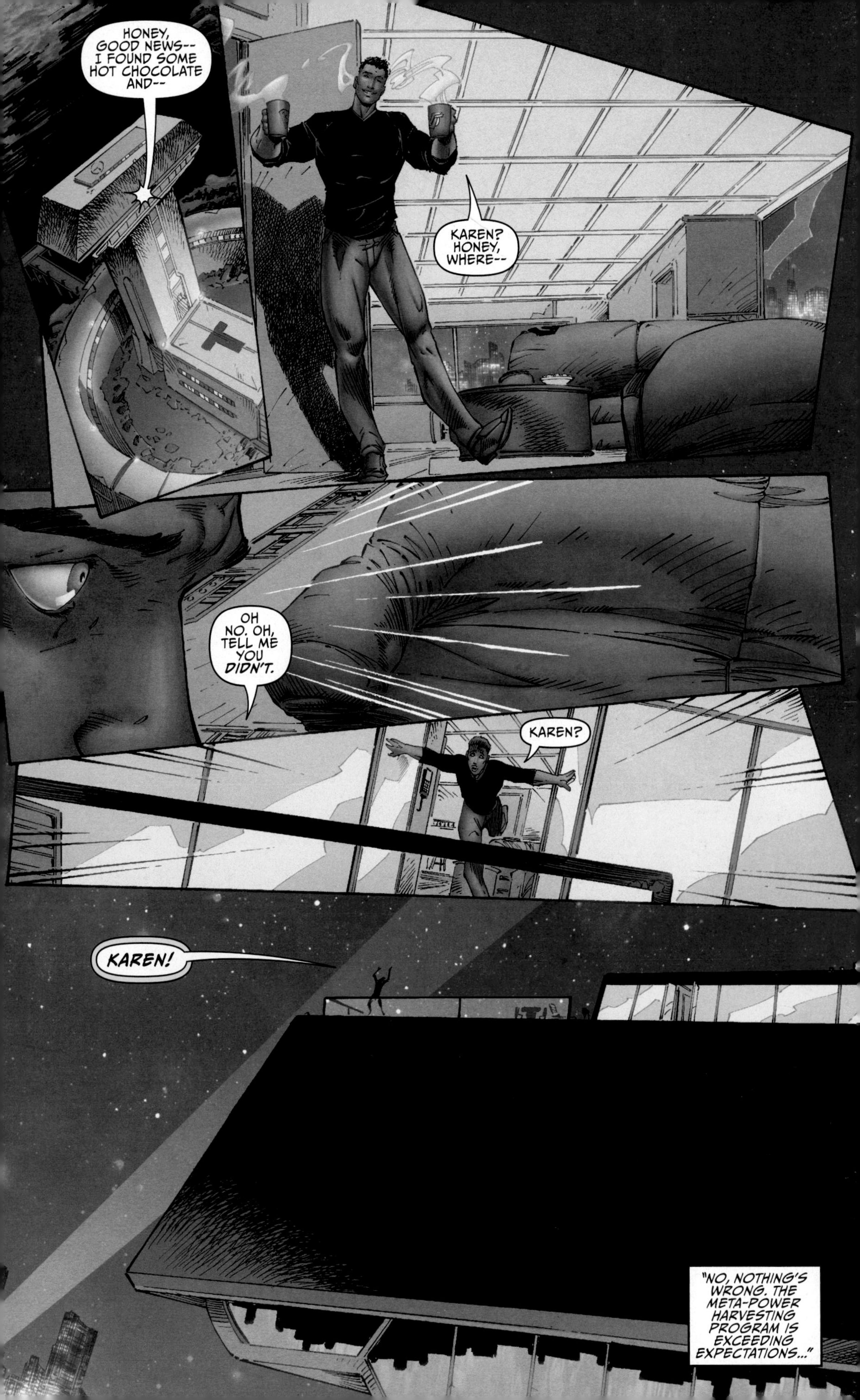
HONEY, GOOD NEWS-- I FOUND SOME HOT CHOCOLATE AND--
KAREN? HONEY, WHERE--
OH NO. OH, TELL ME YOU DIDN'T.
KAREN?
KAREN!
"NO, NOTHING'S WRONG. THE META-POWER HARVESTING PROGRAM IS EXCEEDING EXPECTATIONS..."

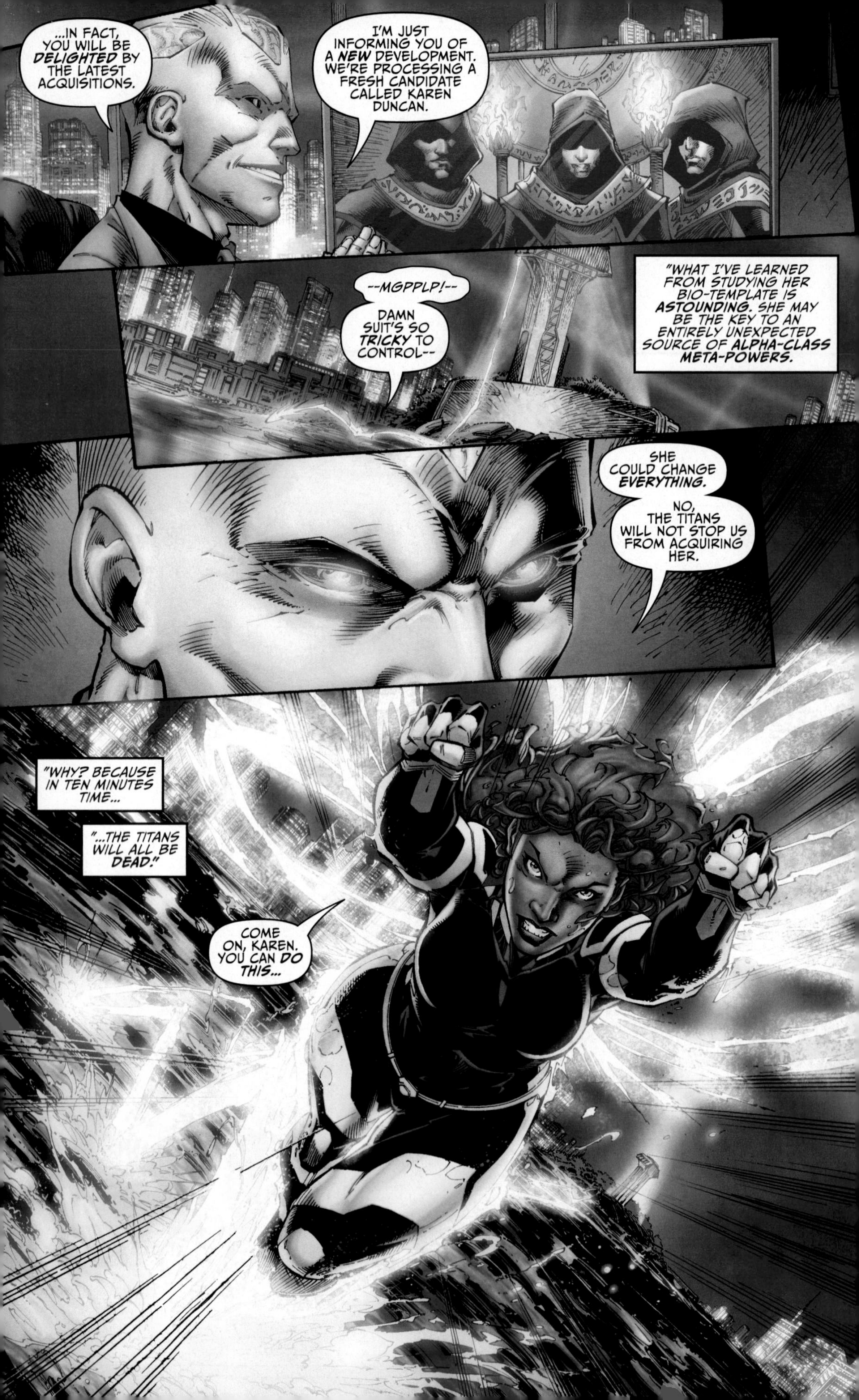

...IN FACT, YOU WILL BE DELIGHTED BY THE LATEST ACQUISITIONS.
I'M JUST INFORMING YOU OF A NEW DEVELOPMENT. WE'RE PROCESSING A FRESH CANDIDATE CALLED KAREN DUNCAN.
--MGPPLP!--
DAMN SUIT'S SO TRICKY TO CONTROL--
"WHAT I'VE LEARNED FROM STUDYING HER BIO-TEMPLATE IS ASTOUNDING. SHE MAY BE THE KEY TO AN ENTIRELY UNEXPECTED SOURCE OF ALPHA-CLASS META-POWERS.
SHE COULD CHANGE EVERYTHING.
NO, THE TITANS WILL NOT STOP US FROM ACQUIRING HER.
"WHY? BECAUSE IN TEN MINUTES TIME...
"...THE TITANS WILL ALL BE DEAD."
COME ON, KAREN. YOU CAN DO THIS...

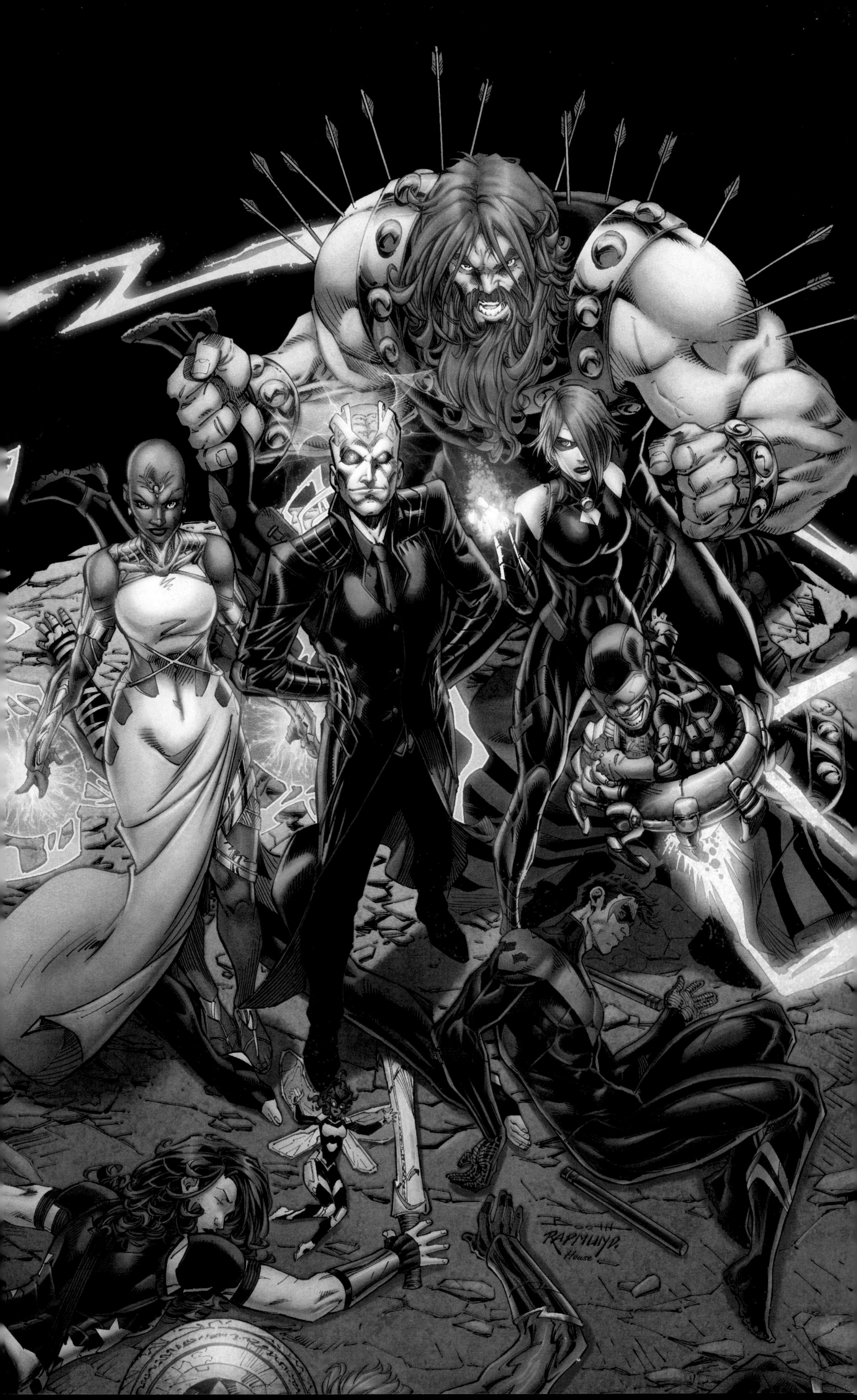

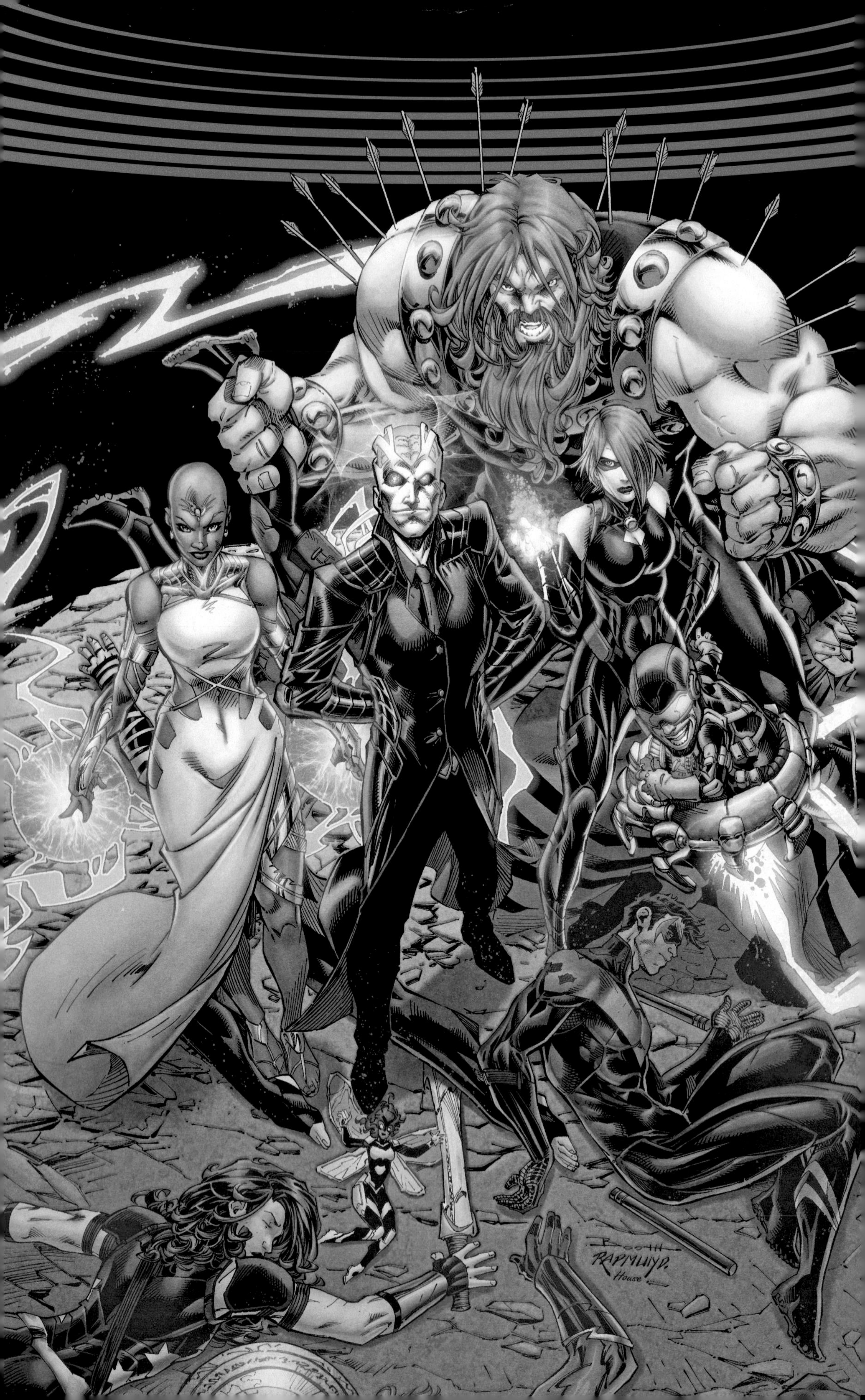
Booth
RAPMUND
House

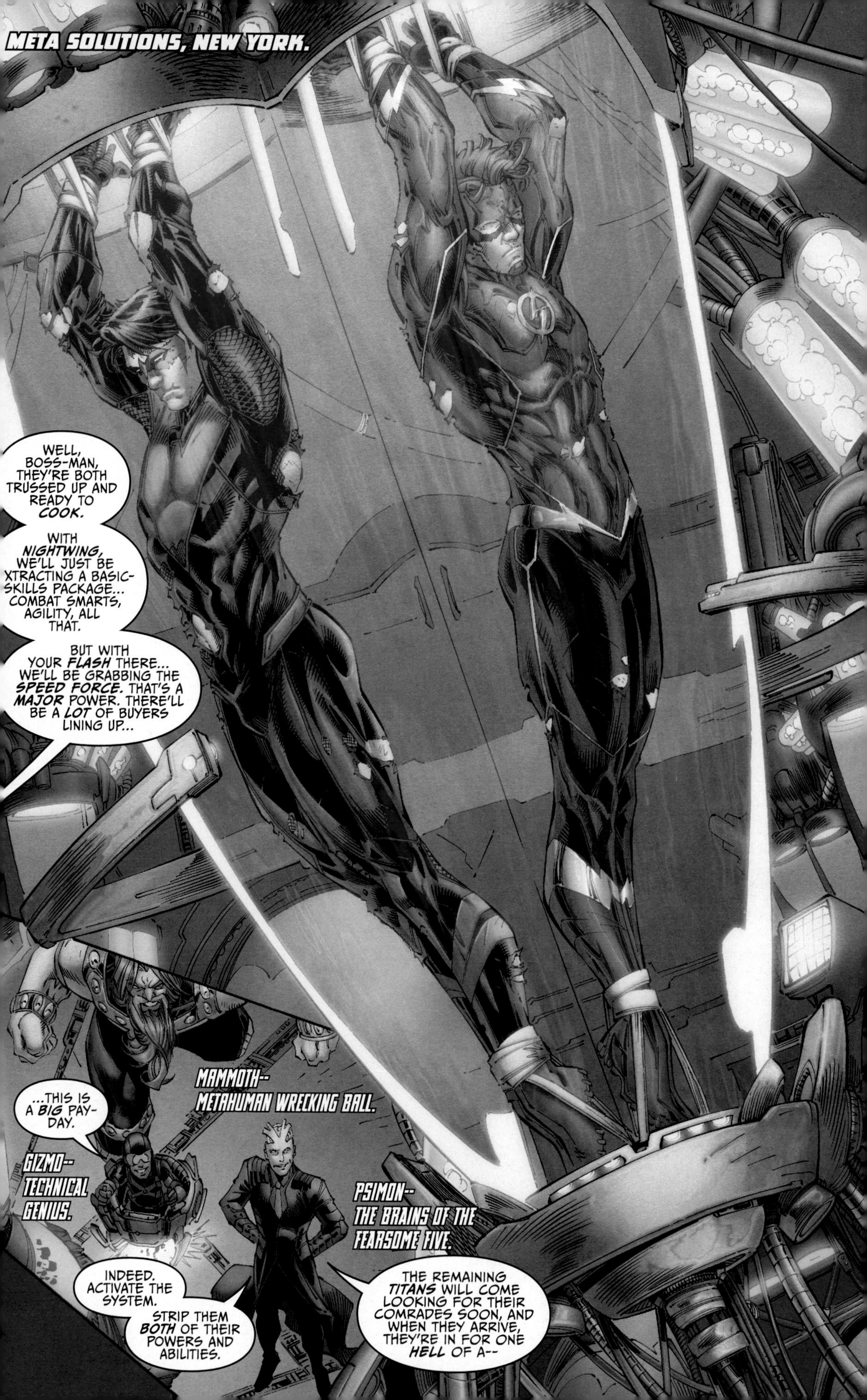
META SOLUTIONS, NEW YORK.
WELL, BOSS-MAN, THEY'RE BOTH TRUSSED UP AND READY TO COOK.
WITH NIGHTWING, WE'LL JUST BE XTRACTING A BASIC-SKILLS PACKAGE... COMBAT SMARTS, AGILITY, ALL THAT.
BUT WITH YOUR FLASH THERE... WE'LL BE GRABBING THE SPEED FORCE. THAT'S A MAJOR POWER. THERE'LL BE A LOT OF BUYERS LINING UP...
...THIS IS A BIG PAY-DAY.
MAMMOTH-- METAHUMAN WRECKING BALL.
GIZMO-- TECHNICAL GENIUS.
PSIMON-- THE BRAINS OF THE FEARSOME FIVE.
INDEED. ACTIVATE THE SYSTEM.
STRIP THEM BOTH OF THEIR POWERS AND ABILITIES.
THE REMAINING TITANS WILL COME LOOKING FOR THEIR COMRADES SOON, AND WHEN THEY ARRIVE, THEY'RE IN FOR ONE HELL OF A--

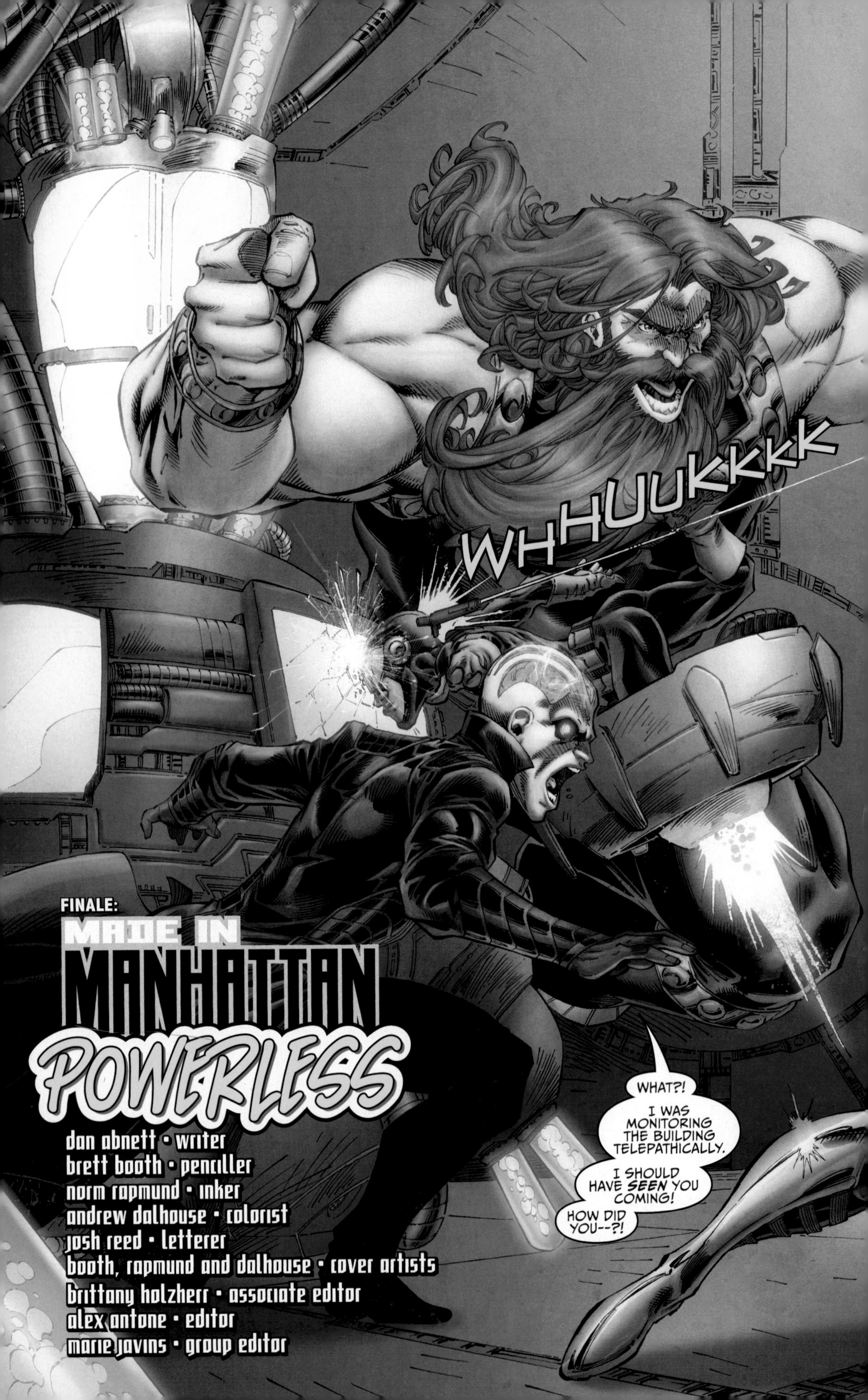
WHHUUKKKK
FINALE:
MADE IN MANHATTAN
POWERLESS
dan abnett • writer
brett booth • penciller
norm rapmund • inker
andrew dalhouse • colorist
josh reed • letterer
booth, rapmund and dalhouse • cover artists
brittany holzherr • associate editor
alex antone • editor
marie javins • group editor
WHAT?!
I WAS MONITORING THE BUILDING TELEPATHICALLY.
I SHOULD HAVE SEEN YOU COMING!
HOW DID YOU--?!

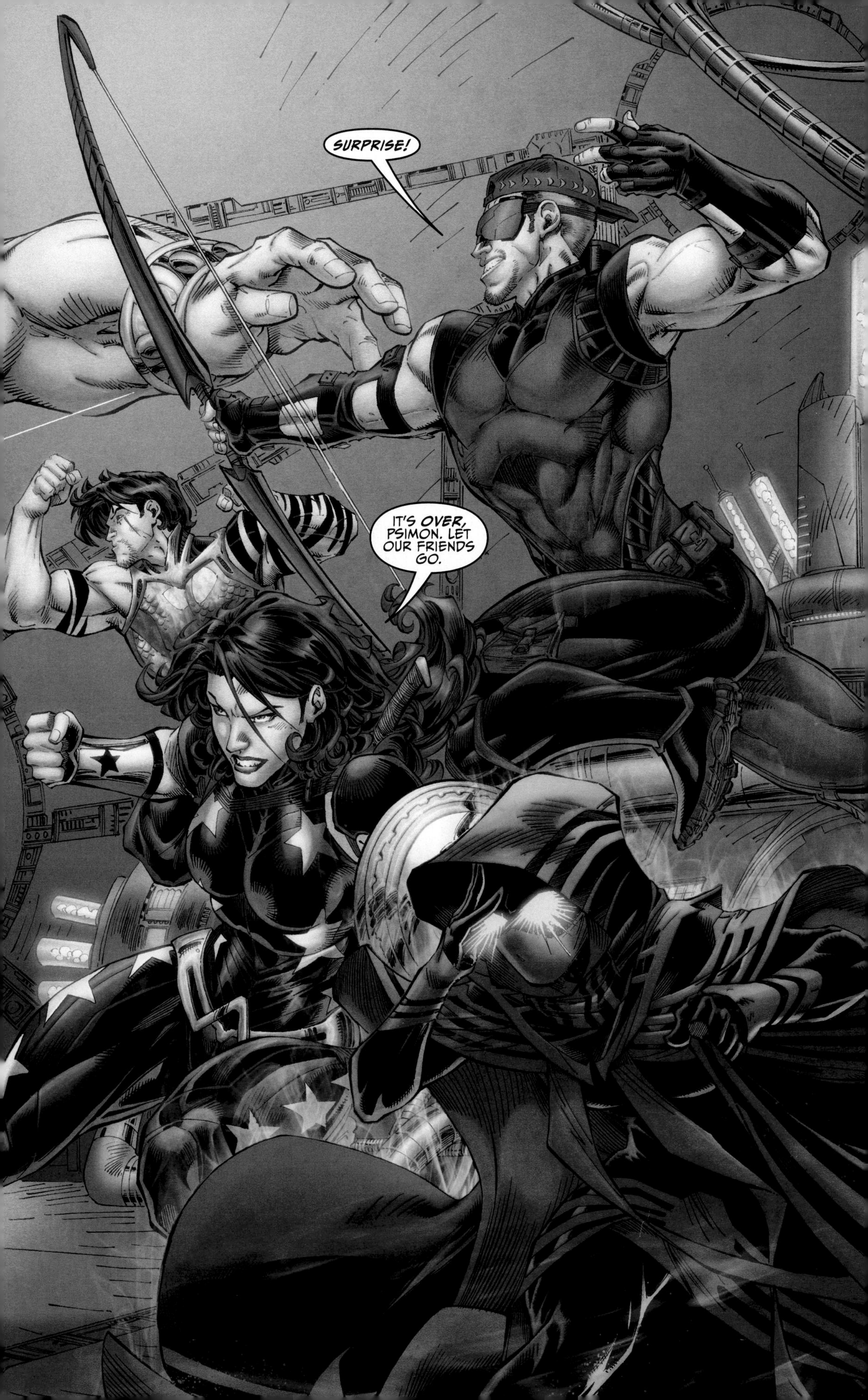
SURPRISE!
IT'S OVER, PSIMON. LET OUR FRIENDS GO.

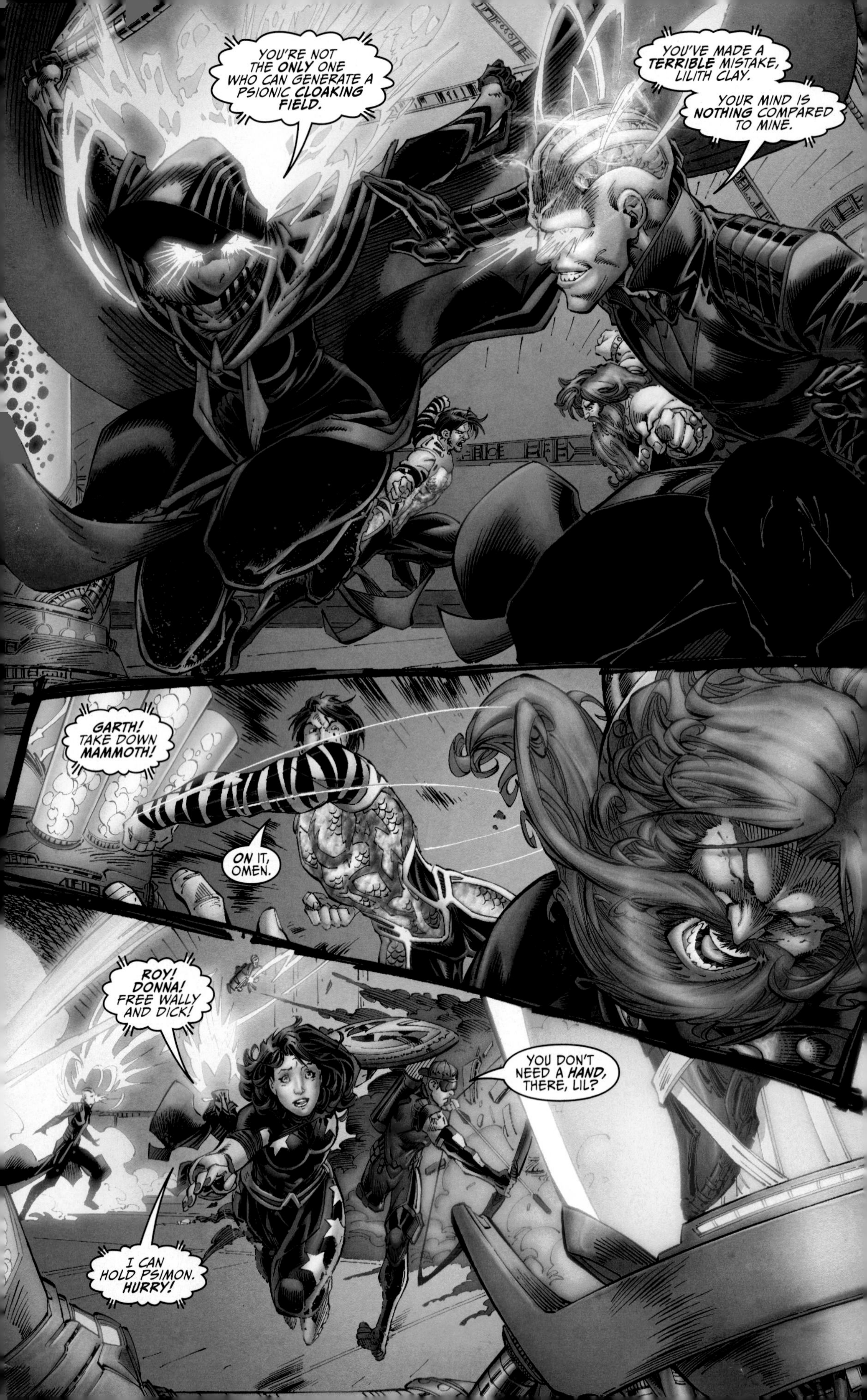
YOU'RE NOT THE ONLY ONE WHO CAN GENERATE A PSIONIC CLOAKING FIELD.
YOU'VE MADE A TERRIBLE MISTAKE, LILITH CLAY.
YOUR MIND IS NOTHING COMPARED TO MINE.
GARTH! TAKE DOWN MAMMOTH!
ON IT, OMEN.
ROY! DONNA! FREE WALLY AND DICK!
YOU DON'T NEED A HAND, THERE, LIL?
I CAN HOLD PSIMON. HURRY!

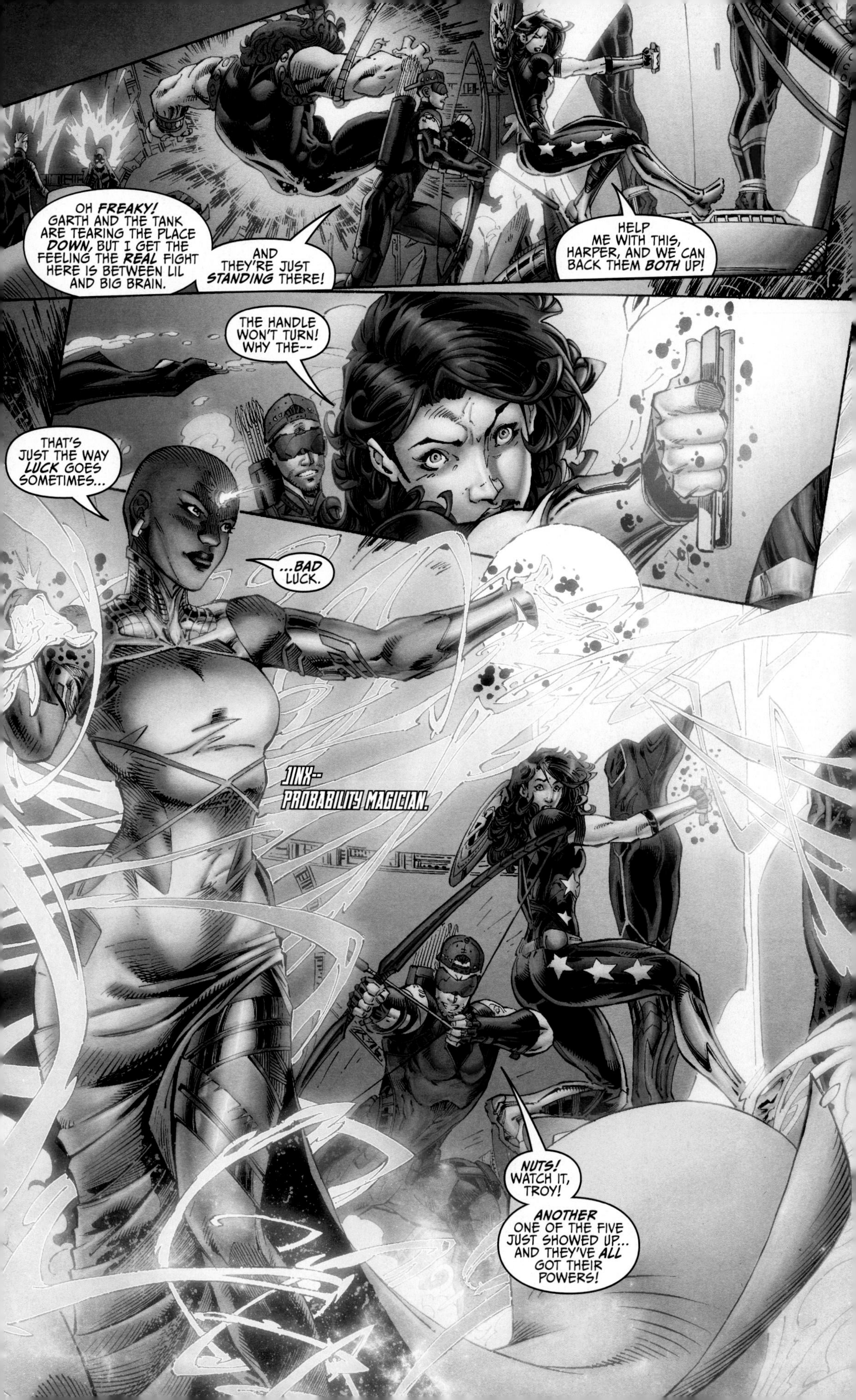
OH FREAKY! GARTH AND THE TANK ARE TEARING THE PLACE DOWN, BUT I GET THE FEELING THE REAL FIGHT HERE IS BETWEEN LIL AND BIG BRAIN.
AND THEY'RE JUST STANDING THERE!
HELP ME WITH THIS, HARPER, AND WE CAN BACK THEM BOTH UP!
THE HANDLE WON'T TURN! WHY THE--
THAT'S JUST THE WAY LUCK GOES SOMETIMES...
...BAD LUCK.
JINX-- PROBABILITY MAGICIAN.
NUTS! WATCH IT, TROY!
ANOTHER ONE OF THE FIVE JUST SHOWED UP... AND THEY'VE ALL GOT THEIR POWERS!

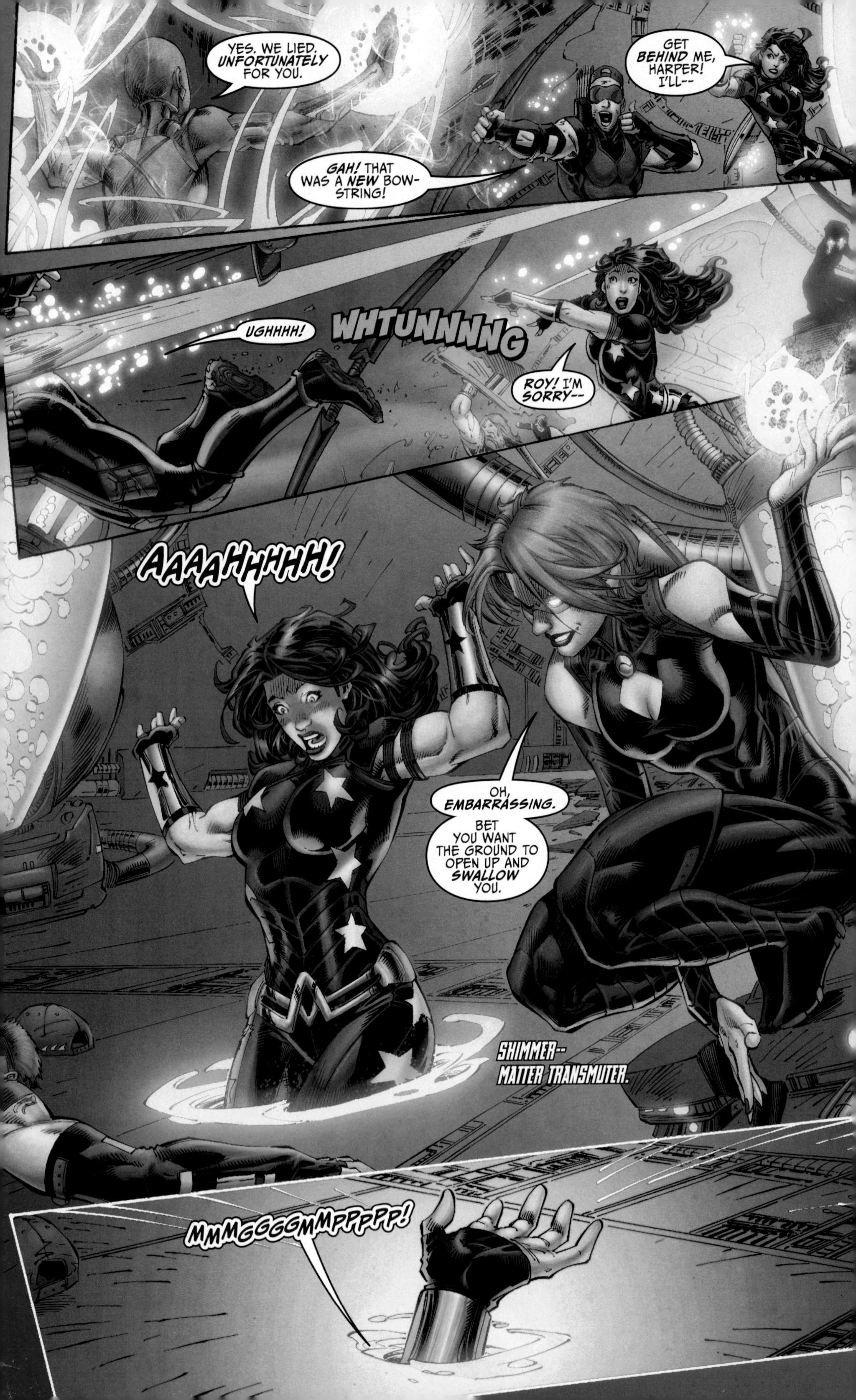
YES. WE LIED. UNFORTUNATELY FOR YOU.
GET BEHIND ME, HARPER! I'LL--
GAH! THAT WAS A NEW BOW-STRING!
UGHHHH!
WHTUNNNNG
ROY! I'M SORRY--
AAAAHHHHH!
OH, EMBARRASSING.
BET YOU WANT THE GROUND TO OPEN UP AND SWALLOW YOU.
SHIMMER--
MATTER TRANSMUTER.
MMMGGGGMMPPPPP!

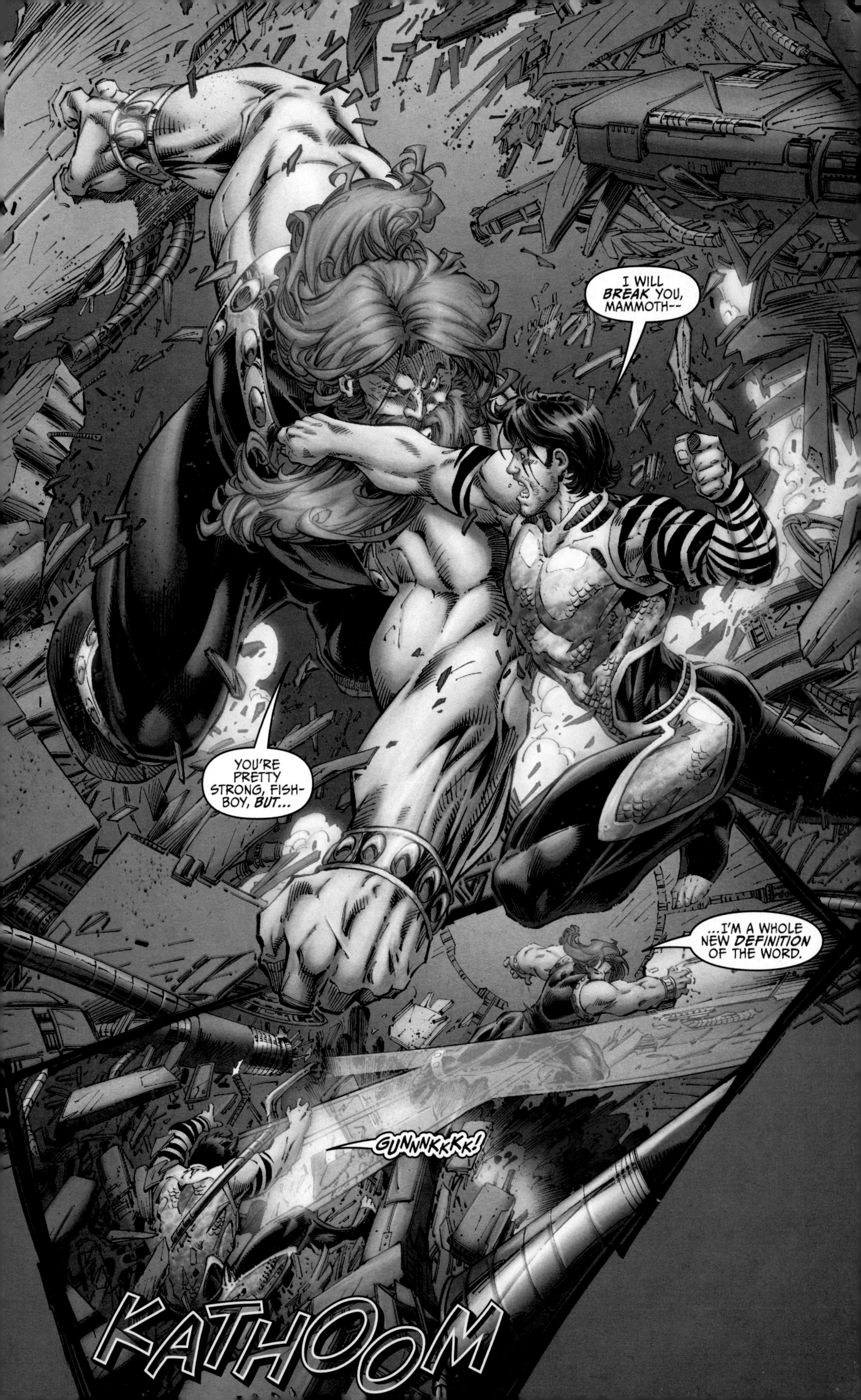
I WILL *BREAK* YOU, MAMMOTH--
YOU'RE PRETTY STRONG, FISH-BOY, *BUT*...
...I'M A WHOLE NEW *DEFINITION* OF THE WORD.
GUNNNKKKK!
KATHOOM

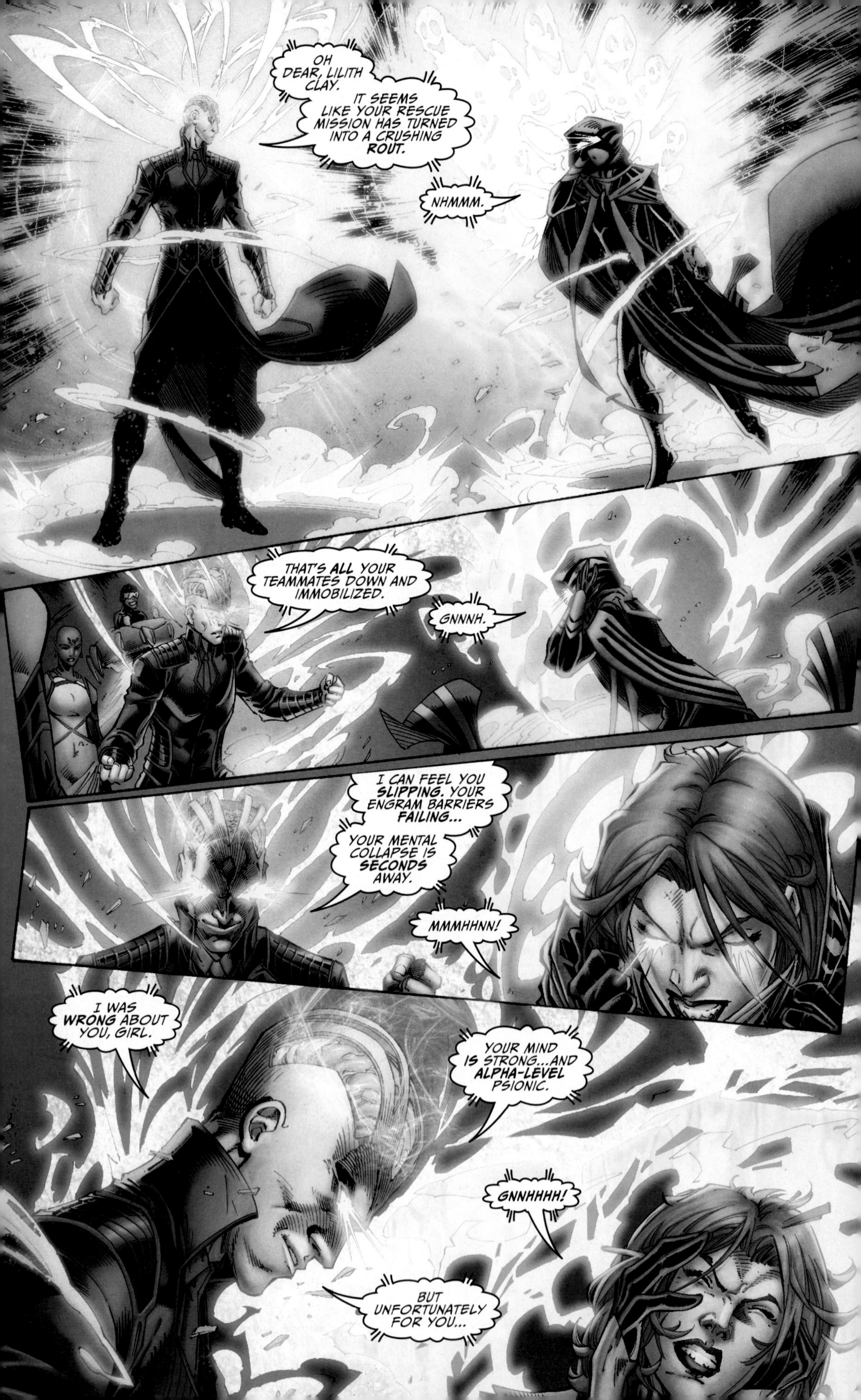

OH DEAR, LILITH CLAY.
IT SEEMS LIKE YOUR RESCUE MISSION HAS TURNED INTO A CRUSHING ROUT.
NHMMM.
THAT'S ALL YOUR TEAMMATES DOWN AND IMMOBILIZED.
GNNNH.
I CAN FEEL YOU SLIPPING. YOUR ENGRAM BARRIERS FAILING...
YOUR MENTAL COLLAPSE IS SECONDS AWAY.
MMMHHNN!
I WAS WRONG ABOUT YOU, GIRL.
YOUR MIND IS STRONG...AND ALPHA-LEVEL PSIONIC.
GNNHHHH!
BUT UNFORTUNATELY FOR YOU...

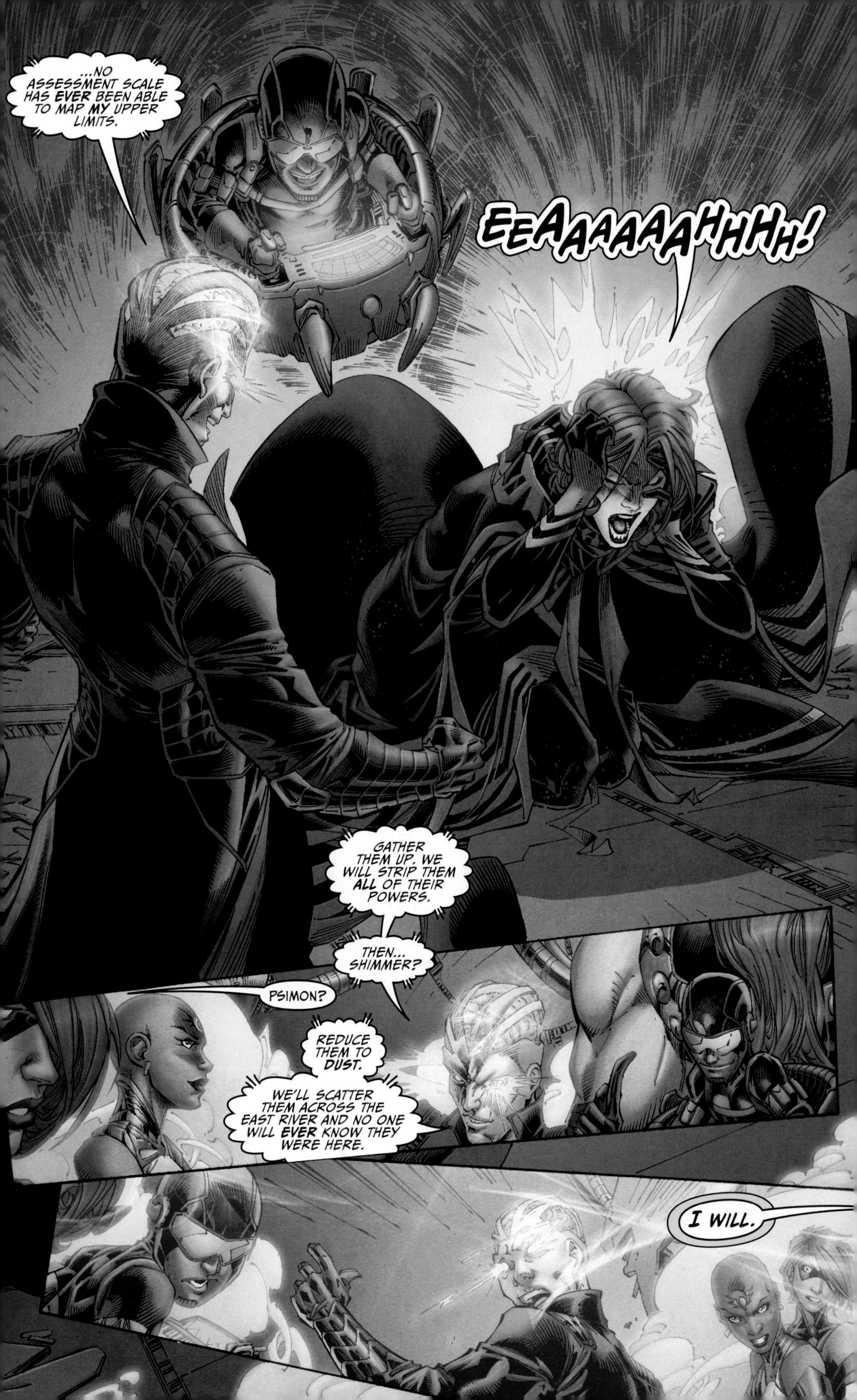
...NO ASSESSMENT SCALE HAS EVER BEEN ABLE TO MAP MY UPPER LIMITS.
EEAAAAAAHHHH!
GATHER THEM UP. WE WILL STRIP THEM ALL OF THEIR POWERS.
THEN... SHIMMER?
PSIMON?
REDUCE THEM TO DUST.
WE'LL SCATTER THEM ACROSS THE EAST RIVER AND NO ONE WILL EVER KNOW THEY WERE HERE.
I WILL.

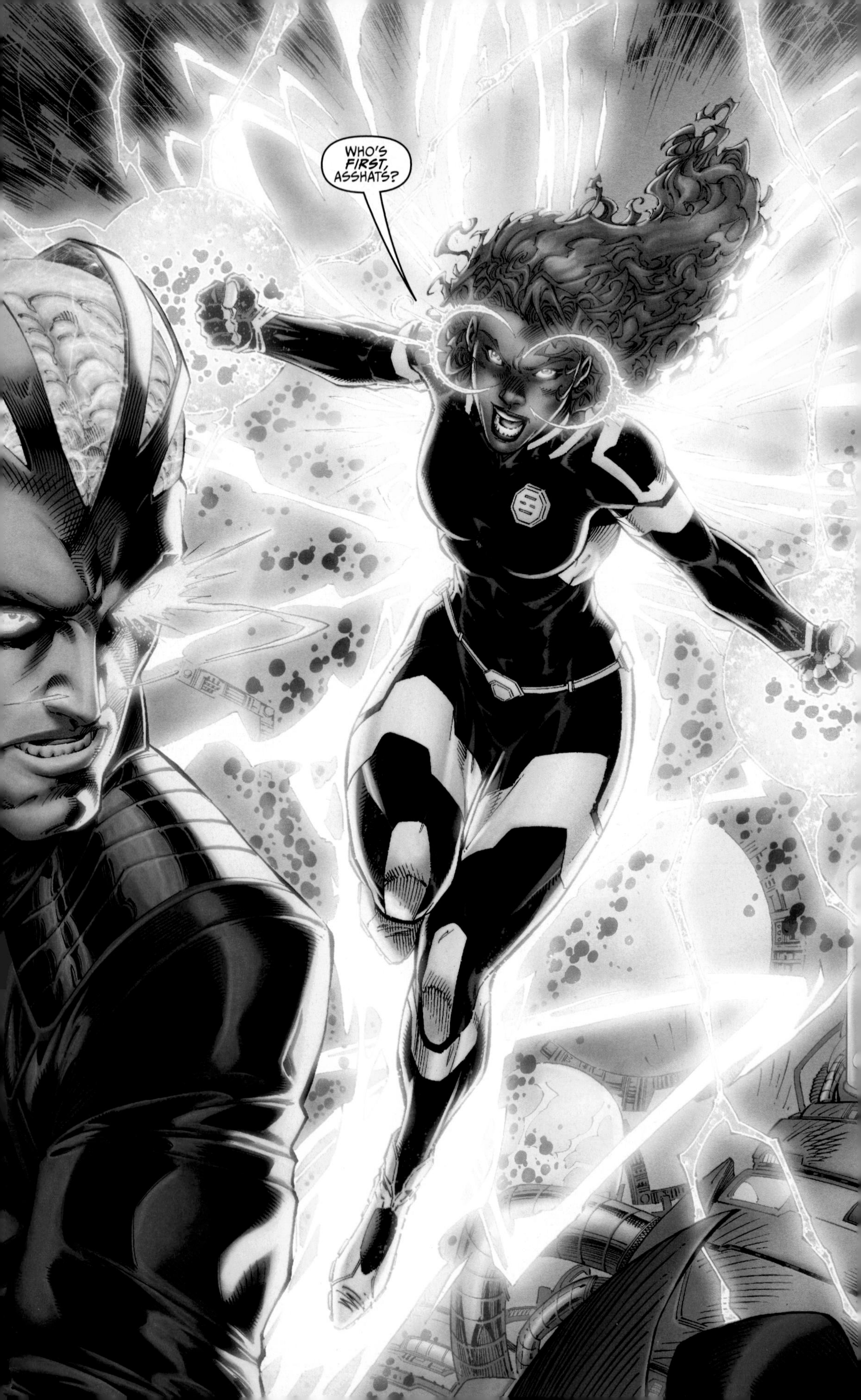
WHO'S *FIRST,* ASSHATS?

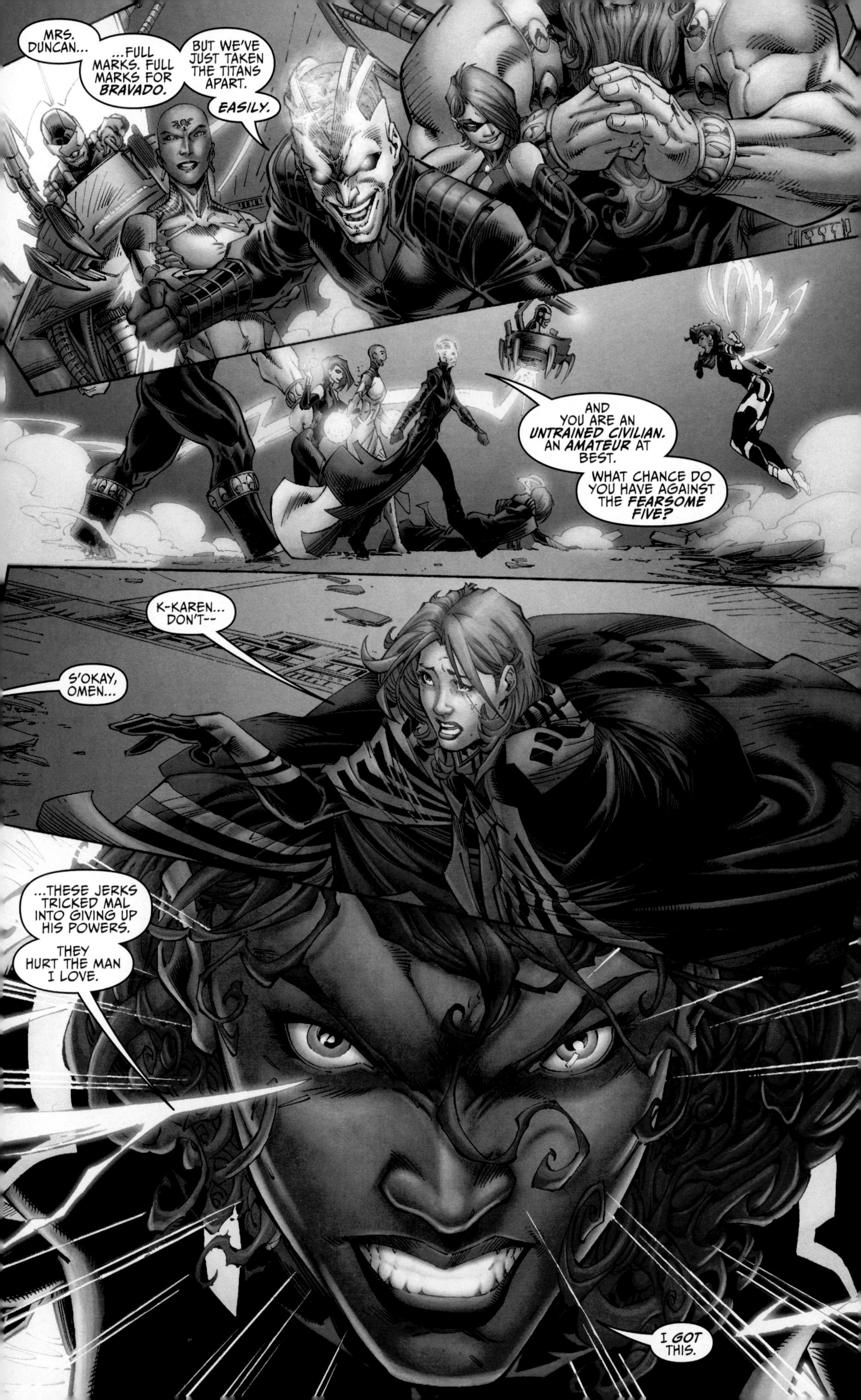
MRS. DUNCAN...
...FULL MARKS. FULL MARKS FOR BRAVADO.
BUT WE'VE JUST TAKEN THE TITANS APART.
EASILY.
AND YOU ARE AN UNTRAINED CIVILIAN. AN AMATEUR AT BEST.
WHAT CHANCE DO YOU HAVE AGAINST THE FEARSOME FIVE?
K-KAREN... DON'T--
S'OKAY, OMEN...
...THESE JERKS TRICKED MAL INTO GIVING UP HIS POWERS.
THEY HURT THE MAN I LOVE.
I GOT THIS.

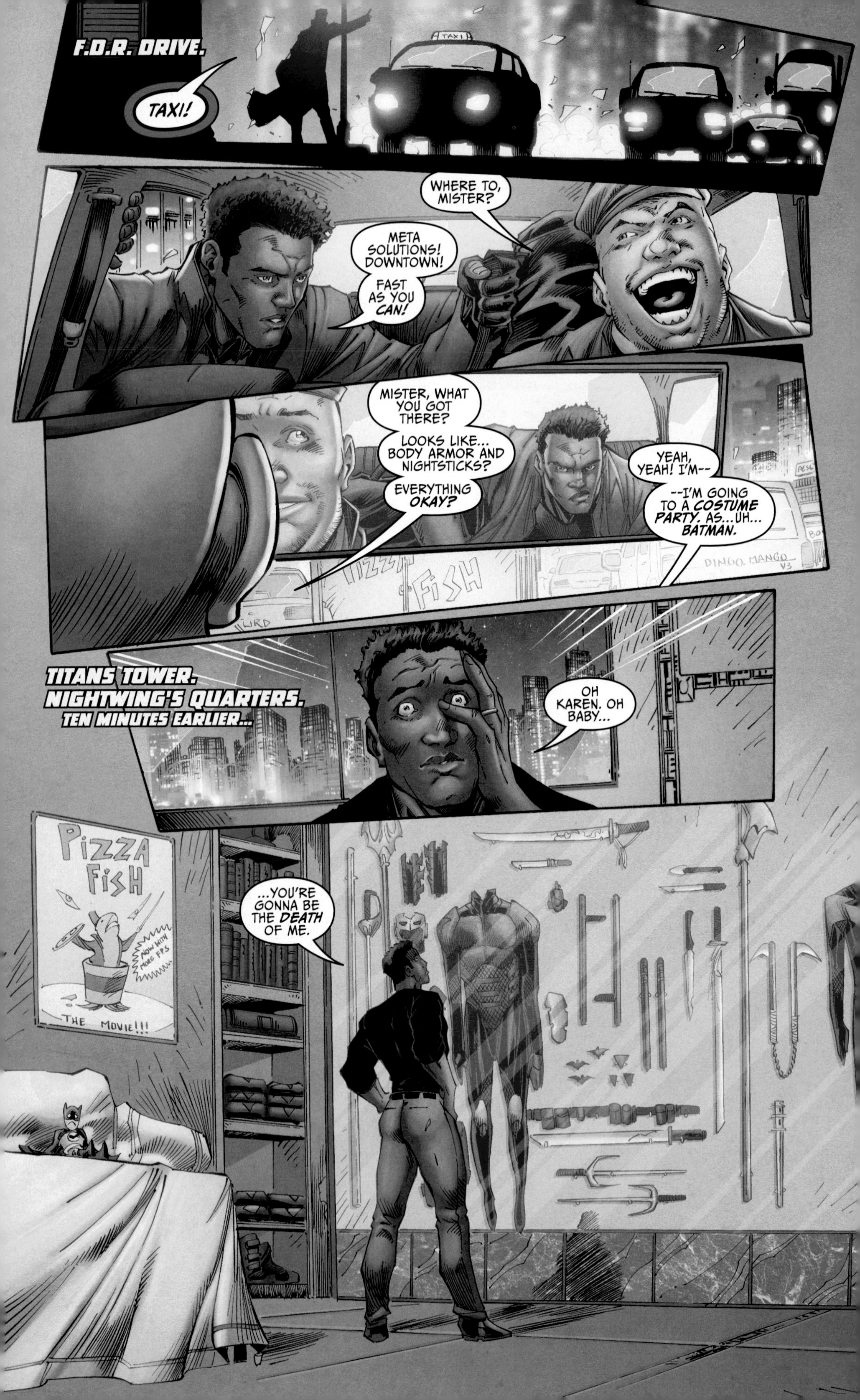
F.D.R. DRIVE.
TAXI!
WHERE TO, MISTER?
META SOLUTIONS! DOWNTOWN!
FAST AS YOU CAN!
MISTER, WHAT YOU GOT THERE?
LOOKS LIKE... BODY ARMOR AND NIGHTSTICKS?
EVERYTHING OKAY?
YEAH, YEAH! I'M--
--I'M GOING TO A COSTUME PARTY. AS...UH... BATMAN.
TITANS TOWER. NIGHTWING'S QUARTERS. TEN MINUTES EARLIER...
OH KAREN. OH BABY...
PIZZA FISH
NOW WITH MORE FPS
THE MOVIE!!!
...YOU'RE GONNA BE THE DEATH OF ME.

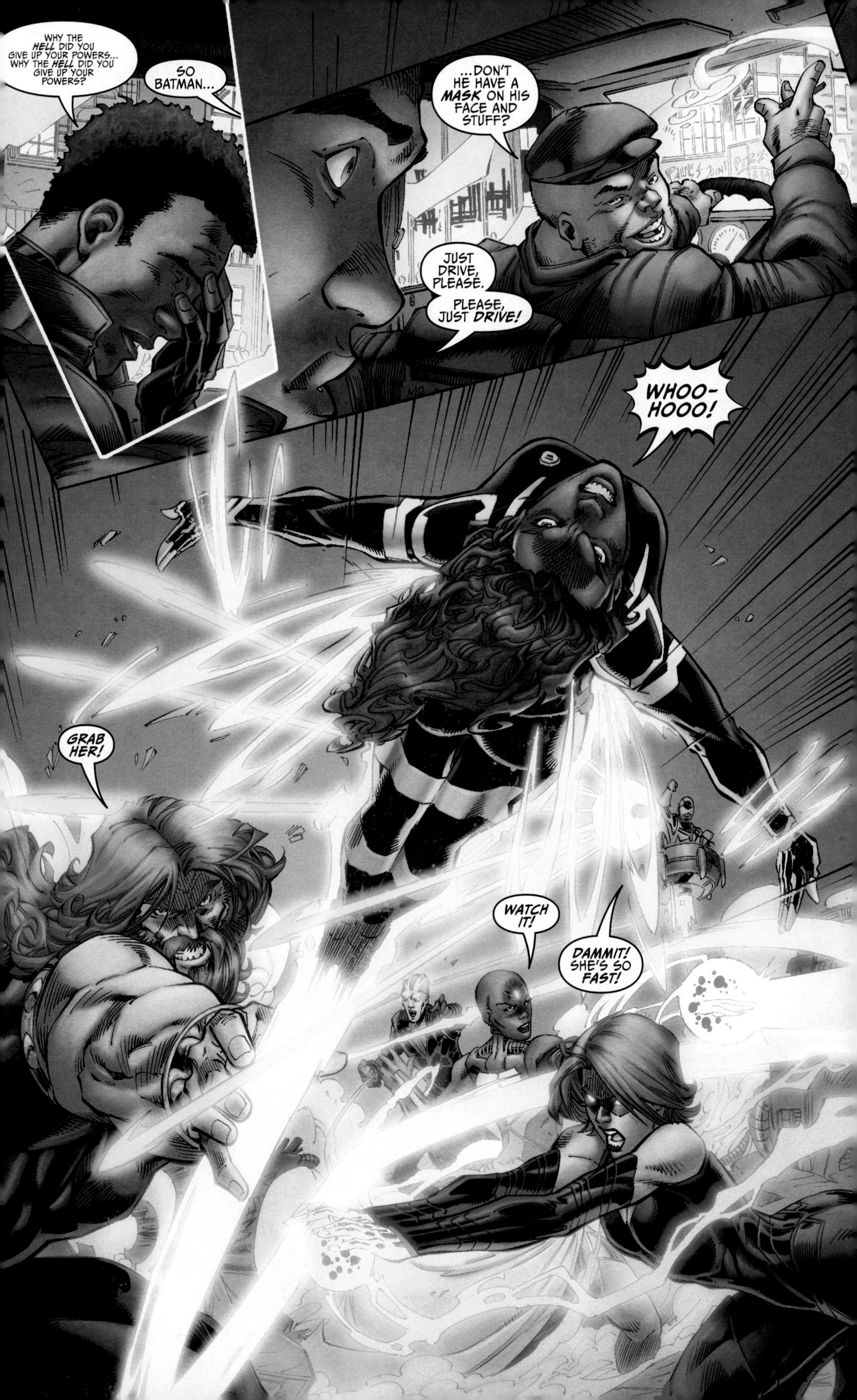
WHY THE HELL DID YOU GIVE UP YOUR POWERS... WHY THE HELL DID YOU GIVE UP YOUR POWERS?
SO BATMAN...
...DON'T HE HAVE A MASK ON HIS FACE AND STUFF?
JUST DRIVE, PLEASE.
PLEASE, JUST DRIVE!
WHOO-HOOO!
GRAB HER!
WATCH IT!
DAMMIT! SHE'S SO FAST!

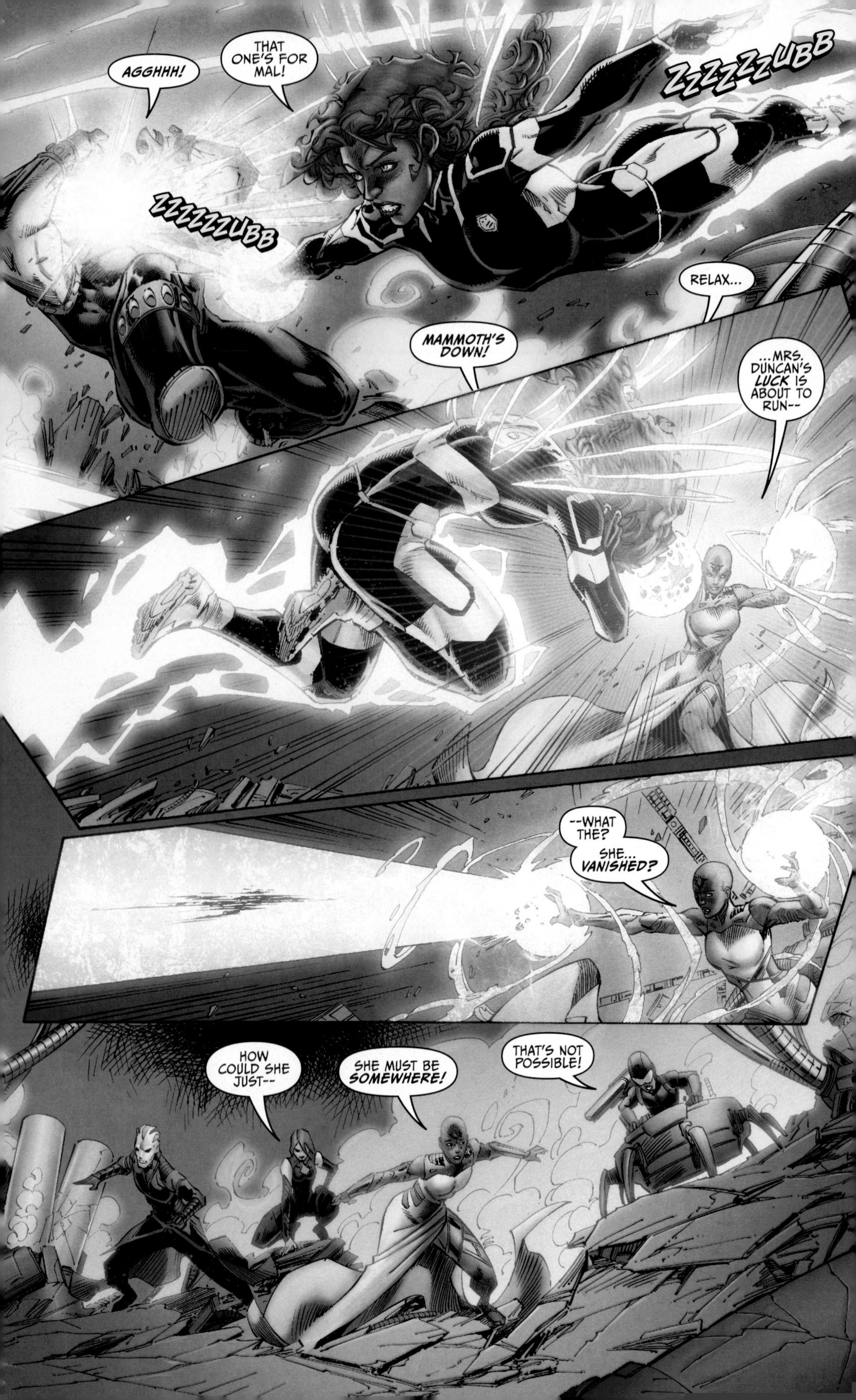
AGGHHH!
THAT ONE'S FOR MAL!
ZZZZZZUBB
ZZZZZZUBB
RELAX...
MAMMOTH'S DOWN!
...MRS. DUNCAN'S LUCK IS ABOUT TO RUN--
--WHAT THE? SHE... VANISHED?
HOW COULD SHE JUST--
SHE MUST BE SOMEWHERE!
THAT'S NOT POSSIBLE!

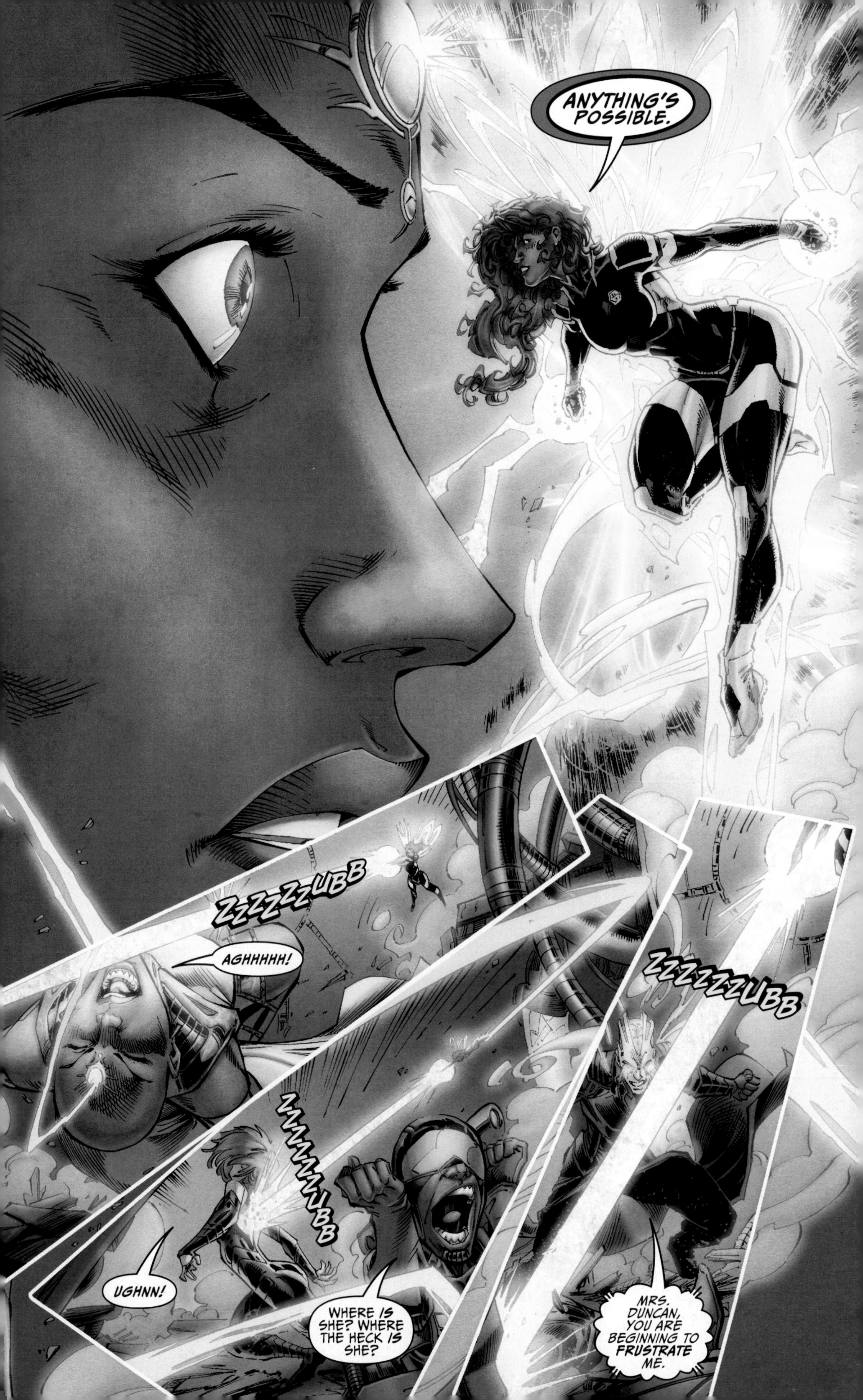
ANYTHING'S POSSIBLE.
ZZZZZZZUBB
AGHHHHH!
ZZZZZZZZUBB
UGHNN!
WHERE IS SHE? WHERE THE HECK IS SHE?
ZZZZZZZZUBB
MRS. DUNCAN, YOU ARE BEGINNING TO FRUSTRATE ME.

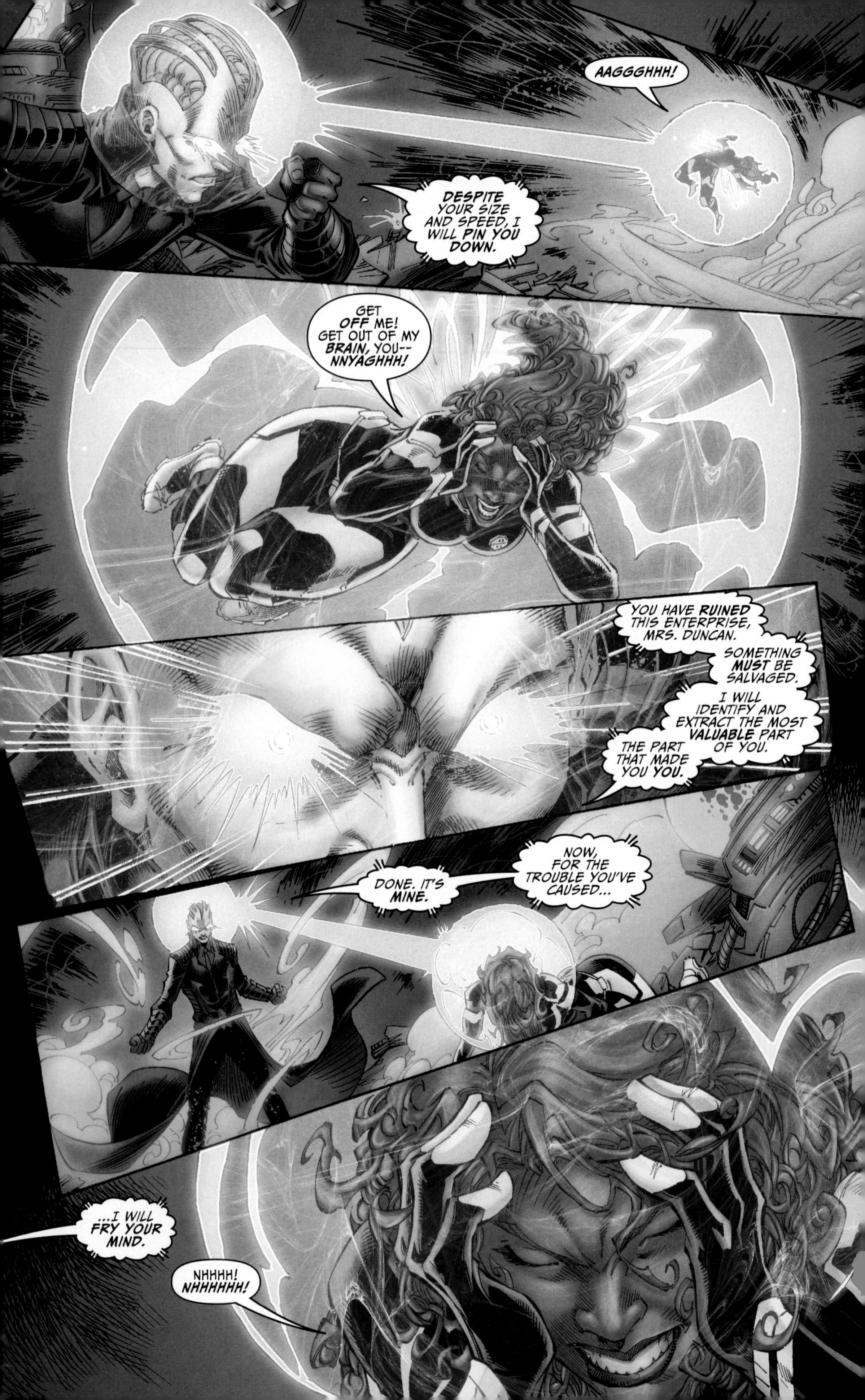
AAGGGHHH!
DESPITE YOUR SIZE AND SPEED, I WILL PIN YOU DOWN.
GET OFF ME! GET OUT OF MY BRAIN, YOU-- NNYAGHHH!
YOU HAVE RUINED THIS ENTERPRISE, MRS. DUNCAN.
SOMETHING MUST BE SALVAGED.
I WILL IDENTIFY AND EXTRACT THE MOST VALUABLE PART OF YOU.
THE PART THAT MADE YOU YOU.
DONE. IT'S MINE.
NOW, FOR THE TROUBLE YOU'VE CAUSED...
...I WILL FRY YOUR MIND.
NHHHH! NHHHHHH!

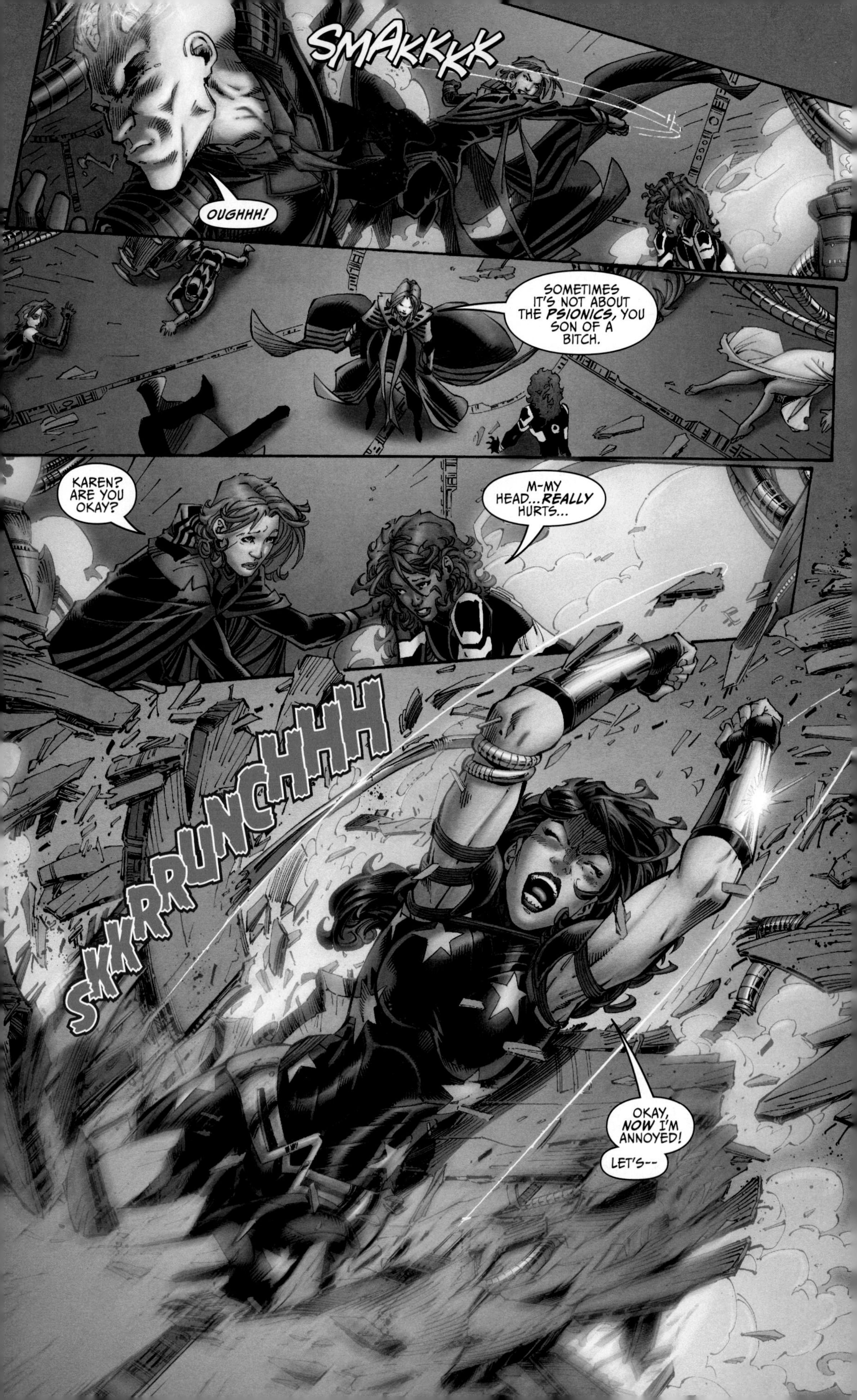
SMAKKKK
OUGHHH!
SOMETIMES IT'S NOT ABOUT THE PSIONICS, YOU SON OF A BITCH.
KAREN? ARE YOU OKAY?
M-MY HEAD...REALLY HURTS...
SKKRRUNCHHH
OKAY, NOW I'M ANNOYED!
LET'S--

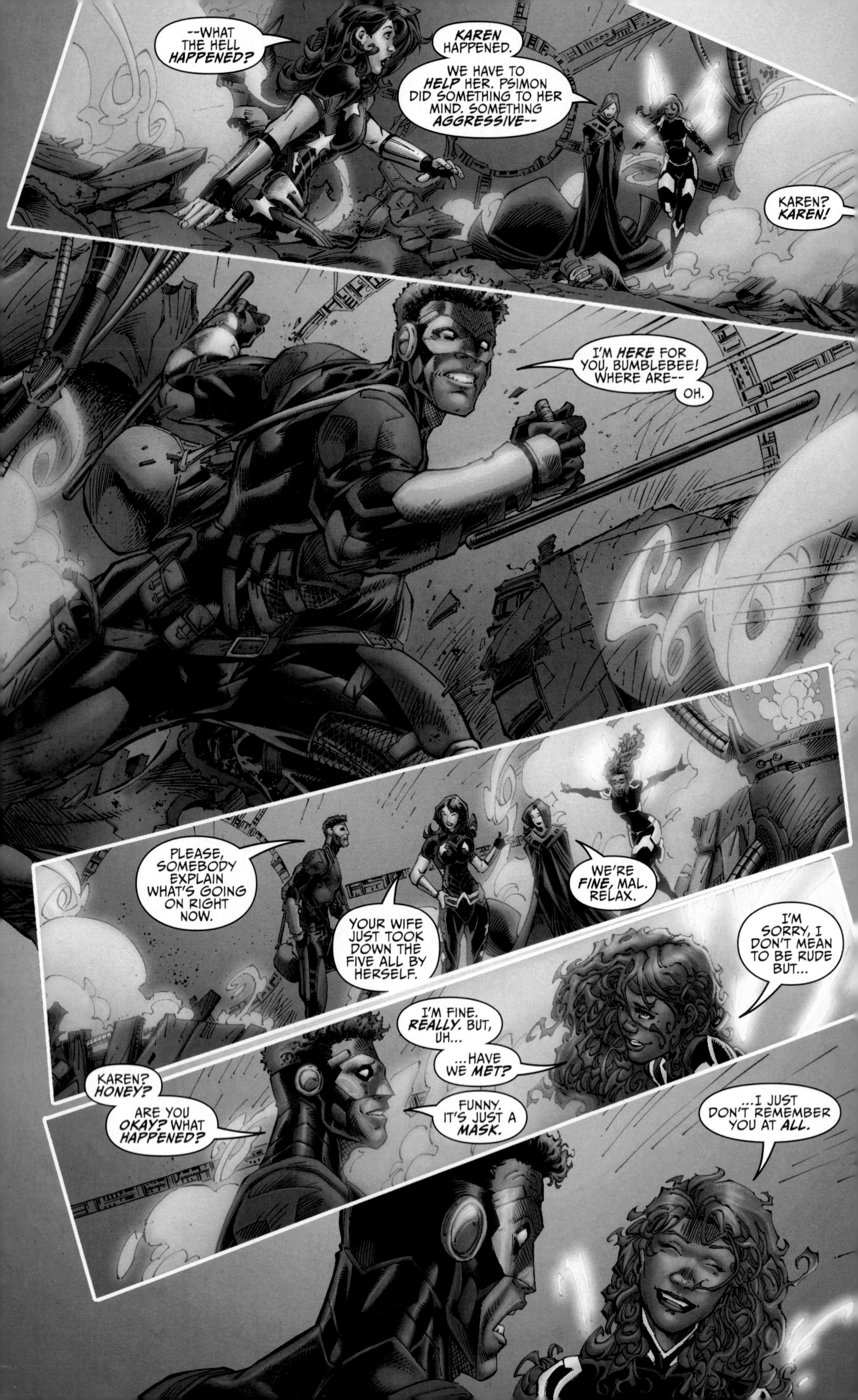

--WHAT THE HELL HAPPENED?
KAREN HAPPENED.
WE HAVE TO HELP HER. PSIMON DID SOMETHING TO HER MIND. SOMETHING AGGRESSIVE--
KAREN? KAREN!
I'M HERE FOR YOU, BUMBLEBEE! WHERE ARE--
OH.
PLEASE, SOMEBODY EXPLAIN WHAT'S GOING ON RIGHT NOW.
YOUR WIFE JUST TOOK DOWN THE FIVE ALL BY HERSELF.
WE'RE FINE, MAL. RELAX.
KAREN? HONEY?
ARE YOU OKAY? WHAT HAPPENED?
I'M FINE. REALLY. BUT, UH...
...HAVE WE MET?
FUNNY. IT'S JUST A MASK.
I'M SORRY, I DON'T MEAN TO BE RUDE BUT...
...I JUST DON'T REMEMBER YOU AT ALL.

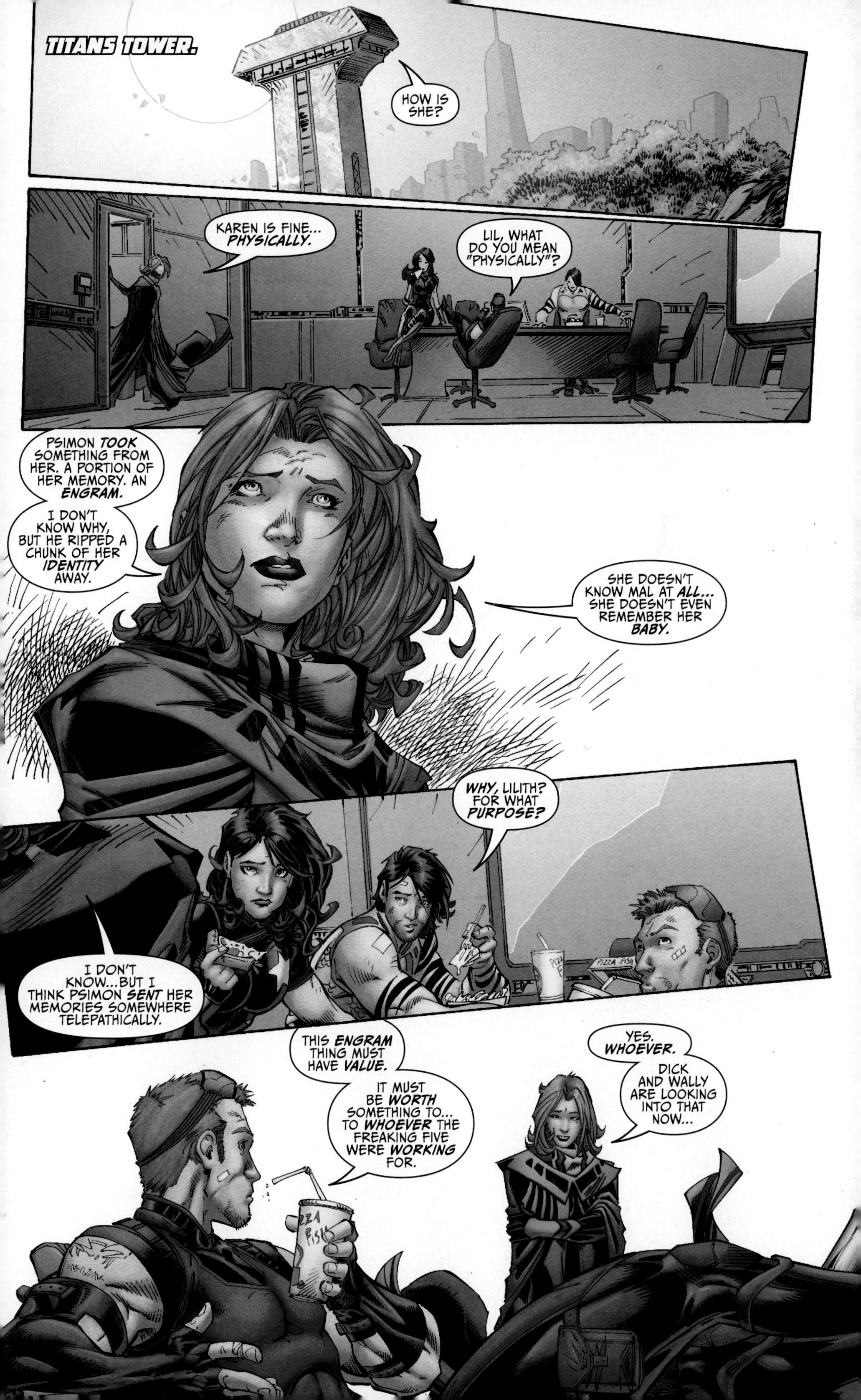
TITANS TOWER.
HOW IS SHE?
KAREN IS FINE... PHYSICALLY.
LIL, WHAT DO YOU MEAN "PHYSICALLY"?
PSIMON TOOK SOMETHING FROM HER. A PORTION OF HER MEMORY. AN ENGRAM.
I DON'T KNOW WHY, BUT HE RIPPED A CHUNK OF HER IDENTITY AWAY.
SHE DOESN'T KNOW MAL AT ALL... SHE DOESN'T EVEN REMEMBER HER BABY.
WHY, LILITH? FOR WHAT PURPOSE?
I DON'T KNOW...BUT I THINK PSIMON SENT HER MEMORIES SOMEWHERE TELEPATHICALLY.
THIS ENGRAM THING MUST HAVE VALUE.
IT MUST BE WORTH SOMETHING TO... TO WHOEVER THE FREAKING FIVE WERE WORKING FOR.
YES. WHOEVER.
DICK AND WALLY ARE LOOKING INTO THAT NOW...

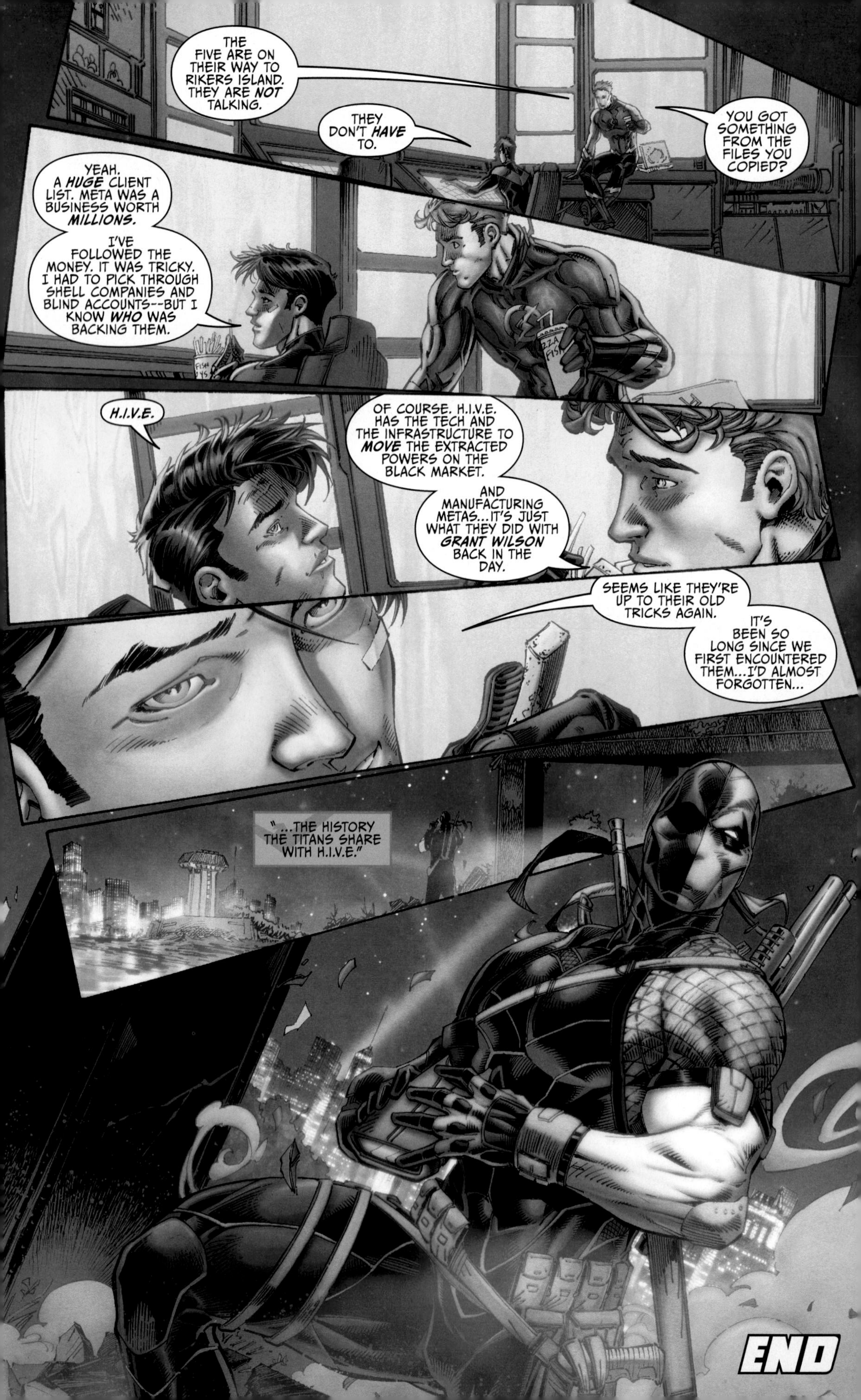
THE FIVE ARE ON THEIR WAY TO RIKERS ISLAND. THEY ARE NOT TALKING.
THEY DON'T HAVE TO.
YOU GOT SOMETHING FROM THE FILES YOU COPIED?
YEAH. A HUGE CLIENT LIST. META WAS A BUSINESS WORTH MILLIONS.
I'VE FOLLOWED THE MONEY. IT WAS TRICKY. I HAD TO PICK THROUGH SHELL COMPANIES AND BLIND ACCOUNTS--BUT I KNOW WHO WAS BACKING THEM.
H.I.V.E.
OF COURSE. H.I.V.E. HAS THE TECH AND THE INFRASTRUCTURE TO MOVE THE EXTRACTED POWERS ON THE BLACK MARKET.
AND MANUFACTURING METAS...IT'S JUST WHAT THEY DID WITH GRANT WILSON BACK IN THE DAY.
SEEMS LIKE THEY'RE UP TO THEIR OLD TRICKS AGAIN.
IT'S BEEN SO LONG SINCE WE FIRST ENCOUNTERED THEM...I'D ALMOST FORGOTTEN...
"...THE HISTORY THE TITANS SHARE WITH H.I.V.E."
END

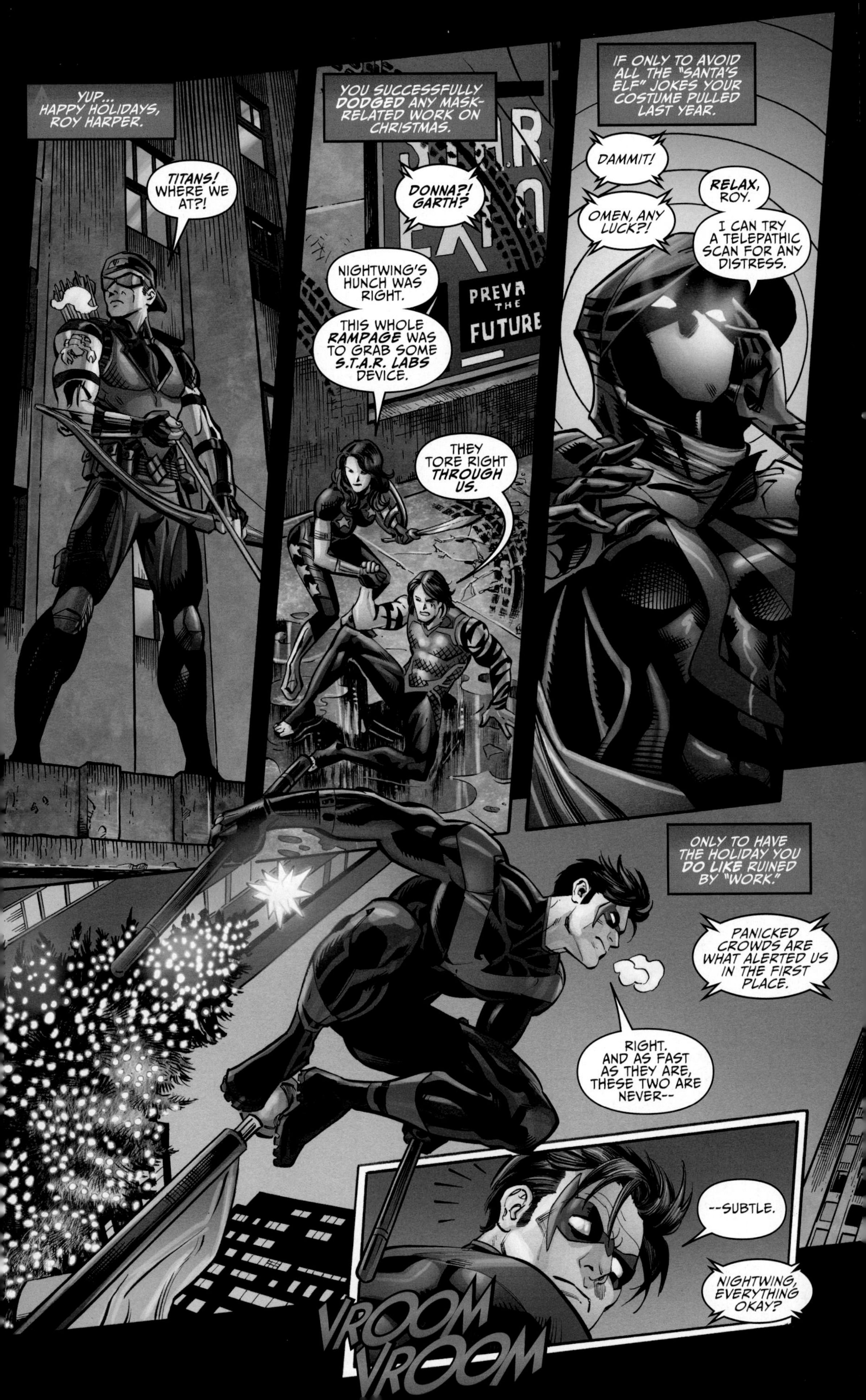
YUP... HAPPY HOLIDAYS, ROY HARPER.
TITANS! WHERE WE AT?!
YOU SUCCESSFULLY DODGED ANY MASK-RELATED WORK ON CHRISTMAS.
DONNA?! GARTH?
NIGHTWING'S HUNCH WAS RIGHT.
THIS WHOLE RAMPAGE WAS TO GRAB SOME S.T.A.R. LABS DEVICE.
PREVA THE FUTURE
THEY TORE RIGHT THROUGH US.
IF ONLY TO AVOID ALL THE "SANTA'S ELF" JOKES YOUR COSTUME PULLED LAST YEAR.
DAMMIT!
OMEN, ANY LUCK?!
RELAX, ROY.
I CAN TRY A TELEPATHIC SCAN FOR ANY DISTRESS.
ONLY TO HAVE THE HOLIDAY YOU DO LIKE RUINED BY "WORK."
PANICKED CROWDS ARE WHAT ALERTED US IN THE FIRST PLACE.
RIGHT. AND AS FAST AS THEY ARE, THESE TWO ARE NEVER--
--SUBTLE.
NIGHTWING, EVERYTHING OKAY?
VROOM VROOM

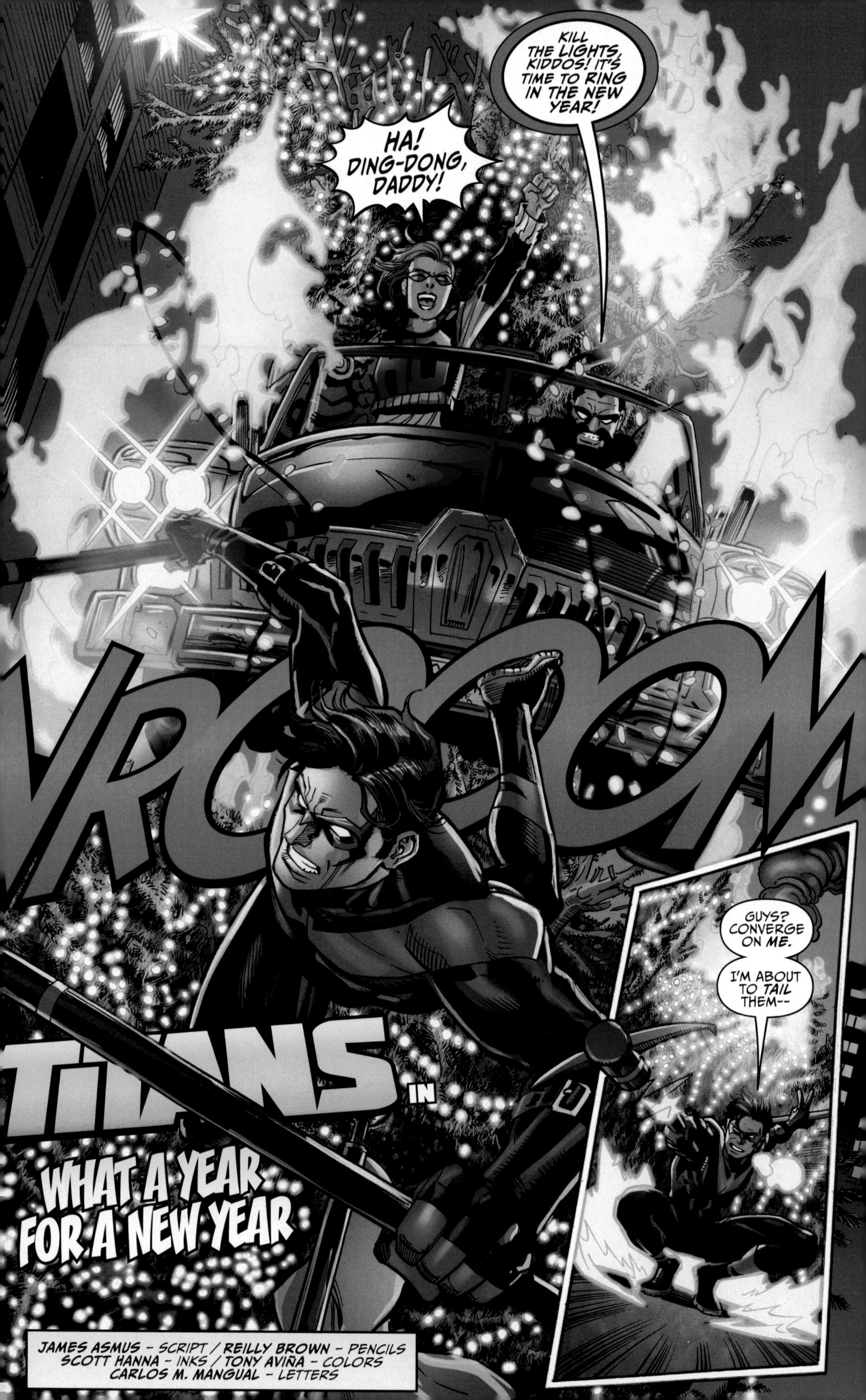
HA! DING-DONG, DADDY!
KILL THE LIGHTS, KIDDOS! IT'S TIME TO RING IN THE NEW YEAR!
VROOOM
GUYS? CONVERGE ON ME.
I'M ABOUT TO TAIL THEM--
TITANS IN
WHAT A YEAR FOR A NEW YEAR
JAMES ASMUS - SCRIPT / REILLY BROWN - PENCILS
SCOTT HANNA - INKS / TONY AVIÑA - COLORS
CARLOS M. MANGUAL - LETTERS

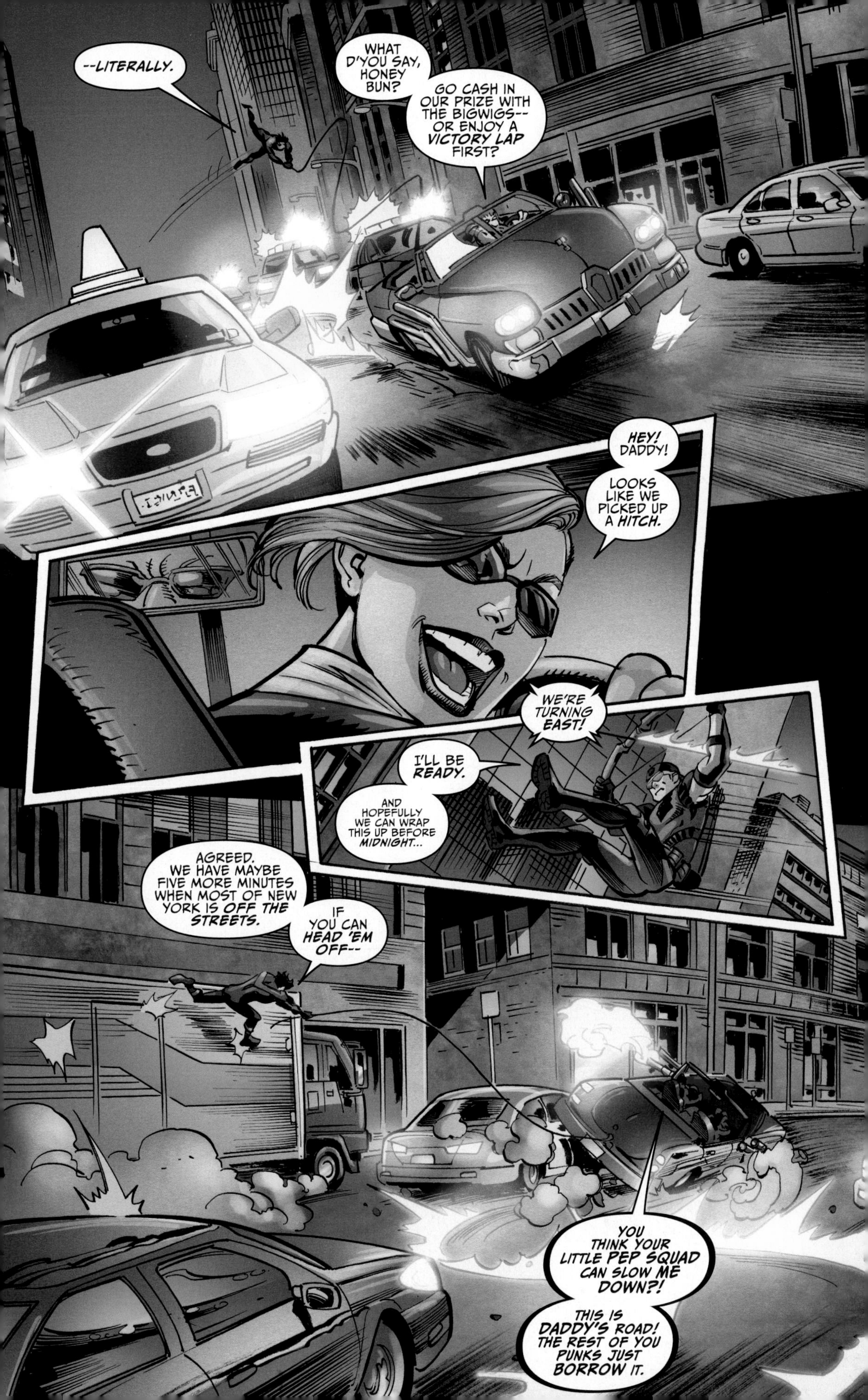
--LITERALLY.
WHAT D'YOU SAY, HONEY BUN?
GO CASH IN OUR PRIZE WITH THE BIGWIGS-- OR ENJOY A VICTORY LAP FIRST?
HEY! DADDY!
LOOKS LIKE WE PICKED UP A HITCH.
WE'RE TURNING EAST!
I'LL BE READY.
AND HOPEFULLY WE CAN WRAP THIS UP BEFORE MIDNIGHT...
AGREED. WE HAVE MAYBE FIVE MORE MINUTES WHEN MOST OF NEW YORK IS OFF THE STREETS.
IF YOU CAN HEAD 'EM OFF--
YOU THINK YOUR LITTLE PEP SQUAD CAN SLOW ME DOWN?!
THIS IS DADDY'S ROAD! THE REST OF YOU PUNKS JUST BORROW IT.

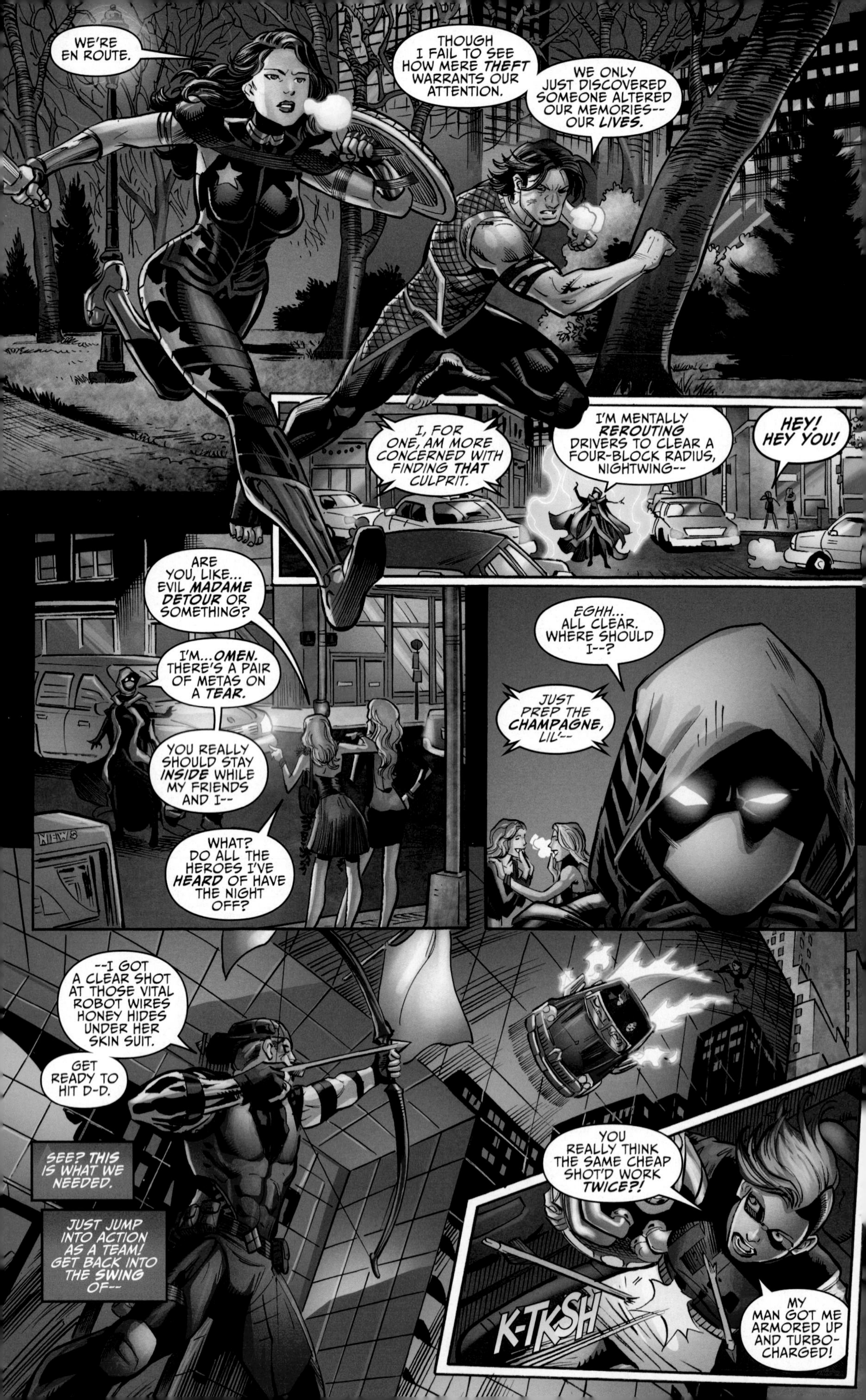
WE'RE EN ROUTE.
THOUGH I FAIL TO SEE HOW MERE THEFT WARRANTS OUR ATTENTION.
WE ONLY JUST DISCOVERED SOMEONE ALTERED OUR MEMORIES-- OUR LIVES.
I, FOR ONE, AM MORE CONCERNED WITH FINDING THAT CULPRIT.
I'M MENTALLY REROUTING DRIVERS TO CLEAR A FOUR-BLOCK RADIUS, NIGHTWING--
HEY! HEY YOU!
ARE YOU, LIKE... EVIL MADAME DETOUR OR SOMETHING?
I'M...OMEN. THERE'S A PAIR OF METAS ON A TEAR.
YOU REALLY SHOULD STAY INSIDE WHILE MY FRIENDS AND I--
WHAT? DO ALL THE HEROES I'VE HEARD OF HAVE THE NIGHT OFF?
EGHH... ALL CLEAR. WHERE SHOULD I--?
JUST PREP THE CHAMPAGNE, LIL'--
--I GOT A CLEAR SHOT AT THOSE VITAL ROBOT WIRES HONEY HIDES UNDER HER SKIN SUIT.
GET READY TO HIT D-D.
SEE? THIS IS WHAT WE NEEDED.
JUST JUMP INTO ACTION AS A TEAM! GET BACK INTO THE SWING OF--
YOU REALLY THINK THE SAME CHEAP SHOT'D WORK TWICE?!
K-TKSH
MY MAN GOT ME ARMORED UP AND TURBO-CHARGED!

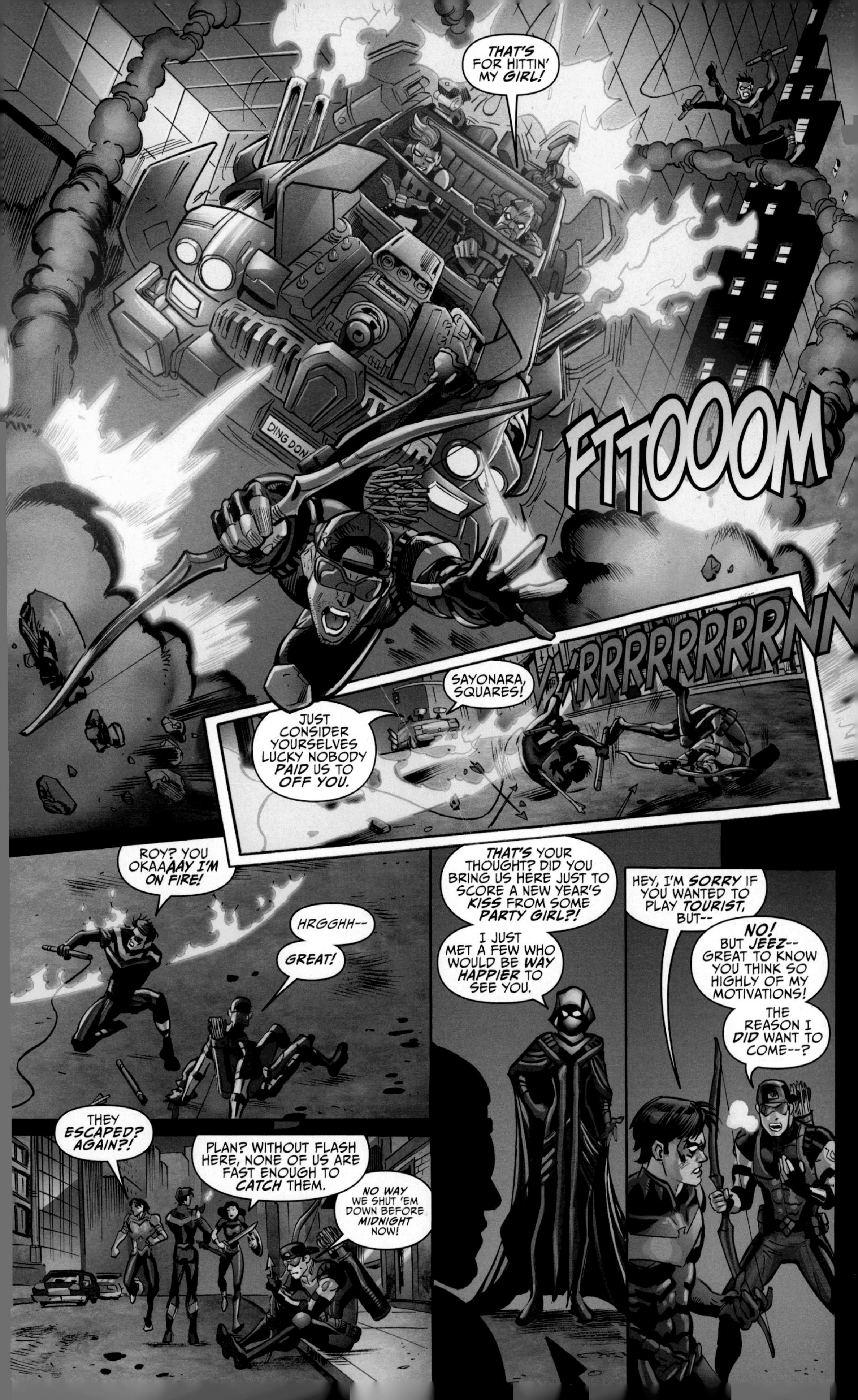
THAT'S FOR HITTIN' MY GIRL!
DING DON
FTTOOOM
VVRRRRRRRRRNN
SAYONARA, SQUARES!
JUST CONSIDER YOURSELVES LUCKY NOBODY PAID US TO OFF YOU.
ROY? YOU OKAAAAY I'M ON FIRE!
HRGGHH--
GREAT!
THEY ESCAPED? AGAIN?!
PLAN? WITHOUT FLASH HERE, NONE OF US ARE FAST ENOUGH TO CATCH THEM.
NO WAY WE SHUT 'EM DOWN BEFORE MIDNIGHT NOW!
THAT'S YOUR THOUGHT? DID YOU BRING US HERE JUST TO SCORE A NEW YEAR'S KISS FROM SOME PARTY GIRL?!
I JUST MET A FEW WHO WOULD BE WAY HAPPIER TO SEE YOU.
HEY, I'M SORRY IF YOU WANTED TO PLAY TOURIST, BUT--
NO! BUT JEEZ-- GREAT TO KNOW YOU THINK SO HIGHLY OF MY MOTIVATIONS!
THE REASON I DID WANT TO COME--?

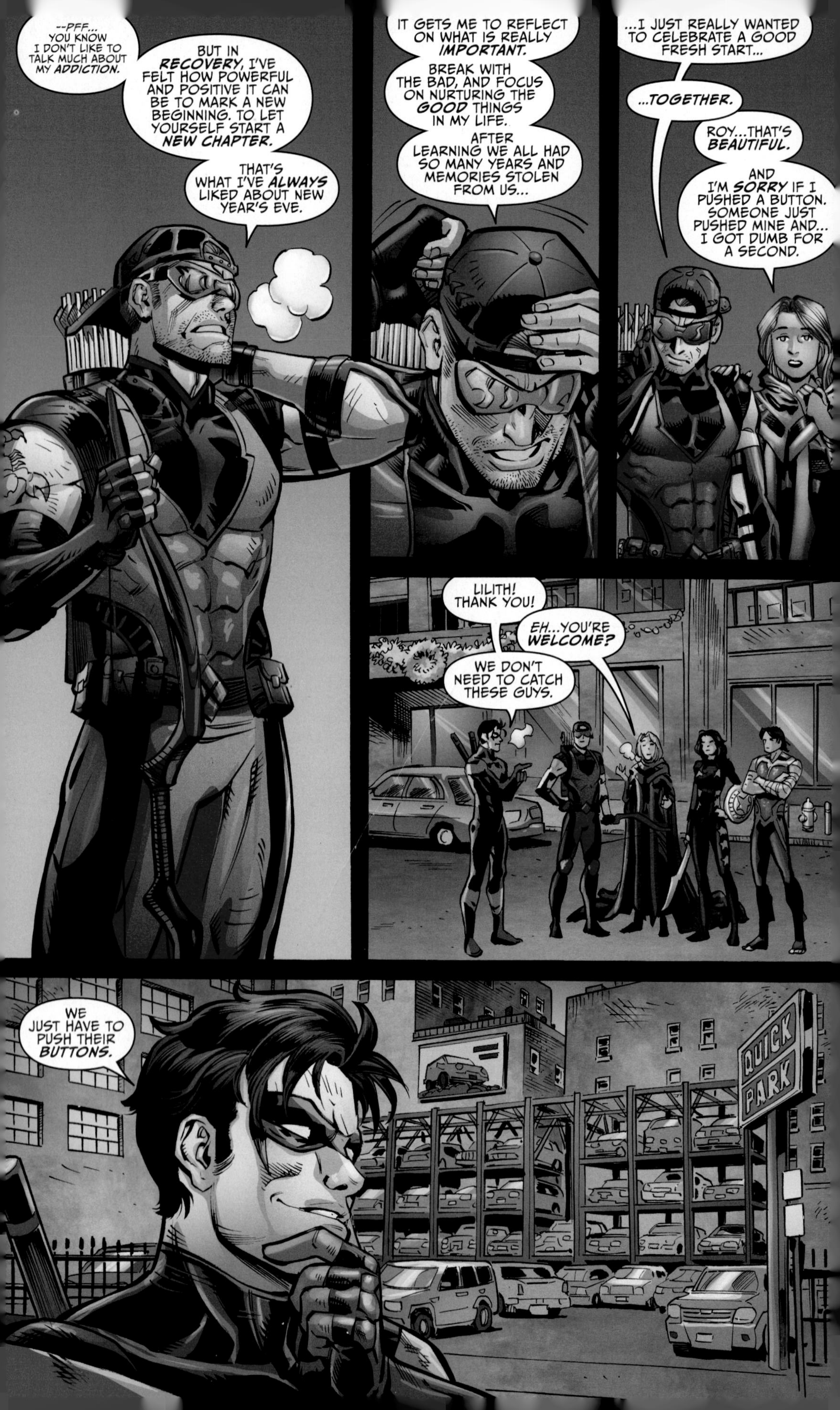
--PFF... YOU KNOW I DON'T LIKE TO TALK MUCH ABOUT MY ADDICTION.
BUT IN RECOVERY, I'VE FELT HOW POWERFUL AND POSITIVE IT CAN BE TO MARK A NEW BEGINNING. TO LET YOURSELF START A NEW CHAPTER.
THAT'S WHAT I'VE ALWAYS LIKED ABOUT NEW YEAR'S EVE.
IT GETS ME TO REFLECT ON WHAT IS REALLY IMPORTANT.
BREAK WITH THE BAD, AND FOCUS ON NURTURING THE GOOD THINGS IN MY LIFE.
AFTER LEARNING WE ALL HAD SO MANY YEARS AND MEMORIES STOLEN FROM US...
...I JUST REALLY WANTED TO CELEBRATE A GOOD FRESH START...
...TOGETHER.
ROY...THAT'S BEAUTIFUL.
AND I'M SORRY IF I PUSHED A BUTTON. SOMEONE JUST PUSHED MINE AND... I GOT DUMB FOR A SECOND.
LILITH! THANK YOU!
EH...YOU'RE WELCOME?
WE DON'T NEED TO CATCH THESE GUYS.
WE JUST HAVE TO PUSH THEIR BUTTONS.
QUICK PARK

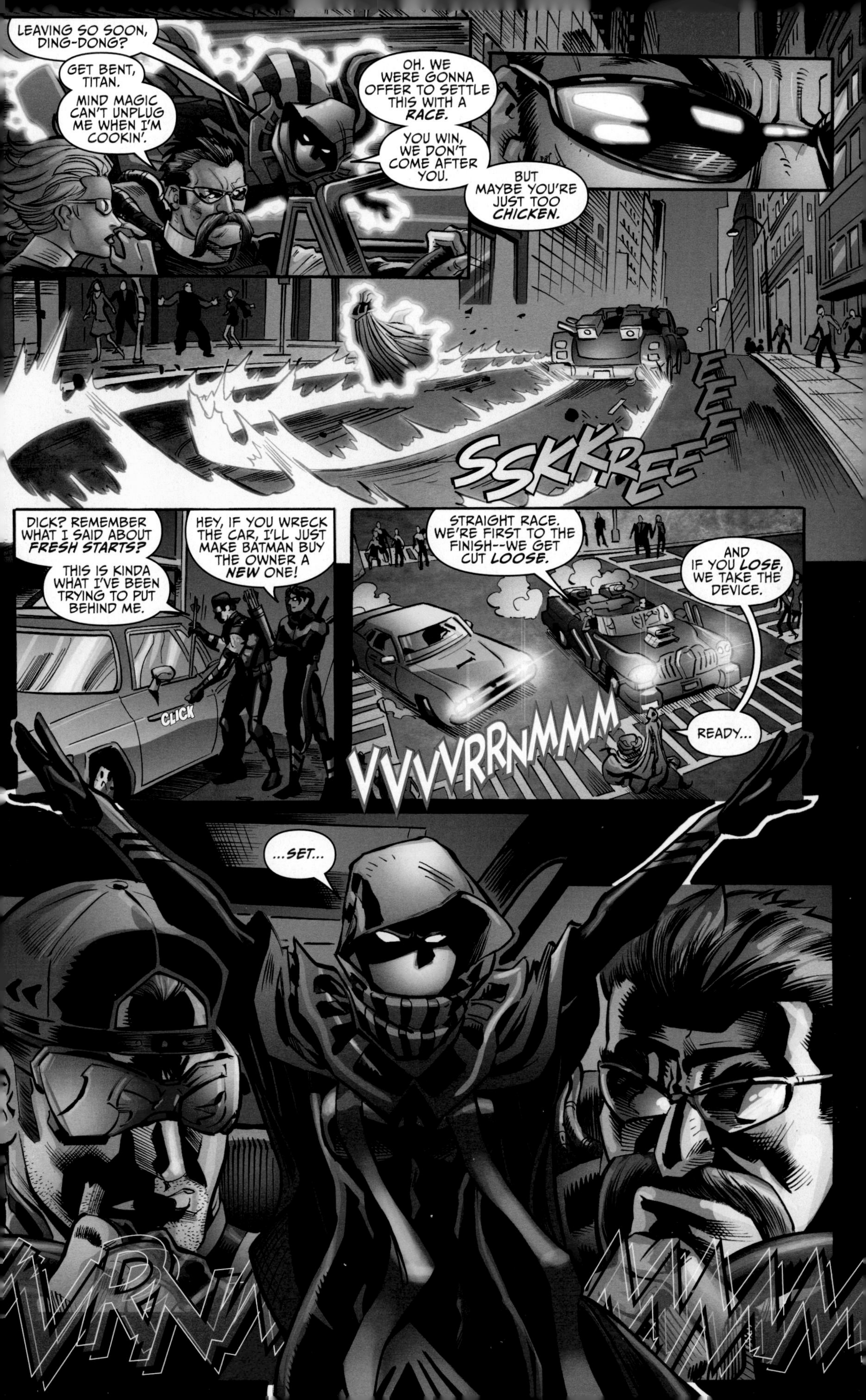
LEAVING SO SOON, DING-DONG?
GET BENT, TITAN.
MIND MAGIC CAN'T UNPLUG ME WHEN I'M COOKIN'.
OH. WE WERE GONNA OFFER TO SETTLE THIS WITH A RACE.
YOU WIN, WE DON'T COME AFTER YOU.
BUT MAYBE YOU'RE JUST TOO CHICKEN.
SSKKREEEEEE
DICK? REMEMBER WHAT I SAID ABOUT FRESH STARTS?
THIS IS KINDA WHAT I'VE BEEN TRYING TO PUT BEHIND ME.
HEY, IF YOU WRECK THE CAR, I'LL JUST MAKE BATMAN BUY THE OWNER A NEW ONE!
CLICK
STRAIGHT RACE. WE'RE FIRST TO THE FINISH--WE GET CUT LOOSE.
AND IF YOU LOSE, WE TAKE THE DEVICE.
READY...
VVVVRRNMMM
...SET...
VRN

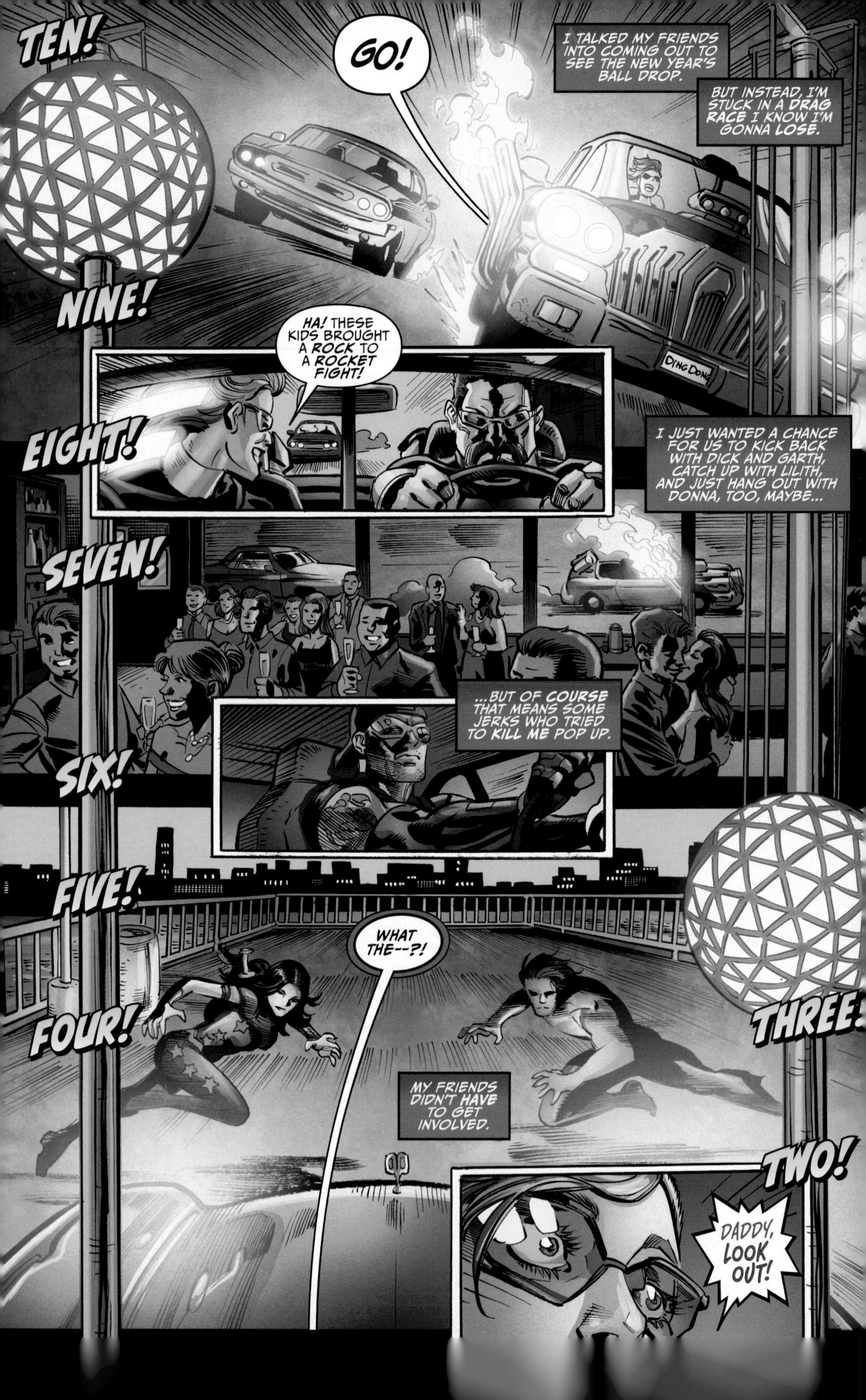
TEN!
GO!
I TALKED MY FRIENDS INTO COMING OUT TO SEE THE NEW YEAR'S BALL DROP.
BUT INSTEAD, I'M STUCK IN A DRAG RACE I KNOW I'M GONNA LOSE.
NINE!
HA! THESE KIDS BROUGHT A ROCK TO A ROCKET FIGHT!
DING DONG
EIGHT!
I JUST WANTED A CHANCE FOR US TO KICK BACK WITH DICK AND GARTH, CATCH UP WITH LILITH, AND JUST HANG OUT WITH DONNA, TOO, MAYBE...
SEVEN!
...BUT OF COURSE THAT MEANS SOME JERKS WHO TRIED TO KILL ME POP UP.
SIX!
FIVE!
WHAT THE--?!
FOUR!
THREE!
MY FRIENDS DIDN'T HAVE TO GET INVOLVED.
TWO!
DADDY, LOOK OUT!

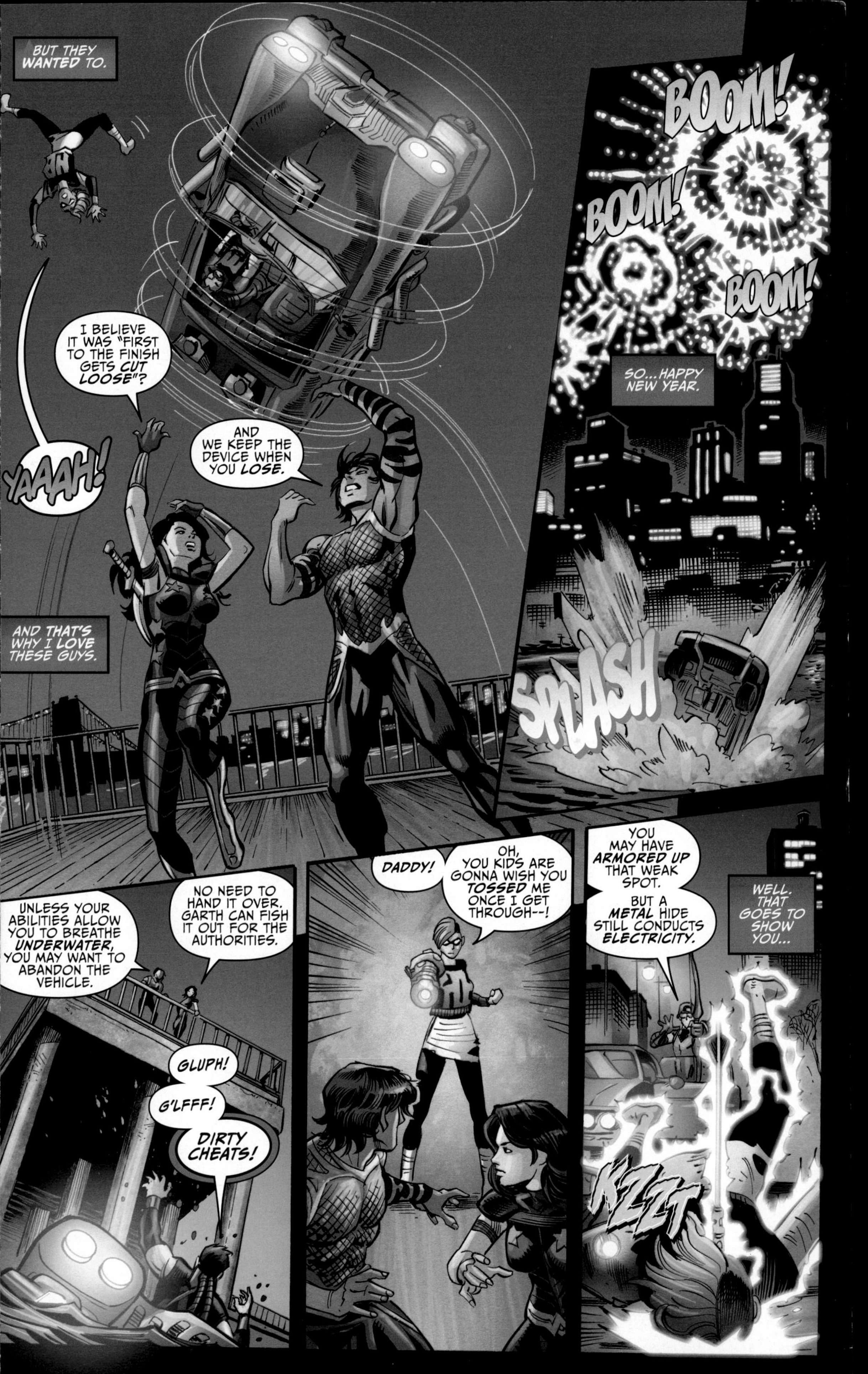
BUT THEY WANTED TO.
I BELIEVE IT WAS "FIRST TO THE FINISH GETS CUT LOOSE"?
AND WE KEEP THE DEVICE WHEN YOU LOSE.
YAAAH!
AND THAT'S WHY I LOVE THESE GUYS.
BOOM!
BOOM!
BOOM!
SO...HAPPY NEW YEAR.
SPLASH
UNLESS YOUR ABILITIES ALLOW YOU TO BREATHE UNDERWATER, YOU MAY WANT TO ABANDON THE VEHICLE.
NO NEED TO HAND IT OVER. GARTH CAN FISH IT OUT FOR THE AUTHORITIES.
GLUPH!
G'LFFF!
DIRTY CHEATS!
DADDY!
OH, YOU KIDS ARE GONNA WISH YOU TOSSED ME ONCE I GET THROUGH--!
YOU MAY HAVE ARMORED UP THAT WEAK SPOT.
BUT A METAL HIDE STILL CONDUCTS ELECTRICITY.
WELL. THAT GOES TO SHOW YOU...
KZZZT

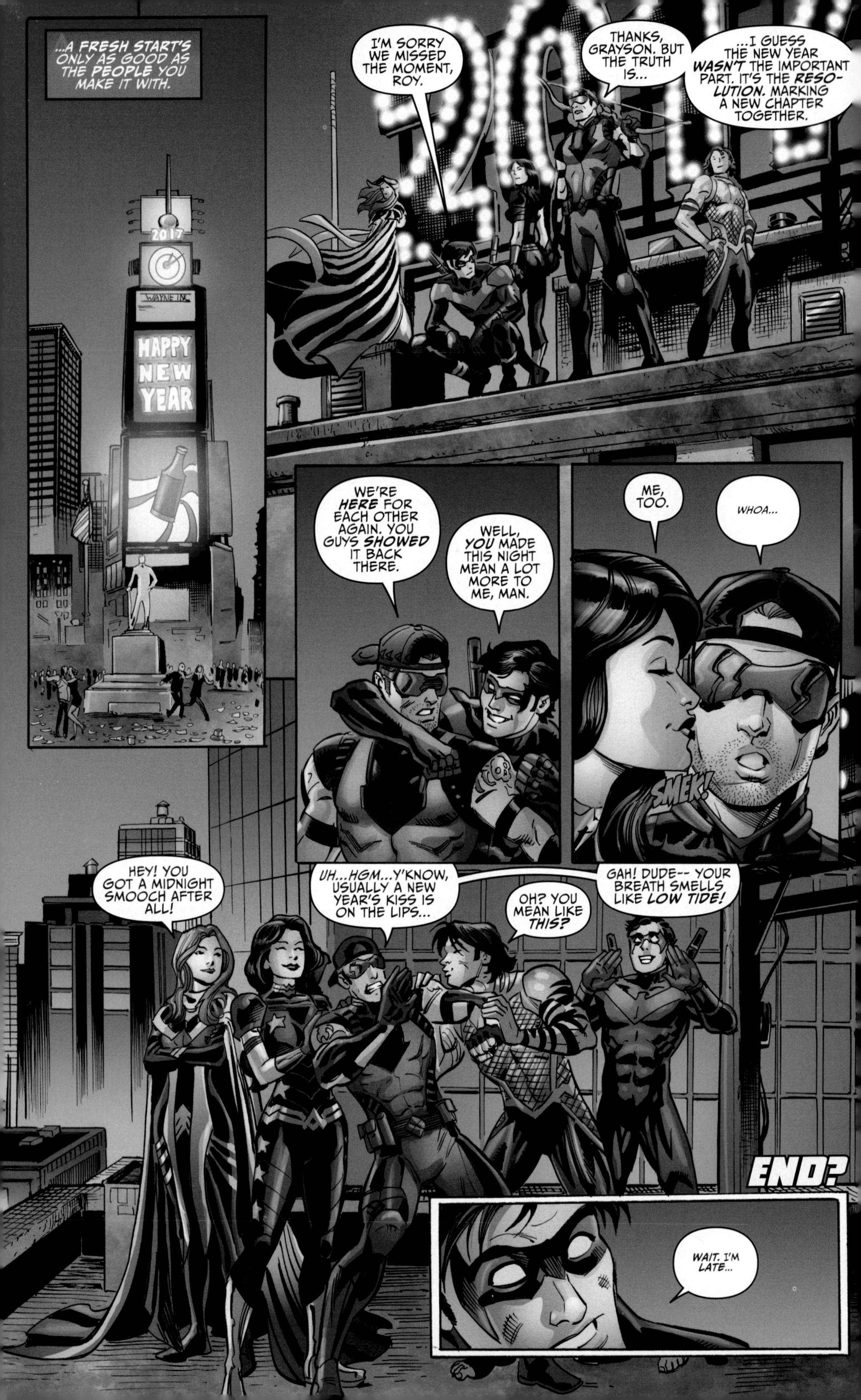

...A FRESH START'S ONLY AS GOOD AS THE PEOPLE YOU MAKE IT WITH.
2017
WAYNE INC.
HAPPY NEW YEAR
I'M SORRY WE MISSED THE MOMENT, ROY.
THANKS, GRAYSON. BUT THE TRUTH IS...
...I GUESS THE NEW YEAR WASN'T THE IMPORTANT PART. IT'S THE RESOLUTION. MARKING A NEW CHAPTER TOGETHER.
WE'RE HERE FOR EACH OTHER AGAIN. YOU GUYS SHOWED IT BACK THERE.
WELL, YOU MADE THIS NIGHT MEAN A LOT MORE TO ME, MAN.
ME, TOO.
WHOA...
SMEK!
HEY! YOU GOT A MIDNIGHT SMOOCH AFTER ALL!
UH...HGM...Y'KNOW, USUALLY A NEW YEAR'S KISS IS ON THE LIPS...
OH? YOU MEAN LIKE THIS?
GAH! DUDE-- YOUR BREATH SMELLS LIKE LOW TIDE!
END?
WAIT. I'M LATE...

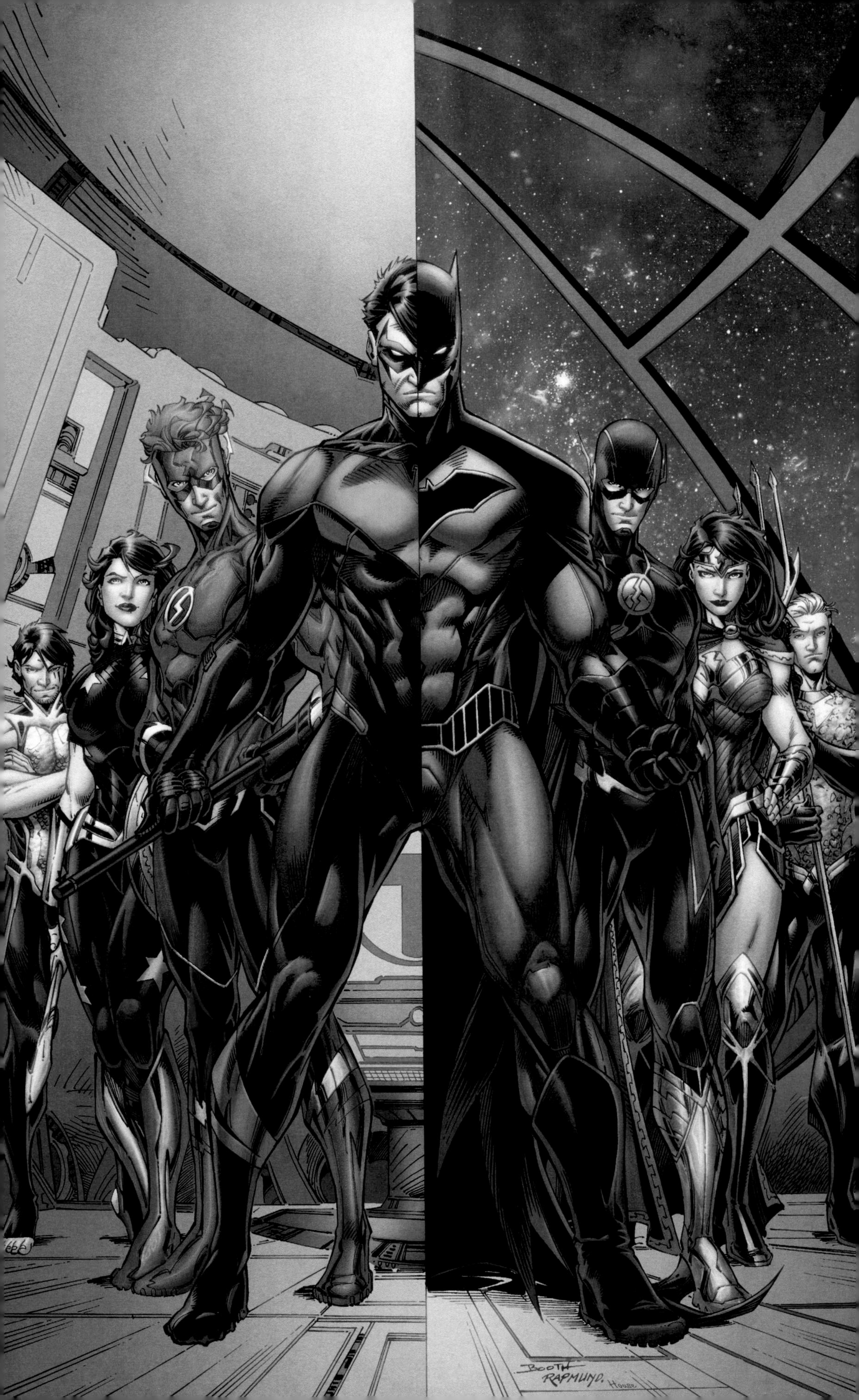
BOOTH
RAPMUND.

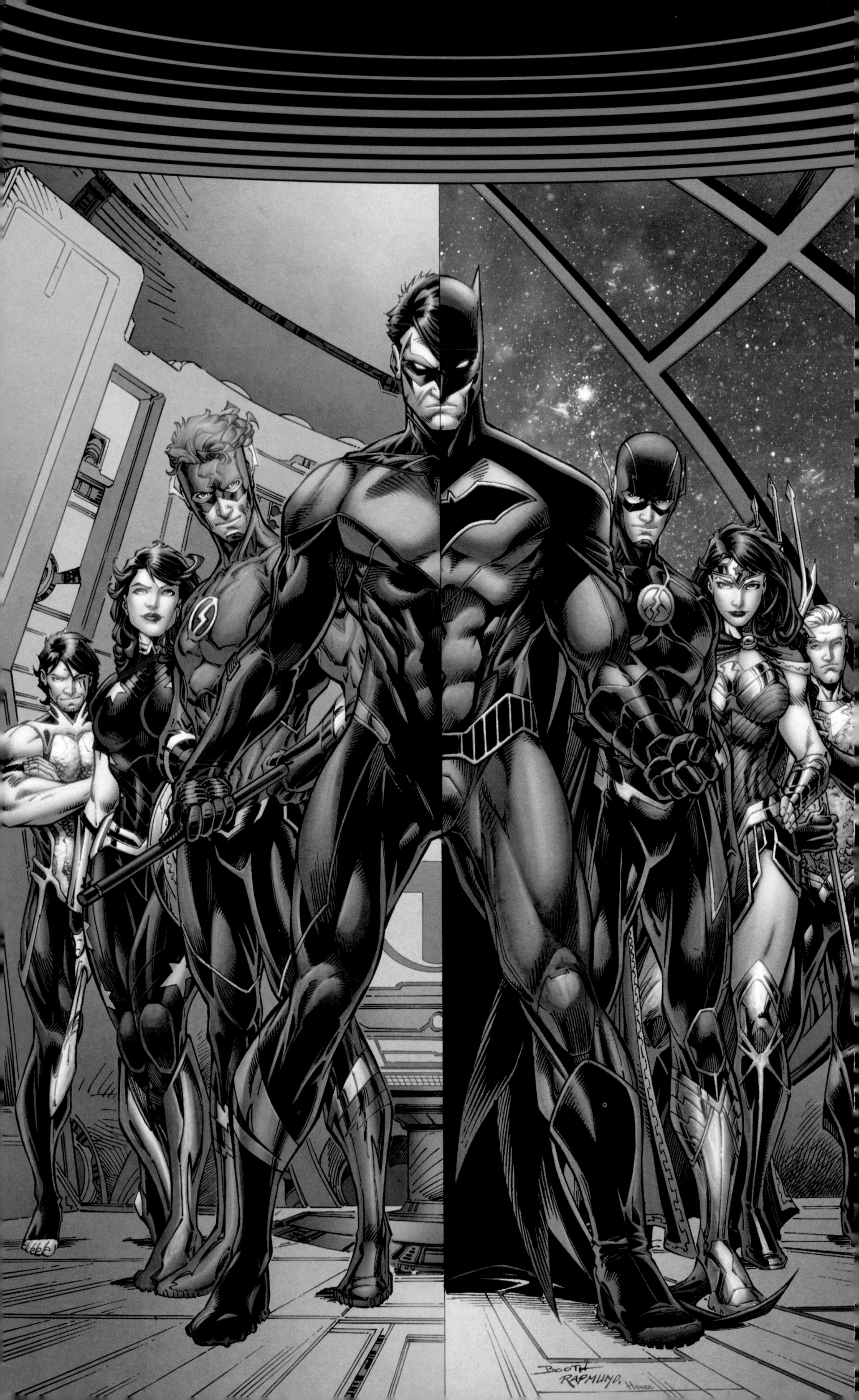
BOOTH
RAPMUND
House

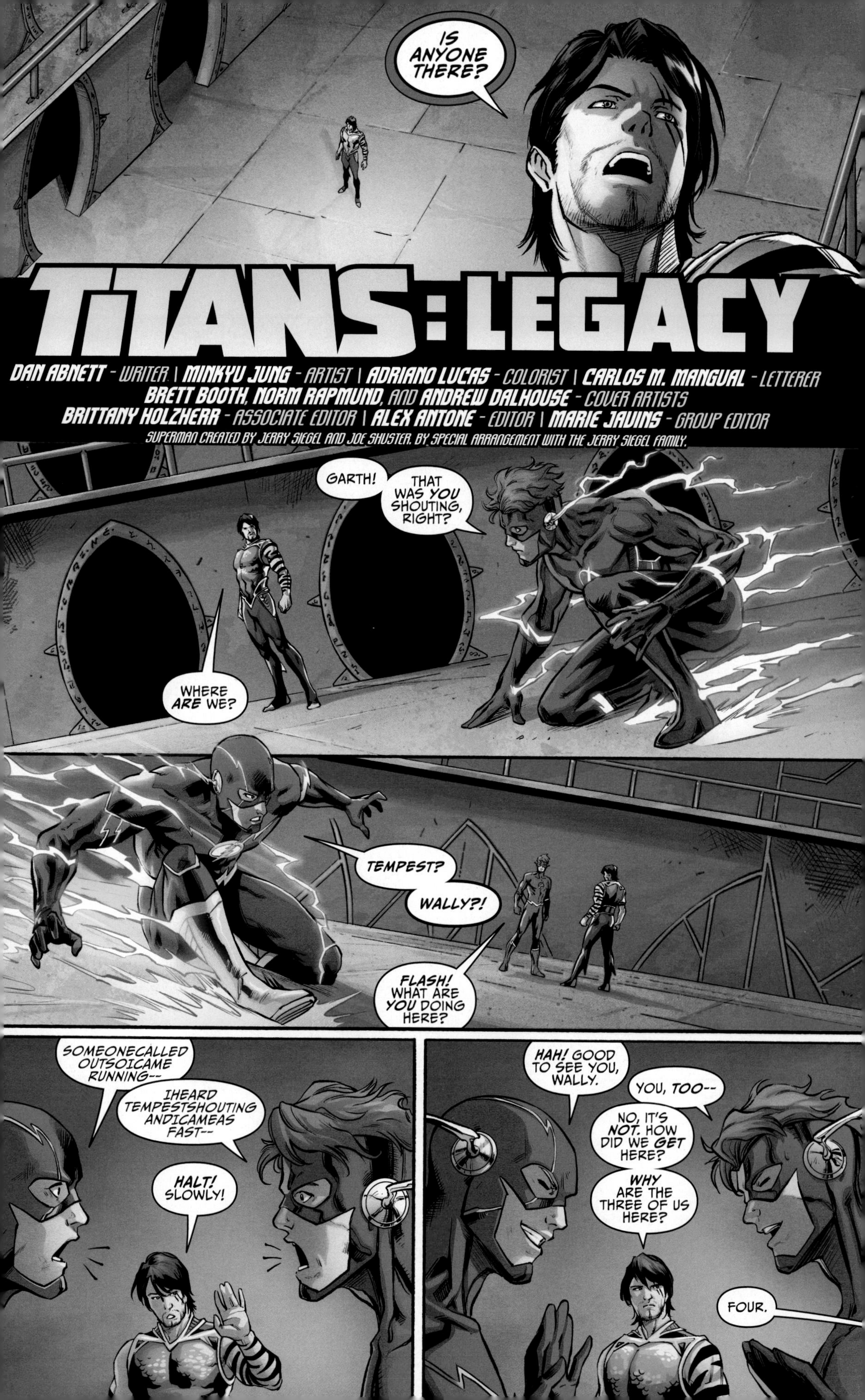
IS ANYONE THERE?
TITANS: LEGACY
DAN ABNETT - WRITER \ MINKYU JUNG - ARTIST \ ADRIANO LUCAS - COLORIST \ CARLOS M. MANGUAL - LETTERER
BRETT BOOTH, NORM RAPMUND, AND ANDREW DALHOUSE - COVER ARTISTS
BRITTANY HOLZHERR - ASSOCIATE EDITOR \ ALEX ANTONE - EDITOR \ MARIE JAVINS - GROUP EDITOR
SUPERMAN CREATED BY JERRY SIEGEL AND JOE SHUSTER. BY SPECIAL ARRANGEMENT WITH THE JERRY SIEGEL FAMILY.
GARTH!
THAT WAS YOU SHOUTING, RIGHT?
WHERE ARE WE?
TEMPEST?
WALLY?!
FLASH! WHAT ARE YOU DOING HERE?
SOMEONECALLED OUTSOICAME RUNNING--
IHEARD TEMPESTSHOUTING ANDICAMEAS FAST--
HALT! SLOWLY!
HAH! GOOD TO SEE YOU, WALLY.
YOU, TOO--
NO, IT'S NOT. HOW DID WE GET HERE?
WHY ARE THE THREE OF US HERE?
FOUR.

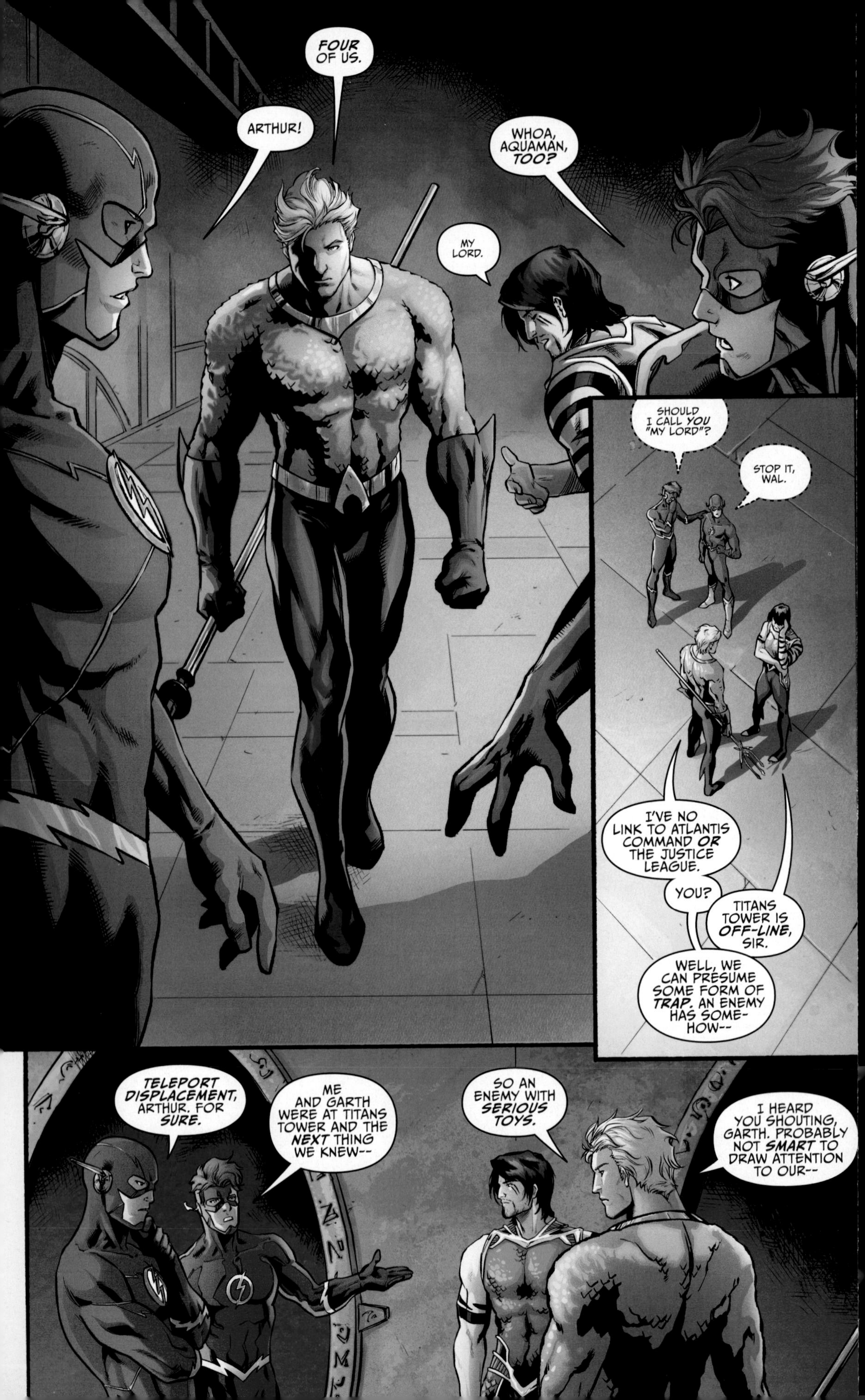
ARTHUR!
FOUR OF US.
WHOA, AQUAMAN, TOO?
MY LORD.
SHOULD I CALL YOU "MY LORD"?
STOP IT, WAL.
I'VE NO LINK TO ATLANTIS COMMAND OR THE JUSTICE LEAGUE.
YOU?
TITANS TOWER IS OFF-LINE, SIR.
WELL, WE CAN PRESUME SOME FORM OF TRAP. AN ENEMY HAS SOME-HOW--
TELEPORT DISPLACEMENT, ARTHUR. FOR SURE.
ME AND GARTH WERE AT TITANS TOWER AND THE NEXT THING WE KNEW--
SO AN ENEMY WITH SERIOUS TOYS.
I HEARD YOU SHOUTING, GARTH. PROBABLY NOT SMART TO DRAW ATTENTION TO OUR--

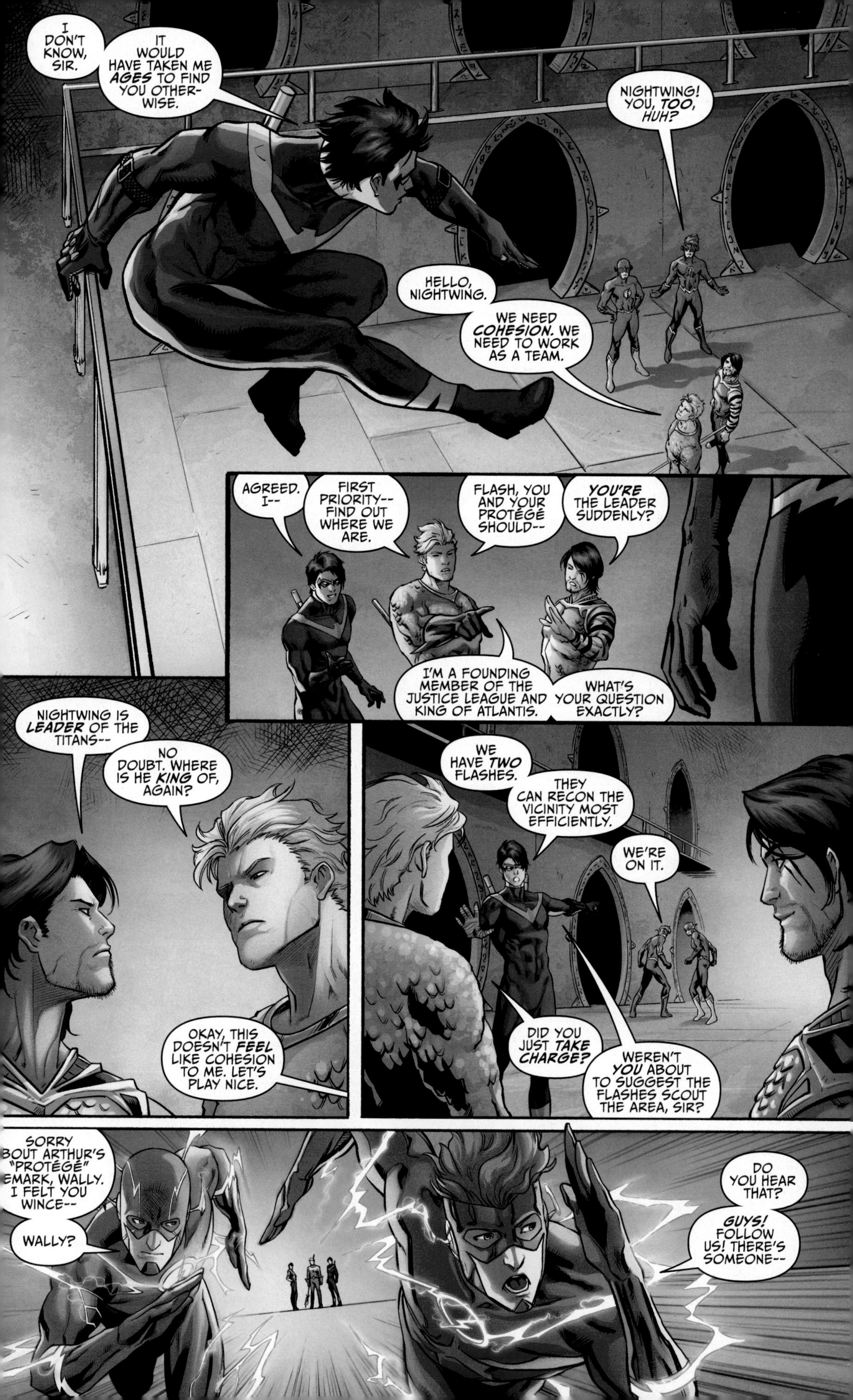
I DON'T KNOW, SIR.
IT WOULD HAVE TAKEN ME AGES TO FIND YOU OTHER-WISE.
NIGHTWING! YOU, TOO, HUH?
HELLO, NIGHTWING.
WE NEED COHESION. WE NEED TO WORK AS A TEAM.
AGREED. I--
FIRST PRIORITY-- FIND OUT WHERE WE ARE.
FLASH, YOU AND YOUR PROTÉGÉ SHOULD--
YOU'RE THE LEADER SUDDENLY?
I'M A FOUNDING MEMBER OF THE JUSTICE LEAGUE AND KING OF ATLANTIS.
WHAT'S YOUR QUESTION EXACTLY?
NIGHTWING IS LEADER OF THE TITANS--
NO DOUBT. WHERE IS HE KING OF, AGAIN?
OKAY, THIS DOESN'T FEEL LIKE COHESION TO ME. LET'S PLAY NICE.
WE HAVE TWO FLASHES.
THEY CAN RECON THE VICINITY MOST EFFICIENTLY.
WE'RE ON IT.
DID YOU JUST TAKE CHARGE?
WEREN'T YOU ABOUT TO SUGGEST THE FLASHES SCOUT THE AREA, SIR?
SORRY BOUT ARTHUR'S "PROTÉGÉ" EMARK, WALLY. I FELT YOU WINCE--
WALLY?
DO YOU HEAR THAT?
GUYS! FOLLOW US! THERE'S SOMEONE--

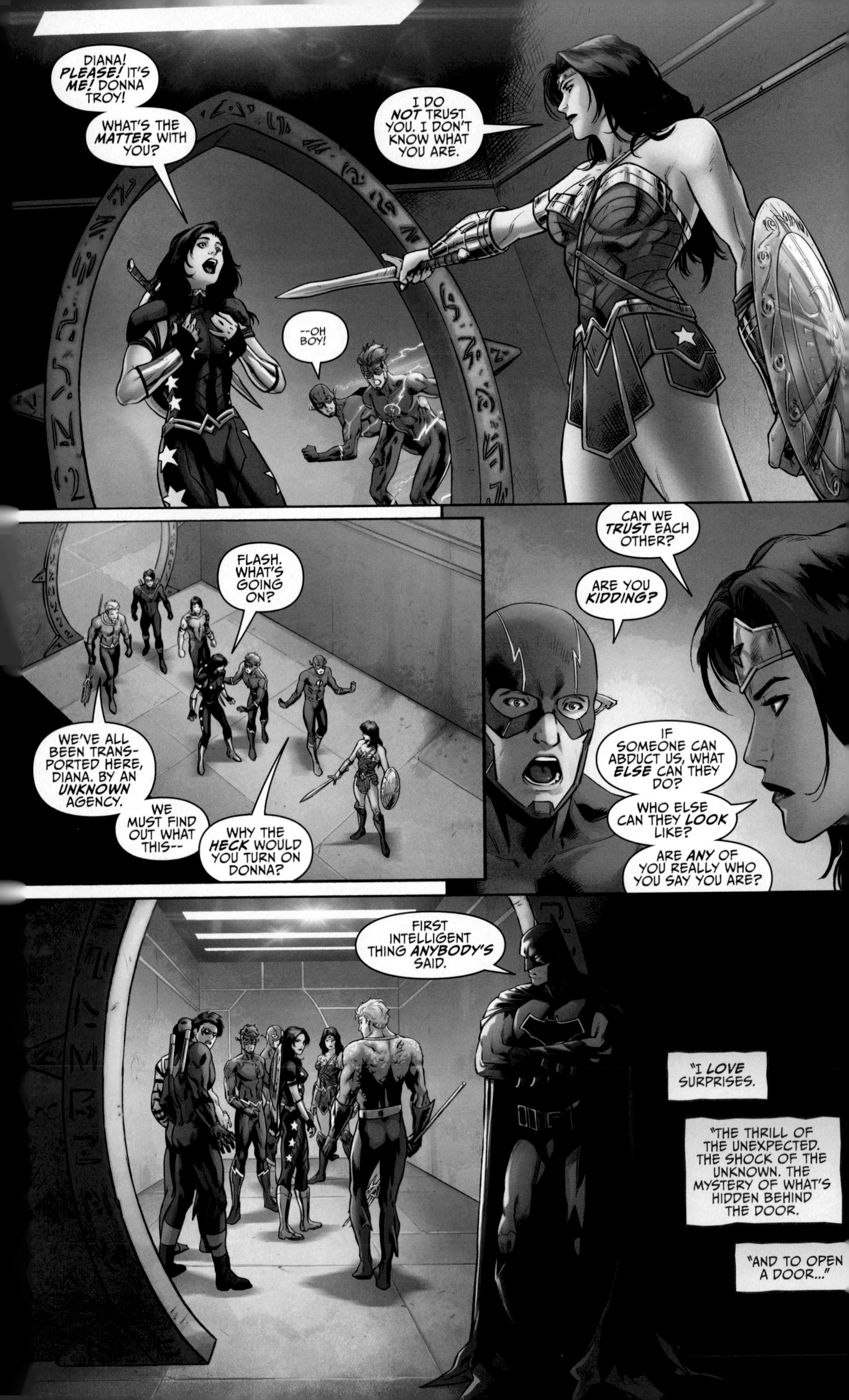
DIANA! PLEASE! IT'S ME! DONNA TROY!
WHAT'S THE MATTER WITH YOU?
I DO NOT TRUST YOU. I DON'T KNOW WHAT YOU ARE.
--OH BOY!
FLASH. WHAT'S GOING ON?
WE'VE ALL BEEN TRANS-PORTED HERE, DIANA. BY AN UNKNOWN AGENCY.
WE MUST FIND OUT WHAT THIS--
WHY THE HECK WOULD YOU TURN ON DONNA?
CAN WE TRUST EACH OTHER?
ARE YOU KIDDING?
IF SOMEONE CAN ABDUCT US, WHAT ELSE CAN THEY DO?
WHO ELSE CAN THEY LOOK LIKE?
ARE ANY OF YOU REALLY WHO YOU SAY YOU ARE?
FIRST INTELLIGENT THING ANYBODY'S SAID.
"I LOVE SURPRISES.
"THE THRILL OF THE UNEXPECTED. THE SHOCK OF THE UNKNOWN. THE MYSTERY OF WHAT'S HIDDEN BEHIND THE DOOR.
"AND TO OPEN A DOOR..."

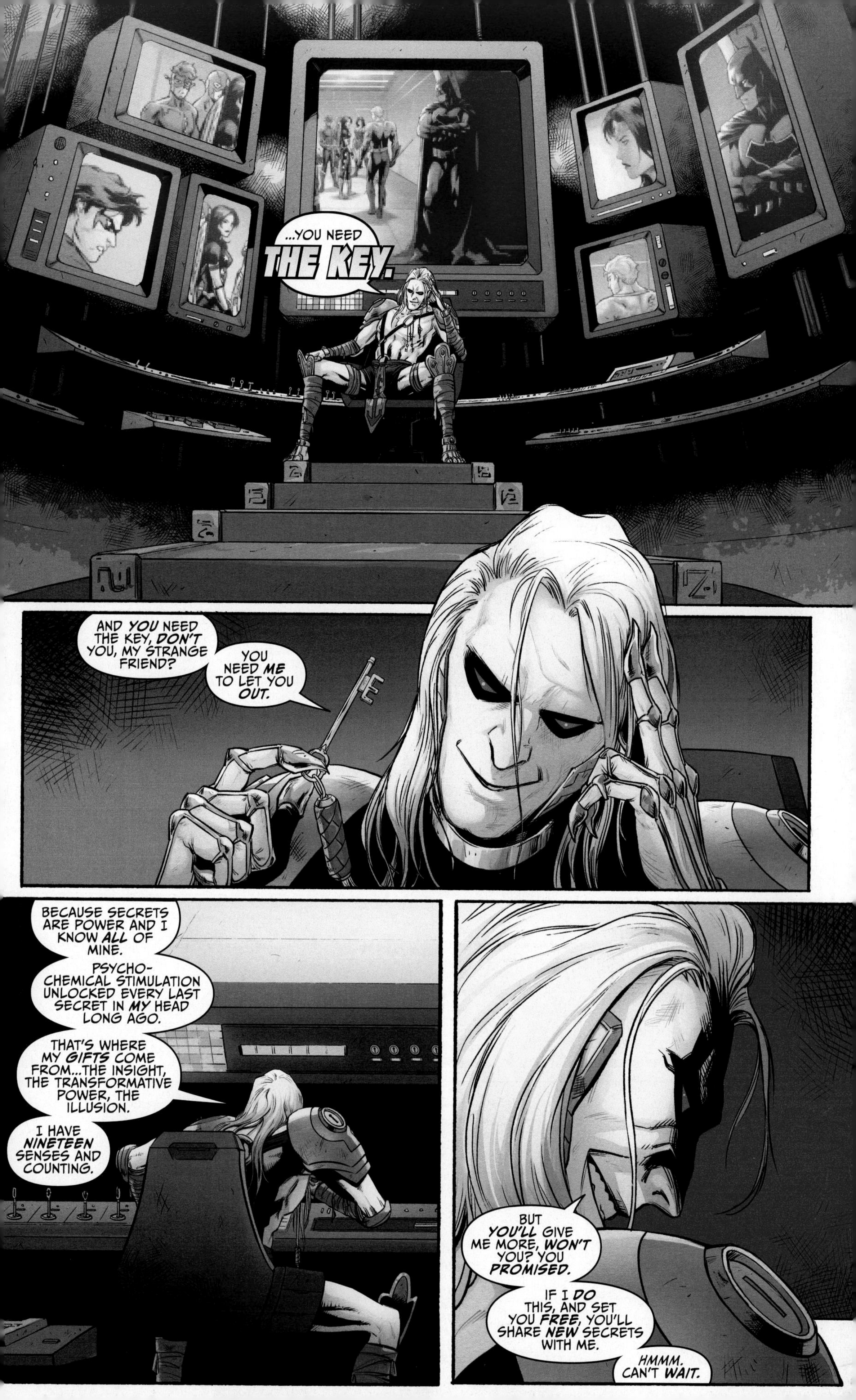
...YOU NEED THE KEY.
AND YOU NEED THE KEY, DON'T YOU, MY STRANGE FRIEND?
YOU NEED ME TO LET YOU OUT.
BECAUSE SECRETS ARE POWER AND I KNOW ALL OF MINE.
PSYCHO-CHEMICAL STIMULATION UNLOCKED EVERY LAST SECRET IN MY HEAD LONG AGO.
THAT'S WHERE MY GIFTS COME FROM...THE INSIGHT, THE TRANSFORMATIVE POWER, THE ILLUSION.
I HAVE NINETEEN SENSES AND COUNTING.
BUT YOU'LL GIVE ME MORE, WON'T YOU? YOU PROMISED.
IF I DO THIS, AND SET YOU FREE, YOU'LL SHARE NEW SECRETS WITH ME.
HMMM. CAN'T WAIT.

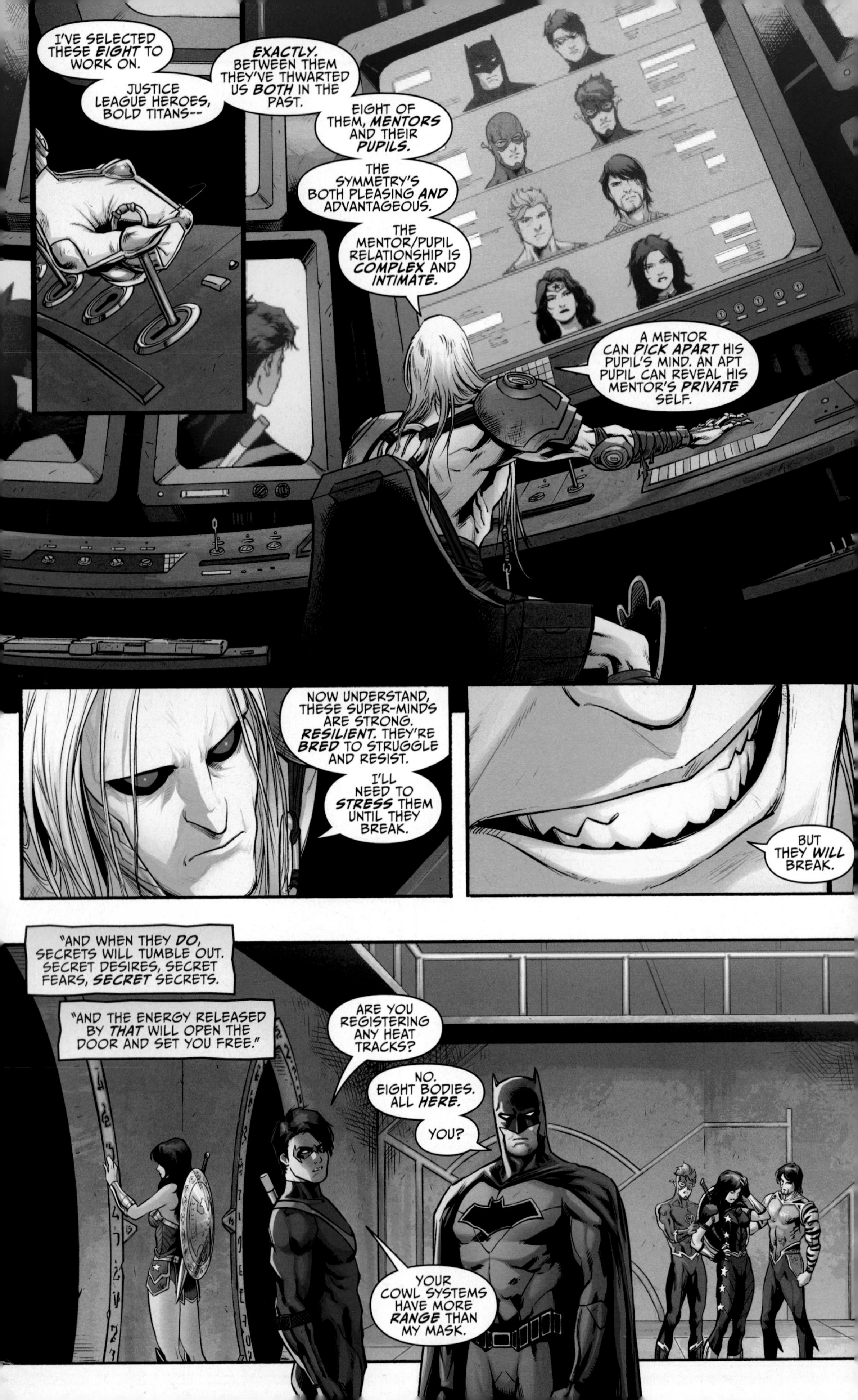
I'VE SELECTED THESE EIGHT TO WORK ON.
JUSTICE LEAGUE HEROES, BOLD TITANS--
EXACTLY. BETWEEN THEM THEY'VE THWARTED US BOTH IN THE PAST.
EIGHT OF THEM, MENTORS AND THEIR PUPILS.
THE SYMMETRY'S BOTH PLEASING AND ADVANTAGEOUS.
THE MENTOR/PUPIL RELATIONSHIP IS COMPLEX AND INTIMATE.
A MENTOR CAN PICK APART HIS PUPIL'S MIND. AN APT PUPIL CAN REVEAL HIS MENTOR'S PRIVATE SELF.
NOW UNDERSTAND, THESE SUPER-MINDS ARE STRONG. RESILIENT. THEY'RE BRED TO STRUGGLE AND RESIST.
I'LL NEED TO STRESS THEM UNTIL THEY BREAK.
BUT THEY WILL BREAK.
"AND WHEN THEY DO, SECRETS WILL TUMBLE OUT. SECRET DESIRES, SECRET FEARS, SECRET SECRETS.
"AND THE ENERGY RELEASED BY THAT WILL OPEN THE DOOR AND SET YOU FREE."
ARE YOU REGISTERING ANY HEAT TRACKS?
NO. EIGHT BODIES. ALL HERE.
YOU?
YOUR COWL SYSTEMS HAVE MORE RANGE THAN MY MASK.

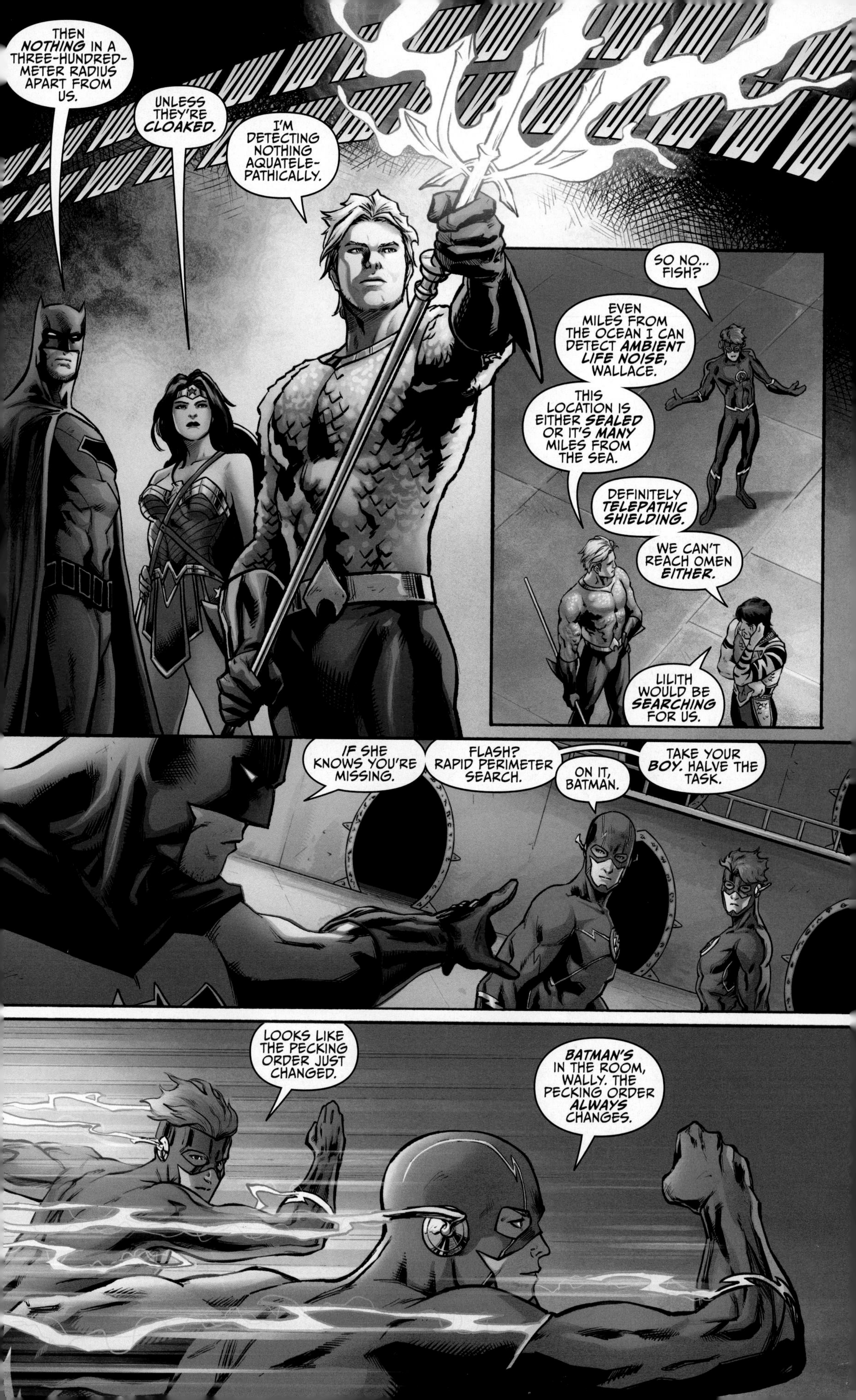
THEN NOTHING IN A THREE-HUNDRED-METER RADIUS APART FROM US.
UNLESS THEY'RE CLOAKED.
I'M DETECTING NOTHING AQUATELE-PATHICALLY.
SO NO... FISH?
EVEN MILES FROM THE OCEAN I CAN DETECT AMBIENT LIFE NOISE, WALLACE.
THIS LOCATION IS EITHER SEALED OR IT'S MANY MILES FROM THE SEA.
DEFINITELY TELEPATHIC SHIELDING.
WE CAN'T REACH OMEN EITHER.
LILITH WOULD BE SEARCHING FOR US.
IF SHE KNOWS YOU'RE MISSING.
FLASH? RAPID PERIMETER SEARCH.
TAKE YOUR BOY. HALVE THE TASK.
ON IT, BATMAN.
LOOKS LIKE THE PECKING ORDER JUST CHANGED.
BATMAN'S IN THE ROOM, WALLY. THE PECKING ORDER ALWAYS CHANGES.

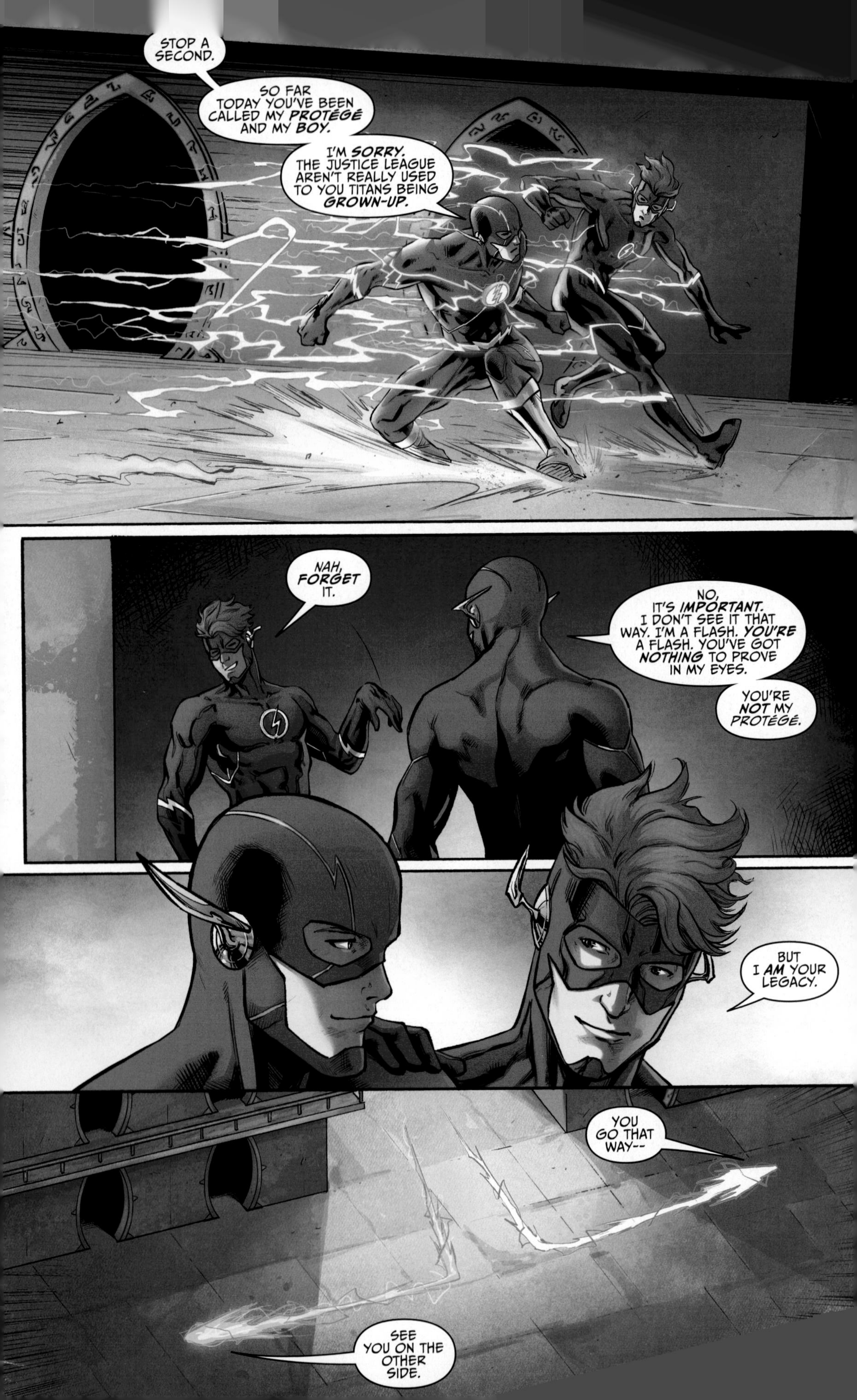

STOP A SECOND.
SO FAR TODAY YOU'VE BEEN CALLED MY PROTÉGÉ AND MY BOY.
I'M SORRY. THE JUSTICE LEAGUE AREN'T REALLY USED TO YOU TITANS BEING GROWN-UP.
NAH, FORGET IT.
NO, IT'S IMPORTANT. I DON'T SEE IT THAT WAY. I'M A FLASH. YOU'RE A FLASH. YOU'VE GOT NOTHING TO PROVE IN MY EYES.
YOU'RE NOT MY PROTÉGÉ.
BUT I AM YOUR LEGACY.
YOU GO THAT WAY--
SEE YOU ON THE OTHER SIDE.

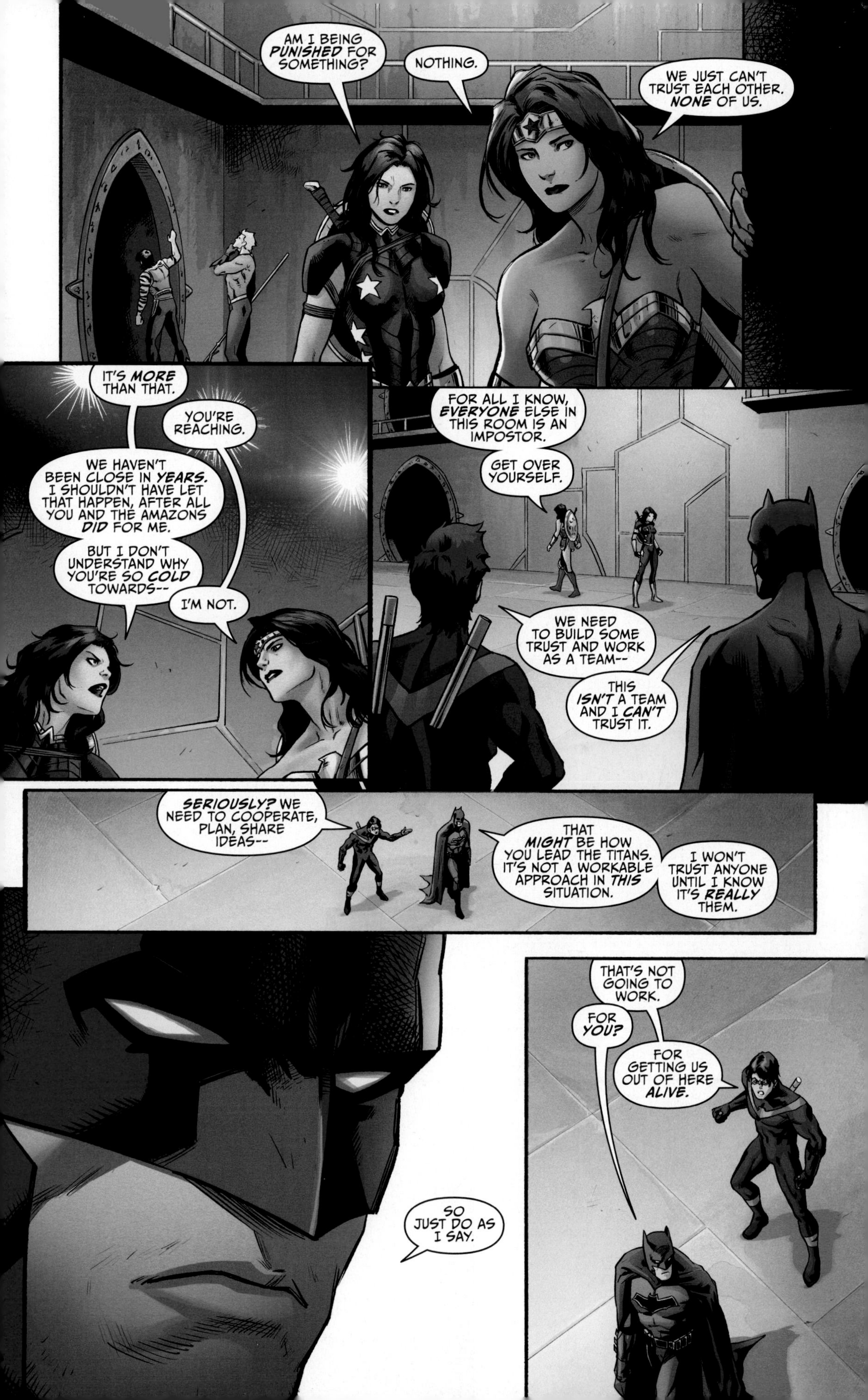
AM I BEING *PUNISHED* FOR SOMETHING?
NOTHING.
WE JUST CAN'T TRUST EACH OTHER. *NONE* OF US.
IT'S *MORE* THAN THAT.
YOU'RE REACHING.
WE HAVEN'T BEEN CLOSE IN *YEARS.* I SHOULDN'T HAVE LET THAT HAPPEN, AFTER ALL YOU AND THE AMAZONS *DID* FOR ME.
BUT I DON'T UNDERSTAND WHY YOU'RE SO *COLD* TOWARDS--
I'M NOT.
FOR ALL I KNOW, *EVERYONE* ELSE IN THIS ROOM IS AN IMPOSTOR.
GET OVER YOURSELF.
WE NEED TO BUILD SOME TRUST AND WORK AS A TEAM--
THIS *ISN'T* A TEAM AND I *CAN'T* TRUST IT.
SERIOUSLY? WE NEED TO COOPERATE, PLAN, SHARE IDEAS--
THAT *MIGHT* BE HOW YOU LEAD THE TITANS. IT'S NOT A WORKABLE APPROACH IN *THIS* SITUATION.
I WON'T TRUST ANYONE UNTIL I KNOW IT'S *REALLY* THEM.
SO JUST DO AS I SAY.
THAT'S NOT GOING TO WORK.
FOR *YOU?*
FOR GETTING US OUT OF HERE *ALIVE.*

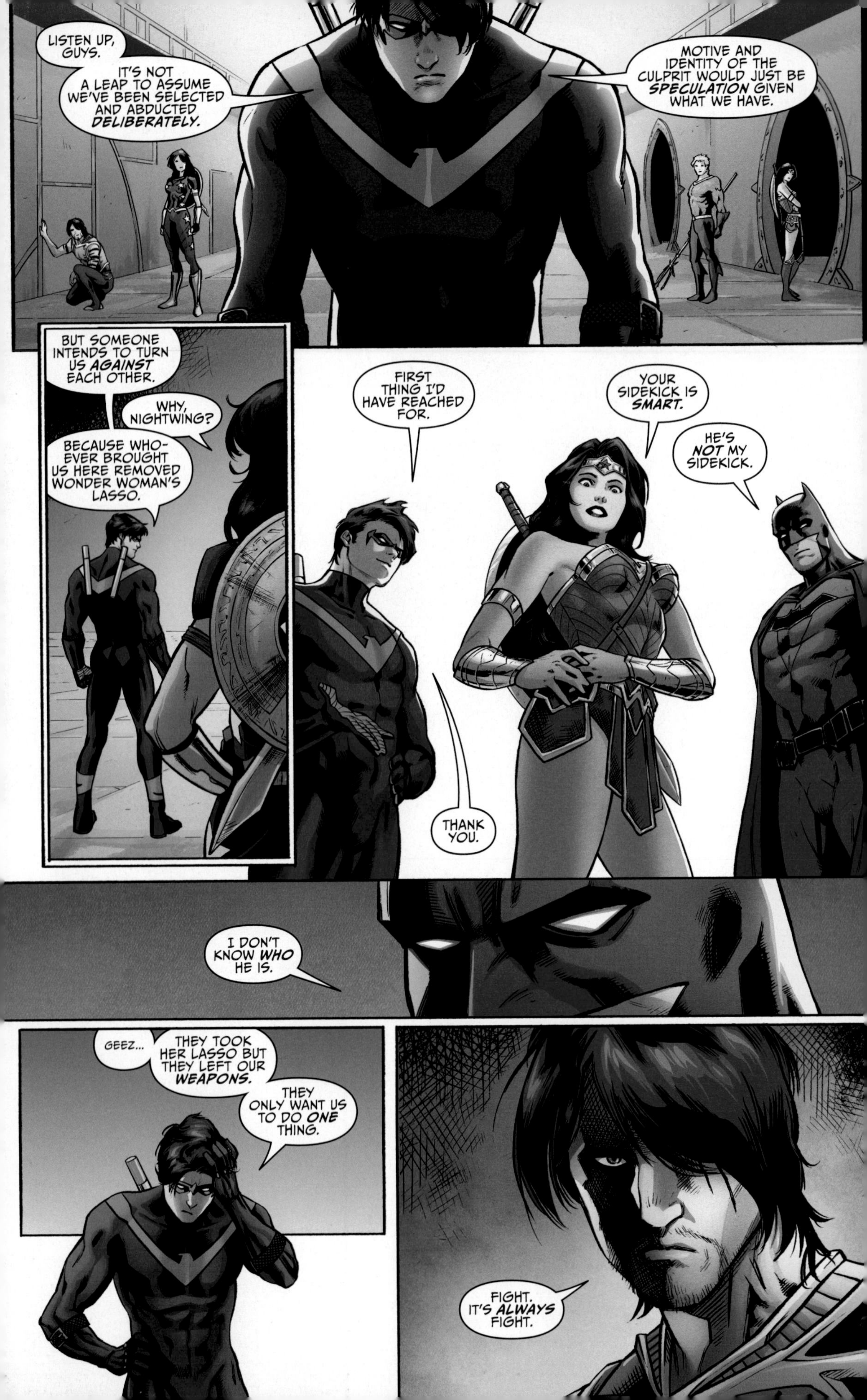
LISTEN UP, GUYS.
IT'S NOT A LEAP TO ASSUME WE'VE BEEN SELECTED AND ABDUCTED DELIBERATELY.
MOTIVE AND IDENTITY OF THE CULPRIT WOULD JUST BE SPECULATION GIVEN WHAT WE HAVE.
BUT SOMEONE INTENDS TO TURN US AGAINST EACH OTHER.
WHY, NIGHTWING?
BECAUSE WHO-EVER BROUGHT US HERE REMOVED WONDER WOMAN'S LASSO.
FIRST THING I'D HAVE REACHED FOR.
YOUR SIDEKICK IS SMART.
HE'S NOT MY SIDEKICK.
THANK YOU.
I DON'T KNOW WHO HE IS.
GEEZ...
THEY TOOK HER LASSO BUT THEY LEFT OUR WEAPONS.
THEY ONLY WANT US TO DO ONE THING.
FIGHT. IT'S ALWAYS FIGHT.

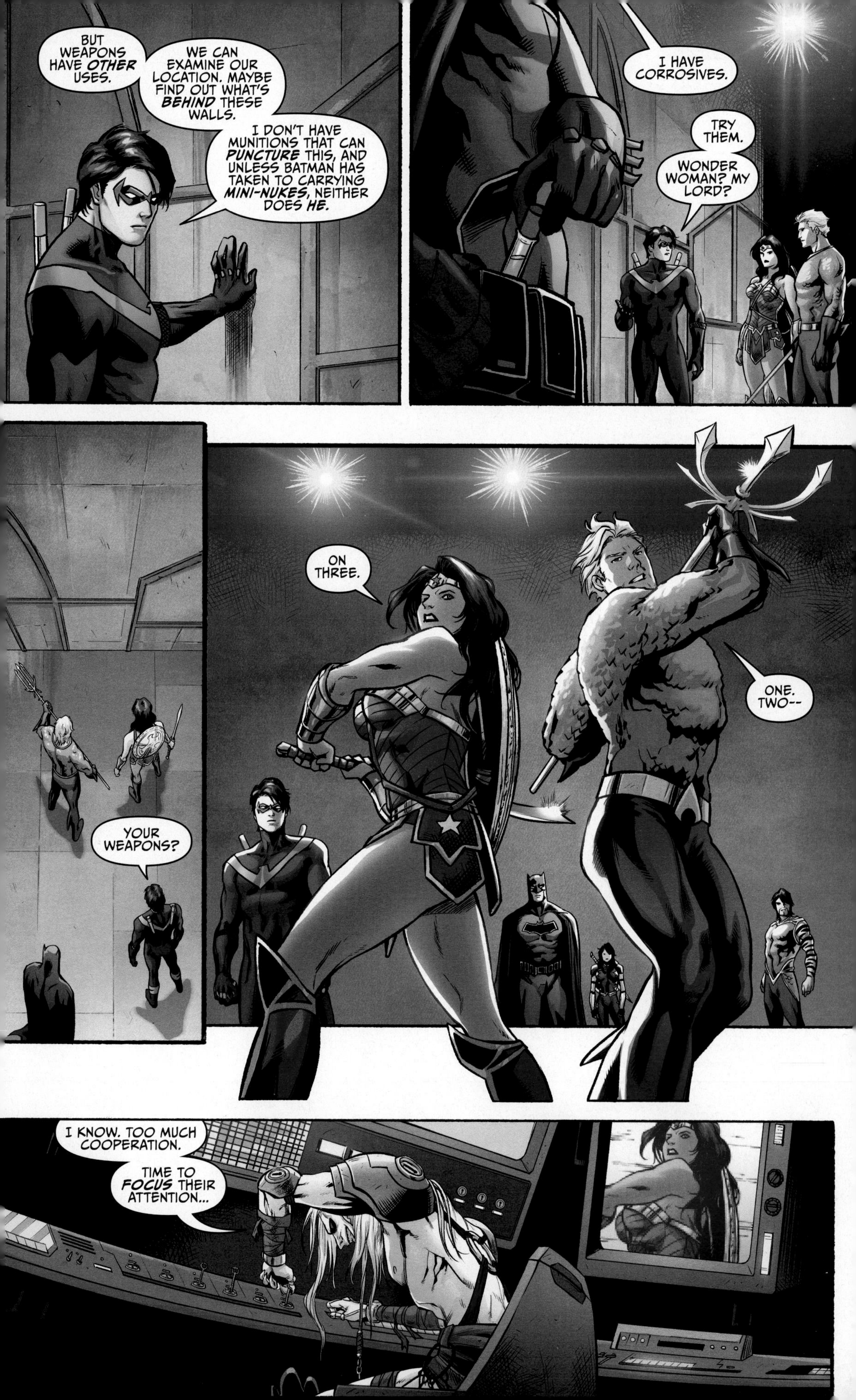

BUT WEAPONS HAVE OTHER USES.
WE CAN EXAMINE OUR LOCATION. MAYBE FIND OUT WHAT'S BEHIND THESE WALLS.
I DON'T HAVE MUNITIONS THAT CAN PUNCTURE THIS, AND UNLESS BATMAN HAS TAKEN TO CARRYING MINI-NUKES, NEITHER DOES HE.
I HAVE CORROSIVES.
TRY THEM.
WONDER WOMAN? MY LORD?
YOUR WEAPONS?
ON THREE.
ONE. TWO--
I KNOW. TOO MUCH COOPERATION.
TIME TO FOCUS THEIR ATTENTION...

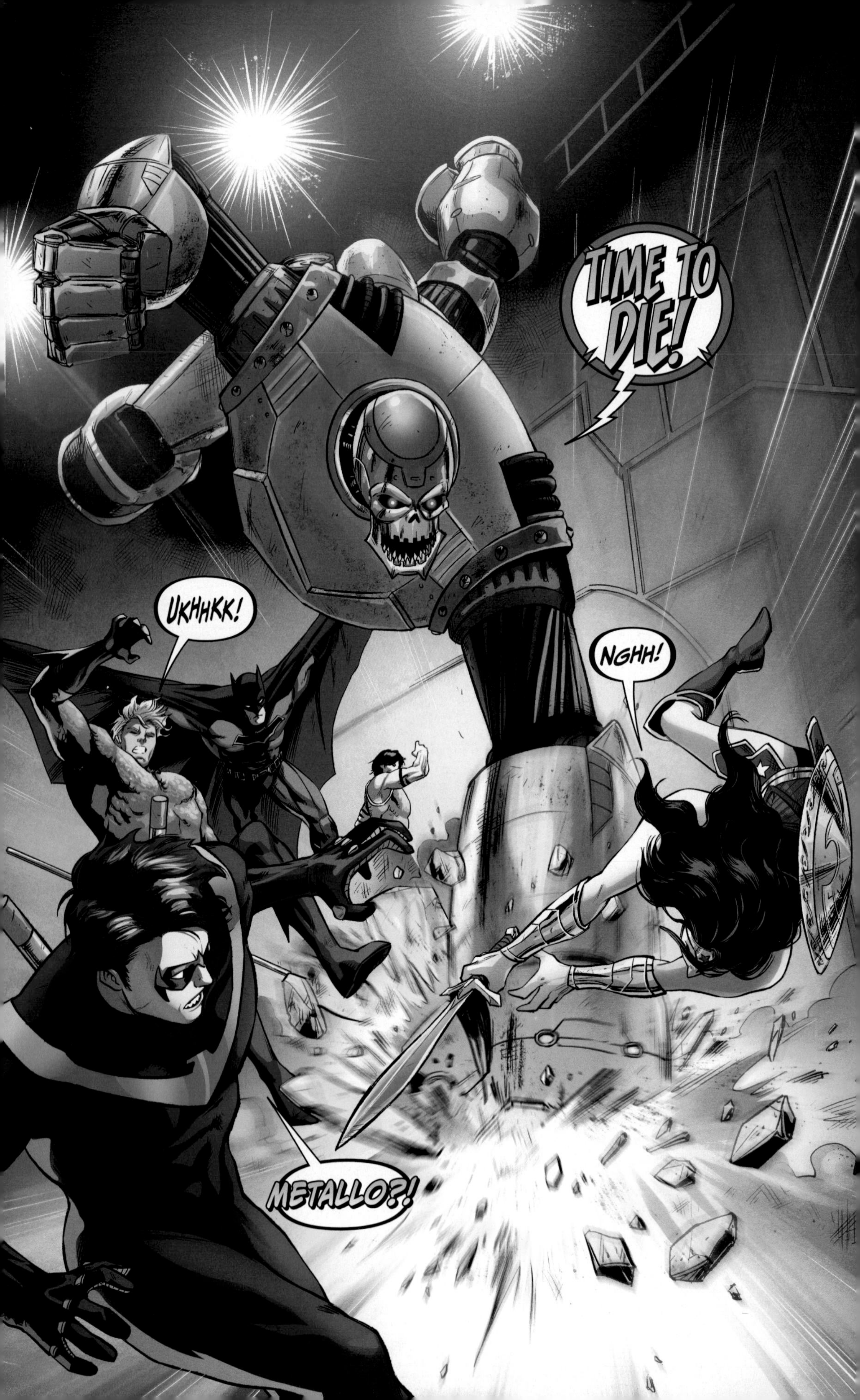
TIME TO DIE!
UKHHKK!
NGHH!
METALLO?!

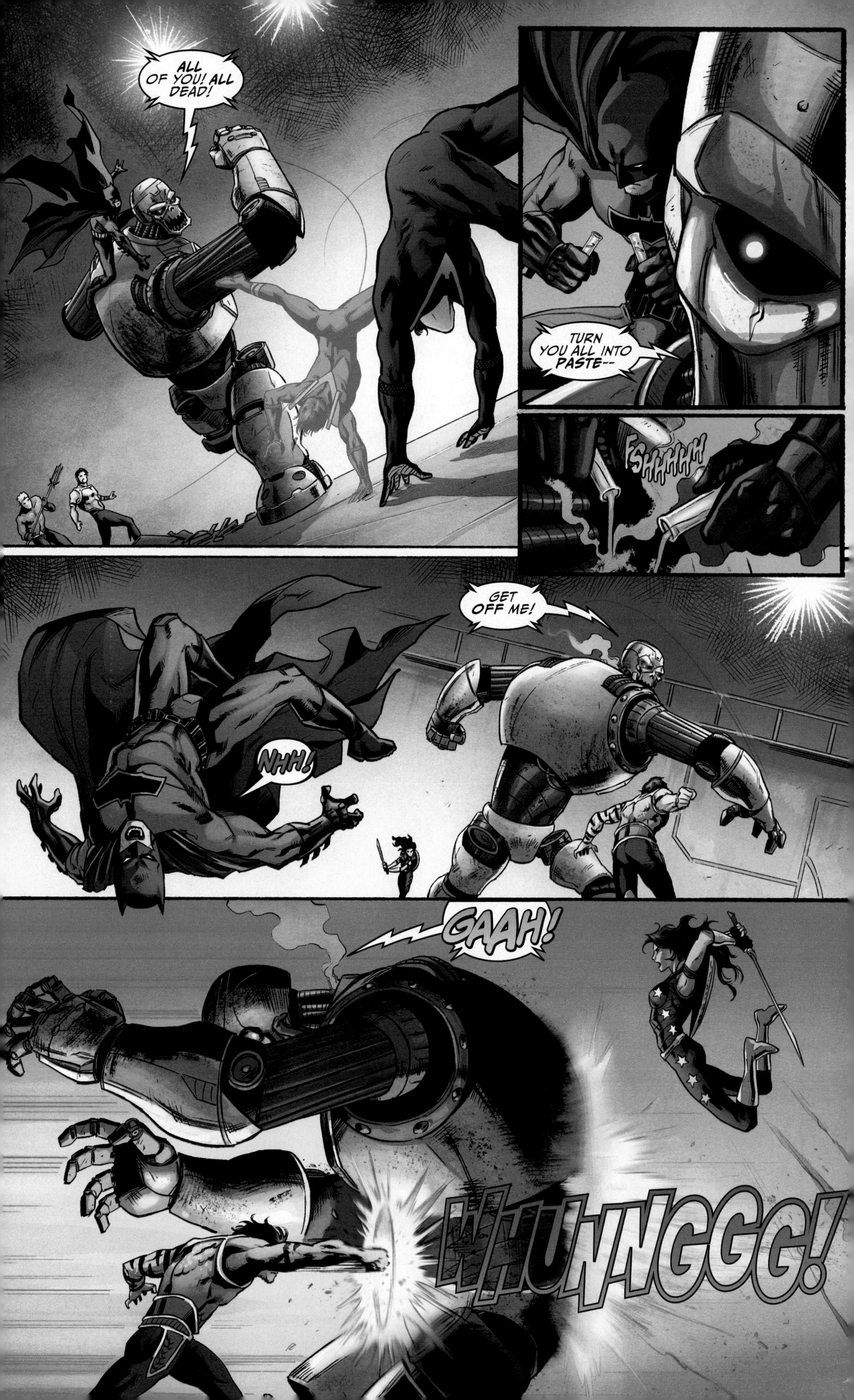
ALL OF YOU! ALL DEAD!
TURN YOU ALL INTO PASTE--
FSHHHHH
GET OFF ME!
NHH!
GAAH!
WHUNNGGG!

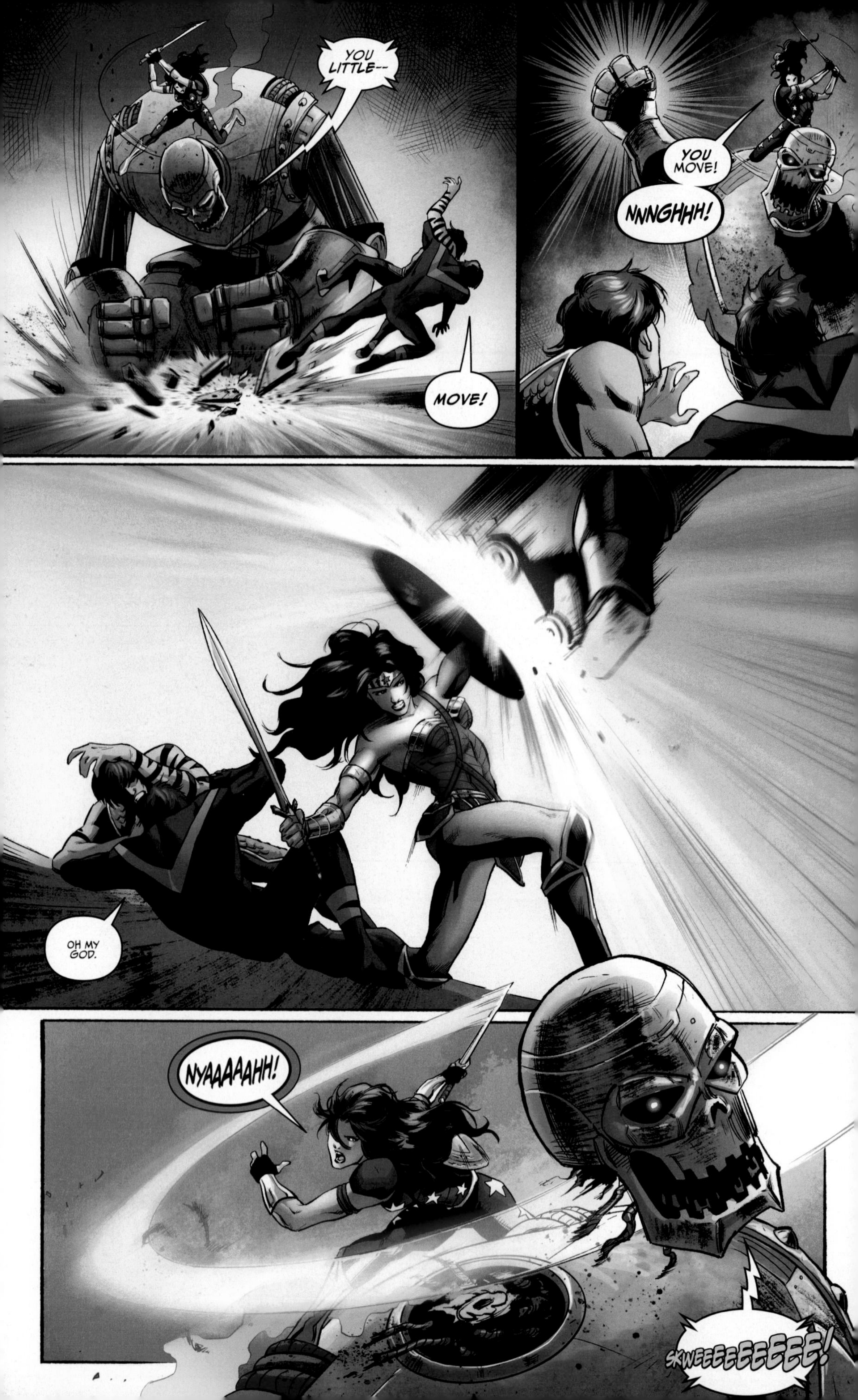
YOU LITTLE--
MOVE!
YOU MOVE!
NNNGHHH!
OH MY GOD.
NYAAAAAHH!
SKWEEEEEEEEEE!

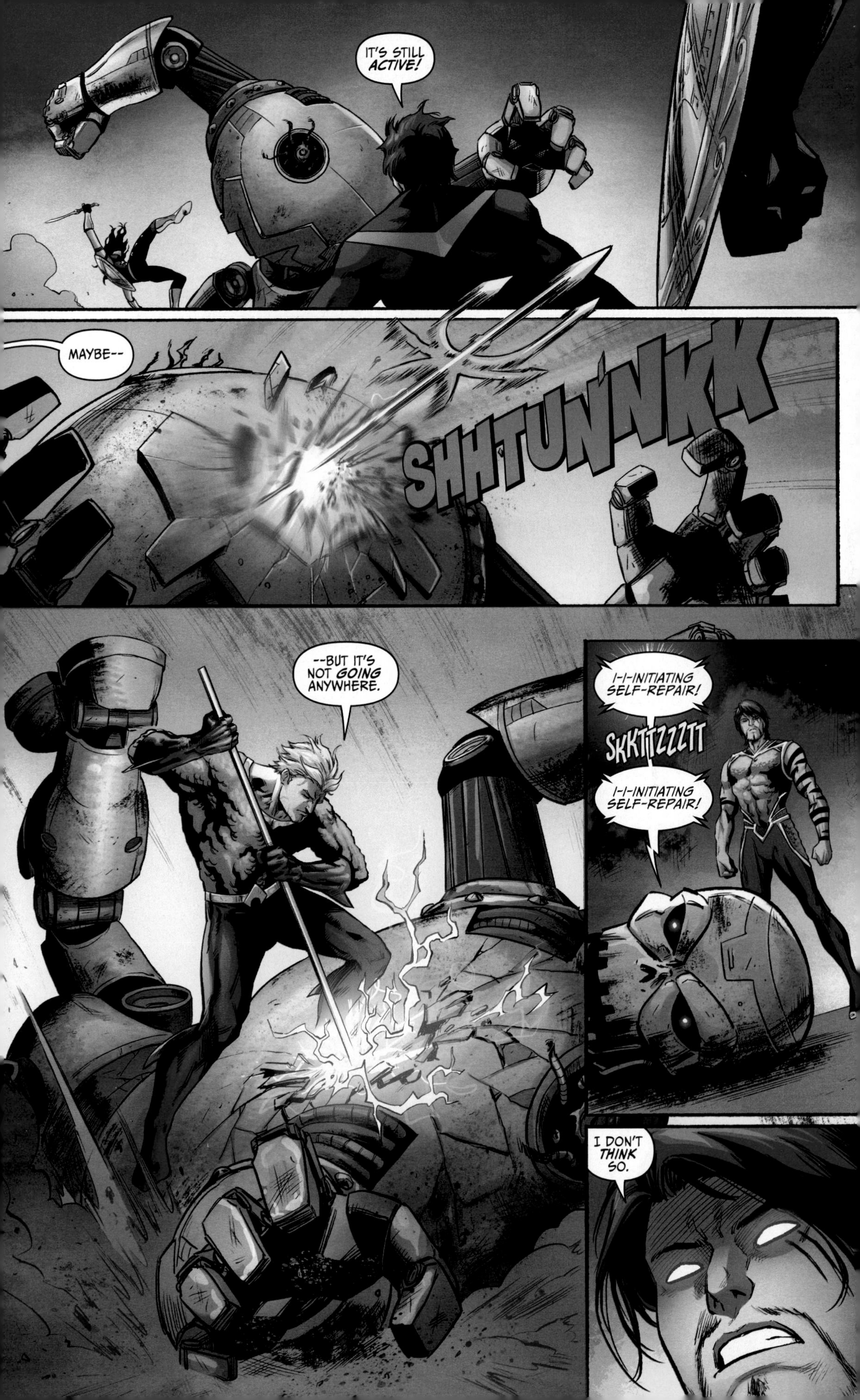
IT'S STILL ACTIVE!
MAYBE--
SHHTUNNKK
--BUT IT'S NOT GOING ANYWHERE.
I-I-INITIATING SELF-REPAIR!
SKKTTZZZTT
I-I-INITIATING SELF-REPAIR!
I DON'T THINK SO.

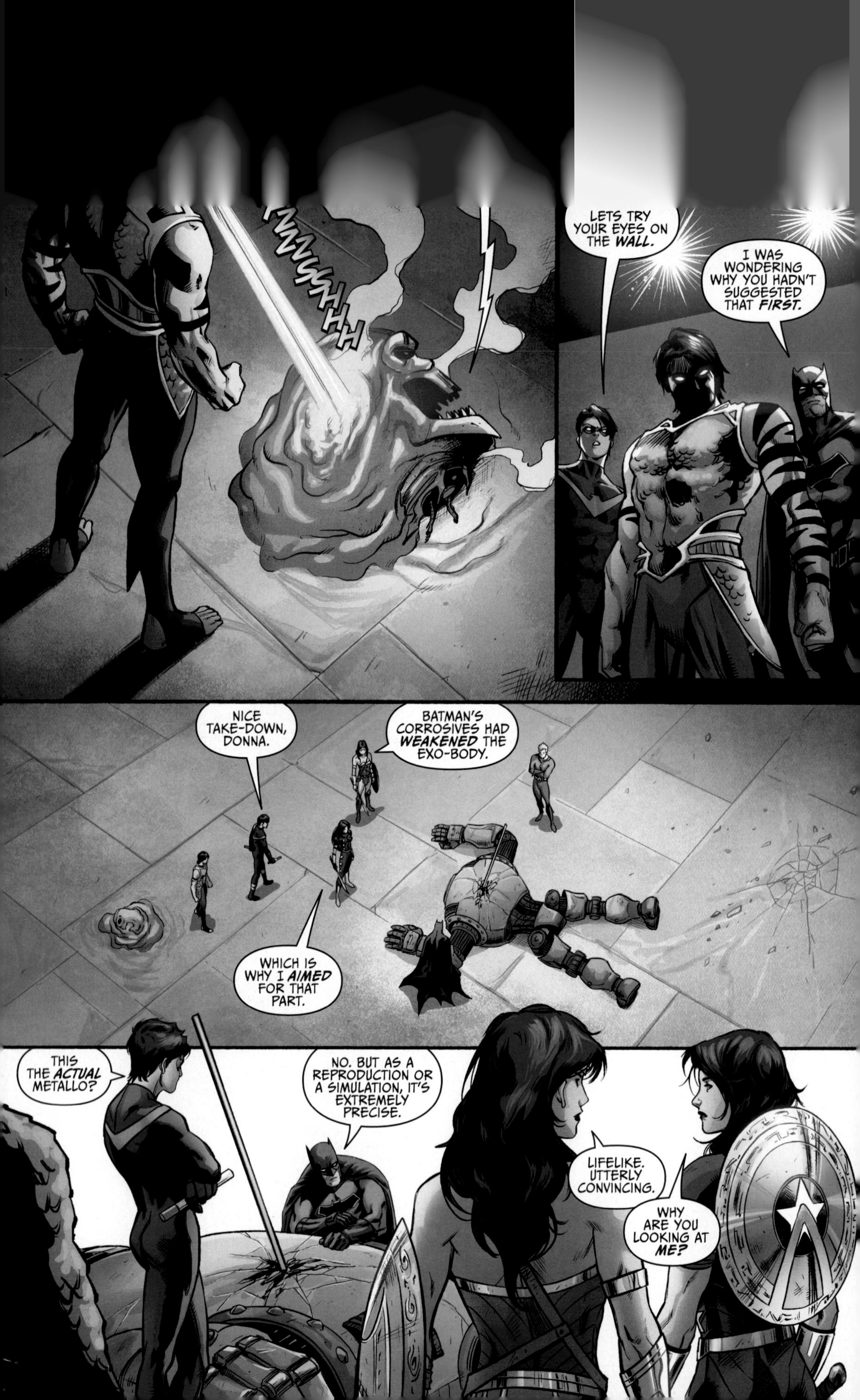
ZZZSSHHH
LETS TRY YOUR EYES ON THE **WALL.**
I WAS WONDERING WHY YOU HADN'T SUGGESTED THAT **FIRST.**
NICE TAKE-DOWN, DONNA.
BATMAN'S CORROSIVES HAD **WEAKENED** THE EXO-BODY.
WHICH IS WHY I **AIMED** FOR THAT PART.
THIS THE **ACTUAL** METALLO?
NO. BUT AS A REPRODUCTION OR A SIMULATION, IT'S EXTREMELY PRECISE.
LIFELIKE. UTTERLY CONVINCING.
WHY ARE YOU LOOKING AT **ME?**

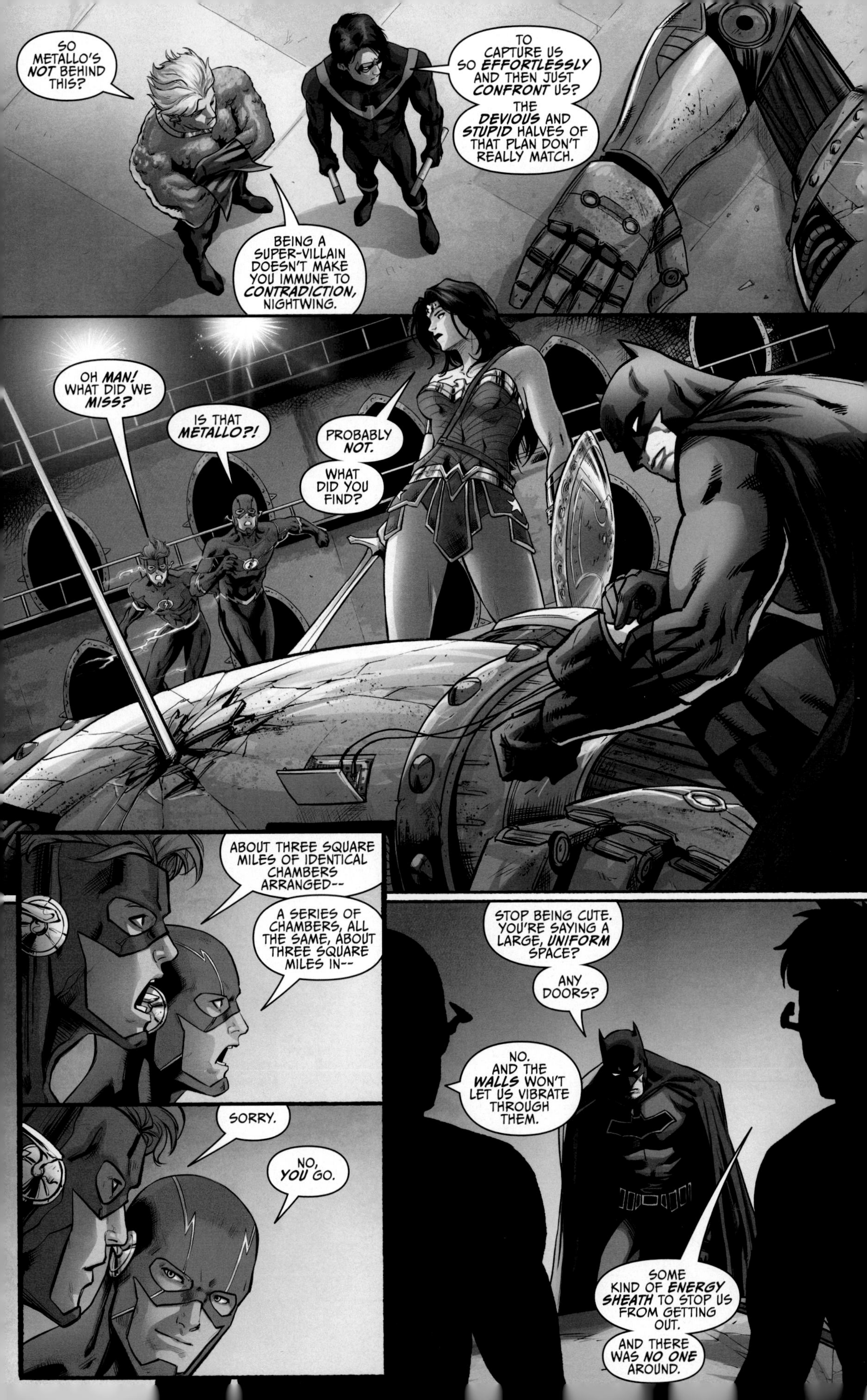
SO METALLO'S NOT BEHIND THIS?
TO CAPTURE US SO EFFORTLESSLY AND THEN JUST CONFRONT US?
THE DEVIOUS AND STUPID HALVES OF THAT PLAN DON'T REALLY MATCH.
BEING A SUPER-VILLAIN DOESN'T MAKE YOU IMMUNE TO CONTRADICTION, NIGHTWING.
OH MAN! WHAT DID WE MISS?
IS THAT METALLO?!
PROBABLY NOT.
WHAT DID YOU FIND?
ABOUT THREE SQUARE MILES OF IDENTICAL CHAMBERS ARRANGED--
A SERIES OF CHAMBERS, ALL THE SAME, ABOUT THREE SQUARE MILES IN--
SORRY.
NO, YOU GO.
STOP BEING CUTE. YOU'RE SAYING A LARGE, UNIFORM SPACE?
ANY DOORS?
NO. AND THE WALLS WON'T LET US VIBRATE THROUGH THEM.
SOME KIND OF ENERGY SHEATH TO STOP US FROM GETTING OUT.
AND THERE WAS NO ONE AROUND.

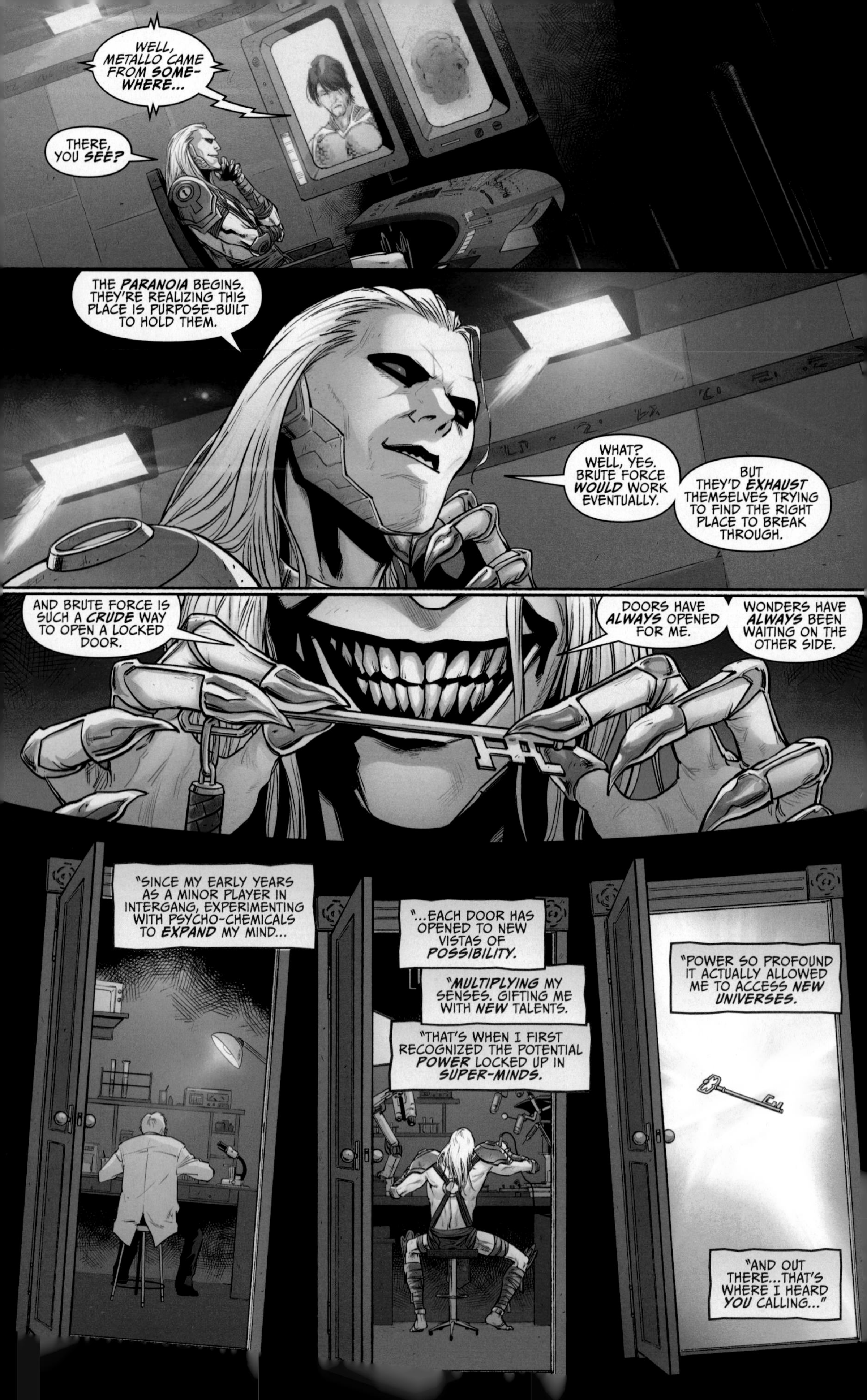
WELL, METALLO CAME FROM SOME-WHERE...
THERE, YOU SEE?
THE PARANOIA BEGINS. THEY'RE REALIZING THIS PLACE IS PURPOSE-BUILT TO HOLD THEM.
WHAT? WELL, YES. BRUTE FORCE WOULD WORK EVENTUALLY.
BUT THEY'D EXHAUST THEMSELVES TRYING TO FIND THE RIGHT PLACE TO BREAK THROUGH.
AND BRUTE FORCE IS SUCH A CRUDE WAY TO OPEN A LOCKED DOOR.
DOORS HAVE ALWAYS OPENED FOR ME.
WONDERS HAVE ALWAYS BEEN WAITING ON THE OTHER SIDE.
"SINCE MY EARLY YEARS AS A MINOR PLAYER IN INTERGANG, EXPERIMENTING WITH PSYCHO-CHEMICALS TO EXPAND MY MIND...
"...EACH DOOR HAS OPENED TO NEW VISTAS OF POSSIBILITY.
"MULTIPLYING MY SENSES. GIFTING ME WITH NEW TALENTS.
"THAT'S WHEN I FIRST RECOGNIZED THE POTENTIAL POWER LOCKED UP IN SUPER-MINDS.
"POWER SO PROFOUND IT ACTUALLY ALLOWED ME TO ACCESS NEW UNIVERSES.
"AND OUT THERE...THAT'S WHERE I HEARD YOU CALLING..."

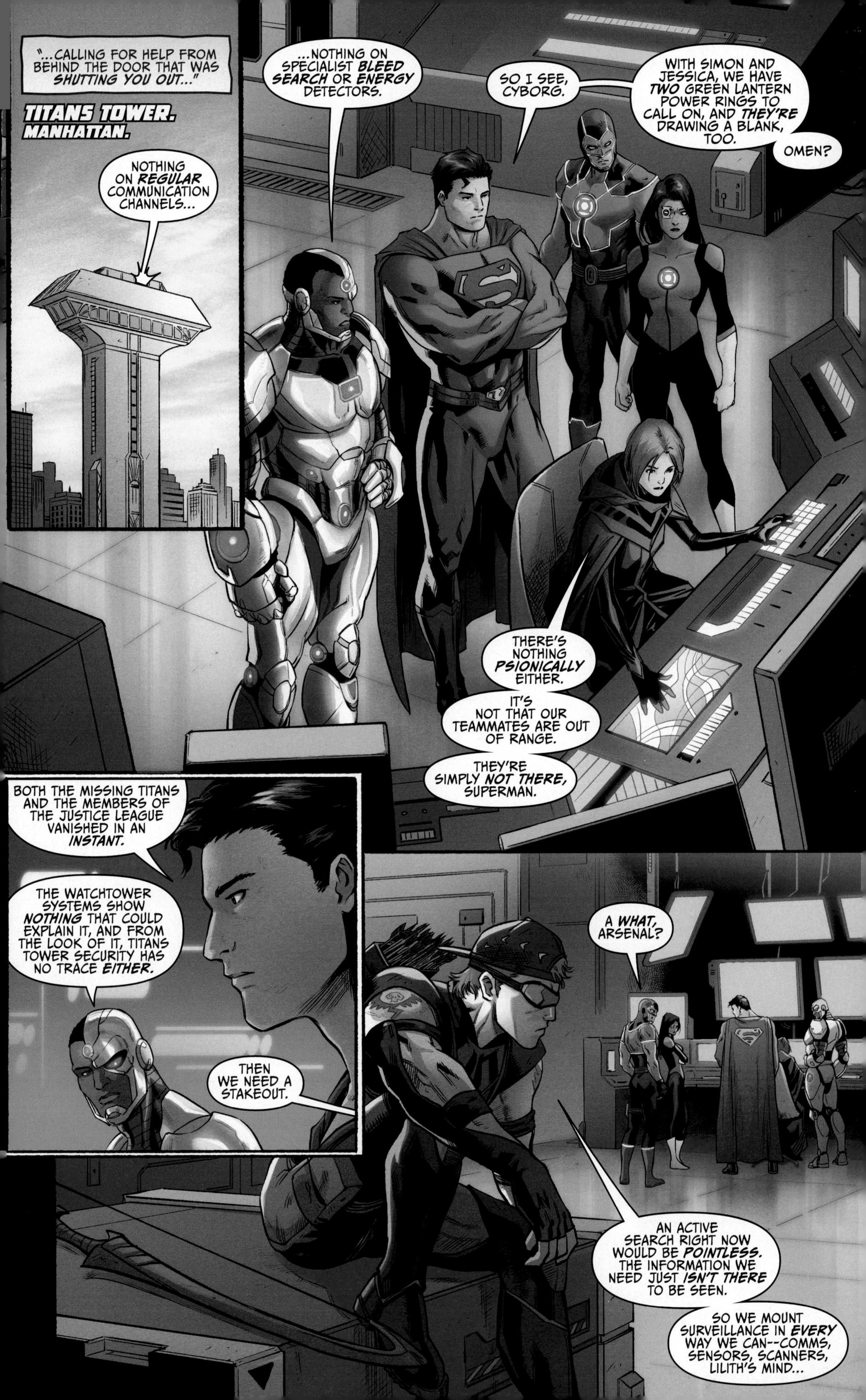
"...CALLING FOR HELP FROM BEHIND THE DOOR THAT WAS SHUTTING YOU OUT..."
TITANS TOWER. MANHATTAN.
NOTHING ON REGULAR COMMUNICATION CHANNELS...
...NOTHING ON SPECIALIST BLEED SEARCH OR ENERGY DETECTORS.
SO I SEE, CYBORG.
WITH SIMON AND JESSICA, WE HAVE TWO GREEN LANTERN POWER RINGS TO CALL ON, AND THEY'RE DRAWING A BLANK, TOO.
OMEN?
THERE'S NOTHING PSIONICALLY EITHER.
IT'S NOT THAT OUR TEAMMATES ARE OUT OF RANGE.
THEY'RE SIMPLY NOT THERE, SUPERMAN.
BOTH THE MISSING TITANS AND THE MEMBERS OF THE JUSTICE LEAGUE VANISHED IN AN INSTANT.
THE WATCHTOWER SYSTEMS SHOW NOTHING THAT COULD EXPLAIN IT, AND FROM THE LOOK OF IT, TITANS TOWER SECURITY HAS NO TRACE EITHER.
THEN WE NEED A STAKEOUT.
A WHAT, ARSENAL?
AN ACTIVE SEARCH RIGHT NOW WOULD BE POINTLESS. THE INFORMATION WE NEED JUST ISN'T THERE TO BE SEEN.
SO WE MOUNT SURVEILLANCE IN EVERY WAY WE CAN--COMMS, SENSORS, SCANNERS, LILITH'S MIND...

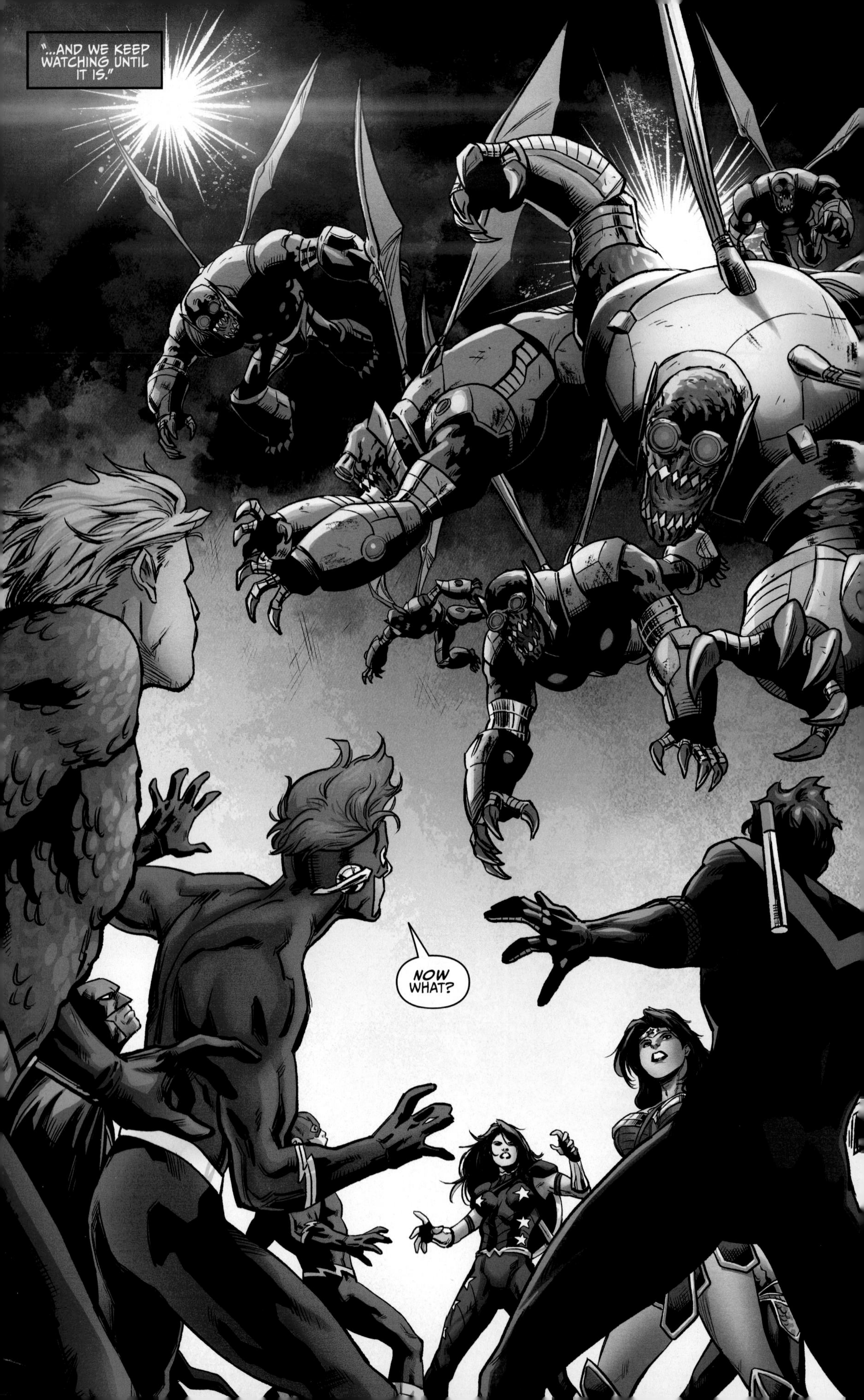
"...AND WE KEEP WATCHING UNTIL IT IS."
NOW WHAT?

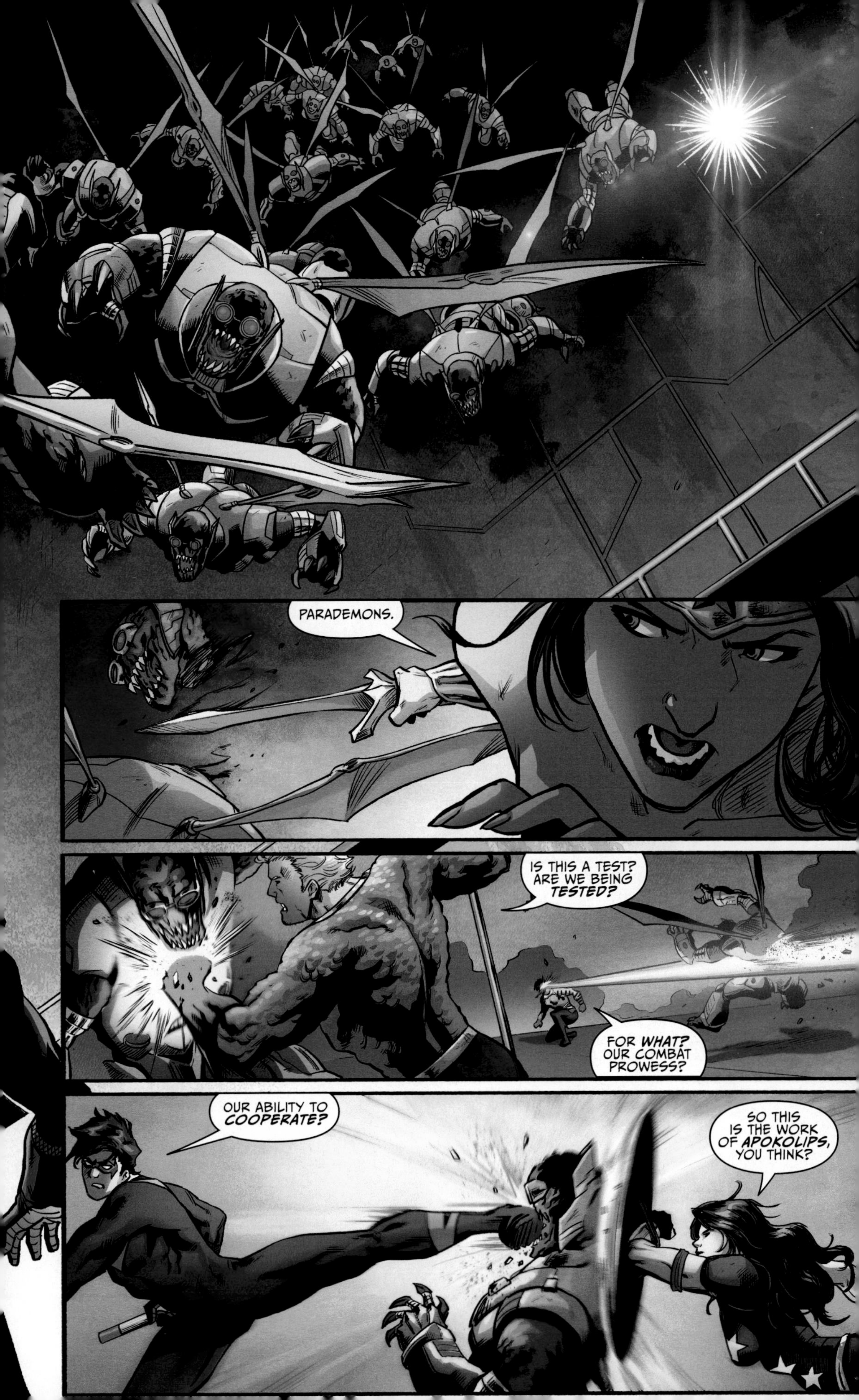
PARADEMONS.
IS THIS A TEST? ARE WE BEING TESTED?
FOR WHAT? OUR COMBAT PROWESS?
OUR ABILITY TO COOPERATE?
SO THIS IS THE WORK OF APOKOLIPS, YOU THINK?

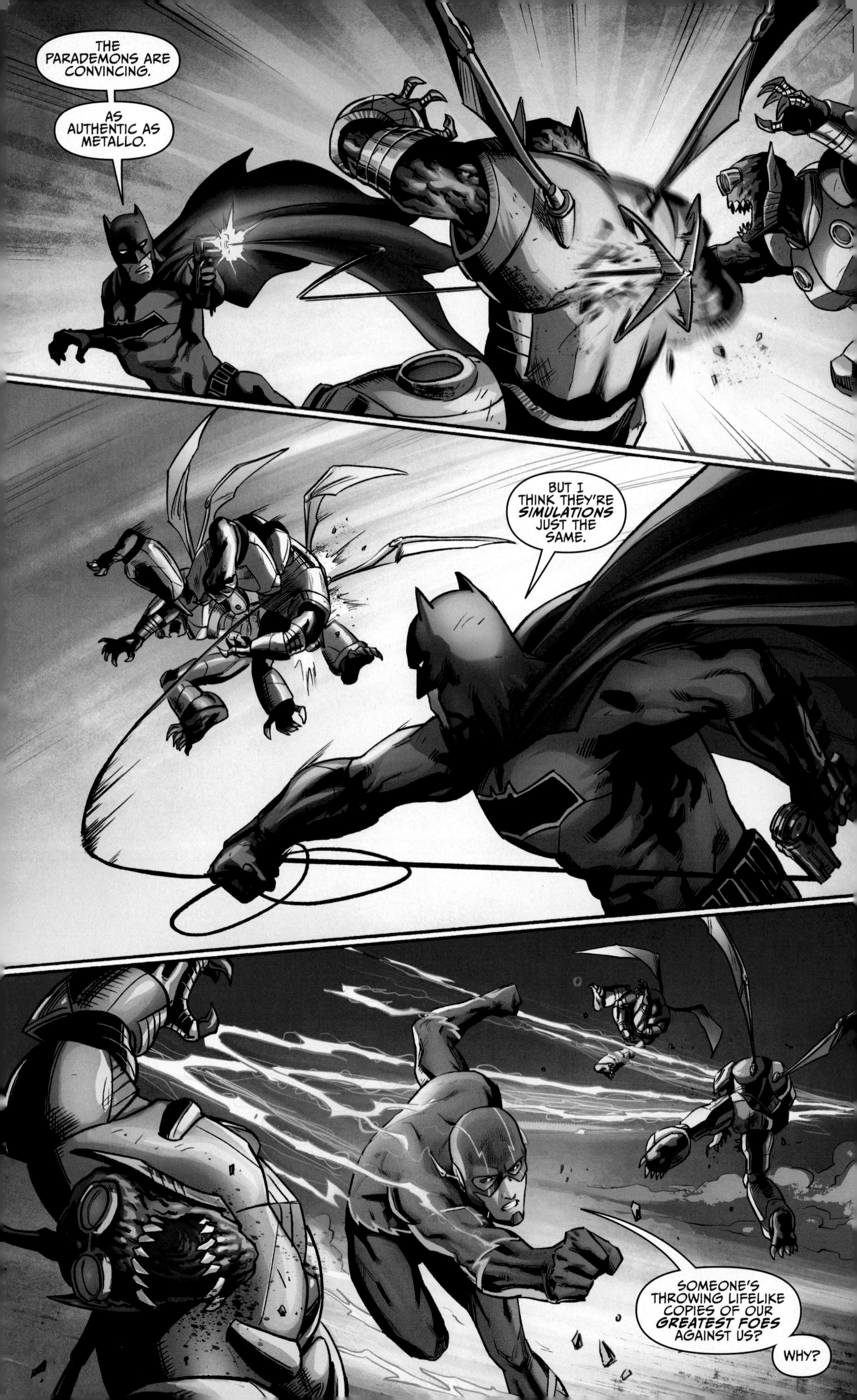
THE PARADEMONS ARE CONVINCING.
AS AUTHENTIC AS METALLO.
BUT I THINK THEY'RE *SIMULATIONS* JUST THE SAME.
SOMEONE'S THROWING LIFELIKE COPIES OF OUR *GREATEST FOES* AGAINST US?
WHY?

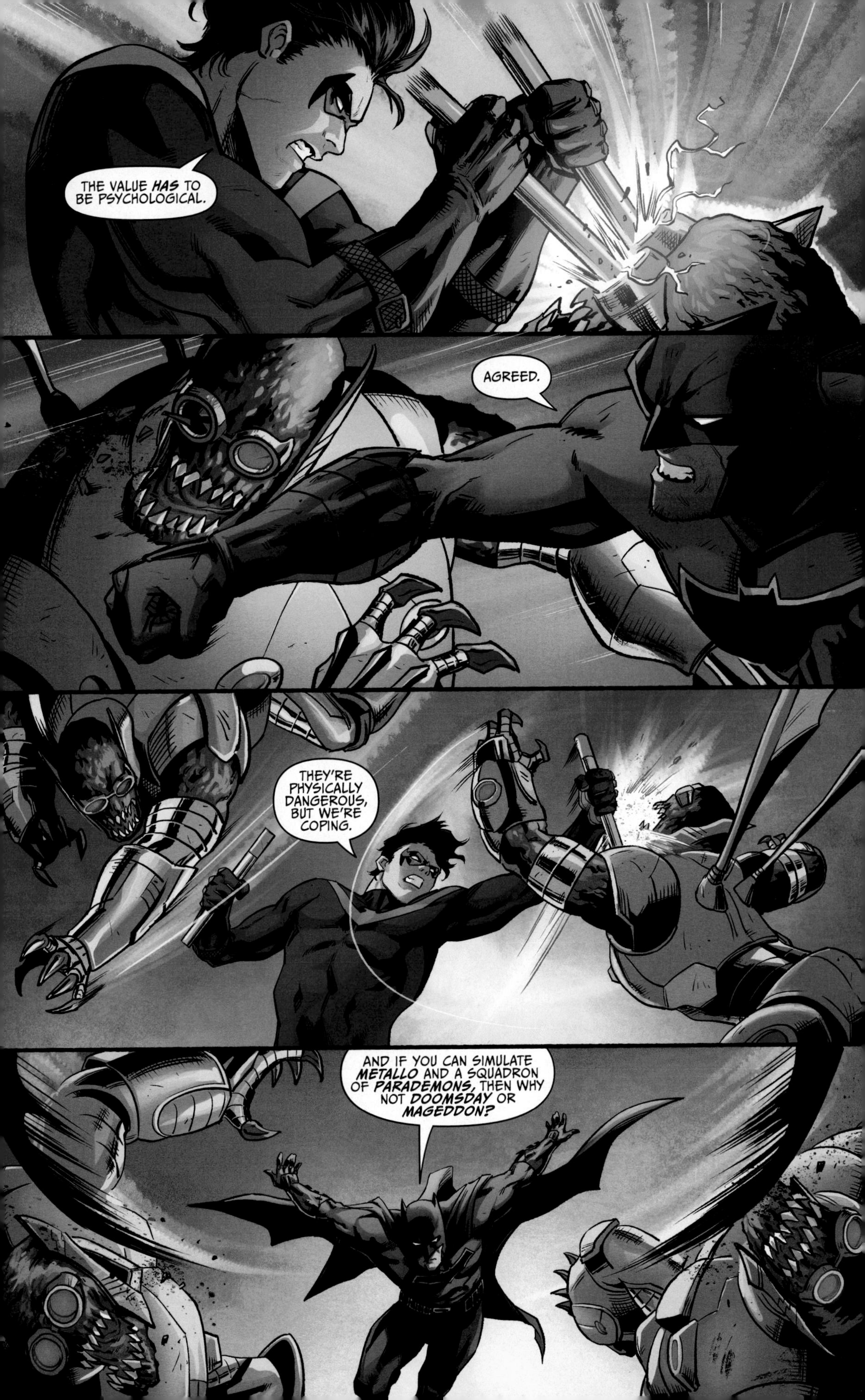
THE VALUE HAS TO BE PSYCHOLOGICAL.
AGREED.
THEY'RE PHYSICALLY DANGEROUS, BUT WE'RE COPING.
AND IF YOU CAN SIMULATE METALLO AND A SQUADRON OF PARADEMONS, THEN WHY NOT DOOMSDAY OR MAGEDDON?

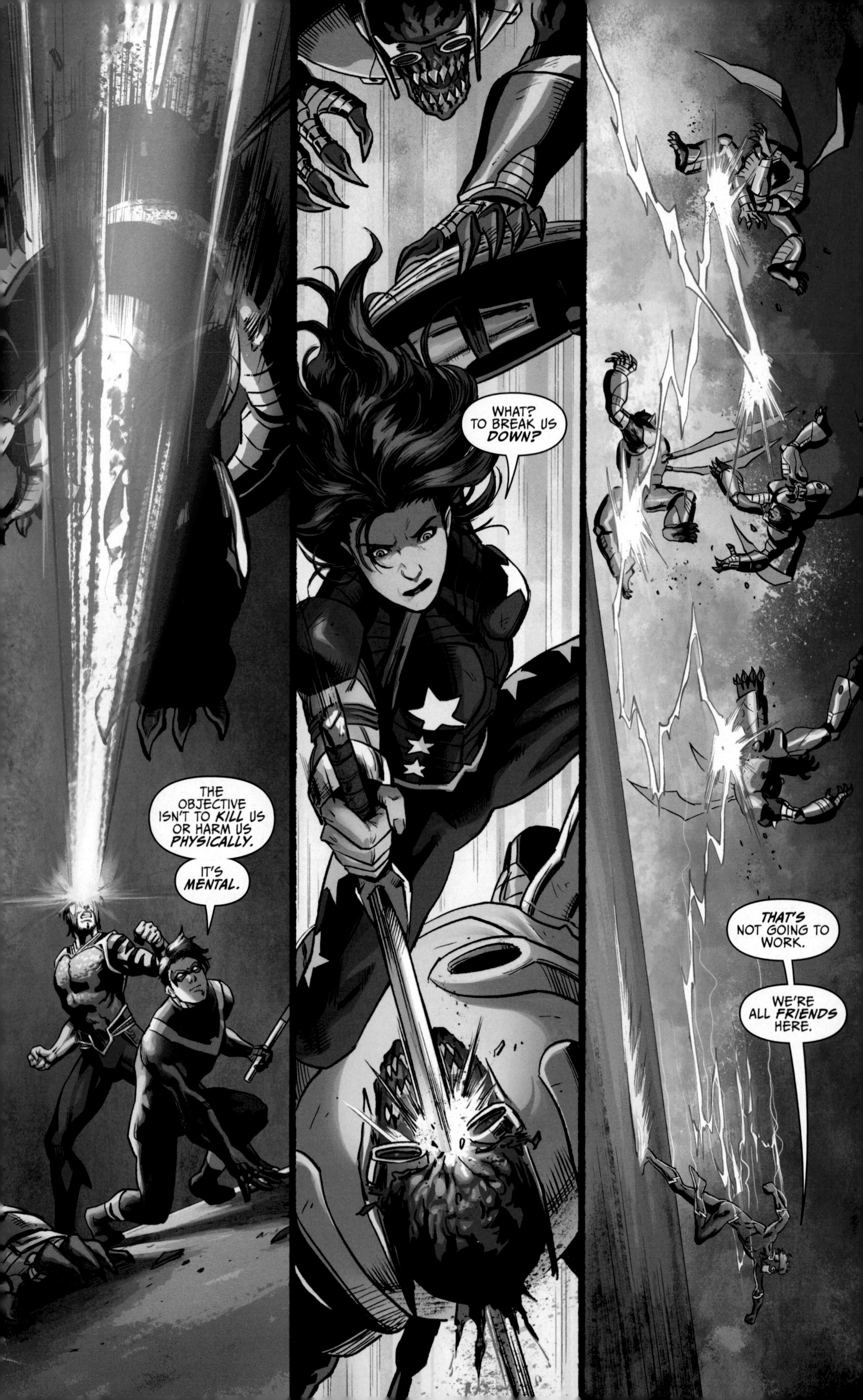
THE OBJECTIVE ISN'T TO KILL US OR HARM US PHYSICALLY.
IT'S MENTAL.
WHAT? TO BREAK US DOWN?
THAT'S NOT GOING TO WORK.
WE'RE ALL FRIENDS HERE.

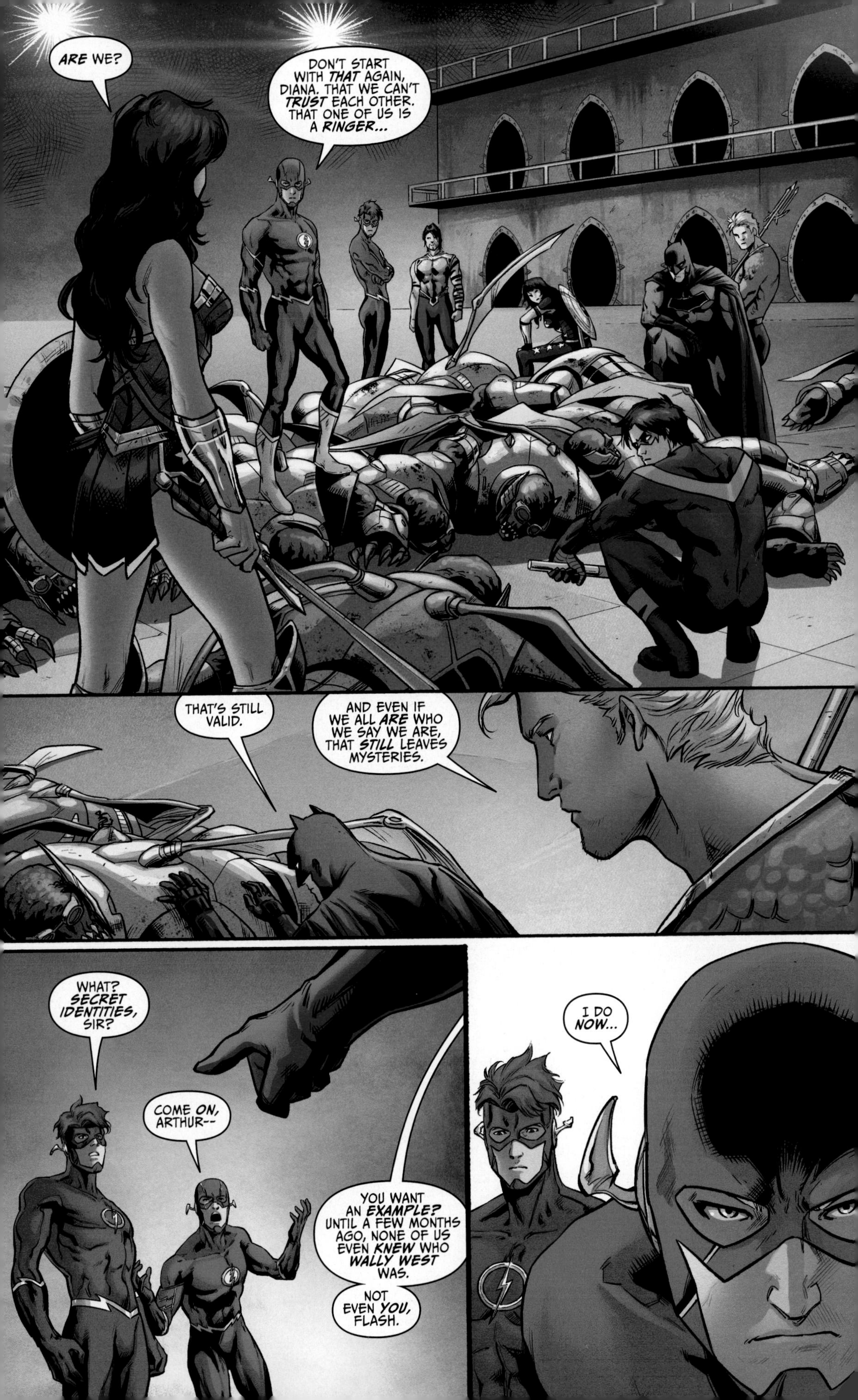
ARE WE?
DON'T START WITH THAT AGAIN, DIANA. THAT WE CAN'T TRUST EACH OTHER. THAT ONE OF US IS A RINGER...
THAT'S STILL VALID.
AND EVEN IF WE ALL ARE WHO WE SAY WE ARE, THAT STILL LEAVES MYSTERIES.
WHAT? SECRET IDENTITIES, SIR?
COME ON, ARTHUR--
YOU WANT AN EXAMPLE? UNTIL A FEW MONTHS AGO, NONE OF US EVEN KNEW WHO WALLY WEST WAS.
NOT EVEN YOU, FLASH.
I DO NOW...

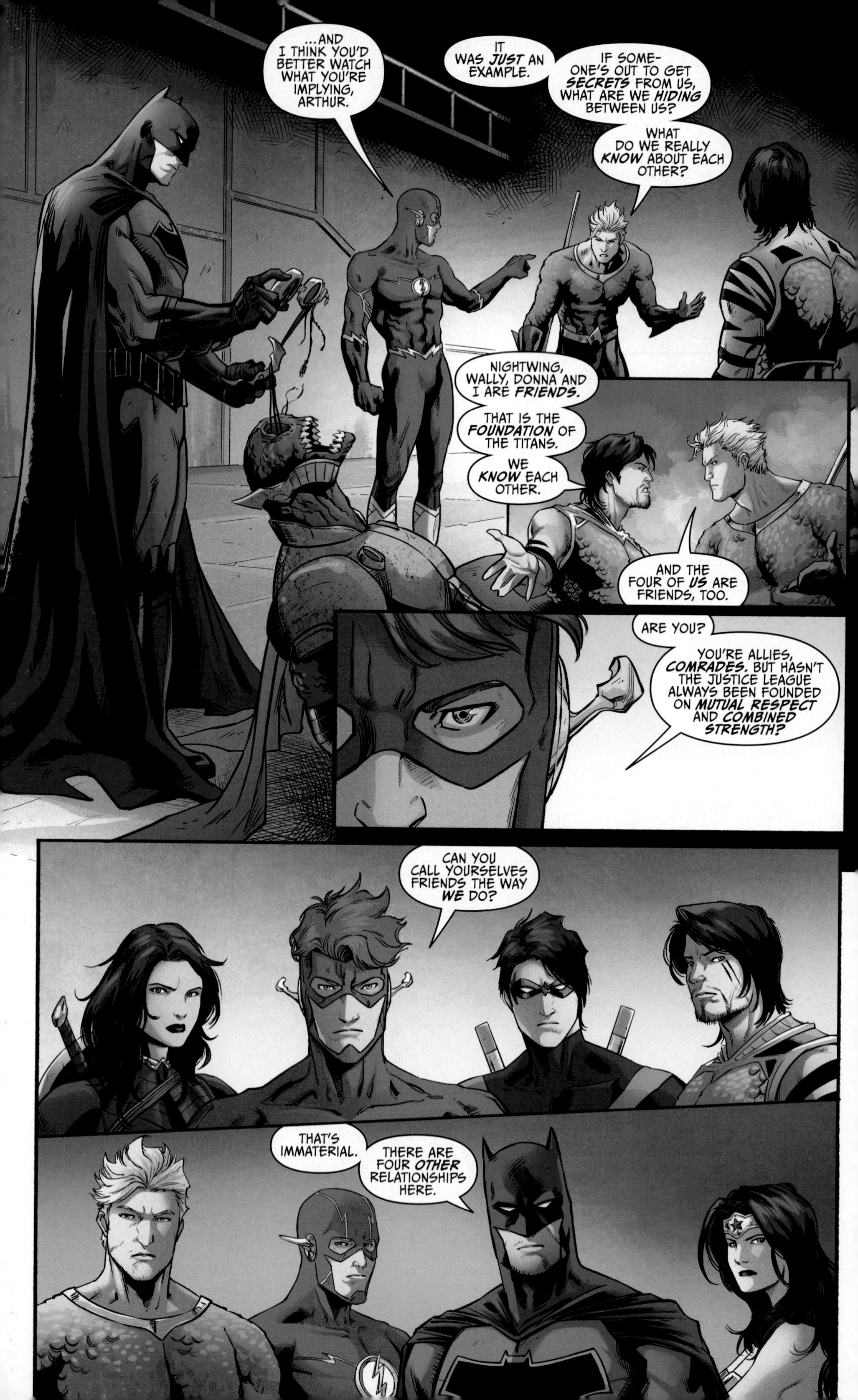

...AND I THINK YOU'D BETTER WATCH WHAT YOU'RE IMPLYING, ARTHUR.
IT WAS JUST AN EXAMPLE.
IF SOME-ONE'S OUT TO GET SECRETS FROM US, WHAT ARE WE HIDING BETWEEN US?
WHAT DO WE REALLY KNOW ABOUT EACH OTHER?
NIGHTWING, WALLY, DONNA AND I ARE FRIENDS.
THAT IS THE FOUNDATION OF THE TITANS.
WE KNOW EACH OTHER.
AND THE FOUR OF US ARE FRIENDS, TOO.
ARE YOU?
YOU'RE ALLIES, COMRADES. BUT HASN'T THE JUSTICE LEAGUE ALWAYS BEEN FOUNDED ON MUTUAL RESPECT AND COMBINED STRENGTH?
CAN YOU CALL YOURSELVES FRIENDS THE WAY WE DO?
THAT'S IMMATERIAL.
THERE ARE FOUR OTHER RELATIONSHIPS HERE.

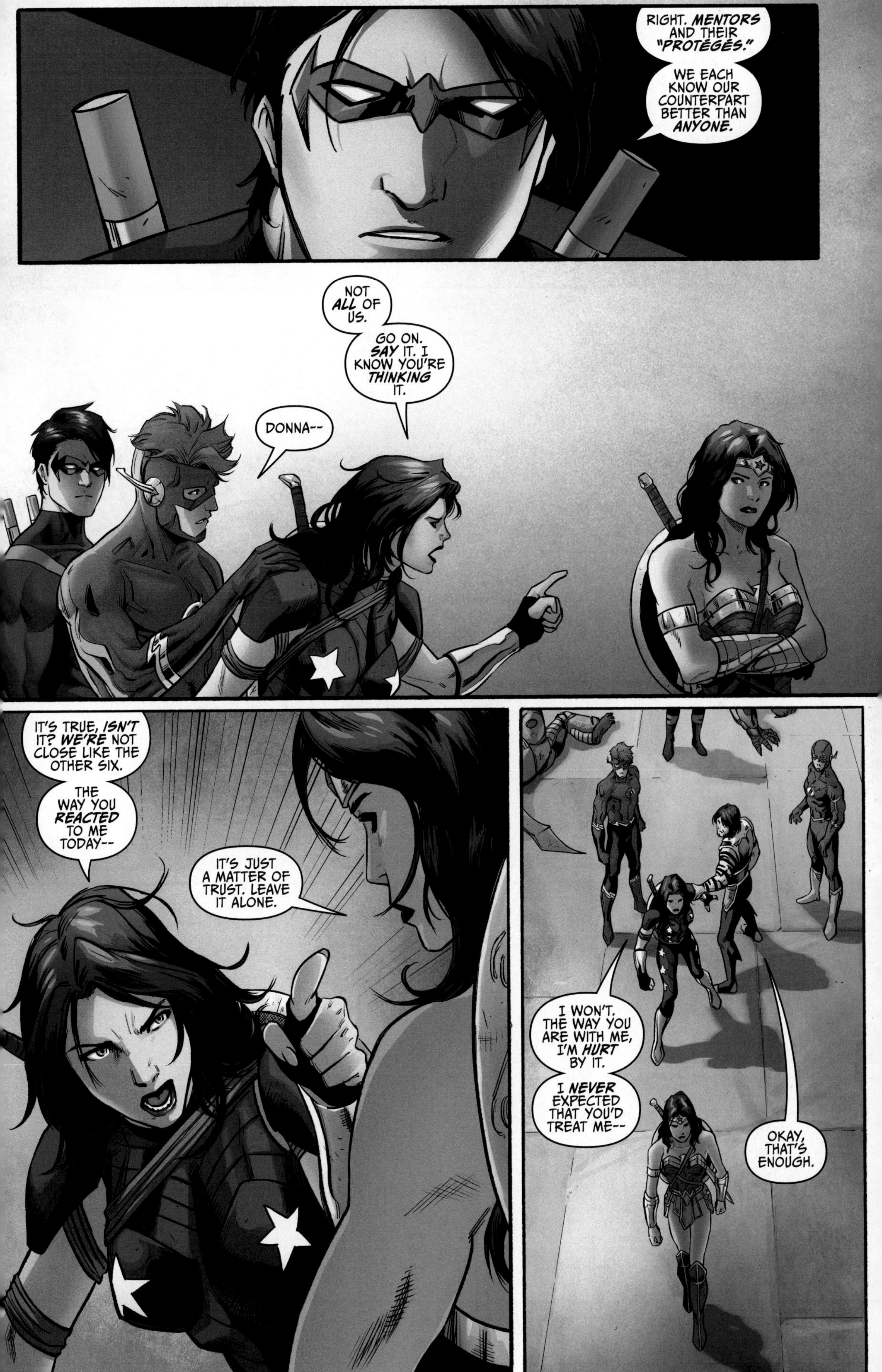
RIGHT. MENTORS AND THEIR "PROTÉGÉS."
WE EACH KNOW OUR COUNTERPART BETTER THAN ANYONE.
NOT ALL OF US.
GO ON. SAY IT. I KNOW YOU'RE THINKING IT.
DONNA--
IT'S TRUE, ISN'T IT? WE'RE NOT CLOSE LIKE THE OTHER SIX.
THE WAY YOU REACTED TO ME TODAY--
IT'S JUST A MATTER OF TRUST. LEAVE IT ALONE.
I WON'T. THE WAY YOU ARE WITH ME, I'M HURT BY IT.
I NEVER EXPECTED THAT YOU'D TREAT ME--
OKAY, THAT'S ENOUGH.

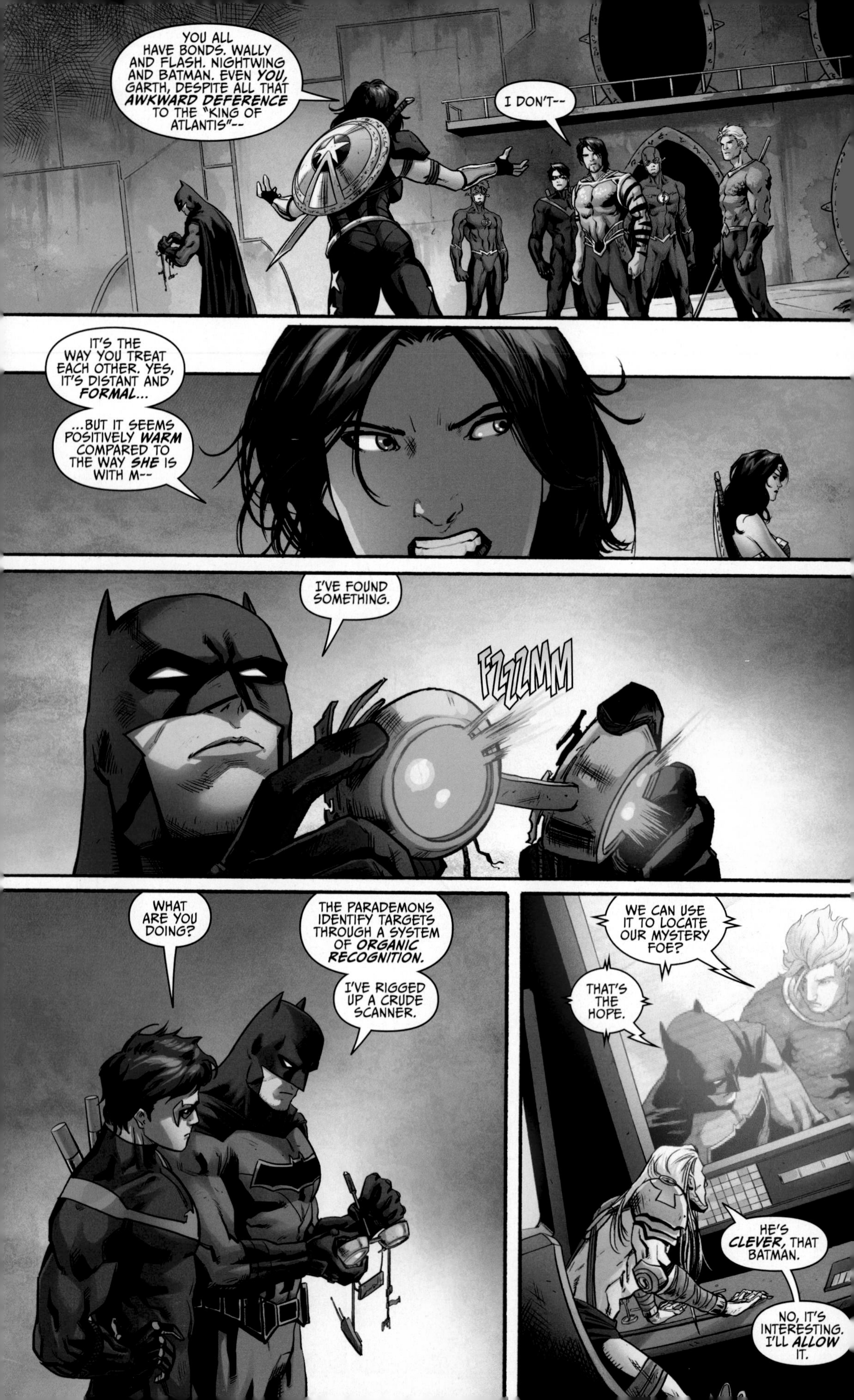
YOU ALL HAVE BONDS. WALLY AND FLASH. NIGHTWING AND BATMAN. EVEN YOU, GARTH, DESPITE ALL THAT AWKWARD DEFERENCE TO THE "KING OF ATLANTIS"--
I DON'T--
IT'S THE WAY YOU TREAT EACH OTHER. YES, IT'S DISTANT AND FORMAL...
...BUT IT SEEMS POSITIVELY WARM COMPARED TO THE WAY SHE IS WITH M--
I'VE FOUND SOMETHING.
FZZZMM
WHAT ARE YOU DOING?
THE PARADEMONS IDENTIFY TARGETS THROUGH A SYSTEM OF ORGANIC RECOGNITION.
I'VE RIGGED UP A CRUDE SCANNER.
WE CAN USE IT TO LOCATE OUR MYSTERY FOE?
THAT'S THE HOPE.
HE'S CLEVER, THAT BATMAN.
NO, IT'S INTERESTING. I'LL ALLOW IT.

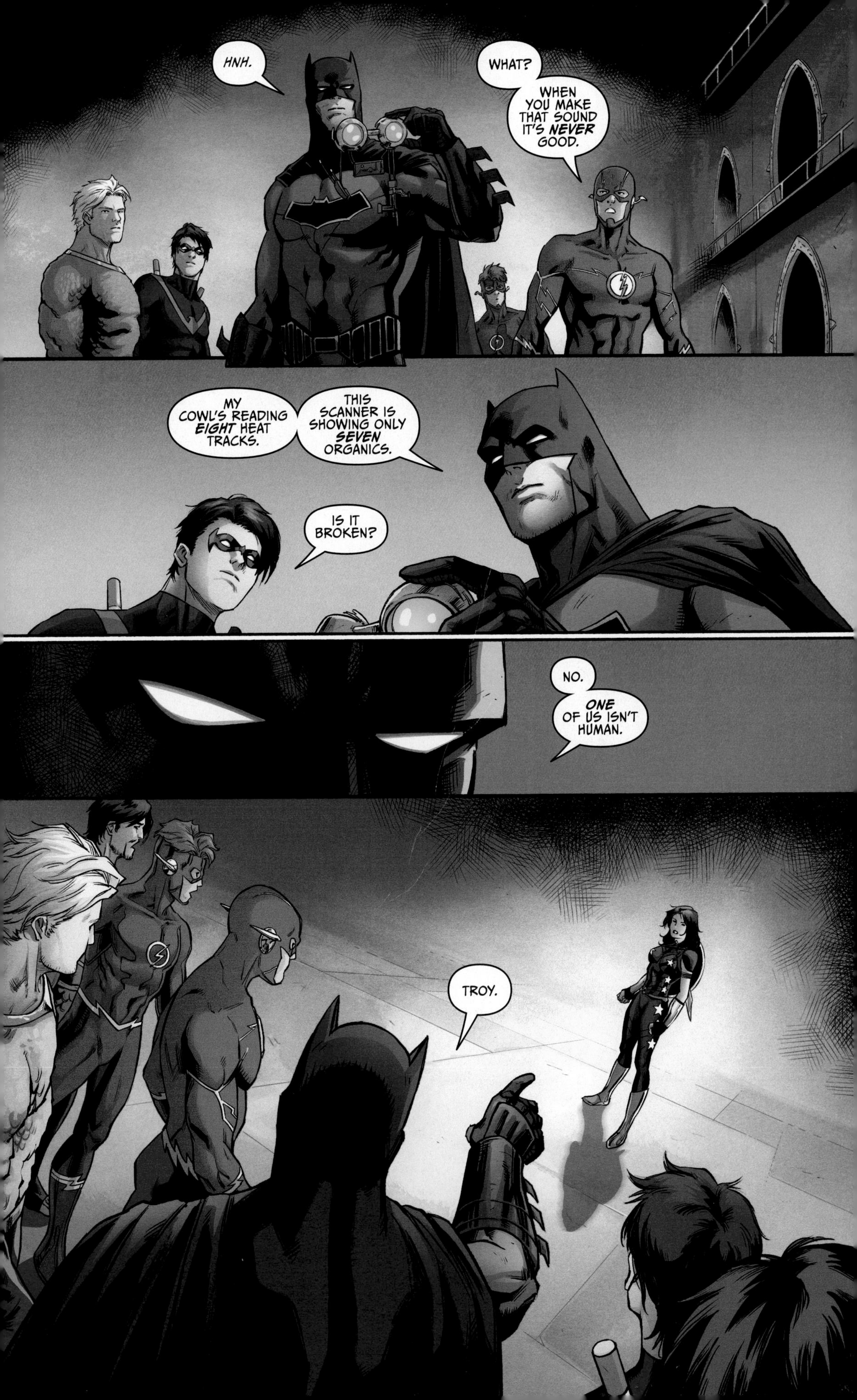
HNH.
WHAT?
WHEN YOU MAKE THAT SOUND IT'S NEVER GOOD.
MY COWL'S READING EIGHT HEAT TRACKS.
THIS SCANNER IS SHOWING ONLY SEVEN ORGANICS.
IS IT BROKEN?
NO.
ONE OF US ISN'T HUMAN.
TROY.

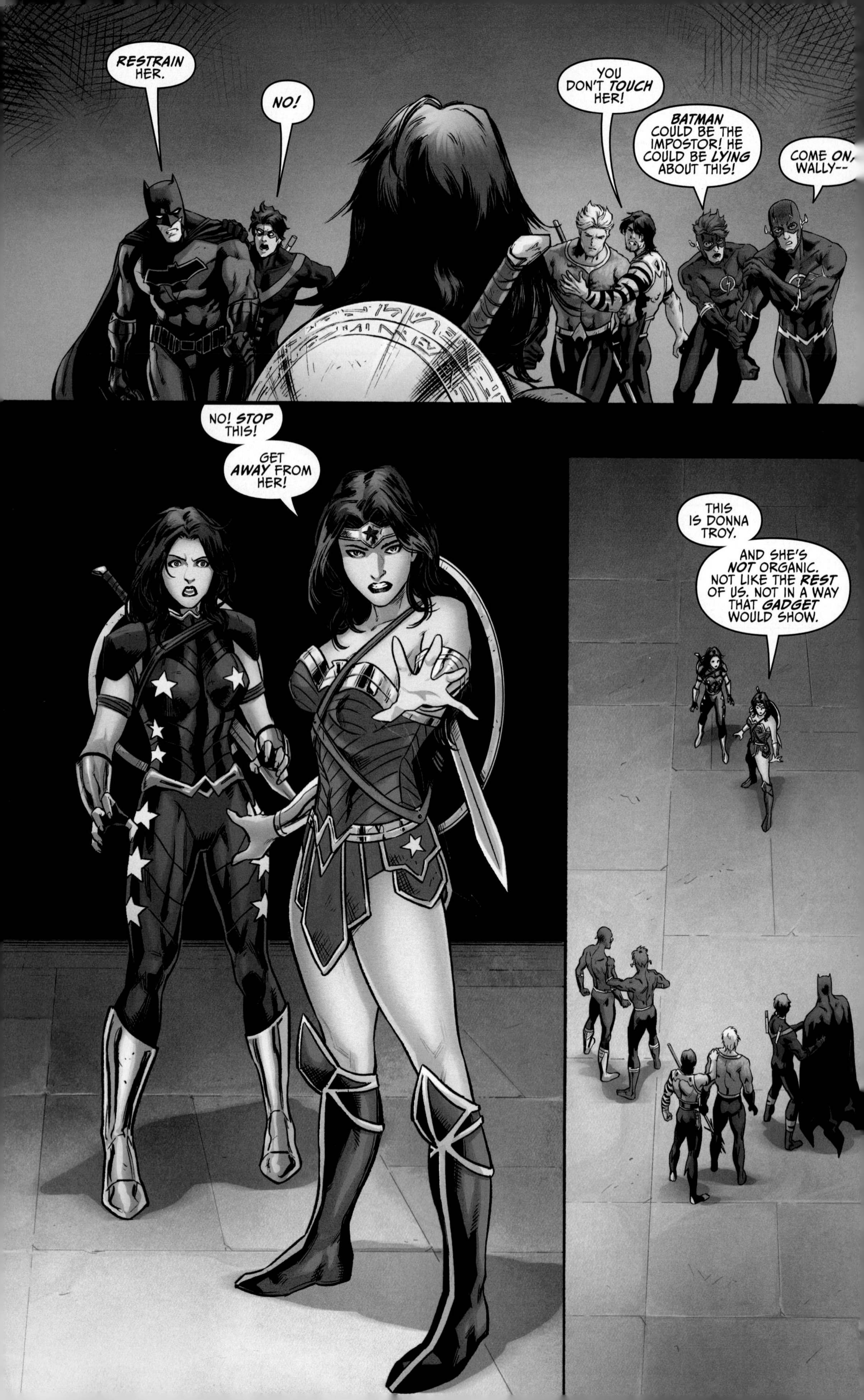
RESTRAIN HER.
NO!
YOU DON'T TOUCH HER!
BATMAN COULD BE THE IMPOSTOR! HE COULD BE LYING ABOUT THIS!
COME ON, WALLY--
NO! STOP THIS!
GET AWAY FROM HER!
THIS IS DONNA TROY.
AND SHE'S NOT ORGANIC. NOT LIKE THE REST OF US. NOT IN A WAY THAT GADGET WOULD SHOW.

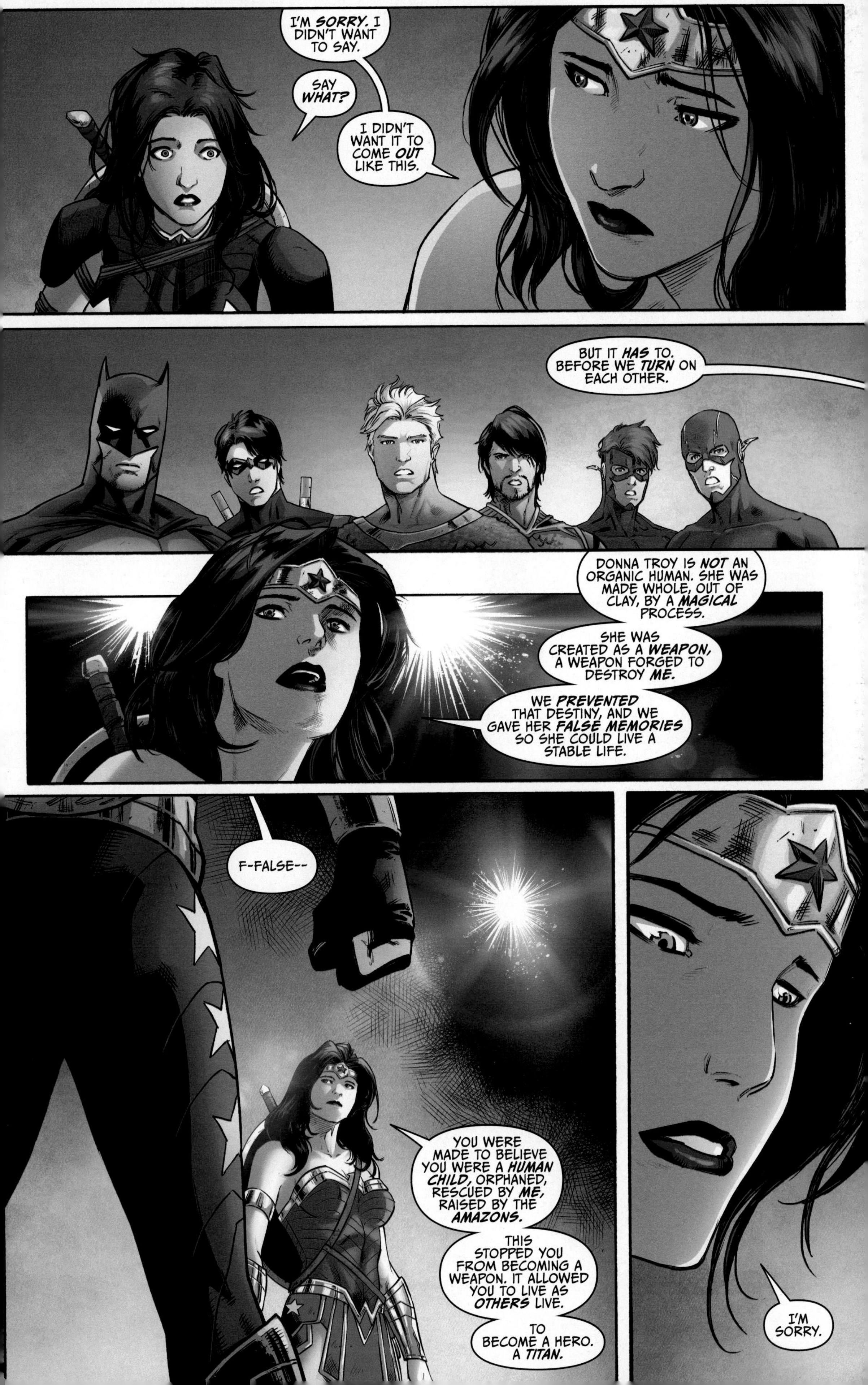
I'M SORRY. I DIDN'T WANT TO SAY.
SAY WHAT?
I DIDN'T WANT IT TO COME OUT LIKE THIS.
BUT IT HAS TO. BEFORE WE TURN ON EACH OTHER.
DONNA TROY IS NOT AN ORGANIC HUMAN. SHE WAS MADE WHOLE, OUT OF CLAY, BY A MAGICAL PROCESS.
SHE WAS CREATED AS A WEAPON, A WEAPON FORGED TO DESTROY ME.
WE PREVENTED THAT DESTINY, AND WE GAVE HER FALSE MEMORIES SO SHE COULD LIVE A STABLE LIFE.
F-FALSE--
YOU WERE MADE TO BELIEVE YOU WERE A HUMAN CHILD, ORPHANED, RESCUED BY ME, RAISED BY THE AMAZONS.
THIS STOPPED YOU FROM BECOMING A WEAPON. IT ALLOWED YOU TO LIVE AS OTHERS LIVE.
TO BECOME A HERO. A TITAN.
I'M SORRY.

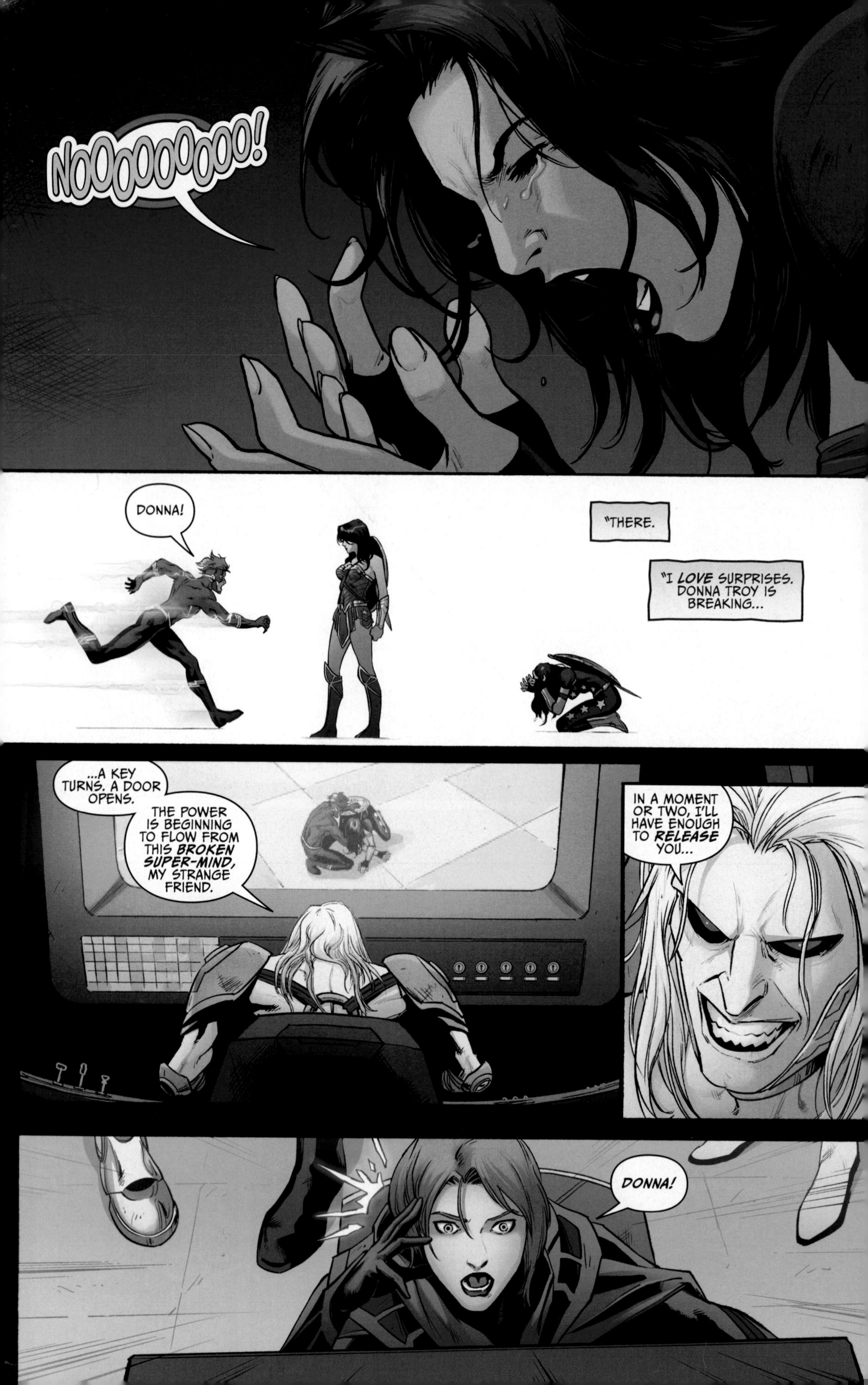
NOOOOOOOOO!
DONNA!
"THERE.
"I LOVE SURPRISES. DONNA TROY IS BREAKING...
...A KEY TURNS. A DOOR OPENS.
THE POWER IS BEGINNING TO FLOW FROM THIS BROKEN SUPER-MIND, MY STRANGE FRIEND.
IN A MOMENT OR TWO, I'LL HAVE ENOUGH TO RELEASE YOU...
DONNA!

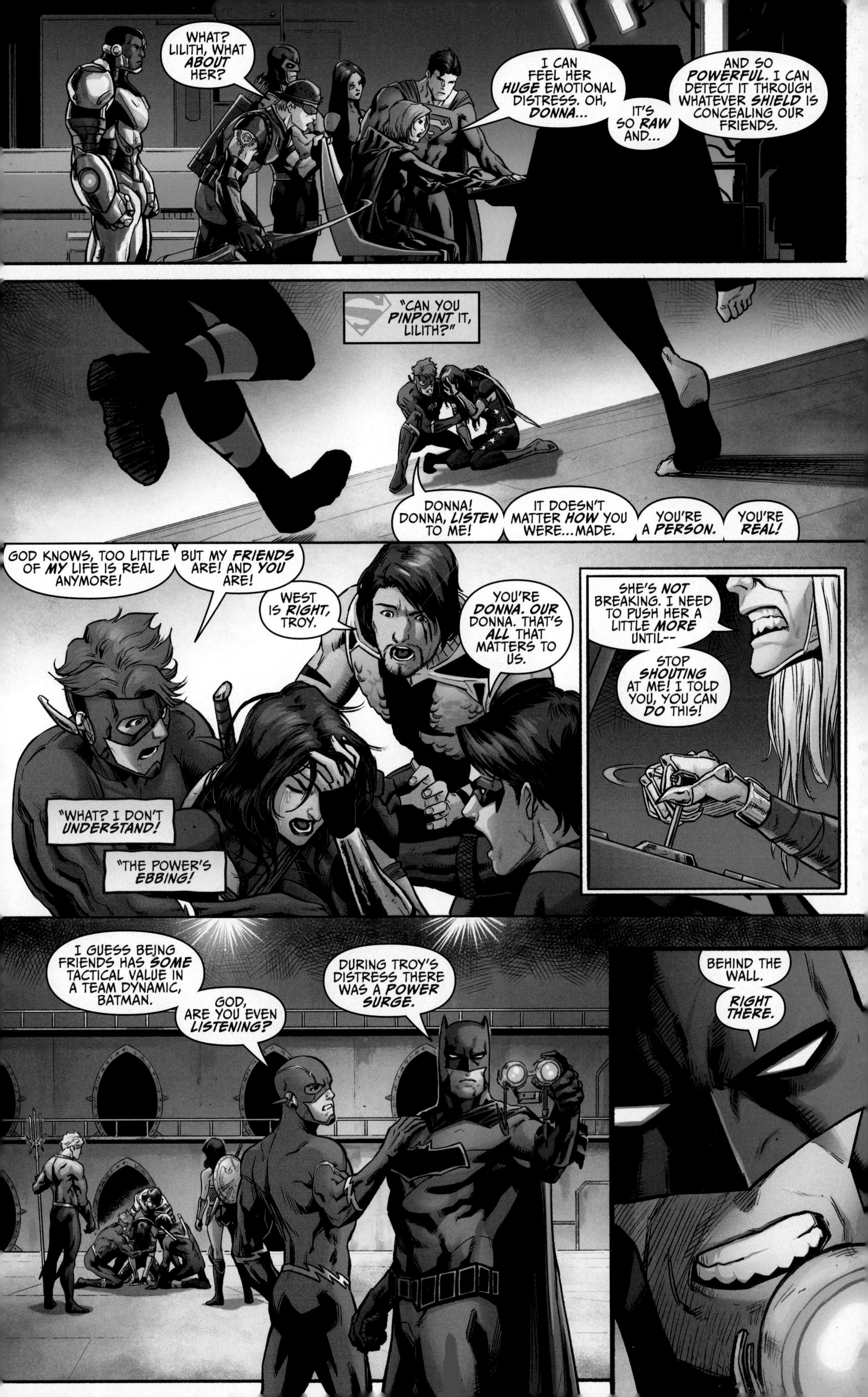
WHAT? LILITH, WHAT ABOUT HER?
I CAN FEEL HER HUGE EMOTIONAL DISTRESS. OH, DONNA...
IT'S SO RAW AND...
AND SO POWERFUL. I CAN DETECT IT THROUGH WHATEVER SHIELD IS CONCEALING OUR FRIENDS.
"CAN YOU PINPOINT IT, LILITH?"
DONNA! DONNA, LISTEN TO ME!
IT DOESN'T MATTER HOW YOU WERE...MADE.
YOU'RE A PERSON.
YOU'RE REAL!
GOD KNOWS, TOO LITTLE OF MY LIFE IS REAL ANYMORE!
BUT MY FRIENDS ARE! AND YOU ARE!
WEST IS RIGHT, TROY.
YOU'RE DONNA. OUR DONNA. THAT'S ALL THAT MATTERS TO US.
"WHAT? I DON'T UNDERSTAND!
"THE POWER'S EBBING!
SHE'S NOT BREAKING. I NEED TO PUSH HER A LITTLE MORE UNTIL--
STOP SHOUTING AT ME! I TOLD YOU, YOU CAN DO THIS!
I GUESS BEING FRIENDS HAS SOME TACTICAL VALUE IN A TEAM DYNAMIC, BATMAN.
GOD, ARE YOU EVEN LISTENING?
DURING TROY'S DISTRESS THERE WAS A POWER SURGE.
BEHIND THE WALL.
RIGHT THERE.

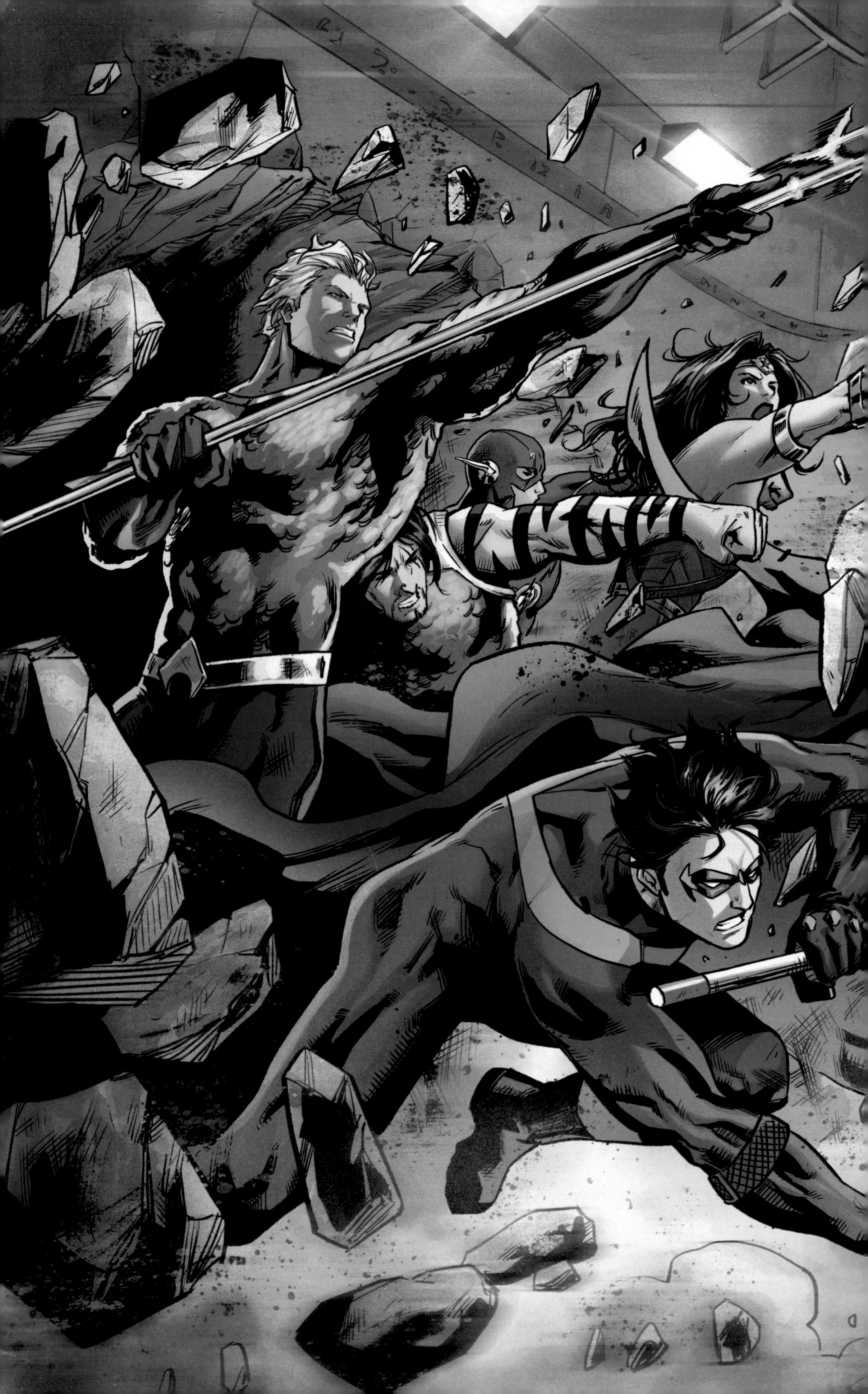

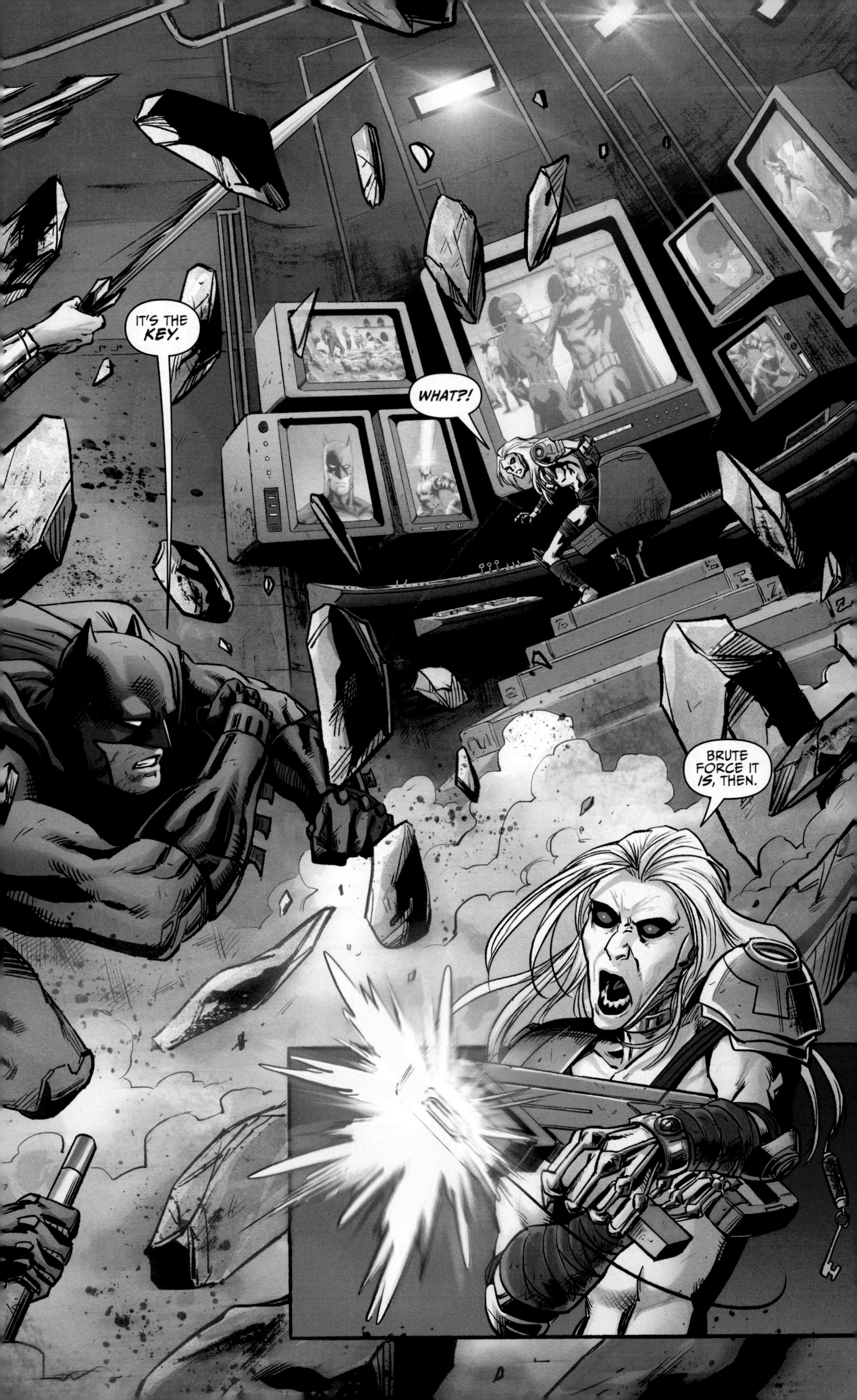
IT'S THE KEY.
WHAT?!
BRUTE FORCE IT IS, THEN.

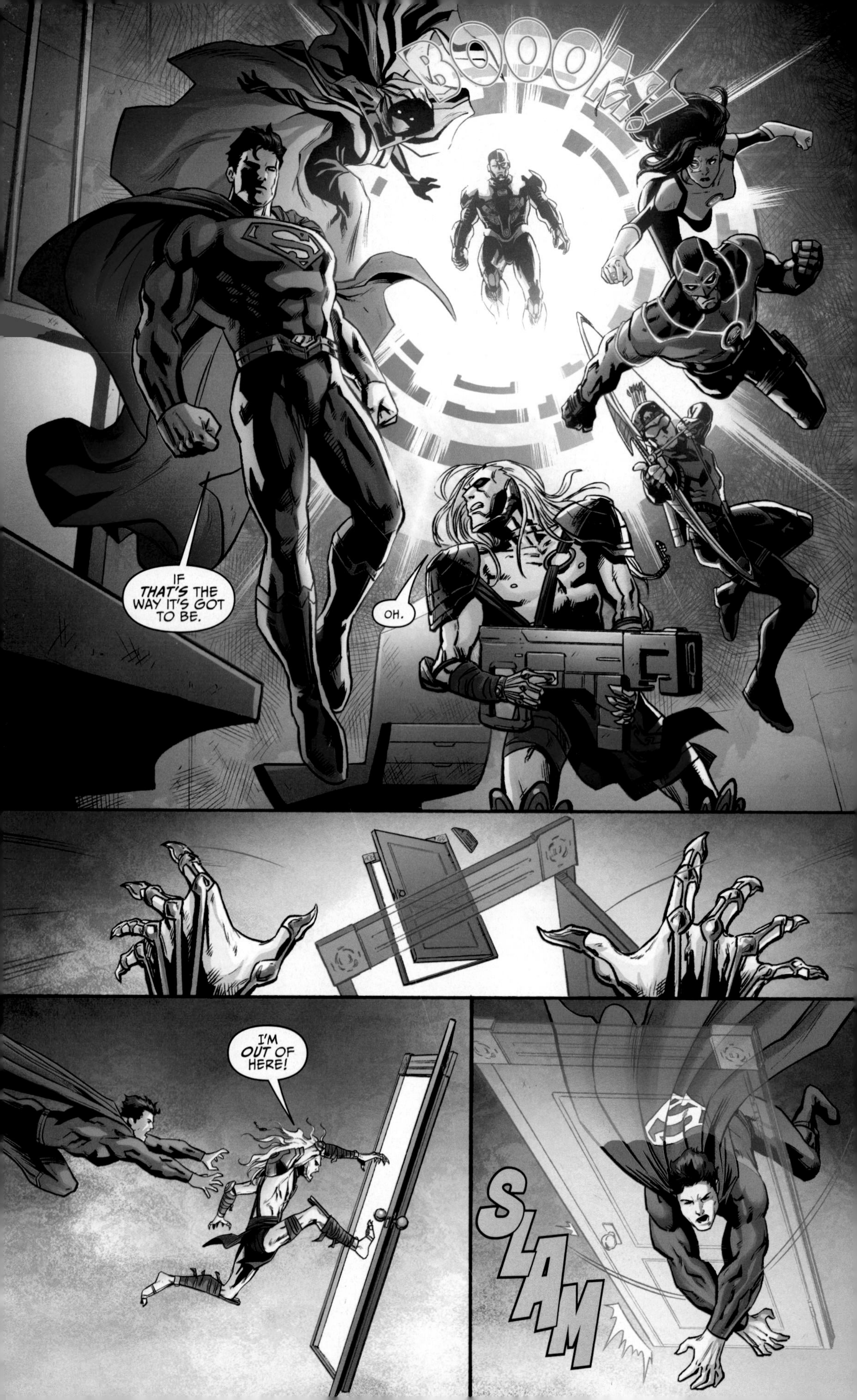
BOOOOM!
IF THAT'S THE WAY IT'S GOT TO BE.
OH.
I'M OUT OF HERE!
SLAM

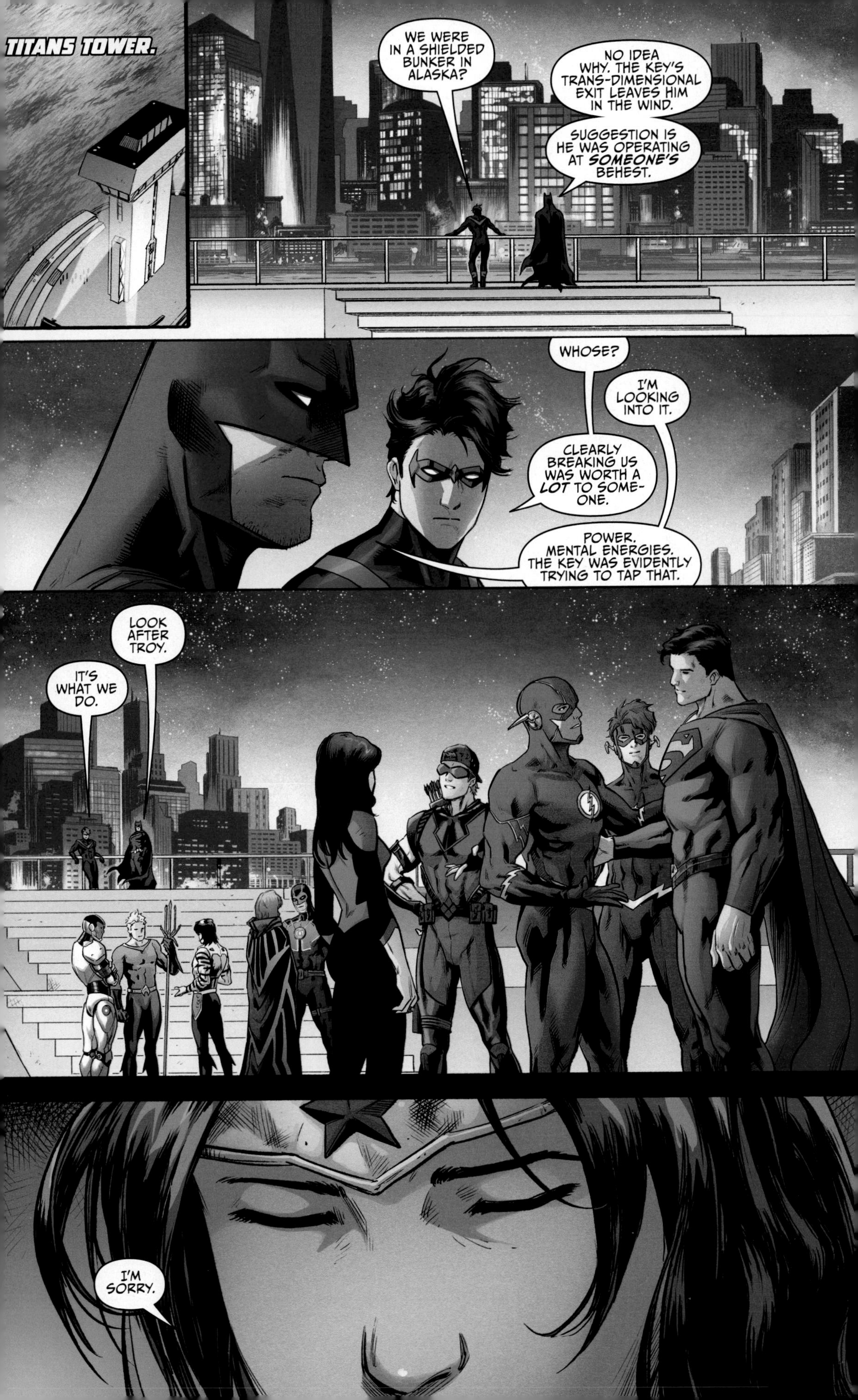
TITANS TOWER.
WE WERE IN A SHIELDED BUNKER IN ALASKA?
NO IDEA WHY. THE KEY'S TRANS-DIMENSIONAL EXIT LEAVES HIM IN THE WIND.
SUGGESTION IS HE WAS OPERATING AT SOMEONE'S BEHEST.
WHOSE?
I'M LOOKING INTO IT.
CLEARLY BREAKING US WAS WORTH A LOT TO SOME-ONE.
POWER. MENTAL ENERGIES. THE KEY WAS EVIDENTLY TRYING TO TAP THAT.
LOOK AFTER TROY.
IT'S WHAT WE DO.
I'M SORRY.

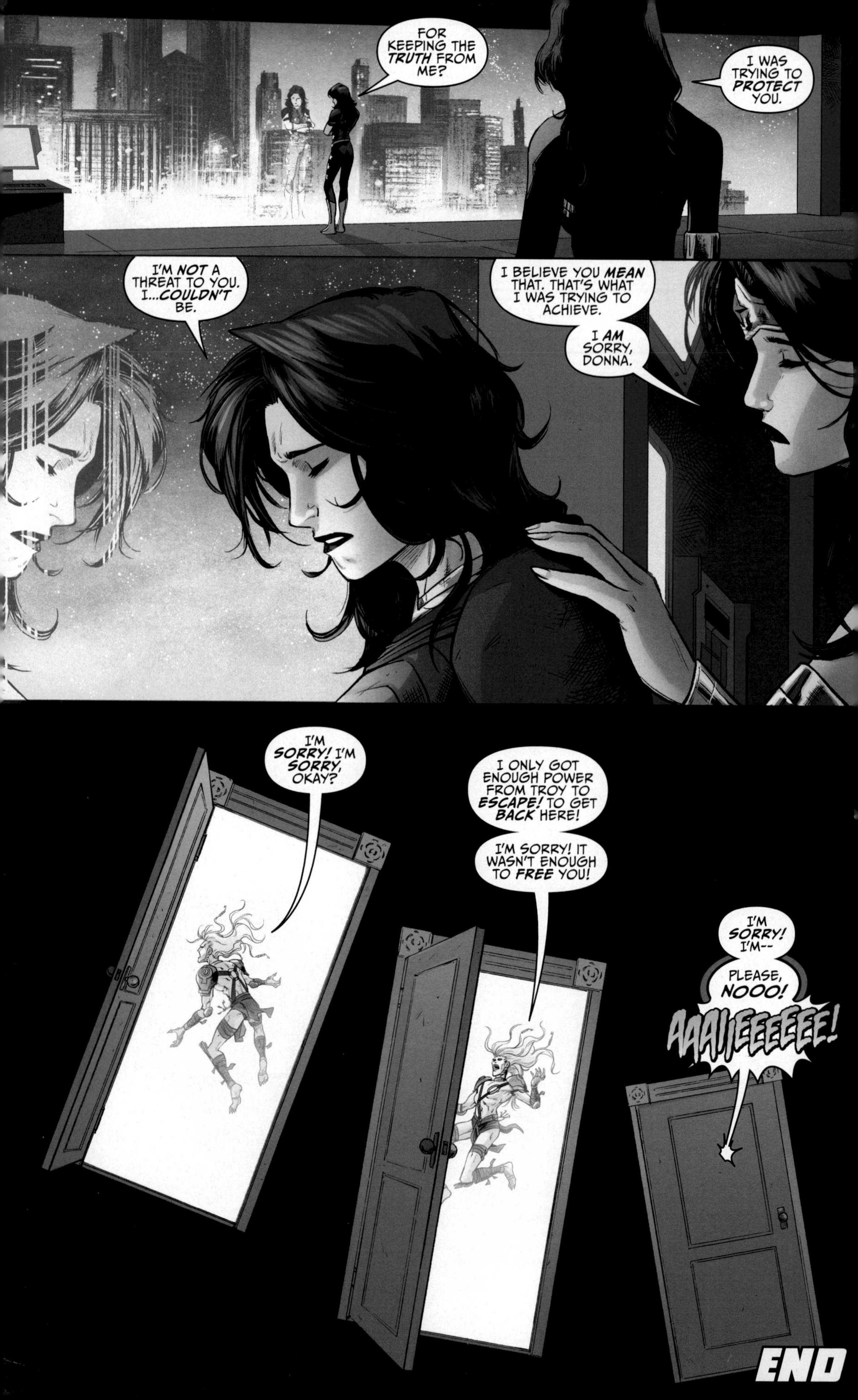
FOR KEEPING THE TRUTH FROM ME?
I WAS TRYING TO PROTECT YOU.
I'M NOT A THREAT TO YOU. I...COULDN'T BE.
I BELIEVE YOU MEAN THAT. THAT'S WHAT I WAS TRYING TO ACHIEVE.
I AM SORRY, DONNA.
I'M SORRY! I'M SORRY, OKAY?
I ONLY GOT ENOUGH POWER FROM TROY TO ESCAPE! TO GET BACK HERE!
I'M SORRY! IT WASN'T ENOUGH TO FREE YOU!
I'M SORRY! I'M--
PLEASE, NOOO!
AAAIIEEEEEEE!
END

VARIANT COVER GALLERY

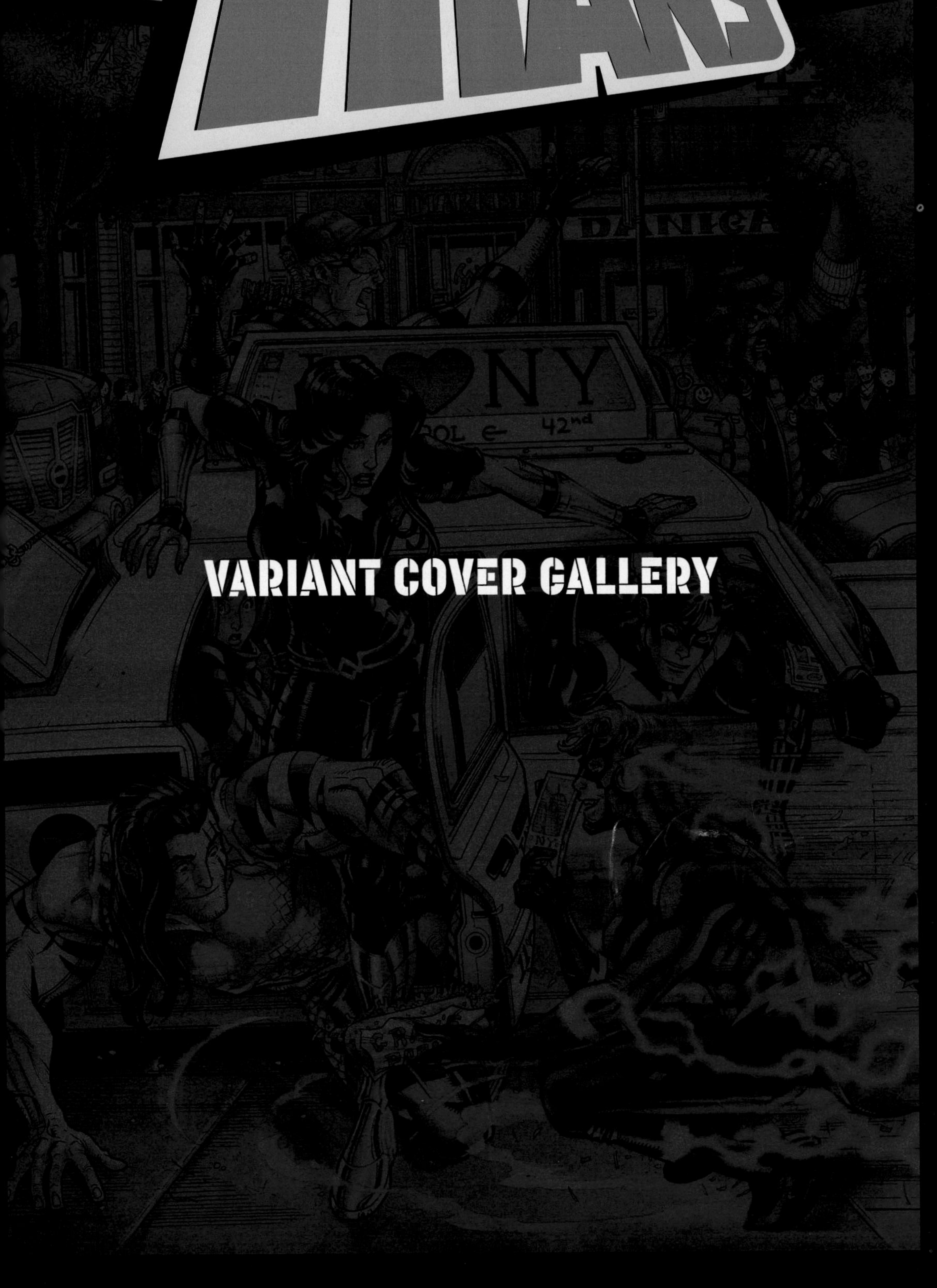

DANICA
NY
42nd

TITANS #7 variant cover by NICK BRADSHAW and ALEX SINCLAIR

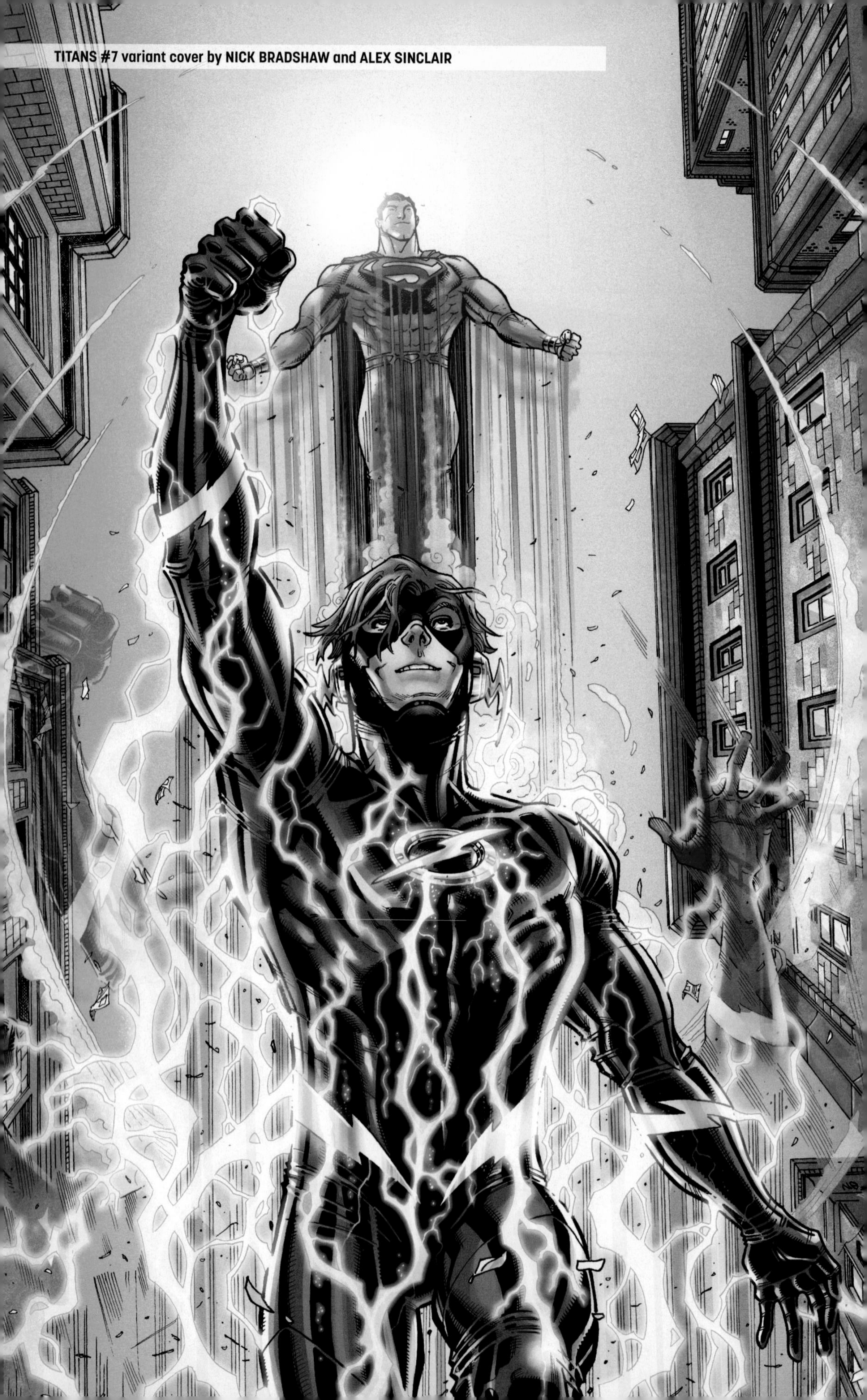

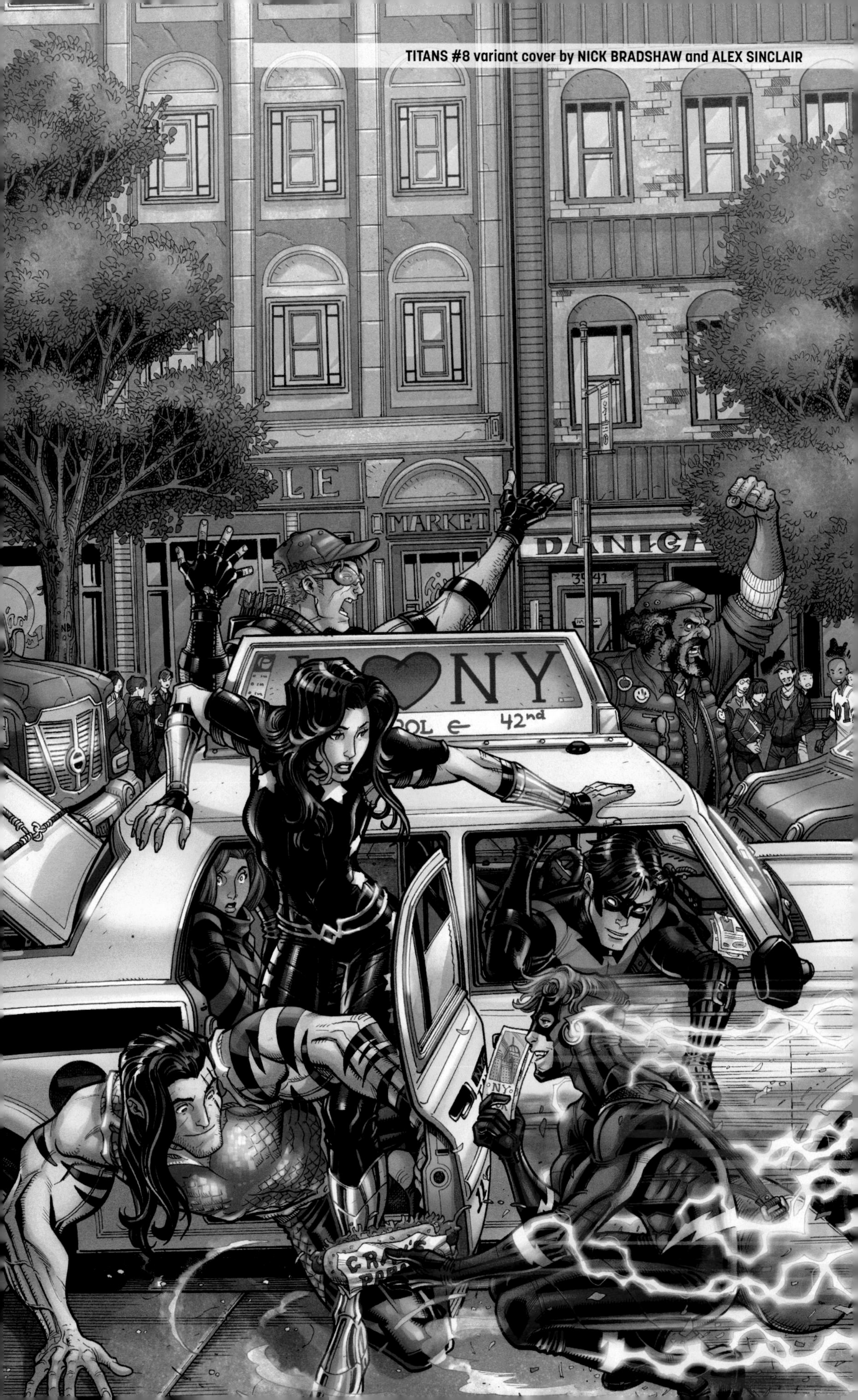
MARKET
3941
NY
42nd
TITANS #8 variant cover by NICK BRADSHAW and ALEX SINCLAIR

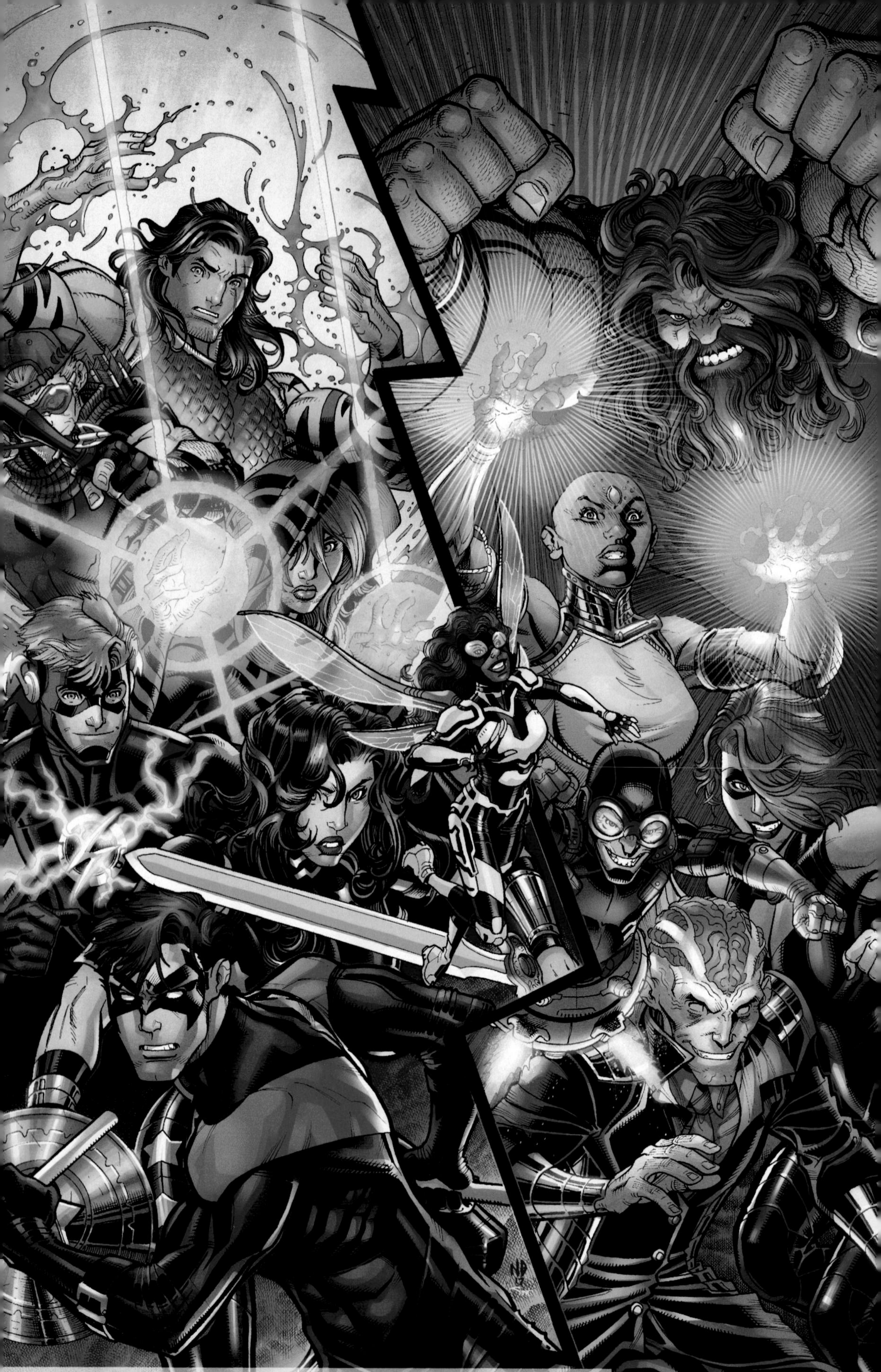

TITANS #9 variant cover by NICK BRADSHAW and ALEX SINCLAIR

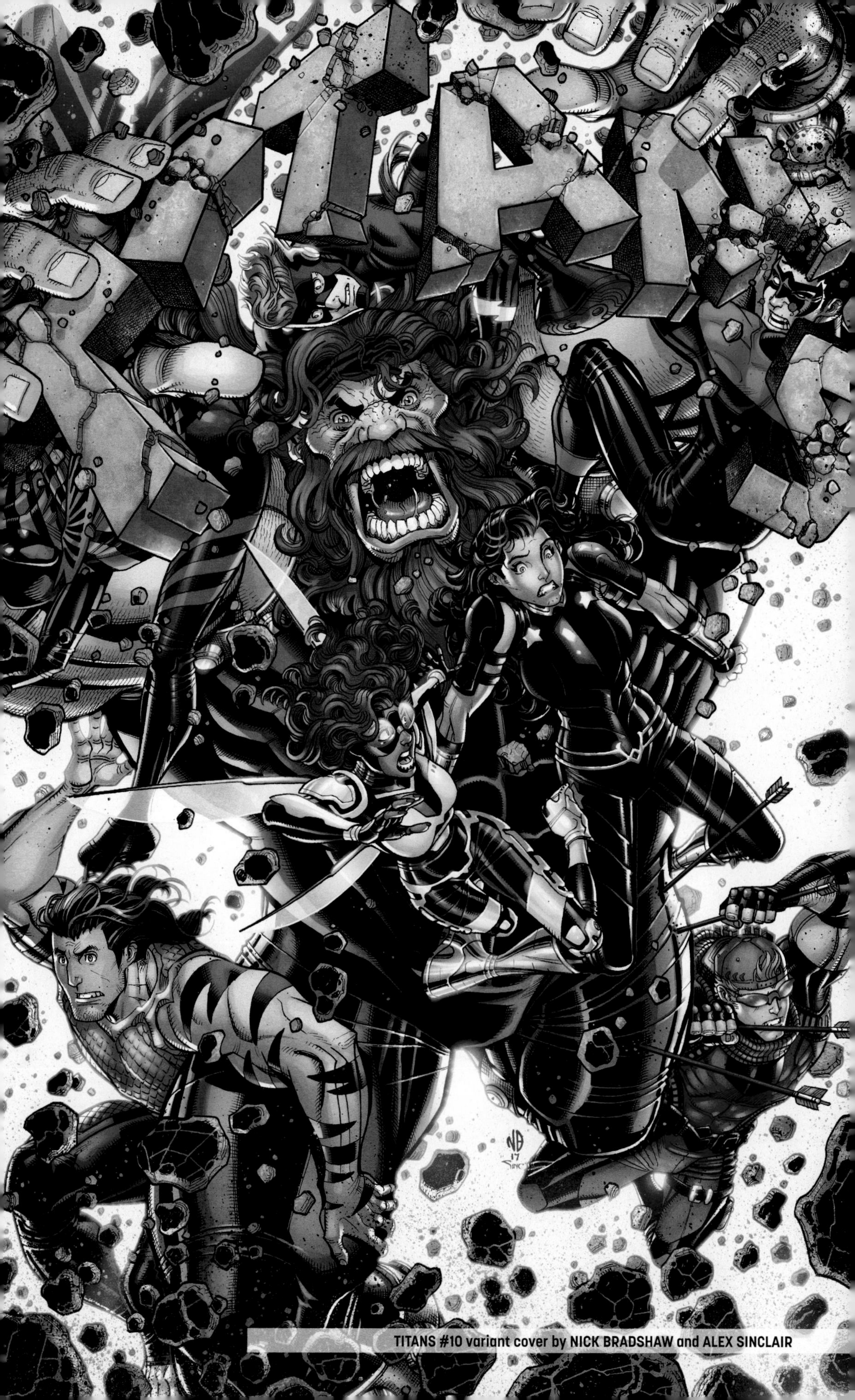

TITANS #10 variant cover by NICK BRADSHAW and ALEX SINCLAIR

Sketch for "Flashstroke" from TITANS ANNUAL #1

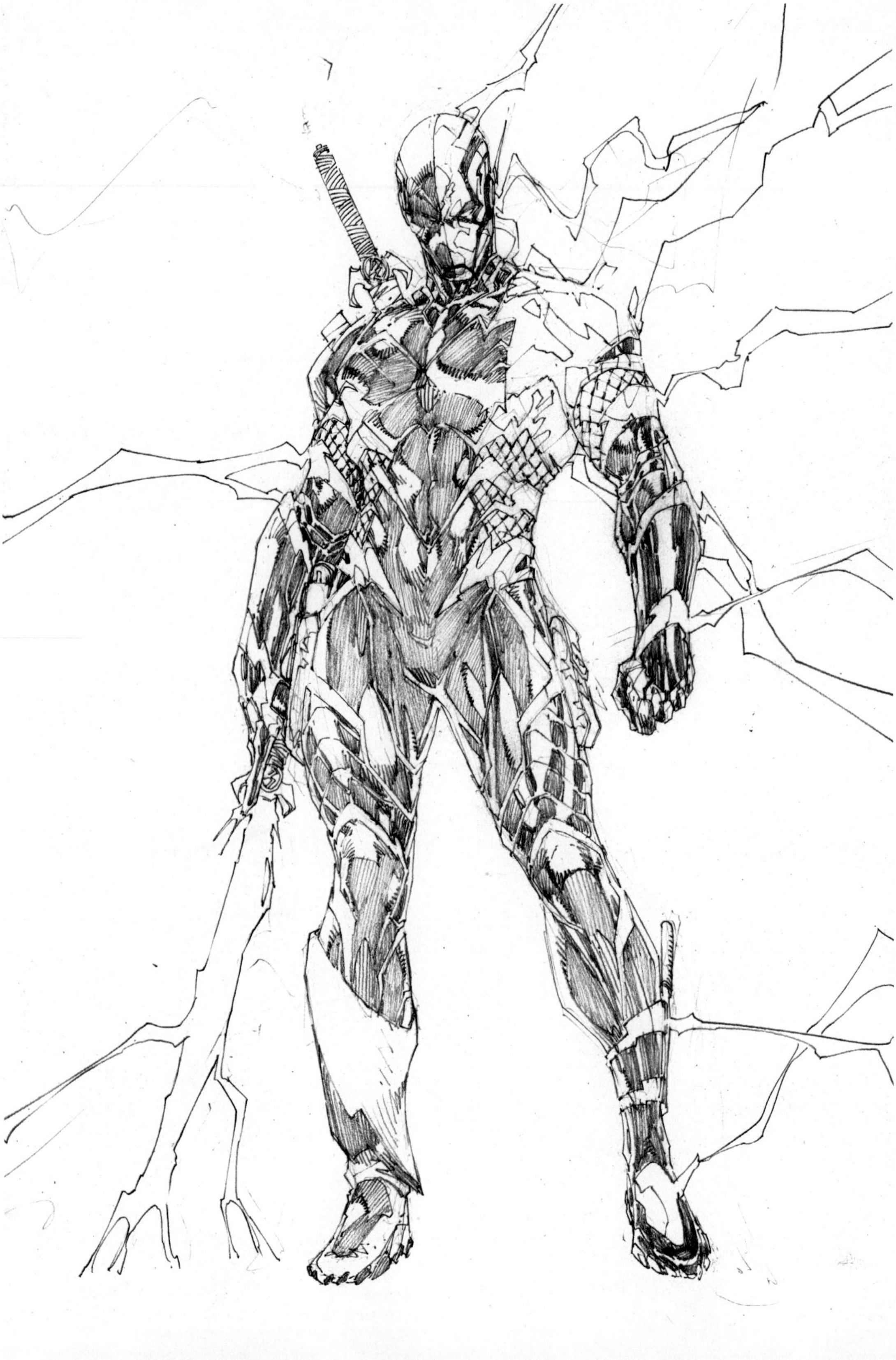

Pencil art for TITANS ANNUAL #1

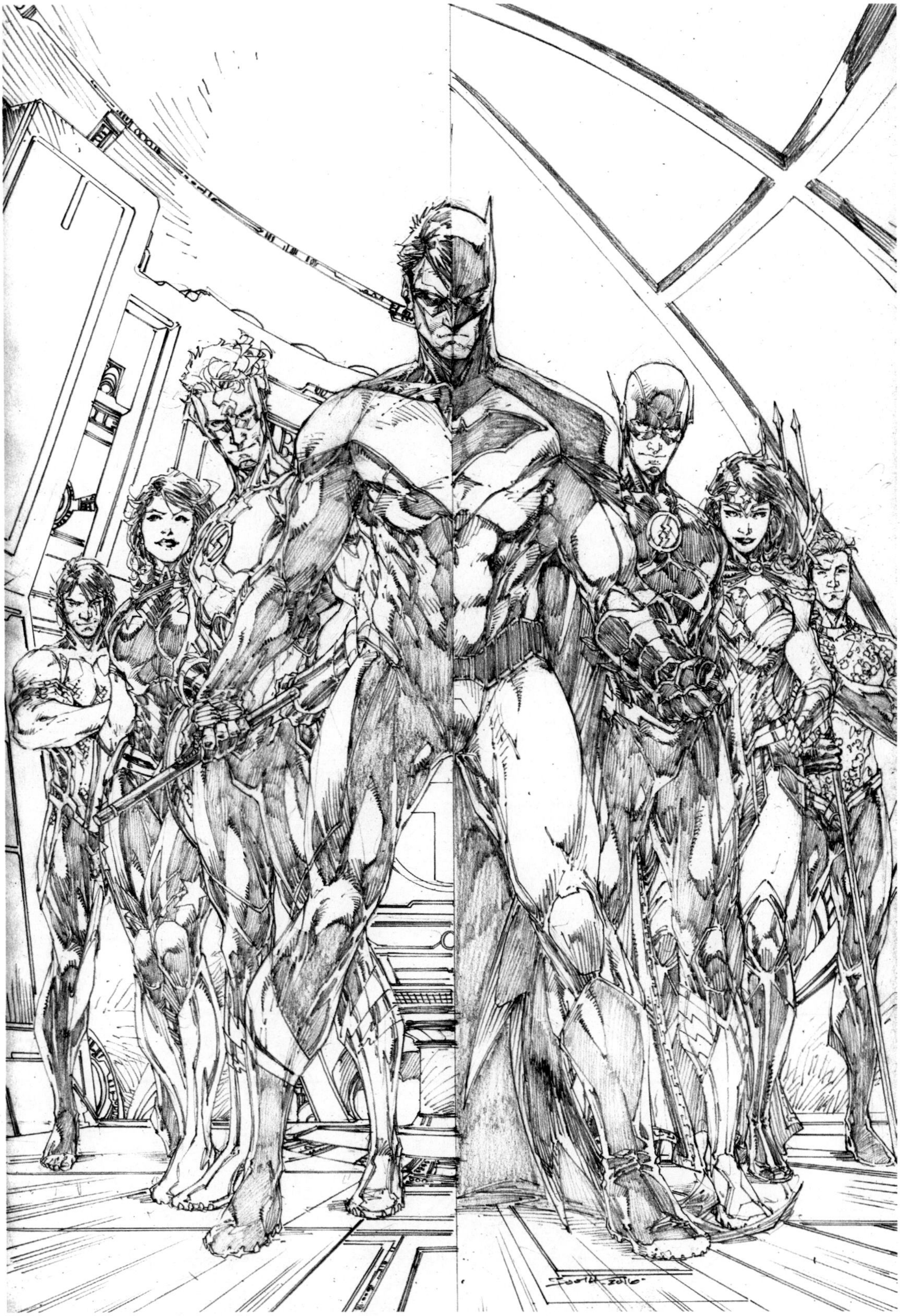

Pencil art for TITANS #8, page 19

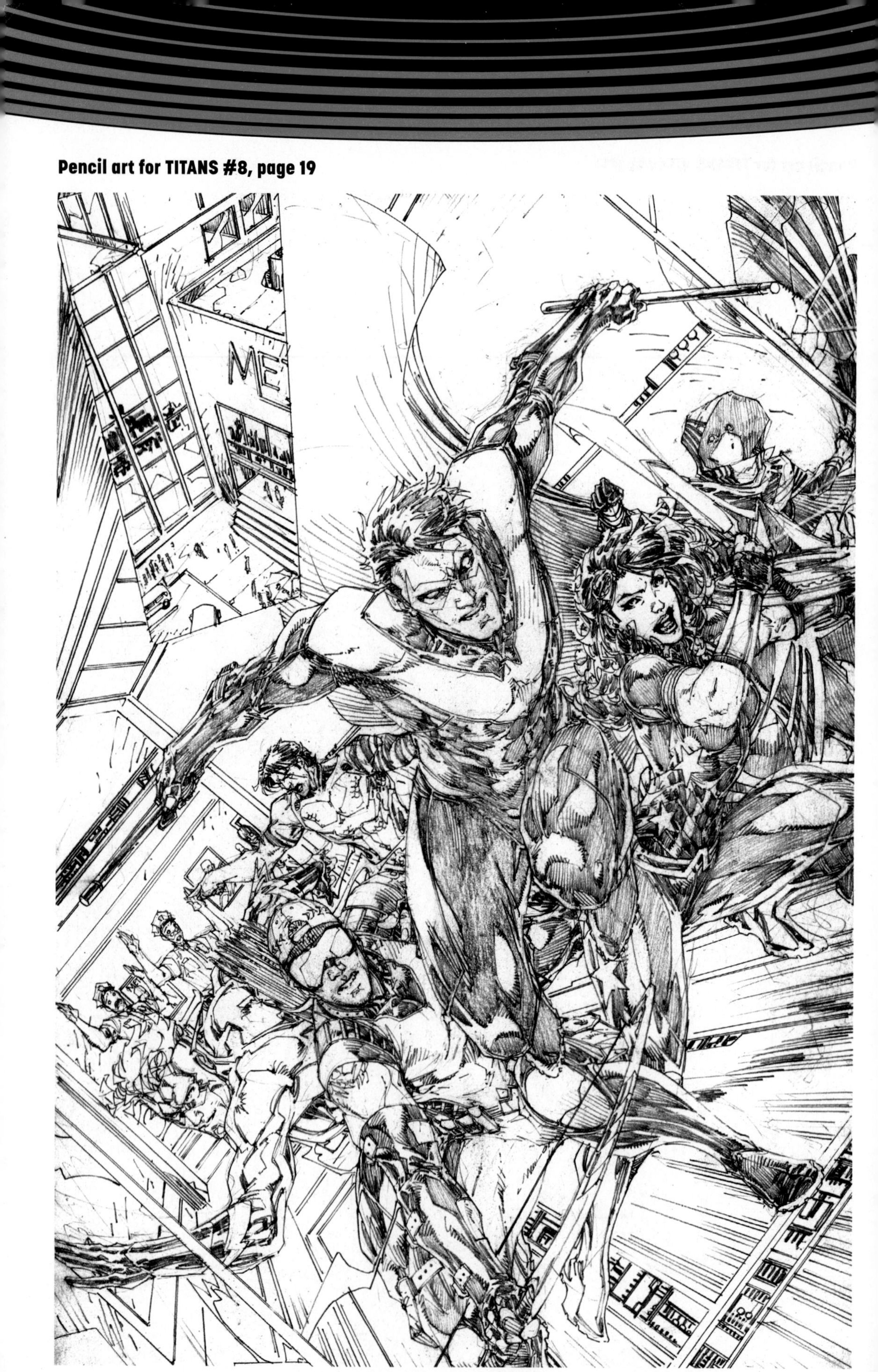

ME